MW00451361

Implementing Cisco IP Telephony and Video, Part 1 (CIPTV1) Foundation Learning Guide

CCNP Collaboration Exam 300-070 CIPTV1, Third Edition

Akhil Behl, CCIE No. 19564

Berni Gardiner, CSI, CCNP Voice

Josh Finke, CCIE No. 25707

Cisco Press

800 East 96th Street

Indianapolis, Indiana 46240 USA

Implementing Cisco IP Telephony and Video, Part 1 (CIPTV1) Foundation Learning Guide

CCNP Collaboration Exam 300-070 CIPTV1, Third Edition

Akhil Behl, Berni Gardiner and Josh Finke

Copyright © 2017 Cisco Systems, Inc.

Published by:
Cisco Press
800 East 96th Street
Indianapolis, IN 46240 USA

All rights reserved. No part of this book may be reproduced or transmitted in any form or by any means, electronic or mechanical, including photocopying, recording, or by any information storage and retrieval system, without written permission from the publisher, except for the inclusion of brief quotations in a review.

Printed in the United States of America

1   16

Library of Congress Cataloging-in-Publication Number: 2016946274

ISBN-13: 978-1-58714-451-6

ISBN-10: 1-587-14451-4

Warning and Disclaimer

This book is designed to provide information about Cisco Unified IP Telephony and Video administration and to provide test preparation for the CCNP Collaboration Exam 300-070 CIPTV1. Every effort has been made to make this book as complete and as accurate as possible, but no warranty or fitness is implied.

The information is provided on an "as is" basis. The authors, Cisco Press, and Cisco Systems, Inc. shall have neither liability nor responsibility to any person or entity with respect to any loss or damages arising from the information contained in this book or from the use of the discs or programs that may accompany it.

The opinions expressed in this book belong to the author and are not necessarily those of Cisco Systems, Inc.

Trademark Acknowledgments

All terms mentioned in this book that are known to be trademarks or service marks have been appropriately capitalized. Cisco Press or Cisco Systems, Inc. cannot attest to the accuracy of this information. Use of a term in this book should not be regarded as affecting the validity of any trademark or service mark.

Special Sales

For information about buying this title in bulk quantities, or for special sales opportunities (which may include electronic versions; custom cover designs; and content particular to your business, training goals, marketing focus, or branding interests), please contact our corporate sales department at corpsales@pearsoned.com or (800) 382-3419.

For government sales inquiries, please contact governmentsales@pearsoned.com.

For questions about sales outside the U.S., please contact intcls@pearson.com.

Feedback Information

At Cisco Press, our goal is to create in-depth technical books of the highest quality and value. Each book is crafted with care and precision, undergoing rigorous development that involves the unique expertise of members from the professional technical community.

Readers' feedback is a natural continuation of this process. If you have any comments regarding how we could improve the quality of this book, or otherwise alter it to better suit your needs, you can contact us through email at feedback@ciscopress.com. Please make sure to include the book title and ISBN in your message.

We greatly appreciate your assistance.

Editor-in-Chief: Mark Taub

Product Line Manager: Brett Bartow

Alliances Manager, Cisco Press: Ron Fligge

Acquistions Editor: Michelle Newcomb

Managing Editor: Sandra Schroeder

Development Editor: Marianne Bartow, Eleanor Bru

Senior Project Editor: Tracey Croom

Copy Editor: Warren Hapke

Technical Editors: Akhil Behl, Berni Gardiner

Editorial Assistant: Vanessa Evans

Cover Designer: Chuti Prasertsith

Composition: codeMantra

Indexer: Erika Millen

Proofreader: Srimathy

Americas Headquarters
Cisco Systems, Inc.
San Jose, CA

Asia Pacific Headquarters
Cisco Systems (USA) Pte. Ltd.
Singapore

Europe Headquarters
Cisco Systems International BV
Amsterdam, The Netherlands

Cisco has more than 200 offices worldwide. Addresses, phone numbers, and fax numbers are listed on the Cisco Website at **www.cisco.com/go/offices.**

CCDE, CCENT, Cisco Eos, Cisco HealthPresence, the Cisco logo, Cisco Lumin, Cisco Nexus, Cisco StadiumVision, Cisco TelePresence, Cisco WebEx, DCE, and Welcome to the Human Network are trademarks; Changing the Way We Work, Live, Play, and Learn and Cisco Store are service marks; and Access Registrar, Aironet, AsyncOS, Bringing the Meeting To You, Catalyst, CCDA, CCDP, CCIE, CCIP, CCNA, CCNP, CCSP, CCVP, Cisco, the Cisco Certified Internetwork Expert logo, Cisco IOS, Cisco Press, Cisco Systems, Cisco Systems Capital, the Cisco Systems logo, Cisco Unity, Collaboration Without Limitation, EtherFast, EtherSwitch, Event Center, Fast Step, Follow Me Browsing, FormShare, GigaDrive, HomeLink, Internet Quotient, IOS, iPhone, iQuick Study, IronPort, the IronPort logo, LightStream, Linksys, MediaTone, MeetingPlace, MeetingPlace Chime Sound, MGX, Networkers, Networking Academy, Network Registrar, PCNow, PIX, PowerPanels, ProConnect, ScriptShare, SenderBase, SMARTnet, Spectrum Expert, StackWise, The Fastest Way to Increase Your Internet Quotient, TransPath, WebEx, and the WebEx logo are registered trademarks of Cisco Systems, Inc. and/or its affiliates in the United States and certain other countries.

All other trademarks mentioned in this document or website are the property of their respective owners. The use of the word partner does not imply a partnership relationship between Cisco and any other company. (0812R)

About the Authors

Akhil Behl is a pre-sales manager with a leading service provider. His charter involves an overarching technology portfolio encompassing IoT, collaboration, security, infrastructure, service management, cloud, and data center. He has thirteen-plus years of experience working in leadership, advisory, business development, and consulting positions with various organizations; leading global accounts; while driving business innovation and excellence. Previously, he was in a leadership role with Cisco Systems.

Akhil has a Bachelor of Technology degree in electronics and telecommunications from MAIT College, IP University, Delhi, India, and a master's degree in business administration from Symbiosis Institute, Pune, India. Akhil holds dual CCIE in Collaboration and Security, PMP, ITIL, VCP, TOGAF, CEH, ISO/IEC 27002, and many other industry certifications.

He has published several research papers in national and international journals, including IEEE, and has been a speaker at prominent industry forums such as Interop, Enterprise Connect, Cloud Connect, Cloud Summit, Cisco Sec-Con, IT Expo, Computer Society of India, Singapore Computer Society, CommunicAsia, Total Security Conference, and Cisco Networkers.

Akhil is the author of the following Cisco Press books:

- *CCIE Collaboration Quick Reference*

- *Securing Cisco IP Telephony Networks*

- *Implementing Cisco IP Telephony and Video (Part 2)*

He is a technical editor for Cisco Press and other publications. Akhil can be reached at akbehl@technologist.com

Berni Gardiner is an independent telecommunications consultant and a long-time certified Cisco Instructor. Berni began her career in the software development arena in the 1980s and moved into the service provider arena in 1990, collaborating on building the first commercial ISP in her home province of Prince Edward Island, Canada. Building on the success of the provincial network, Berni was key in developing one of the first Canadian national ISP offerings.

Berni became a Certified Cisco Systems Instructor in 1998 and continues to combine contract instruction and course development with a career in telecommunications consulting. Her primary focus is in the collaboration product line and Quality-of-Service implementations. Berni holds a number of certifications including CCSI and CCNP Voice.

She has authored a number of white papers and blogs for Global Knowledge. She can be reached at bernigardiner@hotmail.com.

Josh Finke, CCIE No. 25707, is the engineering and services manager for Iron Bow Technologies, a Cisco Gold and Master Unified Communications Partner. Josh was previously a lead instructor and director of operations for Internetwork Expert, a leading CCIE training company. Josh has multiple certifications, including the Cisco Voice CCIE, CCNP, CCDP, CCNA, CCDA, and Cisco Meeting Place Specialist. Josh specializes in Cisco UC, routing & switching, and network design. Josh started working with Cisco networking technologies in 2000 and later became one of the youngest Voice CCIEs in the world. He lives with his wife in Seattle, Washington.

Dedications

I would like to dedicated this book first to my family, my wonderful and beautiful wife Kanika and my lovely sons Shivansh and Shaurya, for their love, patience, sacrifice, and support while writing this book. They have been very kind and supporting as always during my journey to write yet another book. Moreover, my loving wife Kanika has been pivotal while writing the book. She reviewed my work and suggested amendments and improvements.

To my parents, Vijay Behl and Ravi Behl, for their continuous love, encouragement, guidance, and wisdom. To my brothers, Nikhil Behl and Ankit Behl, who have always been there to support me in all my endeavors. To all my extended family and friends, thank you for the support and love during my journey.

And I would like to thank God for all his blessings in my life.

—*Akhil*

I would like to dedicate this book to Ralph for his patience and support during the late hours and weekend writing marathons. To my children and grandchildren, thank you for understanding the occasional hours and days when mom and grandmom became unavailable to join in with family activities. All of your support and encouragement carried me through this project.

—*Berni*

Acknowledgments

Akhil Behl:

I would like to thank the following amazing people and teams for helping me write this book.

A special Thank You to the Cisco Press editorial team: Brett Bartow—Executive Editor, for seeing the value and vision in the proposed title and providing me the opportunity to write this title; Michelle Newcomb—Acquisitions Editor; Marianne Bartow—Development Editor; Ellie Bru—Development Editor, and Vanessa Evans—Editorial Assistant, for their support and guidance throughout the writing of this book. It is my sincere hope to work again with them in the near future. And my gratitude and thanks to everyone else in the Cisco Press production team, for their support and commitment.

I would like to thank my mentors and my peers who have guided me and stood by me all these years. Thank you to all my managers and peers from Cisco who have been supportive of what I wanted to do and helped me achieve it.

And lastly but most importantly, to all those special people—my relatives and my friends; who stood by me during the highs and lows of life.

Berni Gardiner:

I would like to acknowledge and thank the Cisco Press editorial team: Brett Bartow for providing me the opportunity to join this project, Michelle Newcomb, Ellie Bru and Marianne Bartow for patiently keeping me on track and Vanessa Evans for taking care of the business end of things. Thank you to my co-authors for their comments and directions. Thank you to the unseen team members who work behind the scenes to put together the finished product. All of your help has been tremendously appreciated.

Contents at a Glance

Contents

Command Syntax Conventions

The conventions used to present command syntax in this book are the same conventions used in Cisco's Command Reference. The Command Reference describes these conventions as follows:

- **Boldface** indicates commands and keywords that are entered literally as shown. In actual configuration examples and output (not general command syntax), boldface indicates commands that are manually input by the user (such as a show command).

- *Italics* indicate arguments for which you supply actual values.

- Vertical bars (|) separate alternative, mutually exclusive elements.

- Square brackets [ ] indicate optional elements.

- Braces { } indicate a required choice.

- Braces within brackets [{ }] indicate a required choice within an optional element.

Note This book covers multiple operating systems, and a differentiation of icons and router names indicate the appropriate OS that is being referenced.

Reader Services

Register your copy at www.ciscopress.com/title/9781587144516 for convenient access to downloads, updates, and corrections as they become available. To start the registration process, go to www.ciscopress.com/register and log in or create an account*. Enter the product ISBN 9781587144516 and click Submit. When the process is complete, you will find any available bonus content under Registered Products.

*Be sure to check the box that you would like to hear from us to receive exclusive discounts on future editions of this product.

Introduction

Professional career certifications have been a critical part of the computing IT industry for many years and will continue to become more important. Many reasons exist for these certifications, but the most popularly cited reason is that of credibility and the knowledge to get the job done.

All other considerations held equal, a certified employee/consultant/job candidate is considered more valuable than one who is not. CIPTV1 sets stage with the above objective in mind and helps you learn and comprehend the topics for the CCNP Collaboration CIPTV1 exam. At the same time, it prepares you for real world configuration of Cisco's Audio and Video technology.

Goals and Methods

The most important goal of this book is to provide you with knowledge and skills in Cisco Collaboration solution, with focus on deploying the Cisco Unified Communications Manager (CUCM).

CUCM features, CUCM-based call routing, Cisco IOS Voice Gateways, Cisco Unified Border Element (CUBE), and Quality of Service (QoS). All of these are associated and relevant to building and maintaining a robust and scalable Cisco Collaboration solution. Subsequently, another obvious goal of this book is to help you with the Cisco IP Telephony and Video (CIPTV) Part 1 Exam, which is part of the Cisco Certified Network Professional Voice (CCNP) Collaboration certification. The methods used in this book are designed to be helpful in both your job and the CCNP Collaboration exam. This book provides questions at the end of each chapter to reinforce the chapter's concepts and content.

The organization of this book helps you discover the exam topics that you need to review in more depth, fully understand and remember those details, and test the knowledge you have retained on those topics. This book does not try to help you pass by memorization, but truly learn and understand the topics by going in-depths of the very concepts and architecture of Cisco Collaboration. The Cisco IP Telephony Part 1 Exam is one of the foundation topics in the CCNP Collaboration Certification. The knowledge contained in this book is vitally important for you to consider yourself a truly skilled Cisco Collaboration engineer or professional. The book helps you pass the Implementing Cisco IP Telephony and Video Part 1 exam by using the following methods:

Helps you discover which test topics you have not mastered

Provides explanations and information to fill in your knowledge gaps

Connects to real-world case studies and scenarios which are useful beyond the exam in the real life implementation tasks

Who Should Read This Book?

This book is written to be both a general CUCM book as a foundation for Cisco Collaboration and a certification preparation book. It provides you with the knowledge required to pass the CCNP Voice Cisco IP Telephony and Video Exam for in CCNP Collaboration Exams Series CIPT Part 1.

Why should you want to pass the CCNP Voice Cisco IP Telephony exam? The first CIPT test is one of the milestones toward getting the CCNP Voice certification. The CCNP Collaboration could mean a raise, promotion, new job, challenge, success, or recognition. But ultimately you determine what it means to you. Certifications demonstrate that you are serious about continuing the learning process and professional development. Today's technology is evolving at a rapid rate. It is impossible to stay at the same level while the technology around you is constantly advancing. Engineers must continually retrain themselves, or will find themselves with out-of-date commodity-based skill sets. In a fast growing technology like Collaboration; where new solutions are presented and created every day, it is most vital to keep to the pace of change.

How This Book Is Organized

- **Chapter 1, "Understanding Cisco Unified Communications Manager Architecture,"** sets the stage for this book by introducing the very central focus of the Cisco Collaboration solution—CUCM. This chapter covers the nuts and bolts of CUCM architecture and gives an overview of CUCM deployment models.

- **Chapter 2, "Cisco Unified Communications Manager Deployment Models,"** gives an insight to the CUCM deployment models; which help you understand where and why you should position a certain deployment model in a Cisco Collaboration solution as well as the merits and limitations of each model. This helps you comprehend the content not just for the exam but also for real life customer consulting and architecture definition of a Cisco Collaboration solution.

- **Chapter 3, "Cisco Unified Communications Manager Services and Initial Configuration Settings,"** gives an overview of the various initial settings that must be done to bring a CUCM server/cluster online and make it useable for a Cisco Collaboration solution. Some settings are very critical from a design and deployment perspective while others from a functional perspective and all of these are covered in detail.

- **Chapter 4, "Deploying Endpoints and Users in Cisco Unified Communications Manager,"** gives an insight to deploying users and multitude of endpoints in the gambit of Cisco Collaboration solution to support small to medium to large enterprise deployments.

- **Chapter 5, "Deploying IP Phone Services in Cisco Unified Communications Manager,"** helps lay a solid foundation of IP Phone services; which in any successful deployment is necessary for offering state-of-art-services to the end users.

- **Chapter 6, "An Overview of Dial Plan Design and Implementation in Cisco Unified Communications Manager,"** describes the various dial plan elements and gives an overview of the dial plan pertinent to CUCM. This chapter discusses a dial plan from an internal dial plan to a globalized + E.164-based dial plan and lays the foundation for call routing.

- **Chapter 7, "Implementing Cisco Unified Communications Manager Call Routing and Digit Manipulation,"** gives an insight to call routing elements such as route patterns, route groups as well as cover the basis of digit manipulation both from an internal and external call perspective. Call routing and digit manipulation are some of the most basic yet complex constructs in a dial plan which are covered at length in this chapter.

- **Chapter 8 "Implementing Calling Privileges in Cisco Unified Communications Manager,"** gives an insight to deployment locks and keys (partitions and Calling Search Spaces) which form the basis of allowing and disallowing internal or external calling access for the users.

- **Chapter 9, "Implementing Call Coverage in Cisco Unified Communications Manager,"** explains the concepts and implementation of various call coverage mechanisms at play in CUCM based audio and video solutions.

- **Chapter 10, "Implementing Media Resources in Cisco Unified Communications Manager,"** discusses the concept and implementation of various media resources ranging from audio media call resources to video call media resources. These media resources enable what would otherwise be a very daunting task of mixing audio/video streams or playing around with a range of codecs, and so on.

- **Chapter 11, "Cisco Video Conferencing,"** describes the deployment various video conferencing options and tools (platforms) available in Cisco Collaboration solution. The chapter lays the foundation for Cisco TelePresence Conductor, Cisco TelePresence Server, and discusses other platforms that enable rich media conferencing experience.

- **Chapter 12, "Quality of Service in Cisco Collaboration Solution,"** expands on the basics of Quality of Service (QoS) and defines the QoS tools, mechanisms, and ways in which audio or video calls can be handled in much better way as opposed to non-preferential treatment.

- **Chapter 13, "Implementing Cisco IOS Voice Gateways and Cisco Unified Border Element,"** discusses the very basis of how a Cisco Collaboration solution connects with the outside world such as PSTN and IT Service Provider. This chapter details the various voice and video protocols at play in a Cisco Collaboration solution and the role of Cisco Voice Gateways and Cisco Unified Border Element (CUBE). Moreover, the chapter discusses the features by which intuitive user and administrative experience are offered by these platforms.

- **Appendix A, "Answers to the Review Questions,"** allows you to check the validity of your answers at the end of each chapter as you review the questions.

Icons Used in This Book

Buildings

 Branch Office
 Medium Building
 Government Building
 Headquarters
 Home Office
 House

 Small business
 Telecommuter House
 Telecommuter House PC
 Headquarters
 Medium Building
 House
 Branch Office

Computers and Hardware

 Application
  PC
 Softphone
 Web Browser
  Web Server
 Workstation
  IP Communicator
 Laptop
 www Server

  Wireless Laptop
 Web Cluster

Connections

 Line: Circuit-Switched (Lines should always have "Z" this way)
 Line: Ethernet
 Line: Serial (Lines should always have "Z" this way)
 Network Cloud, Dark
 Network Cloud, Standard
 Network Cloud, White
 Ethernet

 Wireless Connection
 RTP Voice Packets
Pipe
 Straight-Through Cable
Rollover (Console) Cable
Crossover Cable
Serial Cable

Firewalls

  Cisco ASA
 Router with Firewall

People

 End User Cisco Works
 End User Female
 End User Female, Video
 End User Male
 End User Male, Video
 Telecommuter

Phones, Multimedia, and Communications

 Fax

 FAX/Phone

 Headphones

 Phone

 Phone 2

 Phone Polycom

 WebCam

Video

Mobile Access IP Phone

 CTS-1000

 CTS-3000

 H.323

 IP Phone

 iPhone

Routers

 Router

 Router (second color)

TDM Router

Voice-Enabled Router

 IP Telephony Router

 CTS-Codec Primary

 CTS-Codec Secondary

 Cisco Telepresence Multipoint Switch

 Access Point

 Local WLAN Controller

Cisco Telepresence Manager

Servers

 Cisco Unified Communications Manager

 Communication Server

 Voice-Enabled Communications Server

Cisco Unity Connection

Cisco Meeting Place

Gateway

MCU

Software conference bridge

Directory Server

 SIP Server

 Cisco Unified IM & P

 Cisco Unified Border Element (CUBE)

 Cisco Unified Communications Manager Cluster

 Cisco Unified Communications 500 Series for Small Business

Switches

 Data Center Switch

 FC Switch

 ISDN Switch

Multilayer Switch with Text

PBX

PBX Switch

 Workgroup Switch

 Voice-Enabled Workgroup Switch

ATA

 IOS SLB

 Data Center Switch

 Nexus 1000

UCS 5108 Blade Chassis

6100 Series Fabric Interconnect

Nexus 4000

Nexus 2000

Nexus 5000

Chapter 1

Understanding Cisco Unified Communications Manager Architecture

A Cisco Collaboration deployment relies on Cisco Unified Communications Manager for its call-processing and call-routing functions. Understanding the role that Cisco Unified Communications Manager plays in a converged Collaboration network from a system, software, and hardware perspective is necessary to successfully install, configure, operate, and maintain a Cisco Collaboration solution.

This chapter describes the role of Cisco Unified Communications Manager in a Cisco Collaboration solution, including its features, functions, architecture, deployment, and redundancy options.

Chapter Objectives

Upon completing this chapter, you will understand Cisco Unified Communications Manager architecture and be able to meet the following objectives:

- Describe the main components of a Cisco Collaboration solution

- Describe Cisco Unified Communications Manager (CUCM) functions and features

- Describe Cisco Unified Communications signaling and media flows

- Provide an overview of Cisco Unified Communications deployment models

- Provide an overview of Cisco Unified Communications redundancy

Overview of the Cisco Collaboration Solution

This section provides a high-level overview of the Cisco Collaboration solution. A layered solution approach, as illustrated by Figure 1-1, provides a clean delineation of functionality between major solution components. The foundation is built on the enterprise network consisting of quality of service (QoS)–enabled Cisco routers and switches and a virtualized server/application environment. Additional focus is placed on providing collaborative access to external entities, such as mobile workforce, customers, suppliers, and teleworkers.

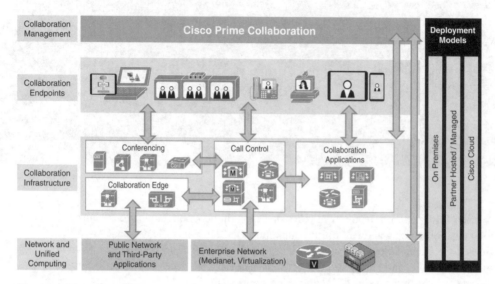

Figure 1-1   *Cisco Collaboration Solution Overview*

The Collaboration Edge provides the entry point for a call from an external source into the corporate network and is based on Cisco Expressway Core (Expressway-C) and Edge (Expressway-E) devices providing firewall traversal and secure communications functionality.

Note   Cisco Expressway solution and its features are covered in detail in *Implementing Cisco IP Telephony and Video, Part 2*.

At the core of the Collaboration Infrastructure is the call control component (that is, CUCM) providing access to a number of Collaboration applications. An extensive portfolio of Collaboration endpoints provides audio and video communication capabilities to address a wide array of user requirements.

Cisco Prime Collaboration provides management and analytics capabilities to allow system administrators complete control across the multiple layers of functionality.

The Cisco Collaboration solution fully integrates communications by enabling data, voice, and video to be transmitted over a single network infrastructure (converged network) using standards-based IP. Leveraging the framework that is provided by Cisco IP hardware and software products, the Cisco Unified Communications system has the capability to address current and emerging communications needs in the enterprise environment. The Cisco Collaboration solution is designed to optimize feature functionality, reduce configuration and maintenance requirements, and provide interoperability with a wide variety of other applications. The Cisco Collaboration solution provides and maintains a high level of availability, QoS, and security for the network and consists of these three main elements:

■ **Collaboration infrastructure:** Routing and switching technologies are the basis for a successful Collaboration solution. Adding QoS mechanisms together with Medianet services provides an infrastructure that is capable of recognizing various services and prioritizing traffic according to its needs. Cisco Collaboration Systems Release 10 includes completely virtualized deployment models that are based on VMware vSphere ESXi Hypervisor, where application nodes run as virtual machines on Cisco UCS (or supported third-party) servers. The Cisco Collaboration infrastructure also includes security mechanisms that protect the system at each level, and a wide variety of tools, applications, and products to monitor and manage the system.

Note   To learn more about Cisco UC Security, refer to *Securing Cisco IP Telephony Networks*.

■ **Collaboration applications and services:** The Cisco Collaboration solution incorporates a number of advanced applications and services that start with CUCM as the basis of the Collaboration portfolio and include the following:

■ **IM and Presence:** The Cisco Instant Messaging (IM) and Presence Service enables Cisco Jabber, CUCM applications, and third-party applications to increase user productivity by determining the most effective form of communication to help connect collaborating partners more efficiently.

■ **Collaborative conferencing:** Cisco WebEx incorporates audio, high-definition video, and real-time content sharing in a platform that provides easy setup and administration of meetings, interactive participation in the meeting, and the ability to join the meeting from any type of device such as an IP phone, a tablet device, or a desktop computer.

■ **Cisco TelePresence:** Cisco TelePresence technology brings people together in real time without the expense and delay of travel. The Cisco TelePresence portfolio of products includes an array of high-definition video endpoints ranging from individual desktop units to large multiscreen immersive video systems for conference rooms. Cisco TelePresence products are designed to interoperate with other Cisco Collaboration products such as Cisco WebEx and Cisco Unified IP phones with video capability.

■ **Voice messaging:** Cisco products such as Cisco Unity Connection and Cisco Unity Express (CUE) provide several voice messaging options for large and small Collaboration systems respectively. Also, these products offer the ability to integrate with third-party voice-mail systems using standard protocols.

■ **Customer contact:** Cisco Unified Contact Center products such as Cisco Unified Contact Center Express (UCCX) and Cisco Unified Contact Center Enterprise (UCCE) provide intelligent contact routing, call treatment, and multichannel contact management for customer contact centers. Cisco Unified Customer Voice Portal (CVP) can be installed as a standalone Interactive Voice Response (IVR) system, or it can integrate transparently with the contact center to deliver personalized self-service for customers. In addition, Cisco SocialMiner is a powerful tool for engaging with customers through social media.

- **Call recording:** Cisco MediaSense captures, preserves, and mines conversations for business intelligence and provides real-time monitoring of customer conversations with contact center personnel.

- **Collaboration user experience:** Cisco is focused on making its Collaboration technology easy, convenient, and beneficial to use, with particular emphasis on the following enhancements to the user experience:

  - **Collaboration endpoints:** A wide variety of Collaboration endpoints are available, including the Cisco BYOD Smart Solution, which allows users to work from their favorite personal device: smart phone, tablet, or PC.

  - **Mobile Collaboration:** Mobile Collaboration includes features and capabilities such as Extension Mobility, Cisco Jabber, and Single Number Reach.

  - **Social networking:** Social networking includes Cisco WebEx Social.

  - **Applications and services:** In addition to the features already mentioned, Cisco offers application programming interfaces (APIs) that allow development of custom applications.

Figure 1-2 depicts a Cisco Collaboration network that can be envisioned in a large enterprise. It encompasses the elements discussed previously.

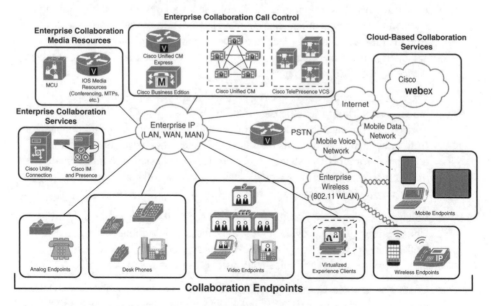

Figure 1-2   *Cisco Collaboration Network in a Large Enterprise*

Note   Cisco Collaboration entities such as CUCM-based call-control, Cisco IM and Presence, IOS gateways, Cisco Unified Border Element (CUBE), Cisco Unified IP Phones, Media Resources, Virtualization of Cisco Collaboration solution elements, Cisco TelePresence-based Video Conferencing, Collaboration Edge (VCS, Expressway), public switched telephone network (PSTN), and ITSP-based SIP Trunking are covered in *Implementing Cisco IP Telephony and Video* Parts 1 and 2. Topics such as WebEx, cloud-based Collaboration solutions, wireless solutions and endpoints, and mobile endpoints are out of scope for the CIPTV1 and CIPTV2 exams and books.

Cisco Unified Communications Manager Function and Features Overview

This section describes the functions that are provided by Cisco Unified Communications Manager.

CUCM extends enterprise telephony features and functions to packet telephony network devices, which include:

- Cisco Unified IP phones and third-party phones
- Media-processing devices
- VoIP gateways
- Multimedia applications

Additional data, voice, and video services that interact with the IP telephony solution through the CUCM API include:

- Converged messaging
- Multimedia conference
- Collaborative conference centers
- Interactive multimedia response systems

From software release 10.0(1) and later, Cisco supports only virtualized deployments of CUCM on Cisco Unified Computing System (CUCS) servers or on a third-party server configuration that is approved by Cisco.

Note   In Release 10.0(1) and later, Cisco does not support deployments of CUCM on Cisco Media Convergence Servers (MCS).

CUCM provides these functions:

- **Call processing:** Call processing refers to the complete process of routing, originating, and terminating calls, including any billing and statistical collection processes.

- **Signaling and device control:** CUCM sets up all the signaling connections between call endpoints and directs devices that include:

  - phones

  - gateways

  - conference bridges to establish and tear down streaming connections

- **Dial plan administration:** The dial plan is a set of configurable elements that CUCM uses to determine call routing. CUCM provides administrators the ability to create scalable dial plans for the users.

- **Phone feature administration:** CUCM extends services and features to IP phones and gateways, such as:

  - hold

  - transfer

  - forward

  - conference

  - speed dial

  - last-number redial

  - call park

- **Directory services:** CUCM uses its own database to store user information. You can authenticate users either locally or against an external directory. You can provision users by directory synchronization. With directory synchronization, you can automatically add users from the directory to the local database. CUCM allows synchronization from the following directories to the database:

  - Microsoft Active Directory 2003

  - Microsoft Active Directory 2008

  - Microsoft Active Directory Application Mode 2003

  - Microsoft Lightweight Directory Services 2008

  - iPlanet Directory Server 5.1

- Sun ONE Directory Server 5.2

- Sun ONE Directory Server 6.x

- OpenLDAP 2.3.39

- OpenLDAP 2.4

- **Programming interface to external applications:** CUCM provides a programming interface for the following:

  - Cisco IP Communicator

  - Cisco Unified IP IVR

  - Cisco Personal Assistant

  - CUCM Attendant Console

- **Backup and restore tools:** CUCM provides Disaster Recovery System (DRS) tools for the following databases:

  - CUCM configuration database

  - Call detail records (CDR)

  - CUCM CDR Analysis and Reporting (CAR) database

Overview of Cisco Unified Communications Manager Signaling and Media Flows

It is important to understand how CUCM performs key functions by tracking the signaling and media path of a basic IP telephony call.

CUCM uses the Session Initiation Protocol (SIP) or the Skinny Client Control Protocol (SCCP) to communicate with Cisco IP phones for call setup and maintenance tasks.

When the call is set up, media exchange occurs directly between the Cisco IP phones using Real-Time Transport Protocol (RTP) to carry the audio.

Example: Basic IP Telephony Call

In Figure 1-3, User A at IP Phone A (left telephone) wants to make a call to IP Phone B (right telephone). User A picks up the handset and dials the number of User B. In this environment, dialed digits are sent to CUCM, the call-processing engine. CUCM searches its dial plan for a matching entry and determines where to route the call.

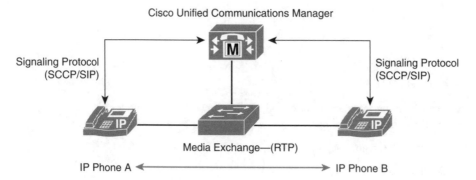

Figure 1-3   *Call Signaling and Media Paths*

> **Note**   Figure 1-3 focuses on the most basic audio call, but in the CUCM environment it is possible to use email-like aliases (known as uniform resource identifier (URI) dialing) to reach the called party.

Using SCCP or SIP, CUCM signals the calling party over IP to initiate a ringback, and Party A hears the ringback tone. CUCM also signals the call to the destination phone, which starts ringing.

User B accepts the call by going off hook. During the final portion of the signaling phase, CUCM examines the capabilities of both endpoints to determine which common elements, such as which codec, are supported by both endpoints. Once a common set of capabilities has been found, CUCM provides each endpoint with the IP address and port number of the other endpoint to establish a direct RTP path between the two stations. User A or User B may now initiate a conversation.

The Cisco IP phones require no further communication with CUCM until either User A or User B invokes a feature, such as call transfer, call conferencing, or call termination.

Figure 1-4 illustrates the call flow for calls leaving the cluster and terminating in the PSTN.

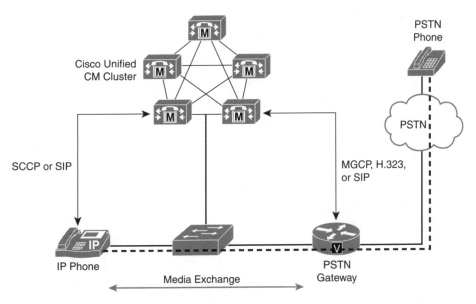

Figure 1-4 *Call Signaling and Media Path for PSTN Calls*

In this scenario, the IP phone user dials a number starting with the access code 9 (as an example for a PSTN/outside line access code). This indicates to CUCM that the call should be routed to the PSTN. The matching route pattern for numbers starting with 9 points to a gateway for call delivery. CUCM signals the gateway with call setup information, and the gateway opens a communication channel through its PSTN connection. Once signaling has completed and the call has been answered, the RTP stream containing the media (voice or video) is set up between the IP phone and the PSTN gateway. The gateway then removes the content from the RTP packet and place it in the appropriate channel for PSTN phone delivery.

Cisco Unified Communications Manager Architecture

This section describes CUCM architecture from the network perspective.

As illustrated in Figure 1-5, CUCM depends on additional network elements to function properly with the Collaboration environment. In particular, the CUCM cluster uses external Network Time Protocol (NTP) and Domain Name System (DNS) servers, plus Dynamic Host Configuration Protocol (DHCP), and Trivial File Transfer Protocol (TFTP) services that are used by the endpoints. These services are described in detail in the sections that follow.

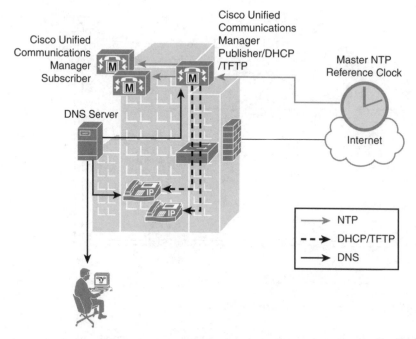

Figure 1-5   *Cisco Unified Communications Manager Architecture—Services Usage*

Cisco Unified Communications Manager Architecture: NTP

CUCM uses NTP to obtain time information from a time server. Only the publisher sends NTP requests to the external NTP server or servers; subscribers synchronize their time with the publisher.

NTP is a protocol for synchronizing computer system clocks over IP networks. NTP has a hierarchical organization that is based on clock strata. Stratum 0 is an extremely precise clock source, such as an atomic clock or radio clock. A stratum 1 server is directly connected to a stratum 0 clock and can provide time information to other (stratum 2) devices, which in turn serves stratum 3 devices. CUCM typically uses stratum 1.

NTP must be enabled and configured during installation of CUCM. At least one external NTP server must be reachable and functioning when installing the CUCM publisher to complete the installation. Cisco recommends using a minimum of three external NTP servers in a production environment.

It is extremely important that all network devices have accurate time information, because the system time on CUCM is relevant in the following situations:

- Cisco IP phones display date and time information. This information is obtained from CUCM.

- Call detail records (CDR) and call management records (CMR), which are used for call reporting, analysis, and billing, include date and time information.

- Alarms and events in log files, as well as trace information in trace files, include time information. Troubleshooting a problem requires correlation of information that is created by different system components (CUCM, Cisco IOS gateway, etc.). This problem solving is only possible if all devices in the network have the same correct time information.

- Some CUCM features are date- or time-based and therefore rely on correct date and time. These features include time-of-day routing and certificate-based security features.

Note Certificates include a validity period. If a system that receives a certificate has an invalid (future) date, it may consider the received certificate to be invalid (expired).

To ensure that all network devices have the correct date and time, it is recommended that all network devices use NTP for time synchronization. The master reference clock should be a stratum 1 NTP server.

Cisco Unified Communications Manager Architecture: DHCP

The CUCM DHCP server is designed to serve IP phones in small deployments (maximum of 1000 devices). It provides a subset of Windows, Linux, or Cisco IOS DHCP server functionality that is sufficient for IP phones, but it should not be used for other network devices (such as PCs).

Note The DHCP server of CUCM must not be used with deployments of more than 1000 registered devices. Even if there are fewer devices, the CPU load of the services must be watched closely. If high CPU load is experienced, the DHCP service should be provided by other devices (for example, a dedicated DHCP server, switch, router, and so on).

Multiple DHCP services can be configured per CUCM cluster. Each CUCM DHCP server can be configured with multiple subnets. In nonattached subnets, DHCP relay must be enabled so that the DHCP requests that were sent out by the clients are forwarded to the DHCP server.

Regardless of whether DHCP is provisioned by CUCM or by an external DHCP server, the same information must be provided to the devices utilizing the service. Aside from offering the basic IP address/gateway information, DHCP also passes an element called Option 150, which contains the IP address of the cluster TFTP server.

The TFTP server, in part, contains configuration files required by endpoints at the beginning of the registration process. Option 150 also provides the ability to configure a secondary TFTP server address.

Cisco Unified Communications Manager Architecture: TFTP

The TFTP server performs an important role in a Cisco Collaboration network. TFTP helps unified communication (UC) endpoints register with Communications Manager. It is the source of files for services such as music on hold (MOH), configuration files for devices such as phones and gateways, binary files for the upgrade of phones as well as some gateways, and various security files. The TFTP server is required because phones and gateways obtain their configuration information from it during registration; otherwise they fail to register to the Communications Manager.

TFTP redundancy is achieved by defining two Option 150 IP addresses in the DHCP scope configuration (as described in the previous section. Depending on the size of the cluster, the administrator can modify the default number of TFTP sessions allowed to improve performance on dedicated TFTP servers. CUCM cluster-based redundancy for call processing services is covered in detail in Chapter 2, "Cisco Unified Communications Manager Deployment Models."

Cisco Unified Communications Manager Architecture: DNS

CUCM can use IP addresses or names to refer to other IP devices in application settings. When names are used, they need to be resolved to IP addresses by DNS.

Both methods have some advantages:

- **Using IP addresses:** The system does not depend on a DNS server, which prevents loss of service when the DNS server cannot be reached. When a device initiates a connection for the first time, the time that is required to establish the connection is shorter, because no name resolution (DNS lookup sent to the DNS server and DNS reply sent back from the server) is required. By eliminating the need for DNS, there is no danger of errors that are caused by DNS misconfiguration. Troubleshooting is simplified because there is no need to verify proper name resolution.

- **Using DNS:** Management is simplified because logical names are simpler to manage than 32-bit addresses. If IP addresses change, there is no need to modify the application settings because they can still use the same names; only the DNS server configuration has to be modified in this case. IP addresses of CUCM servers can be translated toward IP phones, because the IP phone configuration files include server names, not the original server IP addresses (which should appear differently to the IP phone). As long as these names are resolved to the correct (translated) address when IP phones send out DNS requests, the use of Network Address Translation (NAT) is no problem.

In general, due to the additional point of failure that is caused by configuration errors or because of unavailability of the service, the recommendation is not to use DNS with CUCM.

Note   Most IP clients cache the IP address information that is received from the DNS servers to avoid subsequent name resolution requests for the same name

By default, CUCM propagates the machine name and not the IP addresses of its active Cisco CallManager Services. (These hostnames are part of TFTP configuration files for devices such as IP phones.)

Note   DNS reliance refers to the requirement for IP phones to use DNS servers to resolve hostnames of Cisco CallManager Services.

To remove DNS reliance, choose **System > Server** in CUCM Administration, choose each available server from the list, and change the server name to the IP address.

Note   By default, hostnames are also used in phone URLs. When DNS reliance is removed, hostnames that are used in these phone URLs must also be replaced by IP addresses. Phone URLs are configured by using enterprise parameters. Enterprise parameters and their configuration are explained later in this lesson.

Overview of Cisco Unified Communications Manager Deployment Models

This section provides an overview of basic deployment models for CUCM.

Cisco IP telephony supports these deployment models:

- **Single-site (campus):** a CUCM cluster located at a single site or campus where all calls destined outside this location are processed via the PSTN or IP telephony service provider (ITSP)

- **Multisite wide-area network (WAN) with centralized call processing:** A CUCM cluster located at a central campus or data center that provides services to endpoints deployed across multiple locations. Calls between locations use a QoS-enabled WAN as their primary call path.

- **Multisite WAN with distributed call processing:** Multiple sites, each with their own CUCM cluster. Trunks define connections between clusters and calls between clusters use a QoS-enabled WAN as their primary call path.

- **Clustering over the WAN:** A single CUCM cluster where the publisher and one or more subscribers are located at one location while the remaining subscribers may be distributed among other physical locations. Database replication between publisher and subscribers occurs over the WAN and relies on appropriate bandwidth and QoS-enabled connections.

Selection of the deployment model is based on several factors, including the following:

- **Size:** Number of IP phones, CUCM servers, and other resources, such as gateways or media resources (conference bridges, MOH servers, and so on).

- **Geographical distribution:** Number and location of sites. Size of sites also plays a critical role in deciding if a CUCM server should be deployed or if Cisco Unified Communications Manager Express (CUCME) can be deployed.

- **Network characteristics:** Bandwidth and delay of network links, and type of traffic that is carried over the network.

These deployment models, along with design guidelines and a discussion of merits of choosing one over another, are covered in more detail in Chapter 2, "CUCM Deployment Models."

Overview of Cisco Unified Communications Manager Redundancy

This section provides an overview of CUCM redundancy through clustering.

A cluster is a set of networked servers that works together to provide a variety of Cisco Unified Communications Manager services. Dedicated servers can provide database, application, TFTP, and media services such as conferencing and MOH. These services are offered by the subscribers and the publisher and can be shared by all servers.

Figure 1-6 shows the CUCM redundancy model in a CUCM cluster where CUCM B is the primary call processing server (subscriber) and CUCM A (publisher) is the backup call processing server as well as the TFTP server. IP Phone maintains an active signaling connection with the primary call processing server and an active secondary connection with the backup call processing server.

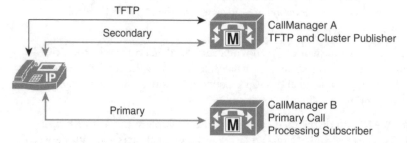

Figure 1-6   *Cisco Unified Communications Manager Redundancy Architecture Overview*

> **Note**   The arrangement shown in Figure 1-6 can be leveraged in a small-sized cluster with a couple of thousand endpoints. TFTP service coresidency with a call processing server is not recommended in larger clusters.

Clustering provides several benefits. It allows the network to scale to tens of thousands of endpoints, provides redundancy in case of network or server failures, and offers a central point of administration. CUCM also supports clusters for load sharing. Database redundancy is available by sharing a common database, whereas call-processing redundancy is provided by CUCM groups.

A cluster utilizes servers in the following manner:

- A cluster consists of one publisher and a total maximum of 20 servers (nodes) running various services, including TFTP, media resources, conferencing, and call processing.

- Call processing (running the Cisco CallManager service) can be enabled on up to eight servers in the cluster.

CUCM redundancy is discussed in detail in Chapter 2, "Cisco Unified Communications Manager Deployment Models."

Chapter Summary

The following list summarizes the key points discussed in this chapter:

- Cisco Collaboration is a comprehensive communications system of voice, video, data, and mobility products and applications over a single network (converged) infrastructure using standards-based IP and a virtualized server and application environment

- CUCM functions include call processing, signaling and device control, dial plan administration, phone feature administration, directory services, and a programming interface

- Cisco Unified Communications Manager uses an Informix Dynamic Server database, with configuration information in the database replicated from the first node (publisher) to all subsequent nodes (subscribers) within a cluster

- User-facing feature changes are stored locally on the subscriber and replicated to all other servers in the cluster

- Clustering provides redundancy for endpoint registration and media services

Reference

For additional information, refer to the following:

Cisco Systems, Inc. *Cisco Collaboration System 10.x Solution Reference Network Designs (SRND)*. San Jose, California, 2015. http://www.cisco.com/c/en/us/td/docs/voice_ip_comm/cucm/srnd/collab10/collab10.html

Review Questions

Use the questions here to review what you learned in this chapter. The correct answers are found in Appendix A, "Answers to the Review Questions."

1. Which layer of the Cisco Unified Communications components is responsible for delivering a dial tone?

   a. Endpoints

   b. Applications

   c. Call control

   d. Infrastructure

2. What is the name of the server in a CUCM cluster that maintains a read/write copy of the entire database?

   a. Member server

   b. Domain controller

   c. Subscriber

   d. Publisher

3. What protocol is responsible for transporting VoIP?

   a. Skinny Client Control Protocol (SCCP)

   b. H.323

   c. Real-Time Transport Protocol (RTP)

   d. Real-Time Transport Control Protocol (RTCP)

   e. Media Gateway Control Protocol (MGCP)

   f. Skinny Gateway Control Protocol (SGCP)

4. How many call-processing agents can be active in a CUCM cluster?

   a. 20

   b. 4

   c. 8

   d. 9

   e. 2

5. How many TFTP servers can be in a CUCM cluster?

   a. 20

   b. 4

   c. 8

   d. 9

   e. 2

6. How many servers can be in a CUCM cluster?

   a. 20

   b. 4

   c. 8

   d. 9

   e. 2

7. True or false? CUCM always relies on an LDAP database for user information.

   a. True

   b. False

8. Which of the following are signaling protocols use to communicate between CUCM and IP Phones? (Choose two.)

   a. MGCP

   b. SCCP

   c. H.323

   d. SIP

   e. RTP

9. Which server contains endpoint configuration files?

   a. Publisher

   b. Subscriber

   c. TFTP server

   d. DHCP server

10. Which deployment model allows for servers from a single cluster to be located across multiple physical locations?

   a. Single Site—Extended

   b. Centralized Multisite

   c. Clustering over the WAN

   d. Distributed Multisite

Chapter 2

Cisco Unified Communications Manager Deployment Models

This chapter introduces the Cisco Unified Communications Manager (CUCM) deployment models and architectures that ensure redundancy and provide high availability for call processing and other services. The different redundancy models explored in this chapter can be applied to the different deployment models to provide fault tolerance for CUCM and its services.

Chapter Objectives

Upon completing this chapter, you will understand the CUCM deployment and redundancy options and be able to meet the following objectives:

- Identify the supported CUCM deployment options.

- Describe the characteristics of a CUCM single-site deployment, and identify the reasons for choosing this deployment option.

- Describe the characteristics of a CUCM multisite deployment with centralized call processing, and identify the reasons for choosing this deployment option.

- Describe the characteristics of a CUCM multisite deployment with distributed call processing, and identify the reasons for choosing this deployment option.

- Describe the characteristics of a CUCM multisite deployment with clustering over the WAN, and identify the reasons for choosing this deployment option.

- Describe the Cisco Collaboration Edge solution for teleworkers and remote workers

- Explain how call-processing redundancy is provided in a CUCM cluster, and identify the requirements for different redundancy scenarios.

Cisco Collaboration Network Overview

In a typical Cisco collaboration network, there can be multiple possibilities from campus to remote sites. Figure 2-1 gives an overview of a typical large enterprise Cisco collaboration campus network where the Cisco collaboration services are available in the campus (headquarters) network.

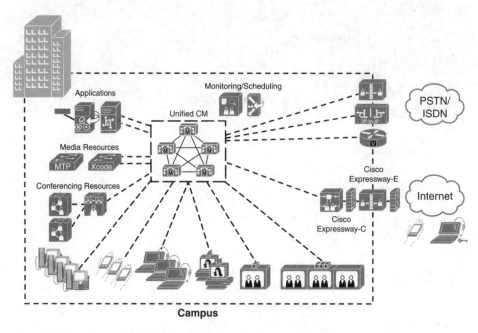

Figure 2-1   *Cisco Collaboration Solution Campus Deployment in a Large Enterprise*

Figure 2-2 shows the campus and a branch (or remote) site; with a subset of campus collaboration services available at the branch/remote site.

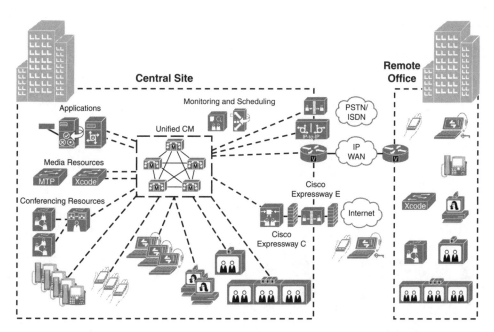

Figure 2-2 *Cisco Collaboration Solution Deployment at Campus and Branch in a Large Enterprise*

As discussed previously, the collaboration network and the associated collaboration services vary from one organization to another. Some of the factors considered are:

■ Number of branch or remote sites

■ Call control configuration (centralized/distributed)

■ Services available for branch or remote sites

■ Teleworking options

The following sections cover CUCM deployment models to support various organization/network/service requirements.

CUCM: Single-Site/Campus Deployment

As illustrated in Figure 2-3, the single-site model for CUCM consists of a CUCM cluster located at a single site or campus with no telephony services provided over a WAN.

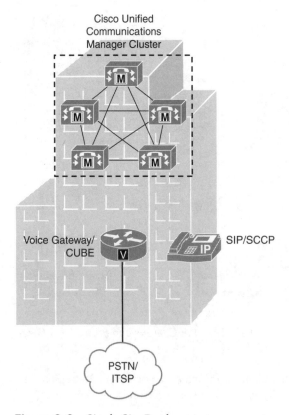

Figure 2-3   *Single-Site Deployment*

All CUCM servers, applications, and digital signal processor (DSP) resources are located in the same physical location or at multiple physical buildings with local-area networks (LAN) or metropolitan-area network (MAN)–based connectivity. LANs are normally defined as having connectivity speeds of 1000 Mbps (1 Gbps) and above, while MANs are typically in the multi-megabit range. In this model, calls beyond the LAN or MAN use the public switched telephone network (PSTN). Besides the voice gateway, Cisco Unified Border Element (CUBE) can also be used to connect all PSTN traffic via IT Service Provider (ITSP) cloud.

Note   ITSP-based PSTN connectivity leverages Session Initiation Protocol (SIP), which is the most popular and prevalent endpoint and media gateway protocol. SIP is described in detail later in this book.

Each cluster supports a maximum of 40,000 IP phones. If there is a need to deploy more than 40,000 IP phones in a single-site configuration, multiple clusters can be implemented inside a LAN or within a MAN and connected through intercluster trunks. Gateway trunks that connect directly to the PSTN manage external calls. If an IP WAN exists between sites, it is used to carry data traffic only; no telephony services are provided over the WAN.

Note   Cisco Business Unit (BU)-supported configurations are available for mega-cluster implementations that can support up to 80,000 devices with 21 servers in a single cluster. Such configurations are subject to review by Cisco Account Team and Cisco BU.

Design Guidelines for Single Site/Campus Model

To accommodate future scalability, Cisco recommends that best practices specific to the distributed and centralized call-processing models be used in a single-site deployment.

Current calling patterns within the enterprise must be understood. How and where are users making calls? If calling patterns indicate that most calls are intrasite, using the single-site model will simplify dial plans and avoid having to provision additional dedicated bandwidth for voice across the IP WAN.

Because Voice over Internet Protocol (VoIP) calls are within the LAN or campus network, it is assumed that bandwidth is not a concern. Using G.722 or G.711 codecs for all endpoints will eliminate the need for DSP resources for transcoding, and those resources can be allocated to other functions, such as conferencing and Media Transfer Protocols (MTPs).

All off-net calls will be diverted to the PSTN (via voice gateway or CUBE) or sent to the legacy private branch exchange (PBX) for call routing if the PSTN resources are being shared during migratory deployments.

To ensure successful operations, a network infrastructure designed for high-availability, fault-tolerant connectivity options should be utilized. In addition, reliable Power over Ethernet (PoE), quality of service (QoS) mechanisms, and monitoring services are recommended. When designing a single campus deployment, do not oversubscribe CUCM to scale larger installations. A single-site deployment does not always equate to a single cluster. If the site has more than 40,000 IP phones, install multiple clusters and configure ICTs between the clusters (or provision mega-cluster).

Benefits of Centralized Call Processing Model

A single infrastructure for a converged network solution provides significant cost benefits and enables CUCM to take advantage of the many IP-based applications in the enterprise.

Single-site deployment allows each site to be completely self-contained. Calls between sites will be routed over the PSTN. Extra provisioning of WAN bandwidth is not needed. Dial plans are also easier to provision. There are no service issues in the event of an IP WAN failure or insufficient bandwidth, and there is no loss of call-processing service or functionality.

In summary, the main benefits of the single-site model are as follows:

- Ease of deployment

- A common infrastructure for a converged solution

- Simplified dial plan

- No transcoding resources are required, due to the use of a single codec

Multisite Deployment with Centralized Call Processing

The multisite deployment with centralized call-processing model consists of a centralized CUCM cluster that provides services for many sites and uses the IP WAN to transport IP telephony traffic between the sites.

The IP WAN also carries call-control signaling between the CUCM cluster at the central site and the IP phones at the remote sites.

Figure 2-4 illustrates a typical centralized call-processing deployment, with a CUCM cluster at the central site or data center and a QoS-enabled IP WAN to connect all the sites. The remote sites rely on the centralized CUCM cluster to manage their call processing. Applications such as voice mail and interactive voice response systems are typically centralized as well to reduce the overall costs of administration and maintenance.

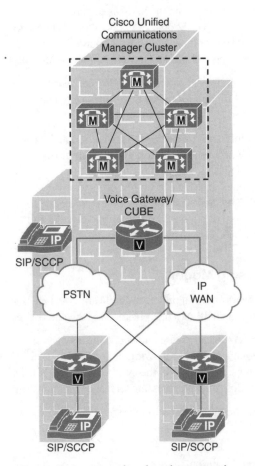

Figure 2-4   *Centralized Multisite Deployment*

The Cisco Unified Survivable Remote Site Telephony (SRST) and E-SRST features that are available in Cisco IOS gateways provide call-processing services to remote IP phones during a WAN outage. When the IP WAN is down, the IP phones at the remote branch office can register to the local Cisco Unified SRST router. The Cisco Unified SRST router can process calls between registered IP phones and send calls to other sites through the PSTN. Figure 2-5 gives an overview of remote site SRST/E-SRST deployment with centralized call processing. The same arrangement however, will work if there are different CUCM clusters (distributed call processing or clustering over WAN) with one or more remote sites.

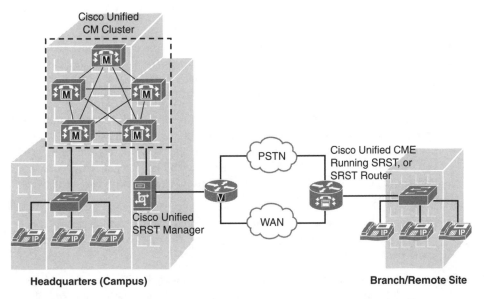

Figure 2-5 *Cisco Unified SRST/E-SRST Deployment with Centralized Call Processing*

Note Topics of SRST, E-SRST, CAC, and AAR are discussed in detail in *Implementing Cisco IP Telephony and Video, Part 2* (CIPTv2).

To avoid oversubscribing the WAN links with voice traffic, causing deterioration of the quality of established calls, Call Admission Control (CAC) is used to limit the number of calls between the sites.

Centralized call-processing models can take advantage of automated alternate routing (AAR) features. AAR allows CUCM to dynamically reroute a call over the PSTN if the call is denied because of CAC.

Design Guidelines for Multisite WAN Model with Centralized Call Processing

Consider the following best practice guidelines when implementing a multisite WAN model with centralized call processing:

- Use a maximum of 2000 locations per CUCM cluster.

- Use a maximum of 2100 H.323 devices (gateways, multipoint control units, trunks, and clients) or 1100 MGCP gateways per CUCM cluster.

- Minimize delay between CUCM and remote locations to reduce voice cut-through delays.

- Use enhanced locations CAC mechanism in CUCM to provide CAC into and out of remote branches. Locations can support a maximum of 40,000 IP phones per cluster when CUCM runs on the largest supported cluster. Another option is to use Resource Reservation Protocol (RSVP)-based CAC between locations.

- Choose appropriate platform for SRST support. There is no limit to the number of IP phones at each individual remote branch. However, the capability that the Cisco Unified SRST feature provides in the branch router limits remote branches to a maximum of 1500 Cisco IP phones on a Cisco 3945E Integrated Services Router during a WAN outage or failover to SRST. Other platforms have different (lower) limits.

- Use high-bandwidth audio (for example, G.711 or G.722) between devices in the same site (intrasite), but low-bandwidth audio (for example, G.729) between devices in different sites (intersite).

- Use high-bandwidth video (for example, 1.5 Mbps with 4CIF or 720p, to 2 Mbps with 1080p) between devices in the same site, but low-bandwidth video (for example, 384 kbps with 448p or CIF) between devices at different sites.

- Use a minimum of 1.5 Mbps or greater WAN link speed. Video is not recommended on WAN connections that operate at speeds lower than 1.5 Mbps.

If a distributed call-processing model is more suitable for the business needs of a customer, the choices include installing a CUCM cluster at the remote branch or running CUCM Express on the branch router.

Benefits of Multisite Deployment with Centralized Call Processing Model

A multisite deployment with centralized call processing saves PSTN costs for intersite calls by using the IP WAN instead of the PSTN. The IP WAN can also be used to bypass toll charges by routing calls through remote site gateways that are closer to the PSTN number that is dialed. This practice is known as Tail End Hop Off (TEHO). TEHO is not permitted in some countries, and local regulations should be verified before implementing TEHO.

This deployment model maximizes the utilization of available bandwidth by allowing voice traffic to share the IP WAN with other types of traffic. Deploying QoS and CAC ensures voice quality. AAR reroutes calls over the PSTN if CAC denies the calls because of oversubscription.

Cisco Extension Mobility can be used within the CUCM cluster, allowing roaming users to use their directory numbers at remote phones as if they were at their home phones.

When the multisite WAN with centralized call-processing deployment model is used, CUCM administration is centralized, and therefore simpler, compared with a multisite WAN with distributed call-processing model where multiple clusters must be separately administered.

Multisite Deployment with Distributed Call Processing

The model for a multisite WAN deployment with distributed call processing consists of multiple independent sites, each with its own CUCM cluster.

An IP WAN carries voice traffic between the distributed clusters. CUCM Session Management Edition (SME) cluster or SIP proxy servers can be used to provide intercluster call routing and dial plan aggregation in multisite distributed call-processing deployments. Cisco CUCM Session Management Edition (SME) is the recommended trunk and dial plan aggregation platform in multisite distributed call processing deployments. SME is essentially a CUCM cluster with trunk interfaces only and no IP endpoints. It enables aggregation of multiple unified communications systems, referred to as leaf systems.

Cisco CUCM SME may also be used to connect to the PSTN and third-party unified communications systems such as PBXs and centralized unified communications applications. Figure 2-6 illustrates a distributed multisite deployment.

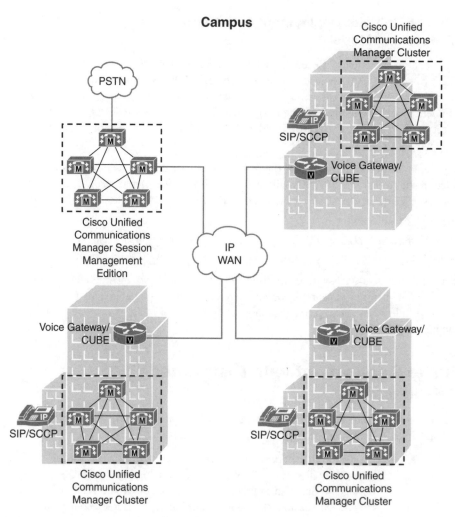

Figure 2-6 *Distributed Multisite Deployment*

Design Guidelines for Multisite Deployment with Distributed Call Processing Model

The multisite model with distributed call processing has the following design characteristics:

- A centralized platform for trunk and dial plan aggregation is commonly deployed. This platform is typically a Cisco Unified Communications Session Management Edition (SME) cluster, although an SIP proxy server (for example, Cisco Unified SIP Proxy (CUSP)) could also be used to provide intercluster call routing and dial plan aggregation in multisite distributed call-processing deployments.

- Centralized services such as centralized PSTN access, centralized voice mail, and centralized conferencing are available. These services can be deployed centrally, thus benefiting from centralized management and economies of scale. Services that need to track end-user status (for example, Cisco IM and Presence) must connect to the CUCM cluster for the users that they serve.

- The use of high-bandwidth audio (for example, G.711 or G.722) between devices within the same site, but low-bandwidth audio (for example, G.729) between devices in different sites.

- The use of high-bandwidth video (for example, 1.5 Mbps with 4CIF or 720p, to 2 Mbps with 1080p) between devices in the same site, but low-bandwidth video (for example, 384 kbps with 448p or CIF) between devices at different sites.

- The use of se a minimum of 1.5 Mbps or greater WAN link speed. Video is not recommended on WAN connections that operate at speeds lower than 1.5 Mbps.

- Call admission control is achieved through Enhanced Locations CAC or RSVP.

Benefits of Multisite Deployment with Distributed Call Processing Model

The multisite deployment with distributed call-processing model is a superset of both the single-site and multisite WAN with centralized call processing models.

The multisite WAN with distributed call-processing model provides the following benefits:

- PSTN call cost savings are possible when the IP WAN is used for calls between sites.

- In this model, you can use the IP WAN to bypass toll charges by routing calls through remote site gateways, closer to the PSTN number that is dialed—that is, TEHO.

- Maximum utilization of available bandwidth is possible by allowing voice traffic to share the IP WAN with other types of traffic.

Clustering over the IP WAN

Cisco supports CUCM clustered over an IP WAN. Figure 2-7 shows the publisher and two subscribers at one location while another pair of subscribers from the same cluster resides at a different location. The QoS-enabled IP WAN connects the two sites. Note the requirement of a round trip time less than 80 ms between the sites. This requirement is in support of database replication occurring between the publisher and all the subscribers in the cluster.

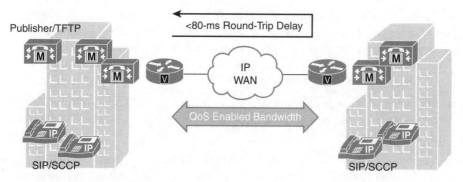

Figure 2-7 *Clustering over the WAN*

Some of the characteristics of this model include:

- Applications and CUCM servers of the same cluster can be distributed over the IP WAN.

- The IP WAN carries intracluster server communication and signaling.

- Limited number of sites:

  - Two to four sites for local failover (two CUCM servers per site)

  - Up to eight sites for remote failover across the IP WAN (one CUCM server per site).

The cluster design is useful for customers who require more functionality than the limited feature set that is offered by Cisco Unified SRST. This network design also allows remote offices to support more IP phones than SRST if the connection to the primary CUCM is lost.

Design Guidelines for Clustering over WAN Deployment Model

Although the distributed single-cluster call-processing model offers some significant advantages, it must adhere to these strict design guidelines:

- Two CUCM servers in a cluster must have a maximum round-trip delay of 80 ms between them. Because of this strict guideline, this design can be used only between closely connected, high-speed locations.

- A minimum of 1.544 Mbps (T1) of bandwidth is required for Intra-Cluster Communication Signaling (ICCS) between each site and every other site that is clustered over the WAN. This bandwidth supports up to 10,000 busy hour call attempts (BHCAs) within the cluster. The BHCA represents the number of call attempts that are made during the busiest hour of the day.

- In addition to the bandwidth required for ICCS traffic, a minimum of 1.544 Mbps (T1) of bandwidth is required for database and other inter-server traffic between the publisher and every subscriber node within the cluster.

- Up to eight small sites are supported using the remote failover deployment model. Remote failover allows you to deploy one server per location. (A maximum of eight call-processing servers are supported in a cluster.) If CUCM fails, IP phones register to another server over the WAN. Therefore, Cisco Unified SRST is not required in this deployment model (although it is supported). The remote failover design may require significant additional bandwidth, depending on the number of telephones at each location.

Benefits of Clustering over WAN Deployment Model

Clustering over the IP WAN provides a combination of the benefits of the two multisite deployment models to satisfy specific site requirements.

Although there are stringent requirements, clustering over the IP WAN offers these advantages:

- Single point of administration for users for all sites within the cluster

- Feature transparency

- Shared line appearances

- Cisco Extension Mobility within the cluster

- A unified dial plan

The clustering over IP WAN design is useful for customers who want to combine these advantages with the benefits that are provided by a local call-processing agent at each site (intrasite signaling is kept local, independent of WAN failures) and require more functionality at the remote sites than is provided by Cisco Unified SRST. This network design also allows remote offices to support more Cisco IP phones than SRST (1500 IP phones using Cisco 3945E Integrated Services Routers) in the event of WAN failure.

These features make clustering across the IP WAN ideal as a disaster-recovery plan for business continuance sites or as a single solution for up to eight small or medium sites.

Collaboration Edge Deployment Model

With increasing focus on teleworking and remote workers, enterprise collaboration resources are required to be extended beyond traditional collaboration borders. This border between an enterprise Unified Communications network and the outside world is referred to as the Collaboration Edge. Collaboration Edge services offer access to enterprise network resources from the outside world via multiple mechanisms. The users can be teleworkers working from home, mobile workers with LTE or Wi-Fi Internet access, or users using collaboration applications such as Jabber to make and receive calls to and from the PSTN or enterprise network. Figure 2-8 gives an overview of a Collaboration Edge solution.

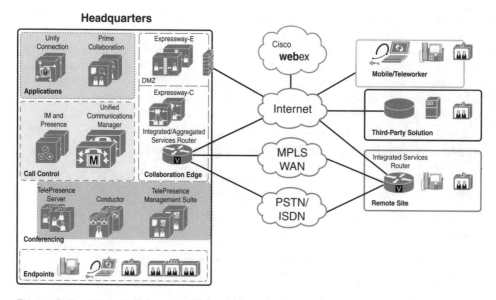

Figure 2-8   *Cisco Collaboration Edge Solution Overview*

The Collaboration Edge solution depends on the requirements of an organization and the technology an organization wishes to leverage. For example, the remote collaboration client access can be categorized into four main categories:

- **VPN-based access:** With endpoints capable of supporting traditional IPsec client or AnyConnect client.

- **VPN-less access:** With clients that traverse the firewall without any VPN client, for example Cisco Expressway solution.

- **Business-to-business communications:** Leveraging CUBE for B2B audio and video calls/conferencing.

- **IP PSTN access:** Leveraging ITSP SIP trunks instead of traditional PSTN trunks. CUBE yet again plays an important and integral part in connecting the enterprise network to ITSP.

> **Note**   Cisco Collaboration Edge solution using Cisco Expressway is addressed in *Implementing Cisco IP Telephony and Video Part 2*. VPN based access is out of scope of this text. For more information on VPN-based access refer to *Securing Cisco IP Telephony Networks*. B2B and IP PSTN access is covered in Chapter 13, "Implementing Cisco IOS Voice Gateways and Cisco Unified Border Element."

The next section addresses CUCM call processing redundancy.

CUCM Call-Processing Redundancy

A cluster is a set of networked servers that can be configured to provide specific services per server. Some cluster servers can be configured to provide CUCM services while other servers can provide Computer Telephony Integration (CTI), Trivial File Transfer Protocol (TFTP), and other media services such as conferencing or music on hold (MOH) These services can be provided by the subscribers and the publisher and can be shared by all servers.

Clustering provides several benefits. It allows the network to scale to up to 40,000 endpoints, provides redundancy in case of network or server failures, and provides a central point of administration. CUCM also supports clusters for load sharing. Database redundancy is provided by sharing a common database, whereas call-processing redundancy is provided by CUCM groups.

A cluster consists of one publisher and a total maximum of 20 servers (nodes) running various services, including TFTP, media resources, conferencing, and call processing. You can have a maximum of eight nodes for call processing (running the Cisco CallManager service).

For a quick recap, a CUCM cluster has a CUCM publisher server that is responsible for replicating the database to the other subscriber nodes in the cluster. The publisher stores the call detail records, and is typically used to make most of configuration change, except starting with CUCM 8.0 where database modifications for user facing call processing features are made on the subscriber servers. The subscriber servers replicate the publisher's database to maintain configuration consistency across the members of the cluster and facilitate spatial redundancy of the database.

To process calls correctly, CUCM needs to retrieve configuration settings for all devices. These settings are stored in a database using an IBM Informix Dynamic Server (IDS). The database is the repository for information such as service parameters, features, device configurations, and the dial plan.

The database replicates nearly all information in a star topology (one publisher, many subscribers). However, CUCM nodes also use a second communication method to replicate run-time data in a mesh topology as shown in Figure 2-9 (every node updates every other node). This type of communication is used for dynamic information that changes more frequently than database changes. The primary use of this replication is to communicate newly registered phones, gateways, and DSP resources, so that optimum routing of calls between members of the cluster and the associated gateways occurs.

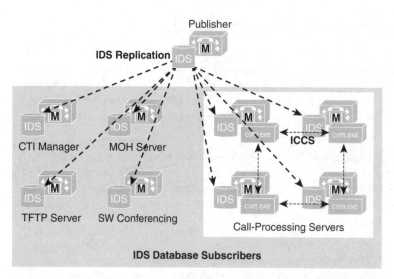

Figure 2-9   *Cisco Unified Communications Manager Database Replication Overview*

Database replication is fully meshed between all servers within a cluster. Static configuration data, because it is created through moves, adds, and changes, is always stored on the publisher and replicated one way from the publisher to each subscriber in the cluster. However, user-facing feature data, for example, Cisco Extension Mobility features, is writeable on a subscriber and are replicated from an updated subscriber to all other servers. All nonuser-facing feature data can be written only to the publisher database and is replicated from the publisher to all subscribers.

User-facing features are typically characterized by the fact that a user can enable or disable the feature directly on their phone by pressing one or more buttons, as opposed to changing a feature through a web-based GUI.

As illustrated in Figure 2-10, user-facing features that are listed below do not rely on the availability of the publisher. The dynamic user-facing feature data can be written to the subscribers to which the device is registered. The data is then replicated to all other servers within the cluster. By allowing the data to be written to the subscriber, the user-facing features can continue to function in the event of a publisher failure.

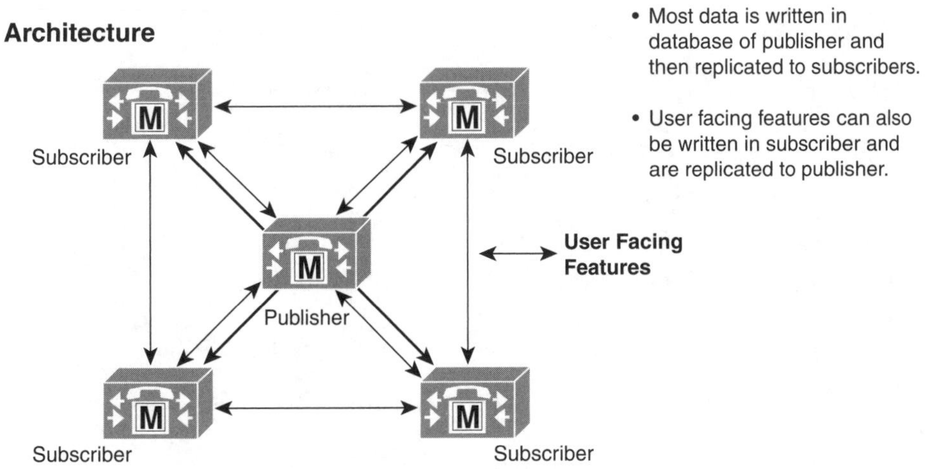

Architecture

- Most data is written in database of publisher and then replicated to subscribers.

- User facing features can also be written in subscriber and are replicated to publisher.

Figure 2-10 *User-Facing Feature Processing*

User-facing features are any features that can be enabled or disabled by pressing buttons on the phone and include the following:

- Call Forward All (CFA)

- Message Waiting Indicator (MWI)

- Privacy Enable/Disable

- Do Not Disturb (DND) Enable/Disable

- Cisco Extension Mobility Login

- Hunt-Group Logout

- Device Mobility

- CTI CAPF status for end users and application users

Therefore, most data (all nonuser-facing feature data) is still replicated in hub-and-spoke style (publisher to subscribers), while user-facing feature data is replicated bidirectionally between all servers.

Cisco Unified Communications Manager Groups: 1:1 Design

A 1:1 CUCM redundancy deployment design, as illustrated in Figure 2-11, guarantees that Cisco IP phone registrations never overwhelm the backup servers, even if multiple primary servers fail concurrently. This design provides high availability and simplifies the configuration. However, the 1:1 redundancy design has an increased server count compared with other redundancy designs and may not be cost-effective.

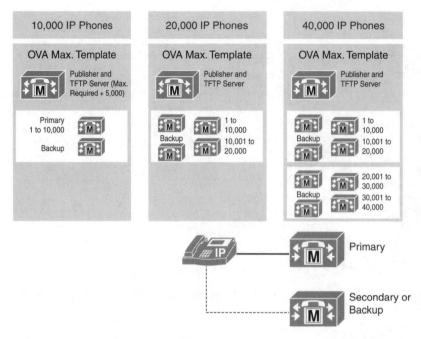

Figure 2-11   *1:1 Redundancy Design*

The other services (dedicated database publisher, dedicated TFTP server, or MOH servers) and media-streaming applications (conference bridge or MTP) may also be enabled on a separate server that registers with the cluster.

Each cluster must also provide the TFTP service, which is responsible for delivering IP phone configuration files to telephones, along with streamed media files, such as MOH and ring files. Therefore, the server that is running the TFTP service can experience a considerable network and processor load.

Depending on the number of devices that a server supports, you can run the TFTP service on a dedicated server, on the database publisher server, or on any other server in the cluster.

In Figure 2-11, an Open Virtualization Archive (OVA) template with the maximum number of users functions as the dedicated database publisher and TFTP server. In addition, there are two call-processing servers supporting a maximum of 10,000 Cisco IP phones. One of these two servers is the primary server; the other server is a dedicated backup server. The function of the database publisher and the TFTP server can be provided by the primary or secondary call-processing server in a smaller IP telephony deployment (fewer than 1000 IP phones). In this case, only two servers are needed in total.

When you increase the number of IP phones, you must increase the number of CUCM servers to support the IP phones. Some network engineers may consider the 1:1 redundancy design excessive because a well-designed network is unlikely to lose more than one primary server at a time. With the low possibility of server loss and the increased server cost, many network engineers choose a 2:1 redundancy design that is explained in the following section.

Cisco Unified Communications Manager Groups: 2:1 Design

Figure 2-12 shows a basic 2:1 redundancy design. While the 2:1 redundancy design offers some redundancy, there is the risk of overwhelming the backup server if multiple primary servers fail. In addition, upgrading the CUCM servers can cause a temporary loss of some services, such as TFTP or DHCP, because a reboot of the CUCM servers is needed after the upgrade is complete.

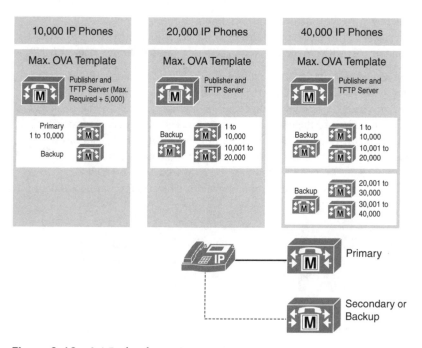

Figure 2-12 *2:1 Redundancy Design*

Network engineers use this 2:1 redundancy model in most IP telephony deployments because of the reduced server costs. If a virtual machine with the largest OVA template is used (shown in Figure 2-11), the server is equipped with redundant, hot-swappable power supplies and hard drives, and it is properly connected and configured, it is unlikely that multiple primary servers will fail at the same time, which makes the 2:1 redundancy model a viable option for most businesses.

As shown in the first scenario in Figure 2-12, when no more than 10,000 IP phones are used, there are no savings in the 2:1 redundancy design compared with the 1:1 redundancy design, simply because there is only a single primary server.

In the scenario with up to 20,000 IP phones, there are two primary servers (each serving 10,000 IP phones) and one secondary server. As long as only one primary server fails, the backup server can provide complete support. If both primary servers failed, the backup server would be able to serve only half of the IP phones.

The third scenario shows a deployment with 40,000 IP phones. Four primary servers are required to facilitate this number of IP phones. For each pair of primary servers, there is one backup server. As long as no more than two servers fail, the backup servers can provide complete support, and all IP phones will operate normally.

Cisco Voice Gateways and Cisco Unified Border Element

Because connectivity to the outside world is of utmost importance in Cisco Collaboration solution, this chapter wouldn't be complete without an overview and a brief discussion of Cisco IOS Voice Gateways and Cisco Unified Border Element (CUBE).

It is important to understand that both traditional voice gateways and CUBE have specific functions (with some degree of overlapping depending on deployment or design). Simply put, a voice gateway terminates time division multiplexing (TDM) signaling and transmits it by way of IP into the network or vice-versa. This allows calls to/from the PSTN network over traditional PSTN trunks, for example, ISDN T1, E1, and BRI trunks. A CUBE on the other hand terminates IP-to-IP calls, with the most common application being a SIP PSTN connection broker for enterprise network with ITSP. CUBE can do protocol interworking, address hiding, and multiple other functions described in the next section.

Note Cisco IOS voice gateways and CUBE and their functionalities, deployment options and protocols are described in detail in Chapter 13, "Implementing Cisco IOS Voice Gateways and Cisco Unified Border Element."

Cisco Voice Gateways

An access digital trunk gateway connects Cisco Unified Communications Manager to the PSTN or to a PBX via digital trunks such as Primary Rate Interface (PRI), Basic Rate Interface (BRI), or E1 R2 channel associated signaling (CAS). Digital E1 PRI trunks may also be used to connect to certain legacy voice mail systems.

Figure 2-13 gives an overview of an IOS voice gateway connecting the enterprise IP network to traditional PSTN network.

Figure 2-13 *Cisco IOS Voice Gateway Overview*

Gateways in a Collaboration network must meet the following core feature requirements:

- **Dual Tone Multifrequency (DTMF) relay capabilities:** DTMF relay capability, specifically out-of-band DTMF, separates DTMF digits from the voice stream and sends them as signaling indications through the gateway protocol (H.323, SCCP, MGCP, or SIP) signaling channel instead of as part of the voice stream or bearer traffic. Out-of-band DTMF is required when a low bit-rate codec is used for voice compression because the potential exists for DTMF signal loss or distortion.

- **Supplementary services support:** Supplementary services are typically basic telephony functions such as hold, transfer, and conferencing.

- **CUCM redundancy support:** CUCM clusters offer CUCM service and application redundancy. The gateways must support the ability to "re-home" to a secondary Cisco Unified Communications Manager in the event that a primary Cisco Unified Communications Manager fails. Redundancy differs from call survivability in the event of a Cisco Unified Communications Manager or network failure.

- **Fax/modem support:** Fax over IP enables interoperability of traditional analog fax machines with IP telephony networks. The fax image is converted from an analog signal and is carried as digital data over the packet network.

From a protocol perspective, CUCM supports the following gateway protocols:

- H.323

- Session Initiation Protocol (SIP)

- Media Gateway Control Protocol (MGCP)

- Skinny Client Control Protocol (SCCP)

Cisco Unified Border Element (CUBE)

Cisco Unified Border Element (CUBE) facilitates simple and cost-effective connectivity between enterprise unified communications with the PSTN world by leveraging Session Initiation Protocol (SIP) trunks to the IT Service Provider (ITSP), also known as the SIP Service Provider. A CUBE is primarily an IP-to-IP gateway that helps connect two or more similar or dissimilar networks, while offering a host of features that a regular voice gateway cannot offer. For example, a CUBE router can connect an H.323 network to SIP network or vice-versa, or a SIP network to a SIP provider. The following are some of the features that CUBE offers:

- Security demarcation, firewalling, DOS protection, and VPN services

- Signaling, protocol, and media interworking (H.323–SIP, SIP–H.323, SIP-SIP)

- Transcoding

- DTMF relay

- Media and signaling control and monitoring
- QoS and bandwidth management
- Co-existence/co-operation with TDM trunking
- Business-to-Business (B2B) audio and video communications

Figure 2-14 gives an overview of CUBE playing a role in B2B communications and connecting Enterprises 1 and 2 to PSTN via ITSP.

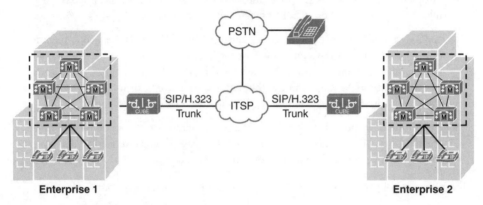

Figure 2-14   *CUBE in B2B Communications*

Chapter Summary

The following list summarizes the key points that were discussed in this chapter:

- Supported CUCM deployment models are Single-Site (Campus), Multisite with Centralized Call Processing, Multisite with Distributed Call Processing, and Clustering over the IP WAN.

- In the Single-Site deployment model, the CUCM, applications, and DSP resources are at the same physical location; all offsite calls are handled by the PSTN.

- The Multisite with Centralized Call Processing model has a single CUCM cluster. Applications and DSP resources can be centralized or distributed. The IP WAN carries call-control signaling traffic, even for calls within a remote site.

- The Multisite with Distributed Call Processing model has multiple independent sites, each with a CUCM cluster; the IP WAN carries traffic only for intersite calls.

- Clustering over the WAN provides centralized administration, a unified dial plan, feature extension to all offices, and support for more remote phones during failover, but it places strict delay and bandwidth requirements on the WAN.

- Clustering provide redundancy. A 1:1 redundancy design offers the highest availability but requires the most resources and is not as cost-effective as 2:1 redundancy.

Reference

For additional information, refer to the following:

- http://www.cisco.com/c/en/us/td/docs/voice_ip_comm/cucm/srnd/collab10/collab10/models.html

Review Questions

Use the questions here to review what you learned in this chapter. The correct answers are found in Appendix A, "Answers to the Review Questions."

1. What is the maximum number of phones supported per CUCM cluster?

   a. 10,000

   b. 7500

   c. 30,000

   d. 40,000 ✓

2. How is call admission control handled in the Centralized Call Processing model?

   a. QoS

   b. H.323 gateway

   c. H.323 gatekeeper

   d. CUCM locations ✓

   e. CUCM regions

3. What technology is used in the Centralized Call Processing model to reroute a call to a remote destination if there is not enough bandwidth to accommodate the call?

   a. Automated alternate routing ✓

   b. Call admission control

   c. Quality of service

   d. Intercluster trunks

4. What technology is used to bypass toll charges by routing calls through remote-site gateways, closer to the PSTN number dialed?

   a. Automated alternate routing

   b. Tail-end hop-off . ✓

   c. Extension mobility

   d. Call admission control

5. Which call-processing model requires the use of SRST to provide backup for IP phones?

   a. Single-Site model

   b. Centralized multisite model

   c. Distributed multisite model

   d. Clustering over the WAN model

6. Gatekeepers are used within which call-processing model?

   a. Single-Site model

   b. Centralized model

   c. Distributed model

   d. Clustering over the WAN model

7. What is the maximum round-trip time requirement between CUCM servers in the Clustering over the WAN model?

   a. 20 ms

   b. 150 ms

   c. 80 ms

   d. 300 ms

8. What is the minimum amount of bandwidth that must be dedicated to database replication in the Clustering over the WAN model?

   a. 900 kbps

   b. 1.544 Mbps

   c. 80 kbps

   d. 2.048 Mbps

9. What platform is recommended to be used as a trunk and dial plan aggregation element?

   a. Cisco Unified SRST

   b. CallManager Express

   c. CUCM Session Management Edition

   d. Cisco Prime Collaboration

10. True or false? Clustering over the WAN allows for up to 20 sites, each with its own subscriber to provide local call control capabilities.

   a. True

   b. False

Cisco Unified Communications Manager Services and Initial Configuration Settings

Cisco Unified Communications Manager (CUCM) configuration includes basic and specific settings, depending on the features and services to be leveraged in an enterprise. This chapter describes how basic settings on CUCM are configured to enable the system and prepare CUCM for endpoint deployment.

Chapter Objectives

Upon completing this chapter, you will be able to activate required CUCM services and settings to enable features, remove Domain Name System (DNS) reliance, and meet the following objectives:

- Identify elements used for general initial configuration

- Describe the difference between network and feature services, and explain how they can be managed using the Cisco Unified Serviceability web interface

- Describe the purpose of enterprise parameters and enterprise phone configuration, and explain key parameters.

- Describe the purpose of service parameters, and explain key parameters

CUCM Deployment Overview

In Release 10.0(1) and later, Cisco supports only virtualized deployments of CUCM (CUCM) on Cisco UCS servers, as illustrated in Figure 3-1, or on a Cisco-approved third-party server configuration. In other words, Cisco does not support deployments of CUCM on Cisco Media Convergence Servers (MCS) starting with Version 10.0(1). Therefore, the VMware vSphere ESXi hypervisor must be deployed for those applications, and they cannot be installed directly on the server (bare metal).

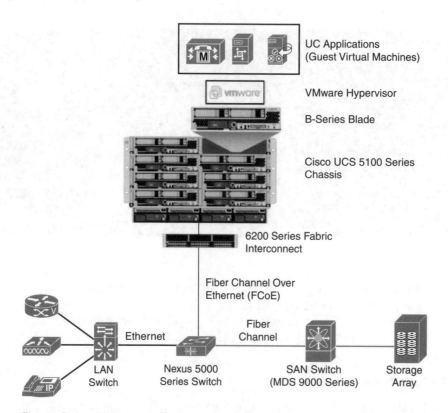

Figure 3-1   *CUCM Installation on VMware and UCS*

References to virtualizing the CUCM environment and supported hardware information are available from the Cisco DocWiki:

   http://docwiki.cisco.com/wiki/UC_Virtualization_Supported_Hardware

A virtual machine template defines the configuration of the virtual machine's virtual hardware, or the "VM configuration." Open Virtualization Format (OVF) is an open standard for describing a VM configuration, and Open Virtual Appliance (OVA) is an open standard to package and distribute those templates. Files in OVA format have an extension of ".ova". Cisco Collaboration applications produce a file in OVA format containing all the required and supported VM configurations for that application. To be TAC-supported, Virtual Machines for Cisco Unified Communications applications must use a VM configuration from the OVA file provided by that application. Two hardware options are available:

■ **Tested Reference Configuration (TRC):** This option provides selected hardware configurations that are based on Cisco UCS platforms. These platforms are tested and documented for specific guaranteed performance, capacity, and application coresidency scenarios that run "full-load" Cisco Collaboration Systems virtual machines. Cisco Business Edition 6000/7000 systems are examples of TRC solutions.

■ **Specification-based hardware:** This option provides more hardware flexibility and, for example, adds support for other Cisco UCS and third-party servers that are listed in the VMware Hardware Compatibility List (available at http://www.vmware.com/resources/compatibility/search.php).

Unlike the Cisco UCS B-Series, the TRCs that are based on the UCS C-Series support local storage for the hypervisor and the application virtual machines on the directly attached storage drives, not on a Fibre Channel Storage Area Network (SAN) storage array. It is possible to use an external storage array with a C-Series server, but the server would then be considered as specifications-based hardware and not as a TRC.

The CUCM application deployment models on virtualized servers are very similar to the deployment models for physical servers, but there are two additional considerations with virtualization: there is no access to the host USB, and there are no serial ports.

Once the CUCM installation process is complete, several additional steps are taken to define the role of each server in the cluster, as well as to define cluster- and service-related parameters, such as:

■ Activate and/or verify CUCM services

■ Understand and configure cluster-wide system parameters

■ Understand and configure per-server and per-cluster service parameters

The following sections take a more detailed look at each of these tasks.

Cisco Unified Communications Manager Services

Each server in a CUCM cluster can fulfill different tasks, such as running a Trivial File Transfer Protocol (TFTP) or music on hold (MOH) server, being the database publisher, processing calls, providing media resources, and so on.

Depending on the usage of a server, different services must be activated on the system. There are two types of services on CUCM servers: feature services and network services.

Feature services can be selectively activated or deactivated per server to assign specific tasks or functions (such as call processing, TFTP, etc.) to a specific server. Feature services can be activated and deactivated by the administrator from **Cisco Unified Serviceability > Tools > Service Activation.** They can be started or restarted from **Cisco Unified Serviceability > Tools > Control Center - Feature Services.** Examples of feature services include Cisco CallManager, Cisco TFTP, or Cisco DirSync. Figure 3-2 gives an overview of the feature services.

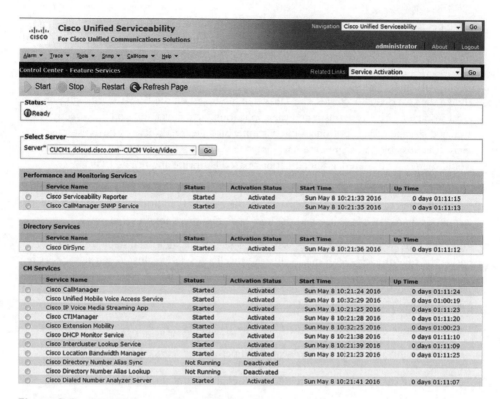

Figure 3-2 *CUCM Feature Services Overview*

Network services are automatically activated and are required for the operation of the server. Network services cannot be activated or deactivated by the administrator, but they can be stopped, started, or restarted from **Cisco Unified Serviceability > Tools > Control Center – Network Services**. Examples of network services are Cisco Discovery Protocol, Cisco Database Replicator, and Cisco Unified Communications Manager Administration. Figure 3-3 gives an overview of network services.

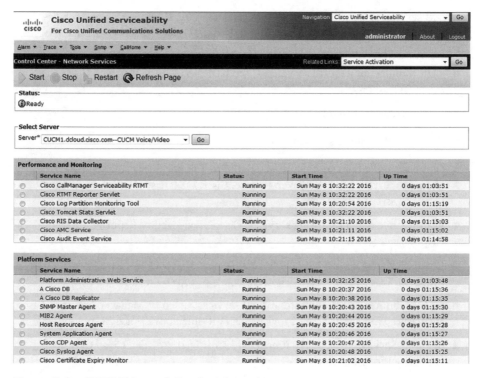

Figure 3-3 *CUCM Network Services Overview*

This list shows the network services by category:

- **Performance and monitoring:** Cisco CallManager Serviceability RTMT (Real-Time Monitoring Tool), Cisco RTMT Reporter Servlet, and so on

- **Backup and restore Services:** Cisco DRF (Disaster Recovery Framework) Local, Cisco DRF Master

- **System services:** Cisco CallManager Serviceability, Cisco CDP (Cisco Discovery Protocol), Cisco Trace Collection Servlet, Cisco Trace Collection Service

- **Platform services:** A Cisco DB (Database), a Cisco DB Replicator, Cisco Tomcat, SNMP (SimpleNetwork Management Protocol) Master Agent, and so on

- **Security services:** Cisco Trust Verification Service

- **DB services:** Cisco Database Layer Monitor

- **SOAP (Simple Object Access Protocol) services:** SOAP–Real-Time Service API (Application Programming Interface), SOAP–Performance Monitoring APIs, and so on

- **CM services:** Cisco CallManager Personal Directory, Cisco Extension Mobility Application, Cisco CallManager Cisco IP Phone Services, Cisco User Data Services, Cisco Change Credential Application, Cisco E911

- **CDR (Call Detail Record) services:** Cisco CDR Repository Manager, Cisco CDR Agent, and so on

- **Admin services:** Cisco CallManager Admin

This list shows the feature services by category:

- **Database and admin services:** Cisco Bulk Provisioning Service, Cisco AXL (Administrative XML Layer) Web Service, Cisco UXL (User XML Layer) Web Service, Cisco TAPS Service

- **Performance and monitoring services:** Cisco Serviceability Reporter, Cisco CallManager SNMP Service

- **CM (CallManager) services:** Cisco CallManager, Cisco TFTP (Trivial File Transfer Protocol), Cisco IP Voice Media Streaming App, and so on

- **CTI (Computer Telephony Integration) services:** Cisco IP Manager Assistant, Cisco WebDialer Web Service, Self Provisioning IVR (Interactive Voice Response)

- **Security Services:** Cisco CTL (Certificate Trust List) Provider, Cisco Certificate Authority Proxy Function

- **Voice Quality Reporter Services:** Cisco Extended Functions

All feature services are disabled by default after CUCM is installed and must be activated manually.

Note   Some services exist as both network services and feature services. The administrator controls the availability of the feature by activating or deactivating the corresponding feature service. CUCM automatically enables the required network services depending on the activated feature services.

Cisco Unified Communications Manager Groups

A CUCM cluster is a collection of virtualized servers that work as a single IP private branch exchange (PBX) system. With CUCM Version 10.0, a cluster may contain as many as 20 server nodes, of which a maximum of eight servers may run the Cisco CallManager service to perform call processing in a cluster. Other servers can be used as TFTP servers or provide media resources such as software conference bridges or MOH.

CUCM groups are used to group servers that run the Cisco CallManager service to provide call-processing redundancy. The concept of CUCM groups was discussed in Chapter 2, "Cisco Unified Communications Manager Deployment Models." A CUCM group is a prioritized list containing up to three call-processing servers. An SRST reference can be added to a CUCM group where the remote site(s) do not have a local CUCM server.

These rules apply to CUCM groups:

- Multiple CUCM groups can exist in the same cluster.

- Each call-processing server can be assigned to more than one CUCM group.

- Each device must have a CUCM group assigned, which will determine the primary and backup servers to which the device can register.

As illustrated in Figure 3-4, Cisco IP phones register with their primary server in the assigned group.

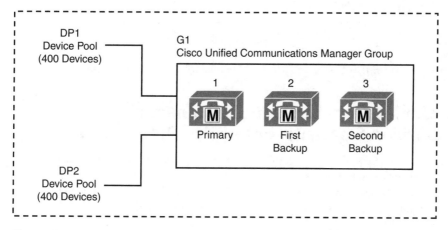

Figure 3-4 *Cisco Unified Communications Manager Group Concept*

The primary server is the first server in the group. When idle, the IP phones and CUCM exchange signaling application keepalives. In addition, Cisco IP phones establish a TCP session with their secondary server and exchange TCP keepalives. When the connection to the primary server is lost (no keepalives received), the IP phone registers to the secondary server. While this is occurring, the IP phone establishes signaling with the tertiary server (if available) in the group. The IP phone continuously tries to re-establish a connection with the primary server; if successful, the IP phone reregisters with the primary server.

Figure 3-5 gives an overview of CUCM Groups.

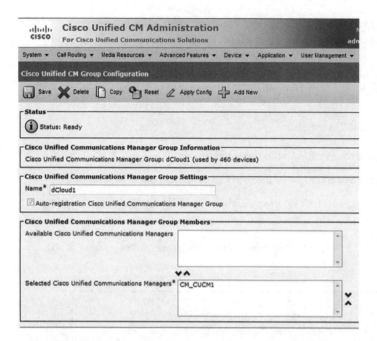

Figure 3-5   *Cisco Unified Communications Manager Group Configuration*

Cisco Unified Communications Manager Configuration Elements: Enterprise Parameters

Enterprise parameters are used to define cluster-wide system settings. These parameters apply to all devices and services in the cluster. After installation, enterprise parameter default values should be verified and modified (if required) before deploying endpoints. Some enterprise parameters specify initial values of device defaults.

Note   Change enterprise parameters only if you are completely aware of the impact of your modifications or if instructed to do so by Cisco TAC.

At the Enterprise Parameters Configuration web page, you will find enterprise parameters that are grouped into categories with the current configuration and the default value shown per parameter.

Note   When DNS reliance is removed, all hostnames within enterprise URL parameters must be changed to IP addresses.

Note   Changes to Enterprise Parameters in CUCM are also reflected in the enterprise parameters for IM&P server.

The following list provides examples of enterprise parameters and their default settings:

- **Cluster ID:** Provides a unique identifier for this cluster

  - Default value = StandAloneCluster

- **Autoregistration Phone Protocol:** Specifies the protocol with which autoregistered phones should boot during initialization

  - Default value = SCCP (Skinny Client Control Protocol)

- **Enable Dependency Records:** Determines whether to display dependency records. Dependency records are a feature of Cisco Unified Communications Manager that allows an administrator to view configuration database records that reference the currently displayed record. Dependency records are useful when you want to delete a configuration entry (for example, a device pool), but the deletion fails because the record is still referenced (for example, by an IP phone). Without dependency records, you would have to check each device to determine if it uses the device pool that you tried to delete.

  - Default value = False

- **CCMUser Parameters:** Used to display or hide user-configurable settings from the CCMUser web page.

- **Phone URL Parameters:** URLs for IP Phone authentication, directory button, services button, etc.

  - Default value = Hostnames used instead of IP addresses

- **User Search Limit:** Specifies the maximum number of users that are retrieved from a search in the Corporate Directory feature on the phone.

  - Default value = 64

Note   To obtain additional information about enterprise parameters, choose **System > Enterprise Parameters** in CUCM Administration and click the question mark symbol (?) at the top right corner of the screen. To obtain additional information about a specific enterprise parameter, click on the parameter itself, and the help file will open directly to the information for that parameter.

Cisco Unified Communications Manager Configuration Elements: Service Parameters and Enterprise Parameters

Service parameters are used to define settings for a specific service on an individual server. An example is the call-processing Cisco CallManager service, which might be activated on only some cluster servers. Some service parameters are defined separately for each server in the cluster, while other parameters may apply to the whole cluster regardless of which server was chosen at the top of the page. An easy way to tell if a parameter will be changed clusterwide is to look at the heading for the group of parameters you are working with. Many groupings say "Clusterwide Parameters," while others may say "parameters for server a.b.c.d .After installation (or activation of feature services), service parameter default values should be verified and modified, if required, before deploying endpoints.

The most important service parameters for the Cisco CallManager service are the following:

- **T302 Timer:** Specifies the interdigit timer for variable-length numbers. Reducing the default value will speed up dialing (shorter postdial delay).

- **CDR and CMR:** Call detail records and call management records (CMR) are the basis for call reporting, accounting, and billing. The service parameters are used to enable CDRs and CMRs (both are disabled by default).

Note   While the CDR service parameter can be easily found by using the search function (the parameter is named CDR Enabled Flag) it is more challenging to find the CMR parameter (the parameter is named Call Diagnostics Enabled).

- **Codecs of Voice Media-Streaming Applications:** Various codecs can be disabled if needed.

Note   By default, not all service parameters are displayed. If you cannot find the service parameter that you want to change, click **Advanced** to see the complete list of available service parameters.

The Change B-Channel Maintenance Status service parameter is an example of a Cisco CallManager service parameter that is not shown by default.

Descriptions for all service parameters can be found by clicking the yellow question mark symbol (?) in the upper right corner (similar to the enterprise parameters) or by clicking on the parameter itself to see help for that parameter directly.

Enterprise parameters deal with clusterwide settings, and service parameters deal with server or service-related settings; device settings include parameters that are tied to individual devices or device pools. Figure 3-6 gives an insight to the enterprise parameters.

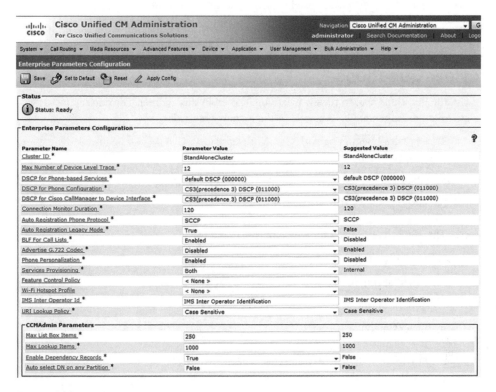

Figure 3-6 *Enterprise Parameters*

Tweaking enterprise parameters is usually required; for example, it may be needed to uniquely identify the cluster from other clusters using **Cluster ID** in an enterprise or to set the default QoS settings by changing **DSCP** for phones and other devices.

> **Note** Unless a change is required or mandated by a configuration procedure, do not change any enterprise or service parameters. Cisco TAC may direct you to do so in certain cases.

Chapter Summary

The following list summarizes the key points discussed in this chapter:

- CUCM initial configuration includes network configuration, activation of feature services, and enterprise and service parameter configuration.

- To avoid DNS reliance by IP phones, change host names to IP addresses.

- Network services are automatically activated, whereas feature services are activated by the CUCM administrator.

- Enterprise parameters are used to define cluster-wide system settings.

- Service parameters are used to configure parameters of specific services.

Review Questions

Use the questions here to review what you learned in this chapter. The correct answers are found in Appendix A, "Answers to the Review Questions."

1. True or false? Beginning with CUCM Release 10.0, CUCM can be installed on physical servers or virtual servers.

   a. True

   b. False ✓

2. The T302 timer is used for which purpose?

   a. Initial digit timeout

   b. Interdigit timeout ✓

   c. Hookflash timer

   d. Ringer timeout

3. What CUCM graphical user interface enables you to activate and deactivate a service from CUCM?

   a. Cisco Unified Serviceability ✓

   b. Control Center

   c. CUCM Administration

   d. Add/Remove Programs

   e. Microsoft Service Console

4. What information does the DHCP option 150 provide?

   a. CUCM publisher IP address

   b. CUCM TFTP server IP address ✓

   c. DHCP server IP address

   d. DNS server IP address

   e. XML service server

5. What default signaling protocol is used for IP Phone Autoregistration?

    a. SIP

    b. SCCP

    c. RTP

    d. RTCP

    e. H.323

    f. MGCP

    g. Ethernet

6. Is the use of a DNS server in an IP telephony environment going to increase or decrease postdial delay?

    a. Increase

    b. Decrease

7. What tool enables you to start, stop, and restart CUCM services from CUCM?

    a. Cisco OS Administration

    b. Control Center

    c. Service Activation

    d. Add/Remove Programs

    e. Microsoft Service Console

8. Which of the following is used to restart network service in CUCM?

    a. Cisco Unified Serviceability

    b. Control Center—Network Services

    c. Service Activation

    d. Control Center—Feature Services

    e. Add/Remove Programs

    f. Microsoft Service Console

9. In CUCM, where can you change the URLs that phone buttons access?

    a. Enterprise parameters

    b. Service parameters

    c. CUCM Serviceability

    d. CUCM Administration

10. Where can call details records and call management records be enabled?

   a. Enterprise parameters

   b. Service parameters

   c. CUCM Serviceability

   d. Cisco Real-Time Monitoring Tool

Chapter 4

Deploying Endpoints and Users in Cisco Unified Communications Manager

An important and implicit task of supporting a Cisco Collaboration solution deployment is managing the endpoints and users. It is important to be able to distinguish between various Cisco Unified Communications endpoints that you might encounter during the course of deploying and administering Cisco Unified Communications Manager (CUCM) cluster(s). Understanding the boot and registration communication between a Cisco Unified IP Phone and CUCM is very valuable for troubleshooting phone registration related issues.

This chapter describes the various models of Cisco Unified IP Phones and discusses how they work within a Cisco Unified Communication solution. It introduces the basic features of Cisco IP Phones, the Cisco IP Phone boot and registration process, and the audio coders-decoders (codecs) that are supported by Cisco IP Phones. The chapter also describes third-party Session Initiation Protocol (SIP) and H.323 endpoints. Moreover, this chapter aims at describing the various user provisioning and management mechanisms available in Cisco Collaboration solution especially in CUCM.

Chapter Objectives

In this chapter you will learn how to implement endpoints and manage user accounts, including integrating CUCM with a corporate LDAP (Lightweight Directory Access Protocol) directory and enabling multiple user privilege levels.

Upon completing this chapter, you will be able to meet the following objectives:

- Compare the endpoints that are supported by CUCM.

- Describe endpoint configuration elements.

- Describe endpoint boot process.

- Compare the types of user accounts that are supported by CUCM.

- Describe the types of LDAP integration.

- Describe LDAP integration features, including mappings, filters, etc.

Cisco Collaboration Solution—Endpoints

Cisco offers a broad range of endpoint products to support the diverse needs of today's collaboration environment. It is important to match the right endpoint to the way each person communicates most effectively. This section provides an overview of endpoint categories and configurations.

Comparison of Endpoints Supported by Cisco Unified Communications Manager

This section provides an overview of audio and video endpoints that can be used with Cisco Unified Communications Manager.

Personal communications styles vary. People who are on the go often rely on mobile devices as a primary means of communication. Executives and managers may need to pull together teams of resources in face to face meetings to accomplish their business goals. Cisco offers a number of endpoints to suit each individual requirement.

Figure 4-1 shows an example of some of the endpoints supported by CUCM.

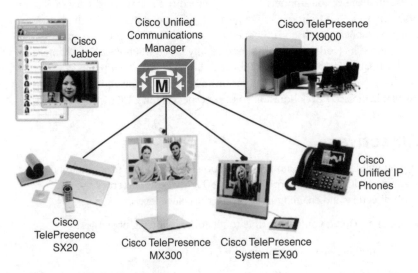

Figure 4-1 *CUCM Endpoints*

Cisco Collaboration endpoints can be grouped as follows:

- Immersive Telepresence
- Telepresence Integration Solutions
- Collaboration Room Endpoints
- Collaboration Desk Endpoints
- IP Phones
- Software Clients

Immersive Telepresence

Immersive Telepresence gives you the feeling of being there in person. The high-quality video, with the size and placement of screens, makes it feel like all participants are sitting around the same table. Some products require custom-built conference rooms, while other products can be placed into any meeting room where conferencing is required.

Immersive products consist of the IX5000, which is a single-row, 6-seat system, and the IX5200, which is a dual-row, 18-seat system. Features include triple 70 inch LCD screens, ultra-high-definition cameras, and support for H.265 video codec. Figure 4-2 shows IX5000 TelePresence system in action.

Figure 4-2   *Cisco IX5000 TelePresence Solution*

Telepresence Integration Solutions

Integration solutions provide the power and flexibility to design a video room of any size using either Cisco or third-party peripherals.

Integration Solutions consist of the Cisco Telepresence SX Series and the Cisco Telepresence Integrator C Series.

The SX Series consists of the SX10 Quick Set and the SX20 Quick Set, which support the needs of small to medium-size conference rooms. The SX80 extends the capabilities to support larger conference rooms and provides three difference camera packages.

The Telepresence Integrator C Series provides three different codec options with varying support for peripherals such as cameras, microphones, and content sources.

Collaboration Room Endpoints

Collaboration room endpoints come in a variety of shapes and sizes, as illustrated in Figure 4-3.

Figure 4-3   *MX700 (left) MX200 (center) Telepresence System 1100 (right)*

Collaboration room endpoints enable you to turn any meeting room into a collaboration hub. This group includes Cisco Telepresence MX Series, as well as the Profile Series and the Telepresence System 1100. These products provide a choice of screen sizes ranging from 42 inch up to 70 inch screens. These typically come as an "all in one" system with fully integrated codecs, displays, cameras, and microphones.

Collaboration Desktop Endpoints

As the name suggests, these endpoints are designed to sit on the desktop. The Desktop Series is composed of the Cisco DX Series (shown in Figure 4-4), Cisco EX Series, and Cisco Telepresence System 500.

Cisco DX650   Cisco DX70   Cisco DX80

Figure 4-4 *DX Series Desktop Endpoints*

These are single screen systems with integrated cameras, microphones, and speakers and a range of display sizes. The DX series are Android based, with built-in Wi-Fi connectivity.

IP Phones

In addition to the telepresence endpoints, Cisco also has an extensive line of IP phones for those instances where the mode of communication may be primarily audio. Some models have cameras attached, while other models can be integrated with external cameras for video conferencing if required. Almost a dozen different IP Phone models are available to suit a diverse set of needs. An example of the different IP Phone models includes the 9900 and 8900 series of phones, which provide standard definition (SD) video capabilities; the 8800 series, which provides high definition (HD) video; and the 7800 series, which provides cost effective voice capabilities. IP Phones 7800 series and 8865 model are shown in Figure 4-5.

Figure 4-5 *7800 Series (left); 8865 (right)*

The key differences between IP phone models are:

- Screen capabilities: resolution, size, color, and touchscreen capability
- List of supported codecs
- Lan port speed, PC port

- Available buttons

- Speakerphone and headset support

- Number of supported lines

- Special services support: HD/SD video, conference station, Wi-Fi

- Supported protocols: SIP vs SCCP

Soft Clients

There are two main categories of software clients: IP Communicator and Cisco Jabber.

The IP Communicator is a Microsoft Windows–based phone application. It provides 8 line keys and 5 soft keys and access to services and applications equal to that of a desk phone. The IP Communicator supports both SIP and SCCP signaling protocols.

Cisco Jabber comes in several forms:

- Cisco Jabber for Windows

- Cisco Jabber for MAC

- Cisco Jabber for Android

- Cisco Jabber Guest

Cisco Jabber for Windows, as illustrated in Figure 4-6 combines contact management, presence status, instant messaging, voice, video, voice messaging, screen sharing and conference capabilities all in one interface on your desktop. Cisco Jabber is built on open standards. It integrates to existing applications to enhance user productivity.

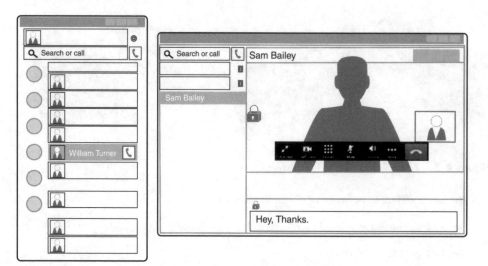

Figure 4-6   *Cisco Jabber for Windows*

For more information on endpoint products, visit cisco.com or consult the endpoint product matrix at the following link: http://www.cisco.com/c/dam/en/us/solutions/collateral/business-video/business-video/endpoint-product-matrix.pdf.

Protocol support varies between different Cisco IP Phone models. Some models support SIP only, other models support SCCP only, while some models support both. For those models that support both protocols, the firmware that is installed on the endpoint will determine the protocol being used.

Legacy video endpoints may support H.323 as their signaling protocol. These endpoints are supported by the Cisco VCS Control product.

Third-party SIP phones can be registered in CUCM and can be authenticated using the directory number (DN) and digest authentication. Cisco IP Phones are uniquely identified in CUCM using the MAC address.

Endpoint Configuration Elements

This section explains the relationship between different phone configuration elements.

Figure 4-7 illustrates a sample list of endpoint configuration elements. The arrows show the assignment of elements.

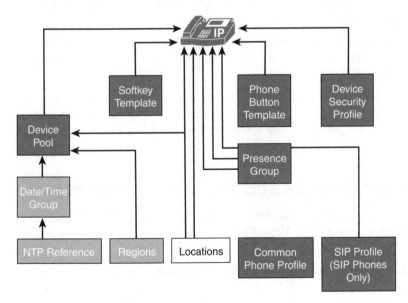

Figure 4-7   *CUCM Endpoint Configuration Elements*

The device pool is one of the components in the IP phone device record. It is a collection of configured elements that can be created once and applied multiple times to various devices and endpoints. The device pool allows IP phones to inherit or acquire settings that have been defined in the various individual elements. The components in the device pool include the following parameters:

- date/time group

- region, which is used for codec selection

- location, which is used for CAC

- local route group, which is used for gateway selection

If a change needs to be made to one of these elements, it can be made once in the device pool and is automatically inherited by all the devices that belong to this device pool at next reset.

For some elements, such as locations, the element can be applied to both the device pool and the phone configuration, in which case the value that is applied to the phone configuration will have higher priority.

In addition to the device pool, there are additional settings that are configured at each phone record. Some of the elements apply only to specific device types. For example, the SIP profile applies only to a SIP phone.

Configuration elements can be divided into mandatory and optional groups. Some mandatory elements may not need to be configured, because there is a default value that is preconfigured.

Mandatory parameters can easily be identified by the asterisk next to the parameter name. If you attempt to save the phone record without having fully configured all mandatory parameters, a popup will inform you that you have missed a required parameter, and the record will not be saved.

Cisco IP Phone Boot-Up and Registration Process

This section describes the boot-up and initial registration process for Cisco Unified SCCP IP Phones and Cisco Unified SIP IP Phones.

Cisco Unified IP Phone Boot-Up and Registration Process—SCCP Phones

Cisco SCCP IP phones follow a specific process when power is applied to the phone. Understanding the boot process is very helpful when troubleshooting phone boot and registration issues. Figure 4-8 shows the Cisco IP Phone boot process.

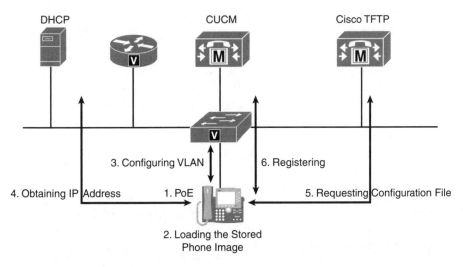

Figure 4-8 *SCCP Phone Boot Process*

The following steps summarize the boot process:

Step 1.   Obtain power. The default option for powering the phone is through Power over Ethernet (PoE). Cisco IP phones do not ship with power adapters; however, it is advisable to purchase a power adapter for your phone models for troubleshooting purposes. When you plug the phone into a properly configured switch port, the Cisco Catalyst switch sends a Fast Link Pulse (FLP) to determine if the phone is connected to an external power source or requires powering up.

Note   FLP goes through a low-pass filter, and upon receiving FLP back, the switch gives the configured level of power on the port. In case the FLP is stopped by the low-pass filter, the switch does not release power to the connected phone.

Once the phone receives power, the buttons on the phone flash on and off in a specific sequence.

Step 2.   Load firmware. The Cisco IP phone has a local firmware image stored in flash. At startup, the phone runs a bootloader that loads the phone image.

Step 3.   Obtain voice/auxillary VLAN. If the Cisco IP phone is connected to a Cisco switch and the switch port has been configured with a voice (auxillary) VLAN, the switch informs the phone of the voice VLAN using Cisco Discovery Protocol (CDP). The IP phone then sends tagged Ethernet frames containing that voice VLAN.

> **Note**   Data from PC port on the phone is sent as untagged frames to the switch.

Step 4.   Obtain IP address. If the Cisco IP phone is configured to use DHCP, it will broadcast a DHCP request. The DHCP server (which can be a Cisco IOS router, CUCM server, or a dedicated DHCP server) should return an IP address and subnet mask, the default gateway, and the IP address of the TFTP server using Option 150 (or option 66) parameter as configured in the DHCP pool. If DHCP is not used, this information must be manually configured on the phone.

> **Note**   For large enterprises DHCP based endpoint deployment is suggested. DHCP option 150 provides the IP addresses of a list of TFTP servers, while DHCP option 66 gives the IP address or the hostname of a single TFTP server.

Step 5.   Obtain a configuration file. The Cisco IP phone will first request its SEP<mac>.cnf.xml file. If the phone has been configured in CUCM, this file will exist on the CUCM TFTP server. If the TFTP server responds with a "file not found" error, the phone then requests XMLDefault.cnf.xml. From the config file, the phone verifies if it has the proper version of firmware and then determines which CUCM to register to. In case the firmware on the phone is older than (or different from) device default firmware defined for the phone model, the phone upgrades (or downgrades) to the firmware version available on the TFTP server.

Step 6.   Register to CUCM. Based on the configuration file CallManager Group List, the phone attempts to register to the highest priority CUCM (the first one in the list) in the CallManager Group. If this registration fails, the phone moves down the list to register to lower priority CUCMs. Upon successful registration, CUCM sends details, such as softkey template, Directory Number (DN), speed dials, etc. to the phone.

Cisco Unified IP Phone Boot-Up and Registration Process—SIP Phones

SIP Phones use a different set of steps to register with CUCM. Steps 1 to 4 are the same as SCCP Phones. For specific steps pertinent to SIP Phone boot-up and registration, refer to the following steps as illustrated in Figure 4-9.

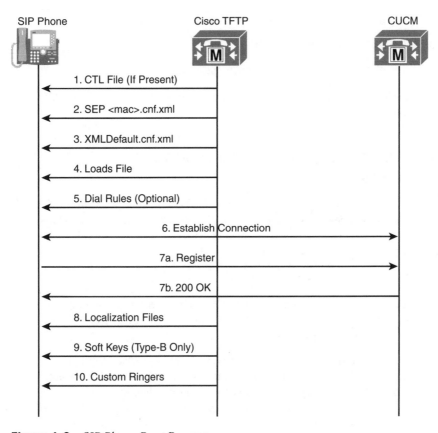

Figure 4-9   *SIP Phone Boot Process*

Step 1.   The phone contacts the TFTP server and requests the Certificate Trust List file (only if the cluster is secured).

Step 2.   The phone contacts the TFTP server and requests its SEP<mac-address>.cnf.xml configuration file.

Step 3.   If the SIP Phone has not been provisioned before boot time, the SIP Phone downloads the default configuration XMLDefault.cnf.xml file from the TFTP server.

Step 4.   The SIP phone requests a firmware upgrade (Load ID file), if one was specified in the configuration file. This process allows the phone to upgrade the firmware image automatically when required for a new version of CUCM.

Step 5.   The phone downloads the SIP dial rules configured for that phone.

Step 6.   The phone establishes connection with the primary CUCM and the TFTP server end to end.

Step 7.   The phone registers with the primary CUCM server listed in its configuration file.

Step 8.   The phone downloads the appropriate localization files from TFTP.

Step 9.   The phone downloads the softkey configurations from TFTP.

Step 10.   The phone downloads custom ringtones (if any) from TFTP.

This completes the basic phone boot-up registration process. The next section addresses the user account management in CUCM.

Cisco Unified Communications Manager User Accounts

User account records are created in CUCM to provide details about phone users, their features and associated devices, and their roles within the CUCM environment. User records are also used by applications to authenticate one application to another when trying to gain access to application resources.

There are two types of user accounts in CUCM:

- **End users:** All end users are associated with a physical person and an interactive login. This category includes all IP telephony users as well as CUCM administrators when using the user groups and roles configurations.

- **Application users:** All application users are associated with Cisco Unified Communications features or applications, such as Cisco Unified Contact Center Express or CUCM Assistant. These applications must authenticate with CUCM, but these internal "users" do not have an interactive login and serve purely for internal communications between applications. Application users can also be created for administrator logins.

The attributes that are associated with end users are separated into three categories:

- Personal and organizational settings:
  - User ID, first name, middle name, last name
  - Manager user ID, department
  - Phone number, mail ID
- Password
- CUCM configuration settings:
  - PIN and SIP digest credentials
  - User privileges (user groups and roles)
  - Associated PCs, controlled devices, and directory numbers
  - Application and feature parameters (Cisco Extension Mobility Profile, Presence Group, Mobility, CAPF, etc.)

> **Note**   Application users are associated with a subset of these attributes.

Users can be provisioned in CUCM either as a local user created in CUCM administration or be imported from a corporate LDAP server. In large organizations, where users are already defined in Microsoft Active Directory (the predominant LDAP Directory application), it may be administratively prohibitive to duplicate these users in CUCM. LDAP synchronization allows administrators to define synchronization agreements with applied filters to limit the scope of imported users.

These are the supported LDAP implementations:

- Microsoft Active Directory 2003 R1/R2 (32-bit)

- Microsoft Active Directory 2008 R1(32-bit)/R2(64-bit)

- Microsoft Active Directory Application Mode 2003 R1/R2 (32-bit)

- Microsoft Lightweight Directory Services 2008 R1(32-bit)/R2(64-bit)

- Sun ONE Directory Server 7.0

- OpenLDAP 2.3.39

- OpenLDAP 2.4

- Oracle Directory Server Enterprise Edition 11gR1

The way a user is created in CUCM determines the method to edit and update the user. If a user was created as a local user, the CUCM administrator can make all changes to the user record through the administration GUI. If a user was synchronized from LDAP, then any changes to the personal and organizational parameters must be made in LDAP and synchronized for CUCM to reflect the changes.

Types of LDAP Integration: Synchronization

The LDAP synchronization feature is employed for user provisioning; it allows central management of accounts on a corporate-wide basis. LDAP provides a specialized database that is optimized to manage a large number of read and search requests and perform occasional write and update requests. This specialized database simplifies end-user provisioning for CUCM administrators.

As illustrated in Figure 4-10, LDAP uses a service called directory synchronization (DirSync) on CUCM to synchronize a number of user attributes (either upon request or periodically) from a corporate LDAP directory. When this feature is enabled, users are automatically provisioned from the corporate directory.

Figure 4-10 shows the synchronization type of LDAP integration.

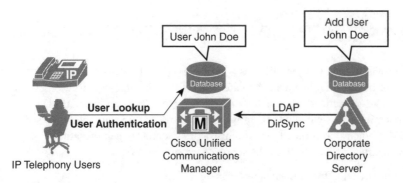

Figure 4-10   *LDAP Integration: Synchronization*

Users and their personal and organizational data are replicated from the LDAP server to CUCM. This information is then visible as read-only in CUCM Administration (CUCM does not copy data back to the LDAP server). All personal and organizational user data is configured in LDAP. There is no schema extension involved in this process.

Note   End users can still be added locally even when LDAP synchronization is enabled.

Note   Application users are never synchronized from LDAP. If an application user id matches an LDAP user being imported, the application user is left intact and the end-user record for the duplicate user id is not created.

Types of LDAP Integration: Authentication

When LDAP authentication is enabled, the local password parameter is removed from the end-user record.

Figure 4-11 shows the communication path for LDAP authentication.

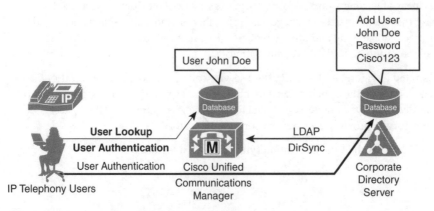

Figure 4-11   *LDAP Integration: Authentication*

With LDAP authentication, CUCM authenticates user credentials against a corporate LDAP directory:

- When this feature is enabled, end-user passwords are not stored in the CUCM database. They are stored in the LDAP directory only.

- Unlike all other parameters, passwords are not replicated to the CUCM database.

CUCM user data (such as associated PCs or controlled devices) is stored in the CUCM database for each individual user. As a consequence, the username must be known in the CUCM database (to assign CUCM user settings to the user) and in the LDAP directory (to assign the password to the user). To avoid separate management of user accounts in these two databases, LDAP synchronization is a prerequisite when configuring LDAP authentication.

LDAP Integration Features: Attribute Mapping

When LDAP synchronization is performed, LDAP directory attributes are mapped to CUCM attributes. The directory attribute data that are mapped to the CUCM user ID must be unique within all entries for that cluster. The data that CUCM imports is all from standard LDAP user attributes.

The **sn** (surname) attribute in LDAP must be populated with data. If it is not populated, that record will not be imported by CUCM.

Some CUCM database fields provide a choice of directory attributes. The administrator can choose only a single mapping for each field. For example, you may use a telephone number or an IP Phone number for the phone number. This setting is the same for all users.

CUCM also allows you to synchronize LDAP directory attributes that are not included in the defaults for the standard user fields to be synchronized. Custom user fields permit you to synchronize LDAP attributes to a customized field that is saved in the CUCM database.

LDAP Integration Feature: Synchronization Agreements and Filters

A search base is an area of the directory that should be considered for synchronization. This is achieved by specifying a position in the directory tree where CUCM begins its search.

CUCM has access to all lower levels, but not to higher levels of the search base.

When users are organized in a structure in the LDAP directory, administrators can use that structure to control which user groups are imported. If a single synchronization agreement specifies the root of the domain, all users of the domain, including service accounts and others, will be synchronized. The search base does not have to specify the domain root. The search base can specify any point in the tree.

The main issue is that customer directory servers are not always clearly organized.

To import data into the CUCM database, the system performs a bind to the LDAP directory using the account that is specified as the LDAP manager distinguished name in the configuration. Reading of the database is done with this account. The account must be available in the LDAP directory for CUCM to log in. It is recommended that you create a specific account with the permission to read all user objects within the subtree that was specified by the user search base.

It is possible to control the import of accounts by limiting read permissions of the LDAP manager distinguished name account or by using LDAP filters.

The example in the Figure 4-12 shows an LDAP synchronization agreement of organizational unit Site 1. It is possible to change the search base to include only users from the organizational subunits Mktg or Eng, but it is not possible to define a search base that will get only users with a user ID that starts with the letter "m." Custom filters enable you to specify such complex rules.

Figure 4-12 shows filtering for LDAP integration.

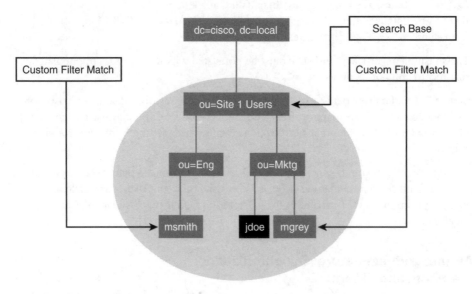

Figure 4-12   *LDAP Integration Filters*

Cisco recommends importing only those directory user accounts to be assigned to Unified Communications resources in each individual cluster. When the number of directory user accounts exceeds the number that is supported for an individual cluster, filtering must be used to choose the subset of users to be associated on that cluster.

Note   A full synchronization is required when the LDAP filter is changed for an agreement.

Search filters allow the definition of search criteria and provide more efficient and effective searches. Unicode strings represent these search filters. Table 4-1 lists some frequently used search filter operators:

Table 4-1   *Search Filter Operators*

Operator	Description
=	Equal to
~=	Approximately equal to
<=	Less than or equal to
>=	Greater than or equal to
&	AND
|	OR
!	NOT

To match a part of a directory number (for example, to look for the groups in two subtrees), use the following filter:

```
(&(objectClass=group)(|(ou:dn:=Chicago)(ou:dn:=Miami)))
```

This filter finds groups that have an organizational unit component in the distinguished name that is either Chicago or Miami.

To exclude entities that match an expression, use an exclamation point (!):

```
(&(objectClass=group)(&(ou:dn:=Chicago)(!(ou:dn:=Boston))))
```

This filter will find all Chicago groups except those that have a Boston organizational unit component. Note the extra parentheses: (!(expression)).

Chapter Summary

The following list summarizes the key points that were discussed in this chapter:

- Cisco CUCM supports a wide spectrum of audio and video endpoints, including third-party devices that communicate via SIP, SCCP, or H.323.

- Compared to previous versions of CUCM, CUCM 10.x supports a wider variety of endpoints, especially video endpoints such as DX, EX, MX, SX, and TX series.

- Some endpoint configuration elements can be applied directly to the device, but also indirectly via other elements such as device pool, SIP profiles, etc.

- Endpoints follow a specific boot process that includes acquiring power, Voice VLAN, DHCP information, and configuration files from a TFTP server.

■ Application users cannot be provisioned or authenticated via an external directory service.

■ LDAP synchronization enables you to import data from the corporate LDAP server into CUCM but does not include passwords.

■ LDAP filters allow for a highly customized selection of users from the corporate directory service, not limited to organizational units, as with the User Search Base parameter.

Review Questions

Use the questions here to review what you learned in this chapter. The correct answers are found in Appendix A, "Answers to the Review Questions."

1. What is used to uniquely identify a Cisco IP Phone?

   a. Directory Number

   b. Digest Authentication

   c. MAC Address

   d. Description

2. What protocols are supported on Cisco IP Phones? (Choose two.)

   a. SCCP

   b. SIP

   c. H.323

   d. MGCP

3. H.323 video endpoints can be registered to which device?

   a. CUCM

   b. VCS Control

   c. IM&P server

   d. Cisco Unified Border Element

4. What two items can be used to authenticate a third-party SIP phone?

   a. Directory Number

   b. MAC Address

   c. Partition

   d. Digest Authentication

   e. Serial Number

5. Which protocol or technology is required to provide the phone with firmware and a configuration file?

   a. Cisco Discovery Protocol

   b. TFTP

   c. FTP

   d. Power over Ethernet

6. What are two types of users that can be created in CUCM? (Choose two.)

   a. End users

   b. GUI users

   c. Administrator users

   d. Application users

   e. Mobility users

7. What protocol or technology is required to provide an IP address, subnet mask, default gateway, and option 150 to a Cisco IP Phone?

   a. DHCP

   b. TFTP

   c. FTP

   d. Power over Ethernet

8. What protocol or technology is required for power delivery to the Cisco IP Phone?

   a. Cisco Discovery Protocol

   b. TFTP

   c. FTP

   d. Power over Ethernet

9. Which protocol is used to communicate the Cisco IP Phone VLAN to the IP Phone?

   a. Cisco Discovery Protocol

   b. TFTP

   c. FTP

   d. Power over Ethernet

10. How are third-party SIP phones authenticated in CUCM?

   a. MAC address

   b. Transport layer security

   c. Digest authentication

   d. Secure hashing algorithm

Chapter 5

Deploying IP Phone Services in Cisco Unified Communications Manager

It used to be that a phone was a phone and a PC was a PC, and each was used for a different purpose. In today's world, those distinctions have blurred and mostly gone away. Your PC can make calls using a softphone application, such as IP Communicator or Cisco Jabber, while some desktop phones can run interactive applications on the phone display. Other endpoints, such as the DX series, are based on the Android operating system to further enhance endpoint functionality.

This chapter discusses the implementation of IP phone services in the Cisco Unified Communications Manager (CUCM) environment.

Chapter Objectives

Upon completing this chapter, you will be able to meet the following objectives:

- Describe general uses of IP phone services.

- Describe IP phone service configuration.

- Describe the IP phone service initiation process.

- Describe how IP phone services are secured.

- Describe IP phone services deployment options.

Overview of Cisco IP Phone Services

Using CUCM Administration, you define and maintain the list of IP phone services that can display on supported models of Cisco Unified IP Phones. IP phone services comprise XML applications or Cisco-signed Java MIDlets that enable the display of interactive content with text and graphics on some Cisco Unified IP Phone models. The Cisco Unified IP phone firmware contains a microbrowser that enables limited web-browsing capability. By running directly on the desktop phone of users, these phone-service applications provide the potential for value-added services and productivity enhancement.

The list of Cisco endpoints that support IP phone services is extensive and includes both Cisco Unified IP Phones and a variety of Cisco Telepresence endpoints. You can view a list of endpoints that support this feature by navigating to Cisco Unified Reporting and running the CUCM Phone Feature List report with the parameters of Product set to All and Feature set to IP Phone Services.

> **Note**   The term phone service refers to an application that transmits and receives content to and from the Cisco Unified IP phone or Telepresence endpoint.

With the exception of the integrated CUCM Extension Mobility and CUCM Assistant application phone services, IP phone services must reside on a separate, off-cluster web server that is not a CUCM web server. Running phone services other than Extension Mobility and CUCM Assistant on the CUCM server node is not supported.

Cisco IP Phone Services Configuration

In Cisco Unified Communications Manager Administration, use the Device > Device Settings > Phone Services menu path to configure IP phone services.

Table 5-1 describes the IP phone service settings that display in the IP Phone Services Configuration window in Cisco Unified Communications Manager Administration.

Table 5-1   *IP Phone Service Settings*

Field	Description
Service Information	.
Service Name	Enter the name of the service. If the service is not marked as an enterprise subscription, the service name will display in areas where you can subscribe to a service; for example, under Cisco Unified Communications Self Care Portal.
	Enter up to 128 characters for the service name.
	For Java MIDlet services, the service name must exactly match the name that is defined in the Java Application Descriptor (JAD) file.
	Note Cisco Unified Communications Manager allows you to create two or more IP phone services with identical names. Cisco recommends that you do not do so unless most or all phone users are advanced, or unless an administrator always configures the IP phone services. Be aware that if AXL or any third-party tool accesses the list of IP phone services for configuration, you must use unique names for IP phone services.

	Note When the service URL points to an external customized URL, you cannot localize the service name as per the device locale of the phone. The service name gets displayed in English alphabets only.
ASCII Service Name	Enter the name of the service to display if the phone cannot display Unicode.
Service Description	Enter a description of the content that the service provides. The description can include up to 50 characters in any language, but it cannot include double quotes ("), or single quotes (').
Service URL	Enter the URL of the server where the IP phone services application is located. Make sure that this server remains independent of the servers in your Cisco Unified Communications Manager cluster. Do not specify a Cisco Unified Communications Manager server or any server that is associated with Cisco Unified Communications Manager (such as a TFTP server or directory database publisher server).

For the services to be available, the phones in the Cisco Unified Communications Manager cluster must have network connectivity to the server.

For Cisco-signed Java MIDlets, enter the location where the JAD file can be downloaded, for example, a web server or the backend application server to which the Java MIDlet communicates.

For Cisco-provided default services, the service URL displays as Application:Cisco/<name of service> by default, for example, Application:Cisco/CorporateDirectory. If you modify the service URL for Cisco-provided default services, verify that you configured Both for the Service Provisioning setting, which displays in the Phone, Enterprise Parameter, and Common Phone Profile Configuration windows. For example, you use a custom corporate directory, so you change Application:Cisco/CorporateDirectory to the external service URL for your custom directory; in this case, change the Service Provisioning setting to Both. |
| Secure-Service URL | Enter the secure URL of the server where the Cisco Unified IP Phone services application is located. Make sure that this server remains independent of the servers in your Cisco Unified Communications Manager cluster. Do not specify a Cisco Unified Communications Manager server or any server that is associated with Cisco Unified Communications Manager (such as a TFTP server or publisher database server).

For the services to be available, the phones in the Cisco Unified Communications Manager cluster must have network connectivity to the server. |

(Continued)

Table 5-1   (*Continued*)

Field	Description
Service Information	
	Note If you do not provide a Secure-Service URL, the device uses the nonsecure URL. If you provide both a secure URL and a nonsecure URL, the device chooses the appropriate URL, based on its capabilities.
Service Category	Select a service application type (XML or Java MIDlet).
	If you choose Java MIDlet, when the phone receives the updated configuration file, the phone retrieves the Cisco-signed MIDlet application (JAD and JAR) from the specified Service URL and installs the application.
Service Type	Choose whether the service is provisioned to the Services, Directories, or Messages button/option on the phone; that is, if the phone has these buttons/options. To determine whether your phone has these buttons/options, see the *Cisco Unified IP Phone Administration Guide* that supports your phone model.
Service Vendor	This field allows you to specify the vendor/manufacturer for the service. This field is optional for XML applications, but it is required for Cisco-signed Java MIDlets.
	For Cisco-signed Java MIDlets, the value that you enter in this field must exactly match the vendor that is defined in the MIDlet JAD file.
	This field displays as blank for Cisco-provided default services.
	You can enter up to 64 characters.
Service Version	Enter the version number for the application.
	For XML applications, this field is optional and is informational only. For Cisco-signed Java MIDlets, consider the following information:
	If you enter a version, the service version must exactly match the version that is defined in the JAD file. If you enter a version, the phone attempts to upgrade or downgrade the MIDlet if the version is different than what is installed on the phone.
	If the field is blank, the version gets retrieved from the Service URL. Leaving the field blank ensures that the phone attempts to download the JAD file every time that the phone reregisters to Cisco Unified Communications Manager as well as every time that the Cisco-signed Java MIDlet is launched; this ensures that the phone always runs the latest version of the Cisco-signed Java MIDlet without you having to manually update the Service Version field.
	This field displays as blank for Cisco-provided default services.
	You can enter numbers and periods in this field (up to 16 ASCII characters).

Enable	This check box allows you to enable or disable the service without removing the configuration from Cisco Unified Communications Manager Administration (and without removing the service from the database).
	Unchecking the check box removes the service from the phone configuration file and the phone.
Enterprise Subscription	This check box allows you to automatically provision the service to all devices in the cluster that can support the service. If you check this check box, you (or an end user) cannot subscribe to the service.
	If this check box is unchecked, you must manually subscribe to the service for it to display on the phone (either in the Phone Configuration window, in BAT, or in the Cisco Unified Communications Self Care Portal).
	Tip This setting displays only when you configure a service for the first time. After you save the service, the check box does not display in the window.
	To identify whether the service is provisioned to all devices in the cluster that can support the service, go to the Find and List IP Phone Services window and display the services. If true displays in the Enterprise Subscription column, you cannot manually subscribe to the service.
	If false displays, you can manually subscribe to the service; for example, an end user can subscribe to the service through the Cisco Unified Communications Self Care Portal.

After you configure the services, you can add services to the phones in the database by subscribing them to each appropriate service if the service is not classified as an enterprise subscription. You can assign the services to the Services, Directory, or Messages buttons/options, if the phone model supports these buttons/options.

Users can log in to Cisco Unified Communications Self Care Portal and subscribe to these services for their Cisco Unified IP Phones if these IP phone services are not classified as enterprise subscriptions.

Cisco IP Phone Services Functions

An IP phone service can be initiated by the end user or by the phone in several ways, as described in the following sections.

- User-initiated (pull)
- Phone-initiated (pull)
- Phone service–initiated (push)

> **Note**   The user-initiated and phone-initiated pull functionalities use the phone's web client to invoke phone services. In contrast, the phone service–initiated push functionality invokes action on the phone by posting content (via an HTTP POST) to the phone's web server (not to its client).

Cisco IP Phone Services Functions: User-Initiated

A user-initiated service occurs when an IP phone user presses the Services or Applications button, which sends a HTTP GET message to CUCM to display a list of user-subscribed phone services.

Figure 5-1 describes the steps between a user initiating a service and CUCM processing the request and fulfilling the delivery of the service application.

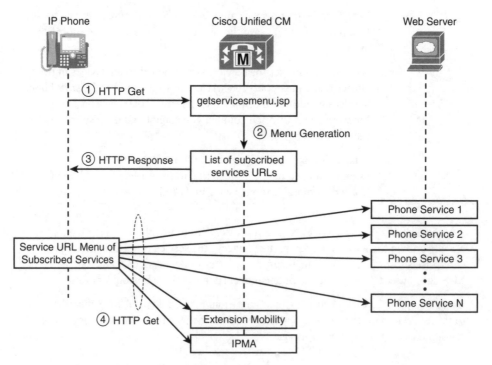

1–Services Provisioning enterprise parameter set to value External URL or Both.

Figure 5-1   *User-Initiated Phone Services*

The steps in Figure 5-1 are as follows:

Step 1.   When a user presses the Services or Applications button, an HTTP GET message is sent from the IP phone to the CUCM getservicesmenu.jsp script, if the Services Provisioning enterprise parameter is set to External URL or Both.

You can specify a different script by changing the URL Services enterprise parameter.

Step 2.   The getservicesmenu.jsp script returns the list of phone service URL locations to which the individual user has subscribed.

Step 3.   The HTTP response returns this list to the IP phone.

Step 4.   Any further phone service menu options chosen by the user continue the HTTP messaging between the user and the web server that contains the selected phone service application.

By default, the Services Provisioning enterprise parameter is set to Internal. With this setting, the IP phone obtains the list of phone services from its configuration file instead of sending an HTTP GET message to CUCM (IP Phone Services begins with Step 4). Some phones, like the Cisco Unified IP Phone 7960, do not have the ability to parse the list of phone services from their configuration file. IP phones that do not have this ability send an HTTP GET message to CUCM to get that list, even if the Service Provisioning enterprise parameter is set to Internal.

CUCM provides the ability to configure a secure IP phone Services URL using HTTPS. This ability was introduced in Release 8.0(1), in addition to a nonsecure URL. Phones that support HTTPS automatically use the secure URL. The following features support HTTPS:

- Cisco Extension Mobility
- Cisco Extension Mobility Cross Cluster (EMCC)
- Cisco Unified Communications Manager Assistant
- Cisco Unified IP Phone Services
- Personal Directory
- Change Credentials

Note   HTTPS access to Cisco Unified IP Phone Services is controlled by the Secured Services URL enterprise parameter. To learn more about secure implementation of CUCM and other Cisco Collaboration applications, refer to the book *Securing Cisco IP Telephony* by Cisco Press.

Cisco IP Phone Services Functions: Phone-Initiated and Phone Service–Initiated

An idle time value can be set within the IP phone firmware, as indicated by the URL Idle Time parameter. When this timeout value is exceeded, the IP phone firmware itself initiates an HTTP GET to the idle URL location that is specified by the URL Idle parameter. This would be an example of a phone-initiated service. Additionally, a phone service application can push content to the IP phone by sending an HTTP POST message to the phone. An example of this would be a service that updates the stock value of the company's shares, which might be of interest to staff members who hold company shares or are compensated in part through a stock option program.

Figure 5-2 details the process of phone or phone service–initiated phone services.

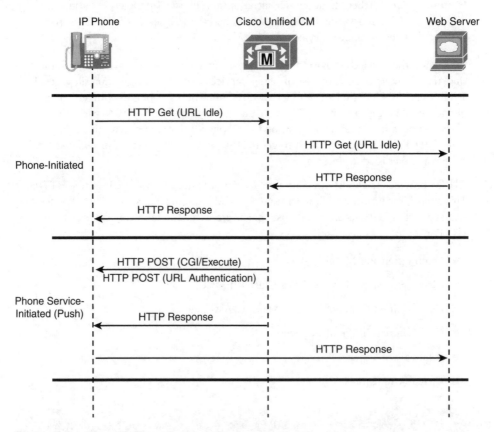

Figure 5-2   *Cisco IP Phone Services Communication Process*

The upper half of Figure 5-2 shows the communication for phone-initiated service, which proceeds with the following steps:

Step 1.   The phone automatically sends an HTTP GET message to the location that is specified in the URL Idle enterprise parameter when the URL Idle Time enterprise parameter is reached.

Step 2.   The HTTP GET message is forwarded via CUCM to the external web server.

Step 3.   The web server sends back an HTTP response containing the content to display.

Step 4.   CUCM relays this content to the phone, and the phone displays the text or image on the screen.

The bottom half of Figure 5-2 shows the communications for phone service–initiated applications using the following steps:

Step 1.   The phone service on the external web server sends an HTTP POST message with a CGI or Execute call to the phone's web server.

Step 2.   Before performing the CGI or Execute call, the phone authenticates the request using the proxy authentication service that is specified by the URL Authentication enterprise parameter. This proxy authentication service provides an interface between the phone and the CUCM directory to validate requests that are made directly to the phone.

Step 3.   If the request is authenticated, CUCM forwards an HTTP response to the phone. The phone's web server then performs the requested action.

Step 4.   The phone returns an HTTP response back to the external web server.

Step 5.   If authentication fails, CUCM forwards a negative HTTP response, and the phone does not perform the requested CGI or Execute action but instead forwards a negative HTTP response to the external web server.

Securing Cisco IP Phone Services

This section explains the Security by Default (SBD) feature and how it applies to secure Cisco IP phone services.

SBD provides these three functions for supported IP phones:

■ Default authentication of TFTP downloaded files (configuration, locale, ring list) that use a signing key

■ Optional encryption of TFTP configuration files that use a signing key

■ Certificate verification for phone-initiated Secure HTTP (HTTPS) connections that use a remote certificate trust store on CUCM called the Trust Verification Service (TVS)

The first two bullets refer to the process of securing the communication between the Cisco IP phone and the TFTP server containing the configuration files. The third bullet applies to any communication between the phone and an HTTPS server where the phone does not have the server's certificate in the Identity Trust List (ITL) file.

The ITL file contains a record for each certificate, and is generated automatically and downloaded by phones at boot or reset. An ITL file is comparable to Certificate Trust List (CTL) file and is downloaded when a Cisco Unified IP Phone first registers with the cluster. In other words, an ITL is a leaner CTL file that is available for Cisco Unified IP Phones to offer initial level of trust with the cluster and consequent protection of signaling and media traffic with CUCM and other IP phones respectively.

If the IP phone service is defined as an HTTPS link, the phone must validate the certificate of the external server. Since the phone's resources are limited, it does not store all possible certificates locally. Instead it uses the ITL certificate of the TVS server to create a secure connection to the TVS service and forward the certificate query to TVS.

TVS is a service that runs on all call processing CUCM servers and acts as a central certificate repository. TVS has access to a broader range of server certificates and can process authentication requests that are received from IP phones when the IP phones don't have the certificate locally.

Note   For an in-depth discussion on SBD, ITL, CTL, CAPF, and other security services available on CUCM, refer to *Securing Cisco IP Telephony Networks*.

Figure 5-3 shows the authentication procedure for an IP phone that is connecting to a secure application server.

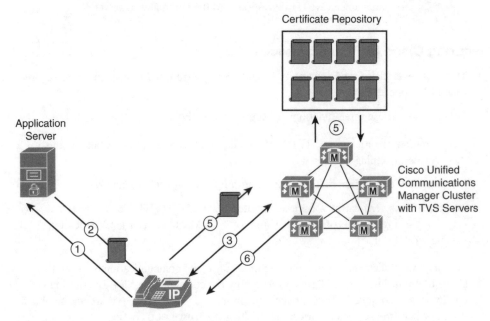

Figure 5-3   *Authentication of Secure IP Phone Services*

These steps take place whenever an SBD-enabled IP phone connects to a secure application server:

Step 1.   The IP phone connects to the secure application server and requests secure communication.

Step 2.   To encrypt the communication, the application server sends its certificate to the IP phone.

Step 3.   The IP phone establishes a Transport Layer Security (TLS) encrypted connection to its configured TVS server. The TVS server sends its certificate to the IP phone the IP phone authenticates the TVS server certificate based on the ITL file of the IP phone.

Step 4.   The IP phone forwards the certificate that was received by the secure application server to the TVS over the encrypted connection that was established in step 3.

Step 5.   The TVS validates the received certificate based on existing certificates that are stored in the TVS certificate repository.

Step 6.   The TVS returns the validation result to the IP phone. If the validation was successful, the IP phone can establish a secure connection with the application server.

Cisco IP Phone Services Deployment Options

This section describes the deployment options that are available for the Cisco IP phone services feature.

In high-availability deployments of Cisco IP phone services, two options are available to provide redundancy:

- **Cisco server load balancing (SLB):** HTTP requests from IP phones are directed to a virtual IP address that is configured on a Cisco server load balancer. The requests are then forwarded to the real IP addresses of the web servers that host the Cisco IP phone Services.

- **Using Domain Name System (DNS) as a redundancy mechanism:** The URLs for Cisco IP phone services that are configured on Cisco Unified Communications Manager use hostnames instead of IP addresses. The DNS server that is responsible for hostname resolution is configured to return multiple IP addresses for a given hostname. This redundancy method requires DNS support on the IP phones.

Figure 5-4 illustrates using SLB to provide redundancy.

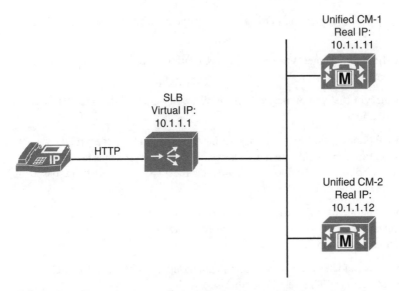

Figure 5-4   *Method for Providing Redundancy for Phone Services*

Cisco does not recommend a redundancy design using DNS A or SRV records with multiple IP listings. With multiple IP addresses returned to a DNS request, the phones must wait for a timeout period before trying the next IP address in the list, and in most cases this results in unacceptable delays to the end user.

Chapter Summary

The following list summarizes the key points that were discussed in this chapter:

- IP phone services can be configured in CUCM and be made available to display on IP phones.

- IP phone services list can be acquired by a phone from its configuration file or by sending an HTTP Get request to CUCM.

- IP phone services can be user initiated, phone initiated or phone service–initiated.

- IP phone service access can be secured and can use SBD to verify server certificates.

- SLB (server load balancing) should be used when deploying high-availability IP phone services.

Review Questions

Use the questions here to review what you learned in this chapter. The correct answers are found in Appendix A, "Answers to the Review Questions."

1. Which statement best describes IP phone services?

   a. Services that are automatically activated but can be stopped, started, and restarted through Control Center—IP phone services.

   b. Applications that provide interactive or non-interactive display of text and/or graphics on a Cisco Unified IP Phone.

   c. Services that enable video, pc port, and web services on a Cisco Unified IP Phone.

   d. Applications that deliver feature services such as call park and call pickup.

2. In which three ways can IP phone services be initiated? (Choose three.)

   a. User-initiated

   b. Serviceability -> control center—IP Phone Services

   c. Phone-initiated

   d. Phone service–initiated

   e. TFTP push initiated

   f. TFTP pull initiated

3. IP phone services support which two of the following protocols? (Choose two.)

   a. HTTPS

   b. ICMP

   c. DCOM

   d. HTTP

   e. RSVP

4. Which IP phone service method sends an HTTP Post message?

   a. User-initiated

   b. Phone-initiated

   c. Phone service–initiated

   d. TFTP pull initiated

5. Phones acquire the list of services to display to the user through which two mechanisms? (Choose two.)

   a. From its configuration file

   b. From the softkey template

   c. From the Service List template

   d. From the CUCM via an HTTP Get request

   e. From the User Subscription List assigned to the phone's device pool

6. Which three features are provided by deploying Security By Default? (Choose three.)

   a. Secure Realtime Transport Protocol (SRTP)

   b. Encrypted TFTP configuration files

   c. Encrypted video streams

   d. Authenticated TFTP configuration files

   e. Secure DHCP

   f. Certificate verification for HTTPS-based IP phone services

7. What is ITL?

   a. Internal Trust List

   b. Internal Trust Location

   c. Identity Template Location

   d. Identity Trust List

8. What does the ITL contain?

   a. Cluster server certificates

   b. Default gateway certificate

   c. CTL files

   d. IP phone services certificates

9. How often does the IP phone receive an ITL file?

   a. When it autoregisters.

   b. When a user selects an IP phone service.

   c. When it goes through the boot process.

   d. When it upgrades to new firmware version.

10. What is the recommended option for IP phone service redundancy?

    a. TFTP Service Load Balancing

    b. Server Load Balancing

    c. DNS SRV records

    d. Dual mode service provisioning

An Overview of Dial Plan Design and Implementation in Cisco Unified Communications Manager

The dial plan is the most important part of any communication system, IP or non-IP. Without a dial plan, an endpoint wouldn't know how it can communicate with another endpoint, whether the latter is local or remote. In order to place or receive calls with an endpoint connected to Cisco Unified Communications Manager (CUCM) or to any external entity, such as another cluster or the public switched telephone network (PSTN), you must first configure the necessary components and connections that compose the basis for a dial plan. The dial plan determines how calls are routed, calling privileges, type of connection they will utilize, such as analog vs Voice over Internet Protocol (VoIP) as well as the entire call flow from endpoint to endpoint. A carefully designed dial plan builds a strong foundation for a successful collaboration network.

Chapter Objectives

Upon completing this chapter, you will be able to meet the following objectives:

- Describe the purpose of a dial plan.

- Describe the knowledge gathering process for dial plan design.

- Provide a high level overview of +E.164 dial plan.

- Describe the components that make up a dial plan in CUCM.

- Compare how dial plan components are deployed across various call control devices.

- Describe dial plan documentation requirements.

Dial Plan Introduction

Although most people are not acquainted with dial plans by name, they use dial plans on a daily basis. As telephony users, people are familiar with the rules of dialing in their own environments. But as a telephony administrator, a person must be familiar with a much broader range of underlying elements as summarized below:

- A dial plan is a carefully planned design defining how to reach devices and services in a collaboration network and in the PSTN. It is different from a numbering plan in that a numbering plan defines formats of numbers, while a dial plan defines all the elements that dictate how to reach that number.

- Ultimately, each dialable entity, such as an endpoint or application, must be categorized by a unique identifier. Endpoint addressing covers how you assign individual numbers, blocks of telephone numbers, or Uniform Resource Identifiers (URIs) to endpoints.

- A dial plan must include information on how to call other numbers. These dial rules typically differ depending on the type of call, such as intrasite, intersite, external, or emergency.

- The dial plan specifies the format in which connected parties are presented and determines appropriate dial plan features and applications, such as classes of service and call coverage.

- A dial plan defines how calls are routed within and outside of a collaboration solution. This process includes analyzing the received digits (digit analysis in CUCM), finding the best matching entry in the call-routing table (translation patterns, route patterns, etc.), choosing the path and device to which the call should be sent (path selection), and what to do if that device is busy or not reachable (reorder tone or an annunciator announcement). This process includes providing called and calling number formats (digit manipulation) based on the call routing decision made.

This chapter provides an overview of each of the dial plan elements such as endpoint addressing, call routing, call coverage, class of service, path selection, and digit manipulation. These are explored in greater detail in the chapters that follow.

Dial Plan Design

If you have the luxury of designing a brand-new dial plan for your Cisco Collaboration solution, you can choose how to structure the various elements within your dial plan. However, in most cases you will end up incorporating an existing dial plan as you migrate your existing infrastructure (e.g., a PABX) to VoIP.

In order to design an effective and scalable dial plan, you must have a good understanding of the following in your collaboration network:

- Types of endpoint addressing, such as numeric addresses, and URIs, such as SIP (Session Initiation Protocol) URIs
  - Identification and avoidance of endpoint address overlaps
  - impact of overlaps on call routing

- Relationship of internally used directory numbers and external (PSTN) E.164 numbers (number masking or direct inward dial (DID) calls)

- E.164 structure (for dial plan normalization)

- Dialing domains

- User's dialing habits

- Emergency dialing requirements

- Cost-avoidance methods (for example, tail-end-hop-off (TEHO) and least-cost routing (LCR))

- NANP dial plan

Endpoint Address Design

Reachability of endpoints registered to a call processing agent, users, and applications is provided by addresses assigned to these addressable entities. In enterprise collaboration networks, you differentiate between numeric addresses and alphanumeric URIs.

Numeric addressing can take any format, as determined by the design process. Endpoints can be identified using a short form directory number, for example extension 50001, or they might be identified using a full +E.164 number format, for example +14165550001.

Building an enterprise address plan or numbering scheme in multisite deployments involves the definition of a typical hierarchical addressing structure with the following characteristics:

- Provides unique numeric addresses for all endpoints, users, and applications in the enterprise.

- Needs to be extensible so that the numbering scheme allows for adding new sites without having to redesign the whole numbering scheme, which would involve address reassignments for existing endpoints, users, and applications.

In the case of using an enterprise numbering plan (users dialing the actual digits that identify a destination), a full enterprise numbering address has three pieces: enterprise address access code (for example, 8), site code (for example, 496), and site subscriber number (for example, 9123); or for example, 8-496-9123. This provides for unique addressing where multiple sites may have overlapping individual extensions.

In the case of using an E.164 numbering plan, good design allows the internal staff to dial a short form of that number and uses a translation pattern to change the extension to the full E.164 format for call delivery. For example, a destination directory number is configured as +14165550001. An internal user dials 50001, and a translation pattern changes the called number 50001 to a called number of +14165550001. The call is now matched to the destination directory number.

URI addressing can be alphanumeric. Alphanumeric addresses based on SIP URIs can also be used to address endpoints, users, and applications. A commonly used scheme for alphanumeric addresses is simplified SIP URIs of the form *user @ host*, where the left-hand side (LHS, user portion) can be alphanumeric and the right-hand side (RHS, host portion) is a domain name. The following examples represent valid alphanumeric addresses based on SIP URIs:

> bob@example.org
>
> bob.home-office@example.org
>
> bob@de.eu.example.org
>
> bob.ex60@example.org
>
> bob.vmbox@example.org
>
> voicemail@de.eu.example.org

All of these URIs can serve as individual alphanumeric addresses for individual endpoints, users, and applications. From the addressing perspective, any hierarchy implied by using dot-separated identifiers (bob.ex60, de.eu.example.org) does not have any impact on the decision of whether any two URIs are considered to be equivalent.

DID Extension Matching Design

When designing endpoint addressing in direct inward dial (DID) environments, the dial plan design should identify whether the numeric endpoint address will be a portion of the DID number or if there is a need to match incoming DID numbers to different internal extensions. An example of matching the DID portion is an incoming DID number that has the format of 4165550001; the associated device may use the last 5 digits of the DID (50001) as its extension. An example of differing DID to extension mapping is an incoming DID number has the format of 4164440001 while the associated directory number is configured as 50001. In this case digit manipulation must change the called number from 4164440001 to 50001.

E.164 Dial Plan Design

E.164 is the global numbering plan that defines country codes to provide uniqueness for all dialable numbers worldwide.

A dialing domain refers to the scope of a more local numbering plan. The United States, Canada, and some Caribbean countries are part of the North American Numbering Plan (NANP), so the dialing domain is the NANP domain. The next section covers the concept of dialing domains.

As a company grows globally, it becomes critical to determine how mobile workers will be required to dial as they travel from office to office in different countries. Each country may have its own numbering plan with its own specific codes for local, long distance, or international dialing.

CUCM can route calls that have been placed to E.164 numbers using a plus sign (+) as a prefix. Support for + dialing is implemented by recognizing the plus sign as dialable pattern that can be part of call-routing entries, such as route patterns or translation patterns. This configuration might be required if international calls are being received with the + character in the called party number information in the call setup.

> **Note**   One of the determinations made during dial plan design is whether the dial plan will be based on E.164 using the "+" number format or whether it will utilize a private dial plan format using local domain number formats and shorter extensions.

For many features, especially if a company is global in nature, building your dial plan based on +E.164 number formats will greatly simplify the configuration and consequently the troubleshooting process.

The key points of a +E.164 dial plan are as follows:

- Users dial numbers in whatever local format they are familiar with, regardless of the office location from which they are dialing. For example, you can dial the headquarters office using 19025550123 from any of your global offices, no matter what country they are in. You no longer have to remember what international dialing codes are used in each country.

  - CUCM, through the use of translation patterns, normalizes or changes the local format numbers (both called and calling) into the +E.164 format. For example, CUCM translates 19025550123 into +19025550123.

  - CUCM attempts to match the +E.164 number against all numbers in the dial plan.

  - The +E.164 dial plan assumes all route patterns, and potentially all other numbers, such as DNs, MeetMe numbers, etc., are in the +E.164 format.

  - Once a pattern or number is matched, CUCM checks to see where the call is destined (endpoint, gateway, trunk, etc.). Once CUCM has determined the final destination device, it then checks to see if it needs to localize, that is, to change the +E.164 number back into a format that the local device requires. If the local device is a gateway connecting to the PSTN, it may be able to send the +E.164 format number if the PSTN provider supports + dialing; otherwise, the numbers will have to be changed to a format the local PSTN supports. For example, if you are in Germany dialing to the United States, the CUCM takes +19025550123 and converts it to the local German format for international dial. The resulting number sent to the German gateway will be 0019025550123.

The details of implementing a +E.164 dial plan are covered more extensively in the *Implementing Cisco IP Telephony and Video* Part 2 (CIPTV2) course material.

Dialing Domains

A dialing domain specifies a group of users or devices sharing the same set of dialing habits (dialing the same strings to reach identical destinations).

Examples of dialing domains include North American Number Plan (NANP), Site 1 dialing domain using 4-digit extensions, or Site 2 dialing domain using 5-digit extensions.

The concept of dialing domains is important because an enterprise dial plan has to implement the same treatment for each dialing domain. All users belonging to any given dialing domain share the same dialing treatment.

To identify dialing domains, it is important to take all dialing habits into consideration (from all possible physical or logical sites). For example, users in two sites in the United States, even though they share the same PSTN dialing habits, would still belong to different dialing domains if you also take into account how on-net calls are placed within the two sites. In a typical enterprise environment, an on-net intrasite call could be supported by dialing four digits, while an on-net intersite call would be placed by using a dial string equivalent to the PSTN dialing habit.

Note   Keep in mind that by dial plan design, forced on-net would still keep the call on-net.

Figure 6-1 gives an insight to the concept of a dialing domain.

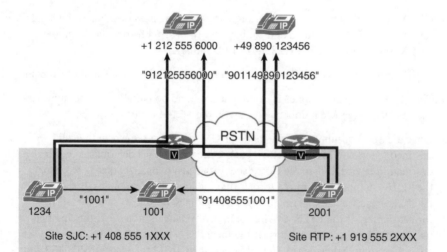

Figure 6-1   *Dialing Domain Overview*

The endpoint 1234 in site SJC and endpoint 2001 in site RTP share the same dialing habit for national destinations. For example, users would be dialing 912125556000 to reach PSTN destination +1 212 555 6000 and dialing 901149890123456 for international destinations to reach PSTN destination +49 890 123456 respectively. The dialing habit to reach endpoint 1001 in site SJC is, however, different for endpoints in RTP than for those in SJC For example, endpoint 1234 in site SJC would dial 1001 (only four digits for an intrasite call), whereas endpoint 2001 in site RTP would need to dial 914085551001 (a full NANAP national number for an intersite call). Therefore, in this example endpoints in site RTP and site SJC belong to different dialing domains.

Understanding User Dialing Habits in Design Considerations

Dialing destinations, such as users, endpoints, and applications, are input using various formats. The numeric +E.164 address +496907739001, for example, could be dialed as any of the following:

- +496907739001

- 9011496907739001 from an enterprise extension in the United States

- 011496907739001 from a land-line phone in the United States

- 006907739001 from an enterprise extension in Germany

- 000496907739001 from an enterprise extension in Italy

- 9001 from a phone in the same office

Good dial plan design is aware of how users dial internal and external numbers and provides elements to recognize calls in these formats and route the call appropriately.

Emergency Dialing Requirements

A dial plan design must address emergency call requirements based on local and national mandates. In NANP, 911 is defined as the number to call for emergencies. In a global environment, different office locations may have different emergency numbers defined; for example, many European countries use 112, Hong Kong uses 999, while Australia uses 000. Additionally, some countries use different codes for different emergency services such as fire, police, and ambulance.

The dial plan must recognize local emergency numbers for each location and route the call to a local PSTN resource with the appropriate caller id to identify the calling location. In environments where extension mobility or device mobility is used, additional steps must be taken to identify the actual physical location of the caller. In these instances, the caller's caller id is not sufficient to identify the caller's location. Additional services such as Cisco Emergency Responder may need to be deployed to manage emergency calls.

Dial Plan Design for Cost-Avoidance Mechanisms

One of the benefits of Voice over IP (VoIP) is the fullest utilization of an enterprise data network to carry voice and video calls in order to save on cost. This is achieved in the following manner:

- **Internal to internal calls:** These calls are typically carried over the data network as a first choice path but can be redirected to utilize the PSTN at a cost as a secondary path. This is often referred to as least-cost routing.

- **Internal to external calls:** These calls are typically routed to a local PSTN gateway or to a SIP service provider for delivery as local, long distance or international calls. However, at times it is possible to route a call such as a long-distance call, by sending it over the data (IP) network to a cluster/gateway that can send it as a local call. This is commonly referred to as tail-end hop-off (TEHO). This type of arrangement helps save toll charges, especially for international calling. Figure 6-2 illustrates as TEHO call from a US cluster to a Europe cluster.

Figure 6-2   *Tail-End Hop-Off (TEHO) Overview*

It is essential to consider legal implications when configuring any cost-avoidance mechanisms. Regulations differ country by country and can be very restrictive in places.

An important aspect for design considerations when utilizing cost-avoidance mechanisms is to determine whether the data network has the capacity to carry the additional flows with proper quality-of-service treatment.

NANP Dial Plan

This section explains the North American Numbering Plan (NANP). The NANP dial plan simplifies the context to understand any dial plan. Table 6-1 gives insight into the NANP.

Table 6-1   *North American Numbering Plan*

Route Pattern	Description
911	Emergency call routing without access code
9.911	Emergency call routing with access code
9.[2–8]11	Three-digit service codes (for example, 411 for information)
9.[2–9]XX XXXX	Seven-digit local dialing

9.[2–9]XX [2–9]XX XXXX	Ten-digit local dialing
9.1[2–9]XX [2–9]XX XXXX	11-digit long-distance dialing
9.011!	International dialing (variable length)
9.011!#	International dialing (variable length with interdigit timeout termination code [#])

Note that the outside access code in NANP is 9.

- **911 and 9.911 (emergency dialing):** The first two route patterns of 911 and 9.911 are both used for emergency call routing in North America. These route patterns are configured with the Urgent Priority check box to avoid any delay in routing the emergency calls.

- **9.[2–8]11 (three-digit service codes):** The three-digit route pattern (plus access code) is used for service codes in the NANP (for example, 411 for general information and 511 for traffic information).

- **9.[2–9]XX XXXX (seven-digit dialing):** This seven-digit route pattern (plus access code) is used for local calling. It may not be supported in all areas however.

- **9.[2–9]XX [2–9]XX XXXX (ten-digit dialing):** This ten-digit route pattern (plus access code) is used to match on ten-digit dialing patterns. This is progressively replaced by the 11-digit long-distance dialing code by carriers.

- **9.1[2–9]XX [2–9]XX XXXX (11-digit long-distance dialing):** This route pattern will signifies a long-distance call. Using the digit discard instructions (DDI) 9 or 1 can be removed, or both can be removed resulting in a ten-digit pattern forwarded to the carrier. The pattern would then be 91.[2-9]XX[2-9]XXXXXX.

Note The dot placement has been moved from before the 1 to after the 1 to ensure that the 1 digit gets stripped out before the call is routed to the carrier so it's a 10-digit call.

- **9.011! and 9.011!# (international dialing):** International dialing from North America requires the international dialing code of 011. International dialing requires a country code next in the dial string. The country code is sometimes referred to as a two-digit code, but international country codes can be three or four digits long, depending on the country being dialed. For example, to dial a number in India, a user from the United States will dial 901191! or 901191!#.

Note # is an interdigit timeout character that signifies that no more digits will be dialed after #. With a number ending with ! in a route pattern, CUCM will wait for interdigit timeout (the default value, 15, is configurable).

More details on route patterns and the special symbols are covered in Chapter 7, "Implementing Cisco Unified Communications Manager Call Routing and Digit Manipulation."

Dial Plan Components and Their Functions

This section describes the components of a dial plan and their functions.

A dial plan defines how calls are (inter)connected between two or more entities participating in the call. Dial plan components include endpoint addressing, call routing and path selection, digit manipulation, calling privileges, and call coverage. Each of these components is summarized here and covered in more detail either in this chapter or in upcoming chapters.

Dial plans contain specific dialing patterns so that users can reach a particular telephone number. Access codes, area codes, specialized codes, and combinations of dialed digits are all part of any particular dial plan. Dial plans that are used with voice-capable routers are defined mainly through dial peer elements, which are used for both inbound and outbound call processing.

Dial plan design requires knowledge of the network topology, current telephone-number dialing patterns, proposed router and gateway locations, and traffic-routing requirements. No standard protocol is defined for the dynamic routing of E.164 telephony addresses. VoIP dial plans have traditionally been configured statically and managed on call processing devices such as Cisco Unified Communications Manager, Cisco gateways, and Cisco Unified Border Element.

A dial plan consists of these components:

- **Endpoint addressing (numbering plan):** Assigning directory numbers to all endpoints (such as IP phones, fax machines, and analog phones) and applications (such as voicemail systems, auto attendants, and conferencing systems).

- **Call routing and path selection:** Defining primary path and potential backup paths for called numbers.

- **Digit manipulation:** Ability to change a number to match the required format for the chosen path.

- **Calling privileges:** Ability to specify which numbers are dialable from a call requesting element, such as a phone, gateway, or trunk.

- **Call coverage:** Ability to signal an incoming call to other devices to promote a higher probability of call answer.

A short overview of each of the elements is provided in the following sections.

Dial Plan Components and Functions: Endpoint Addressing

A fundamental component of the dial plan is endpoint addressing. The dial plan defines what numbers are known locally within the cluster, for example directory numbers, meet me conference numbers or translation patterns, as well as what numbers are reachable by routing calls outside the cluster. The external numbers are defined in route patterns, which specify the path used to deliver a call to the external entity.

Figure 6-3 shows the essence of a scalable endpoint-addressing scheme that logically includes geographical information as part of the endpoint directory number. As seen in Figure 6-3, the DNs for phones are 4 digits. However, they have a full PSTN equivalent—also known as an E.164 number—for routing on the public network.

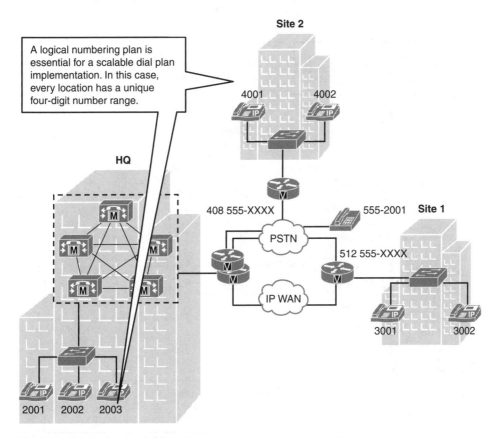

Figure 6-3 *Endpoint Addressing*

In Figure 6-3, the first digit of every endpoint also represents its location. (The digit 2 represents Headquarters, 3 represents Site 1, and 4 represents Site 2.) All endpoints use the same extension length of four digits. Variable extension lengths and overlapping endpoint addresses can make call routing, path selection, or general dial plan implementation much more complex. In this case, the phones can be called via IP network using 4 digits or full E.164 number if the E.164 numbering scheme is used.

Endpoint addressing is covered in more detail in Chapter 7, "Implementing Cisco Unified
Communications Manager Call Routing and Digit Manipulation."

Dial Plan Components and Functions: Call Routing and Path Selection

Enterprise VoIP deployments often have multiple possible paths between dialable
elements when multiple locations are connected using a WAN as well as a PSTN.
Figure 6-4 shows an example of general call routing and path selection in a multisite
environment.

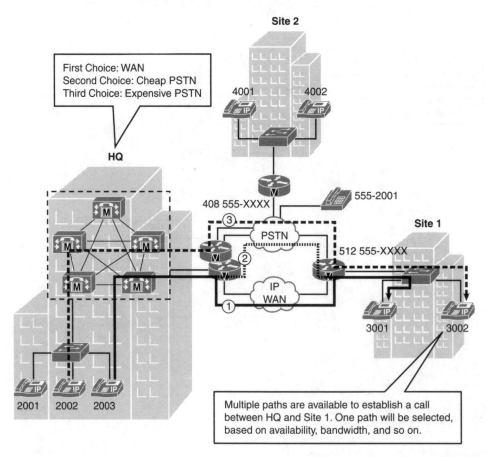

Figure 6-4 *Call Routing and Path Selection*

An important part of every dial plan implementation is call routing and call path
selection. Many factors can be considered when deciding which path to take to connect
two endpoints via WAN or PSTN.

In Figure 6-4, the WAN connection has priority when calls are established between Headquarters and Site 1. If the WAN is unavailable or its bandwidth is exhausted, calls are routed via the first PSTN gateway (cheap PSTN). If the cheap PSTN connection is also unavailable, a third option (with an expensive PSTN gateway connection) is used.

Ideally, the end user will not realize which path was taken to establish the call. A core function of any collaboration solution is to provide this transparency is digit manipulation. The user dials a 4-digit extension, and the system changes the number according to the path the call ultimately takes.

Cisco Unified Communications Manager (CUCM) call routing uses four important components. These come into action once a user dials a number or enters a URI. These four components are:

- **Route pattern:** Route patterns are strings of digits and wildcards configured in CUCM. Route patterns can point directly to a trunk or gateway device or to a route list.

- **Route list:** Route lists are logical groupings of route groups and are referenced by route patterns.

- **Route group:** Gateways and trunks are put into a logical grouping called route groups that one or more route lists can leverage. This allows multiple route patterns to leverage the gateway endpoints or trunks, which wouldn't be possible if the gateway endpoint/trunk was to be assigned directly to one route pattern.

- **Gateway/trunk:** These are the endpoints which connect the Cisco Collaboration network to outside world. Gateways and trunks can be either assigned to a route pattern but the device would not be available for any other route patterns to leverage. If they are assigned to route groups instead, multiple route patterns can use the same device.

Chapter 7, "Implementing Cisco Unified Communications Manager Call Routing and Digit Manipulation," covers these call routing entities in detail.

Dial Plan Components and Functions: Digit Manipulation

Based on endpoint addressing and path selection criteria, a called or calling number may need to be changed to match the formats expected along the path or at the destination. Figure 6-5 shows examples of digit-manipulation requirements in a multisite environment.

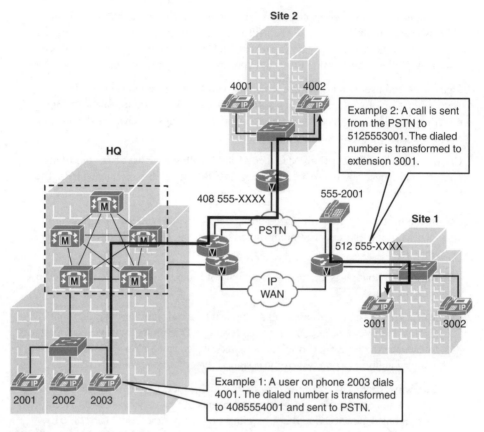

Figure 6-5 *Digit Manipulation*

Many situations require manipulation of called- or calling-party numbers. In the first example in Figure 6-5, a user on phone 2003 dials 4002 to reach a user in Site 2. Headquarters and Site 2 are connected via PSTN only, so the dialed number 4002 must be expanded to a complete PSTN number so that the PSTN can successfully route the call.

The second example shows a scenario in which the complete PSTN called-party number of an incoming call at Site 1 needs to be trimmed to the extension length of four digits.

Digit manipulation can be configured in numerous places, both on the CUCM and on the gateway router. For outgoing calls, manipulation rules can be set at the route pattern level, at the route list level for each route group listed, and at the gateway or trunk level (either directly or through device pools) using transformation calling search spaces (CSS) that define the transformation patterns to be used.

Other elements that may contain digit manipulation rules include endpoints and device pool settings, as well as service parameter settings that can impact number formats for incoming calls.

Which digit manipulation approach is used is in part determined by the approach to the dial plan design. Traditionally, most of the digit manipulation occurred at the route list level for each listed route group. If local route groups are used, then digit manipulation is typically performed at the gateway or trunk level using transformation CSSs.

In the case where a digit manipulation rule exists at multiple levels (for example a prefix that is set at both the route list level for a route group as well as at the gateway using a transformation pattern), the gateway level setting is chosen over the route list level setting. The order of priority from lowest to highest priority looks at the route pattern manipulation rules, which can be overruled by route list level manipulation rules, which will in turn be overruled by a transformation pattern manipulation rule assigned to a gateway, trunk, or endpoint.

Additionally, an administrator must be aware of the fact that once CUCM has released the call to a gateway, the gateway itself may have digit manipulation rules in place that can further change the number before it is sent to the next hop device. Ideally, it is desirable to choose the best approach and be consistent in its use.

Digit manipulation is covered in detail in Chapter 7, "Implementing Cisco Unified Communications Manager Call Routing and Digit Manipulation."

Dial Plan Components and Functions: Calling Privileges

Once the dial plan is configured with all dialable elements, such as endpoints, meet-me conference numbers, and route patterns, the next step is to define which destinations can be dialed by any internal source such as a phone, gateway, or trunk. Figure 6-6 shows examples of different calling privileges in a multisite environment.

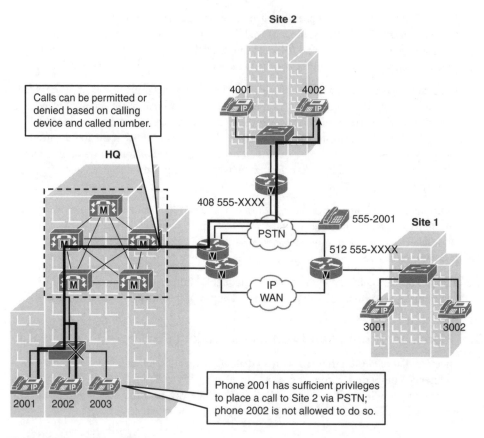

Figure 6-6   *Calling Privileges*

In almost every collaboration network, there is some type of calling privilege that is implemented within a location, between locations, and for calls to the PSTN. Calling privileges are typically designed according to the called and calling numbers. In Figure 6-6, the user on phone 2001 is allowed to establish a call to Site 2 via the PSTN, whereas the user on phone 2002 does not have sufficient privileges to establish calls via the PSTN. This is attained by use of class of service (CoS) using:

■ Partitions

■ Calling search space (CSS)—a list of callable partitions

By way of overview, think of a partition as a lock, and the CSS as the key ring. When a partition is assigned to a number, access to the number is locked. Only those who have that partition in their CSS are allowed to make the call.

Calling privileges are examined in more detail in Chapter 8, "Implementing Calling Privileges in Cisco Unified Communications Manager."

Dial Plan Components and Functions: Call Coverage

Many companies dictate that as many calls as possible should be answered by a live voice instead of being sent directly to voicemail. There are a number of call coverage features that accomplish this goal. Figure 6-7 shows examples of call coverage in a multisite environment.

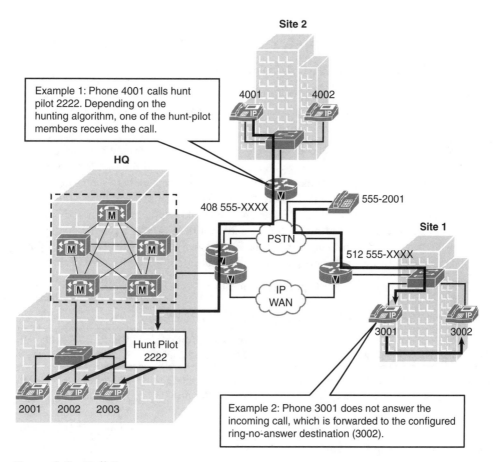

Figure 6-7   *Call Coverage*

In general, call coverage provides functions to process calls that would otherwise be unanswered or sent to voicemail. Features that can be used to facilitate call coverage include forwarding the call to a hunt pilot number or forwarding to another individual such as an operator or a receptionist.

In Example 1 in Figure 6-7, the hunt-pilot number 2222 was created at Headquarters. Calls to this pilot number are distributed among all group members, based on a defined hunting algorithm.

In Example 2, a call to 3001 is unanswered, and so the call is forwarded to extension 3002. Cisco IP phones can be configured to forward calls to different numbers, depending on the reason they are not able to process the call (Busy, No Answer, and so on) and on the origin of the call (on- or off-net).

Call coverage is discussed in more detail in Chapter 9, "Implementing Call Coverage in Cisco Unified Communications Manager."

Comparison of Dial Plan Configuration Elements in a Cisco Collaboration Solution

From a theoretical perspective, all call control systems perform the same basic functions. What differs with each system is the list of commands or elements that need to be configured.

Table 6-1 provides a high-level comparison between CUCM dial plan, IOS router-based dial plan that includes both gateways, and CUBEs (Cisco Unified Border Elements), as well as the call control devices that were introduced from the Tandberg acquisition. Cisco Video Communication Server (VCS) in today's implementations should be used for H.323 endpoint registration only, while all SIP endpoints should register directly to CUCM. The Cisco Expressway series products are a subset of the Cisco VCS product, providing firewall traversal for services such as Mobile Remote Access (MRA). MRA provides the ability for remote Jabber clients to access the internal enterprise VoIP environment.

Table 6-2 lists the dial plan configuration elements of Cisco call control devices.

Table 6-2 *Comparison of Dial Plan Configuration Elements*

Dial Plan Component	CUCM	Cisco IOS (Voice Gateway and CUBE)	Cisco VCS and Cisco Expressway
Endpoint addressing	Directory number, directory URI	Dial peers, ephone-dn voice register pool	IP address, H.323 ID, E.164 alias, directory URI, local zones, prefix
Call routing and path selection	Route patterns, route groups, route lists, translation patterns, partitions, and CSSs	Dial peers	Search rules, CPL scripts, FindMe, neighbor zones, traversal zones, transforms
Digit manipulation	Translation patterns, route patterns, transformation patterns, and settings	Voice translation profiles and rules, dial peer settings	Presearch transform, Search Rules, Call Policy, Pipes, Links

Calling privileges	Partitions and CSSs, FAC	Class of Restriction (COR)	(Integrated part of other configuration elements)
Call coverage	Hunt pilots, hunt lists, line groups, shared lines, call forward settings	Dial peers, hunt groups, call applications	FindMe

Note Cisco IOS-based dial plan elements are covered in Chapter 13, "Implementing Cisco IOS Voice Gateways and Cisco Unified Border Element."

For details on Cisco IOS voice gateways and CUBE, refer to Chapter 13. For detailed discussion on the Cisco VCS and Cisco Expressway series, refer to *Implementing Cisco IP Telephony and Video* Part 2.

Dial Plan Documentation

This section describes what you need to consider when documenting a dial plan.

Dial plans can be very complex and involve a number of different geographic areas and devices. Therefore, good documentation is required and should include information that is relevant to end users, as well as implementation details for administrators and support personnel. Information important to end users includes the dial habits that are applicable to their site, the dial habits that apply when they roam to another site, and their calling privileges.

Documentation is only useful when it is current and accessible. You must make sure that all documentation is well defined and that clear responsibilities and processes are in place to ensure that the documentation is accurate, up-to-date, and easy to understand. Accurate documentation is the basis for troubleshooting, monitoring, planning of changes and enhancements, and redesign.

Chapter Summary

The following key points were discussed in this chapter:

- Dial plan design requires knowledge of endpoint addressing requirements, dialing domain requirements, user dialing habits, emergency dialing requirements, and available call path options.

- A dial plan consists of different elements and functions, such as endpoint addressing, internal and external dial rules, number presentation, and classes of service.

- Dial plans are critical elements to ensuring proper functionality and a reliable experience for users of the collaboration network.

- Call routing and digit manipulation play and important role in Cisco Unified Communications.

- Configuration of dial plan elements is different based on the point of configuration, that is, CUCM vs IOS vs VCS.

- Dial plan documentation must be current and available to assist in administration, planning, and troubleshooting tasks.

Review Questions

Use the questions here to review what you learned in this chapter. The correct answers are found in Appendix A, "Answers to the Review Questions."

1. What is the difference between a dial plan and a numbering plan?

   a. A numbering plan provides the route while a dial plan provides the number format

   b. Nothing, they both refer to the same thing

   c. A dial plan provides the route while a numbering plan provides the number format

   d. NANP defines a dial plan while European countries use a numbering plan.

2. What dial plan element is used to match the dialed digits for call routing to another cluster or the PSTN?

   a. Route pattern

   b. Route list

   c. Route group

   d. Gateway

   e. Trunk

3. What dial plan element can be used for changing the dialed digits?

   a. Directory numbers

   b. Transformation pattern

   c. Hunt pilot

   d. Meet-me numbers

4. Hunt pilots are relevant to which of the following dial plan elements?

   a. Call coverage

   b. Ring tone

    c. Call Waiting

    d. PSTN dial back

    e. IP Manager Assistant

5. Which of the following is an example of a national numbering plan?

    a. NANP

    b. E.164

    c. POTS

    d. ISDN

6. True or false? SIP endpoints use Universal Resource Identifiers for addressing.

    a. False

    b. True

7. A four-digit extension requiring a change to a 10-digit number before being routed across the PSTN is considered which of the following configuration elements?

    a. Digit manipulation

    b. Route pattern

    c. Route group

    d. Number expansion

8. Class of Service uses which two elements? (Choose two.)

    a. Transformation patterns

    b. Partitions

    c. Access codes

    d. Site codes

    e. Calling search spaces

9. Class of Restriction is configured in which device to provide calling privileges?

    a. CUCM

    b. IOS gateway

    c. VCS

    d. Unity connection

10. Which of the following best describes dial plan documentation requirements?

   a. Should be posted to the LDAP server for general consumption

   b. Should be kept up-to-date and available to users and administrators as appropriate

   c. Should be in stored in the corporate knowledge base server

   d. Should be encrypted for security reasons

Implementing Cisco Unified Communications Manager Call Routing and Digit Manipulation

Call routing enables users to reach destinations (numbers/URIs) within and outside of the organization. The process of call routing uses a number of elements as Cisco Unified Communications Manager (CUCM) attempts to determine the feasibility and the final destination of the call. Ultimately it comes down to one of two call types. The call will be routed to an internal number, such as a directory number (DN) of an endpoint or a feature number such as a Meet-Me conference, or the call will be routed via a route pattern through a gateway or trunk for delivery outside the cluster. Endpoint addressing is an important component of a dial plan and mandatory for the routing of internal calls and external calls. Call routing includes a number of components and works in a very hierarchical fashion.

For calls going out of an organization, there are various requirements about the way the calling party or the called party numbers are presented; and this is achieved by digit manipulation in CUCM. CUCM supports a host of digit manipulation mechanisms suited to various requirements and design specifics. Both call routing and digit manipulation work hand-in-hand for successful call placement—both internally and externally in a Cisco Collaboration solution.

This chapter explains the call routing implementation in CUCM, and covers the concept of digit manipulation in CUCM.

Chapter Objectives

Upon completing this chapter you will be able to meet the following objectives:

- Describe how to implement directory numbers and URIs.

- Define call routing and list sources and targets of calls.

- Describe the call routing logic in Cisco Unified Communications Manager.

- Describe the components that enable call routing in Cisco Unified Communications Manager.

- Describe addressing methods, and explain how Cisco Unified Communications Manager analyzes received digits.

- Describe the post-dial delay of variable-length patterns and overlapping patterns, and explain how to solve this problem.

- Describe the various mechanisms in Cisco Unified Communications Manager that allow digit manipulation.

- Describe the implementation of digit manipulation mechanisms such as transformation mask, translation patterns, significant digits, transformation patterns, and prefixing or discarding digits in digit manipulation.

Endpoint Addressing

One of the fundamental steps in defining a dial plan for call routing is to identify the Cisco Unified IP Phones, Cisco Jabber endpoints, or Cisco Telepresence endpoints that will be associated with a cluster.

When CUCM was first designed, Session Initiation Protocol (SIP) was not supported for endpoint registration. SIP support to the phones was first introduced in CUCM release 5.0. One of the benefits that SIP brings is the ability to dial using a name instead of a number. The phones were originally configured only with directory numbers (DNs). Once SIP was introduced, the logical way to implement the name-based calling feature was to map the name, referred to as the URI, to the existing DN.

This section describes how to implement directory numbers and directory URIs.

Figure 7-1 shows endpoints and addressing, both in DN and URI formats.

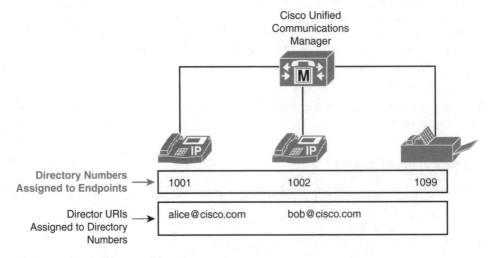

Figure 7-1 *Endpoint Addressing*

In order to reach internal endpoints (such as IP phones or fax machines) and applications (such as voicemail systems, auto-attendants, and conferencing systems), you must assign at least one directory number to each element. In addition, you can assign directory URIs as aliases to directory numbers. By calling a configured directory number or directory URI, you can reach the corresponding device within or outside the organization, provided the dial plan is complete and the route to the destination is known by call-control.

Endpoint Addressing by Numbers

This section describes what you need to consider when implementing endpoint addressing by numbers. Figure 7-2 illustrates directory numbers and E.164 numbering format considerations.

Note   E.164 and +E.164 numbering plans were reviewed in Chapter 6, "Dial Plan Design and Implementation in Cisco Unified Communications Manager." A detailed look at this topic is provided in *Implementing Cisco IP Telephony and Video, Part 2 (CIPTV2)*.

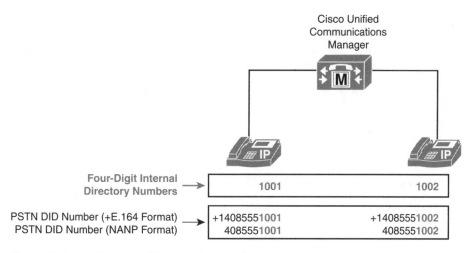

Figure 7-2   *Endpoint Addressing by Number*

Note   Dial plan and numbering plan setup needs immaculate planning and can initially be time consuming. However, the longer terms benefits of having a well-designed dial/numbering plan are invaluable.

First, plan the length of the internally used extension. Depending on the number of required extensions, you may choose longer or shorter extensions. With four-digit extensions, you can theoretically address up to 10,000 endpoints. In reality, this number will be smaller because some leading digits, such as 0 or 9, are used as operator or external line access codes, so they should not be used as the leading digits of an extension.

Typically, the phones should also be reachable from the public switched telephone network (PSTN). You can call internal endpoints from the outside in two ways:

- **Two-stage dialing:** With two-stage dialing, all endpoints share a single PSTN number. When a PSTN user wants to call an internal endpoint, they call the PSTN number of the target company. The communications system (for example, CUCM) accepts the call either by routing the call to the extension of an operator or receptionist or by answering the call with an auto-attendant IVR script that allows the caller then to enter the extension of the desired internal user or to use a dial-by-name search feature.

- **Direct inward dialing (DID):** With DID, each internal phone has its own PSTN number. Ideally, the least significant digits of the external DID range match the internally used extension numbers (1:1 mapping). If a corresponding DID range is not available and your PSTN provider assigns different external numbers, you must map each external number to an internal extension and translate the number accordingly. In other countries, this service may be referred to as direct dial-in (DDI).

The E.164 number format is used in the PSTN environment. E.164 numbers start with a country code and can have a maximum of 15 digits. Globally unique phone numbers are usually written with a plus sign (+) before the phone number to indicate that the number is in international (E.164) format. In Cisco documentation, such numbers are referred to as +E.164 numbers.

To actually dial a PSTN number from a normal fixed-line phone, it may be necessary to use the appropriate access code. Every country has both a national access code, which is used to dial a long-distance number, and an international access code, which is used to dial out of the country. To indicate that a call should be sent to the PSTN instead of being routed within the enterprise, a PSTN access code may be dialed first.

As illustrated in Figure 7-2, the four-digit internal directory numbers are mapped 1:1 to external E.164 numbers.

Dial plan design may dictate that all internal numbers be in the +E.164 number format. This is often the case for global companies or for companies that use certain features that benefit from +E.164 number formats, such as local route groups with device mobility.

In cases where a +E.164 dial plan is implemented, directory numbers may also be in the + format; for example, the DN for a phone may be configured as +19025550123. All other numbers defined in the dial plan, such as Meet-Me numbers, route patterns, etc., would also be defined using the + format. This does not necessarily mean that you have to dial the entire string of numbers when you call your colleague across the hall. You may still be able to dial the five-digit extension of 50123, and the CUCM can have a translation pattern configured to change the 50123 dialed digits to +19025550123, which will now match the configured DN of your colleague's phone.

One significant benefit of +E.164 dial plan formats is that users can dial numbers in their locally known formats and CUCM will convert digit strings into +E.164 format prior to performing dial plan lookup. This is referred to as normalizing the number into a global format.

Once the call matches a route pattern determining which gateway or trunk is used to deliver the call, CUCM then localizes the number, changing it back to the locally known format of the gateway or trunk that will process the call.

Endpoint Addressing by URIs

This section describes how to place calls using a URI.

Directory URIs are aliases to directory numbers. Directory URIs are not assigned to a phone line but are assigned to a directory number (which is assigned to a phone line). A directory URI is also known as an SIP URI.

The format of a URI is (user portion)@(*host portion*), so a URI most often looks like an e-mail address. The host portion can be a domain name or an IP address. You can place calls to URIs from endpoints that support URI dialing by dialing a fully qualified URI or by dialing only the user portion. If you place a call to a URI that is not fully qualified, then CUCM appends the configured Organizational Top Level Domain (OTLD) enterprise parameter to complete the URI. For example, if the OTLD is set for cisco.com and a user simply makes a call to Alice, then CUCM appends the OTLD to create a URI in the form of alice@cisco.com

Note   URI addressing is most common in the video world. It's been there for many years, and Cisco Collaboration 10.x supports SIP URI for video and audio communications with most endpoints.

Ideally, all URIs that are applied to endpoints of a CUCM cluster use the same, globally unique host portion. If you use the same host portion in different clusters, calls between these clusters work only if you implement URI synchronization. URI synchronization among clusters is provided by Intercluster Lookup Service (ILS) and Global Dial Plan Replication (GDPR). ILS and GDPR are covered in detail in *Implementing Cisco IP Telephony and Video, Part 2 (CIPTV2)*.

URIs are not directly applied to a phone or phone line, but they are associated with a directory number. When a call is placed to a locally configured URI, CUCM routes the call to the associated directory number.

The user portion of a directory URI is case sensitive. You can change the user portion to be case insensitive by setting the enterprise parameter URI Lookup Policy to Case Insensitive. The host portion is always case insensitive.

Figure 7-3 shows Jabber client with URI addressing.

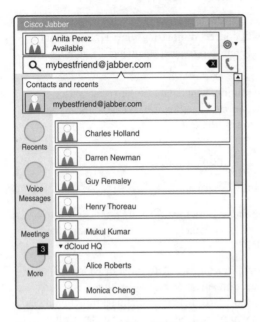

Figure 7-3   *Cisco Jabber URI Addressing*

CUCM allows defining up to five URIs for every DN defined as shown in Figure 7-4.

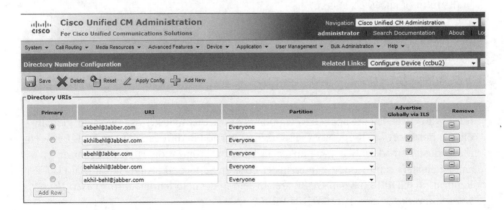

Figure 7-4   *CUCM URI Definition*

The next section covers CUCM-based call routing.

Cisco Unified Communications Manager Call Routing Overview

This section defines call routing and lists sources and targets of calls.

Calls must be routed and interconnected according to the dialed number or URI. Like IP routing, call routing is, by default, destination-based routing. There are three main types of call routing:

- **Intrasite routing:** This type of call routing occurs within a single site.

- **Intersite routing:** This type of call routing type occurs between multiple sites.

  - **On net:** Calls between sites are usually sent over the WAN. Translation patterns can be used to change the format of the called number or the caller id if sites use access codes and site codes to differentiate DNs per site.

  - **Off net:** Calls between sites can be routed over the PSTN if routing over the WAN does not succeed. In this case, digit manipulation is required to change the DN to a PSTN routable number. A route pattern is then used to determine where and how the call is sent to the PSTN.

- **External routing:** Calls to numbers that are not locally defined in the CUCM cluster are routed by matching a route pattern. A route pattern points to the way out of the cluster, either directly through a gateway or trunk or by using the **route list > route group > gateway/trunk** construct.

Figure 7-5 gives an overview of call routing in a typical enterprise network.

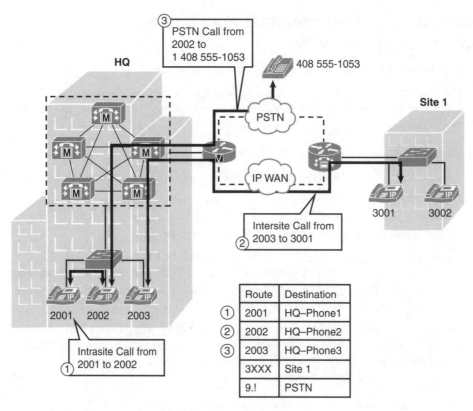

Figure 7-5   *Cisco Collaboration Call Routing Overview*

As seen in Figure 7-5, at HQ the extensions are 2XXX from 2001 to 2003, whereas at Site 1 the extensions are 3XXX, ranging from 3001 to 3002. Any call within the 2XXX dialing domain is an intrasite call, and similarly any call within the 3XXX dialing domain is also an intrasite call. On the other hand, a call between 2XXX and 3XXX or vice versa is an intersite call. Any call outside of the 2XXX and 3XXX dialing domains is an external call going via the gateway to the PSTN (traditional trunk or IP telephony service provider (ITSP) SIP trunk).

CUCM can automatically route calls to internal destinations within the same cluster because CUCM is aware of the configured directory numbers of its associated devices. This scenario can be compared to networks that are directly connected at a router IP routing.

> **Note**   The CUCM call routing database includes the directory numbers of Cisco IP phones and various devices configured in the CUCM cluster. CUCM, however, is not aware of any numbers not explicitly configured and of the devices not registered/configured in the CUCM cluster.

For external destinations, an explicit route—called a route pattern—must be configured. External destinations are PSTN destinations (including off net intersite calls, which are effectively PSTN destinations because they are addressed by their PSTN numbers), other voice over IP (VoIP) domains such as an IP telephony service provider, or another CUCM cluster. A route pattern is equivalent to a static route in an IP router.

To route calls to numbers outside the cluster, the CUCM call routing must match route patterns that point to external destinations.

Regardless of the call routing type, the call routing process itself can be summarized as shown in the following steps:

Step 1.   CUCM receives a call setup request from a local endpoint or from another call control system, such as a remote CUCM cluster, Cisco Unified Communications Manager Express, or a PSTN gateway.

Step 2.   CUCM analyzes the target of the received request to find the best matching entry in its call routing table. The type of analysis depends on the addressing method that is used by the source of the call setup request (digit-by-digit or en bloc) and the address type (number versus URI). Digit-by-digit and en bloc dialing methods are covered in more detail later in this chapter.

Step 3.   CUCM forwards the call setup request to the destination device that is associated with the matched call routing table entry. This destination device can be a local endpoint or another remote call control system.

Sources of Call Routing Requests (Entities Requiring Call Routing Table Lookups)

There are a number of elements that are considered sources of call routing requests. Some, such as IP phones, are an obvious example. Others are not so noticeable. The following list describes sources of call routing requests:

- **Cisco Unified IP Phones, Jabber, or analog phones/endpoints:** when a call is dialed from a phone, CUCM considers the phone as the source of the request.

- **Gateways and trunks:** Gateways and trunks connect the cluster to other clusters, other call processing systems, and to the PSTN or a SIP service provider. When a call comes into the cluster through a trunk or gateway, the CUCM treats the gateway or trunk as the source of the call.

- **Translation patterns:** Translation patterns are almost identical to route patterns, with a couple of notable exceptions. First, a translation pattern can have a null string as the pattern which can be used to configure Private Line Auto Ringdown (PLAR). Second, a route pattern points to a way out of the cluster, while the translation pattern does not. The only role of a translation pattern is to match a dialed destination, change something about the calling or called number, and send the call back for another call routing lookup. At this point, to CUCM, it looks like the translation pattern is the source of the call.

■ **Voicemail ports:** A voicemail system, such as Cisco Unity Connection, allows callers to initiate calls as well as leave voicemail. When a caller dials an extension while in Unity Connection, the call is passed from Unity Connection to CUCM via voice-mail ports if the integration is based on Skinny Client Control Protocol (SCCP). To CUCM, it looks as if the voicemail port is the source of the call.

Note   The distinction between call routing sources and call routing targets is important when implementing features such as calling privileges, call classification, and others.

Call Routing Table Entries (Call Routing Targets)

This section describes call routing table entries, also called call routing targets.

The CUCM call routing table is composed of directory numbers, route patterns, translation patterns, and other entries. The list below shows some examples of call routing table entries.

■ **Directory numbers:** Assigned to endpoints such as Cisco Unified IP Phones, Cisco IP Communicator, etc.

■ **Directory URIs:** Assigned to directory numbers. URIs are associated with a DN rather than a physical or logical device.

■ **Translation patterns:** Used to match a dialed number, change something about the calling or called number, and send it back for another call routing table lookup based on the changed number.

■ **Route patterns/SIP route patterns:** Used to route calls to off-net destinations such as the PSTN or other CUCM clusters. Route patterns typically point to a route list, which contains one or more route groups, each of which can contain one or more gateways or trunks.

■ **Hunt pilot:** Used to route calls to line group members based on a distribution algorithm

■ **Call Park numbers:** Used to place a call on hold and retrieve the same call from another phone by dialing the call park number

■ **Meet-Me numbers:** Used by a conference initiator to initiate a conference by pressing the Meet-Me soft key and dialing the conference number, while all other participants simply dial the same conference number

These entries are all possible call routing targets. If a dialed number matches one of these entries, the call is routed to the appropriate entity. That entity can be a phone line, a trunk, a gateway, a feature, or an application.

For SIP URI–based call routing, only directory URIs and SIP route patterns are applicable. All other examples refer to call routing for numbered targets. However, calls placed to directory URIs can only be routed to a local phone if the directory URI is associated with a directory number. Otherwise, calls to a directory URI will attempt to match a SIP route pattern to determine the location of the receiving endpoint.

Dialing Methods and Digit Analysis

This section describes addressing methods and explains how CUCM analyzes received digits.

Table 7-1 shows the addressing methods that CUCM supports for different devices. Keypad Markup Language (KPML) is a standards-based mechanism that allows SIP phones to provide a digit-by-digit dial experience for SIP phones.

Table 7-1   *Addressing Methods*

Device	Signaling Protocol	Dialing Method
IP Phone	SCCP	Digit-by-digit En bloc (not on type-A phones)
	SIP	En bloc KPML (not on type A phones) SIP dial rules
Gateway	MGCP/SIP/H.323	En bloc Overlap sending and receiving
Trunk	SIP, H.323	En bloc Overlap sending and receiving

Digit-by-digit dialing is achieved when the caller first goes off-hook, hears the dial tone, and then begins to dial the digits. With digit-by-digit dialing, CUCM evaluates dial plan matches after each digit dialed. Therefore, as you dial a number, once you dial enough digits for CUCM to recognize that the number doesn't exist or you do not have permission to dial that number, it presents a fast busy signal at that digit. If you hear a fast busy partway through dialing a number, that may give you a clue as to what to check when you are troubleshooting.

En bloc dialing is achieved when the caller does not go off-hook but first dials all the required digits and then goes off-hook or presses the dial soft key. All the digits are sent to CUCM at the same time, and CUCM compares the entire string against the dial plan to determine reachability. It is possible to get a different result for a call by dialing digit-by-digit versus en bloc.

SCCP phones support both digit-by-digit and en bloc dialing. Figure 7-6 illustrates an SCCP phone dialing 1000.

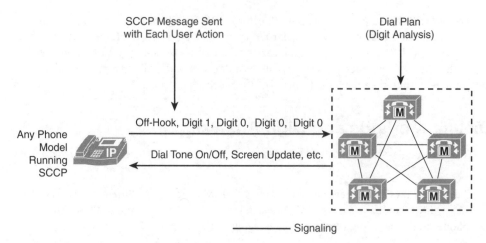

Figure 7-6   *SCCP Phone with Digit-by-Digit Dialing*

Note   Skinny Client Control Protocol (SCCP) is a stimulus/response protocol in which the endpoint sends user input (stimulus) and expects some type of response from the call-control server (CUCM) instructing the endpoint about what to do.

In SIP, you can use en bloc dialing or Keypad Markup Language (KPML). In en bloc dialing, the whole dialed string is sent in a single SIP INVITE message. KPML provides the digit-by-digit dial experience for SIP phones. KPML allows digits to be sent one by one. If you have configured SIP dial rules for the SIP phone, they are processed inside the SIP phone as the user dials. Therefore, a SIP phone can detect invalid numbers and play a reorder tone, without sending any signaling messages to CUCM. If dialed digits match an entry of a SIP dial rule, the dialed string is sent in a single SIP INVITE message to CUCM. If CUCM requires more digits, KPML can be used to send the remaining digits one by one, from the SIP phone to CUCM.

Older SIP phones (Type A), such as 7905, 7912, 7940, and 7960 models, support SIP dial rules but do not support KPML. Newer SIP phone models and Type B phones, for example 79×1, 79×2, 79×5, and 7970 models, support both dial rules and KPML. If a phone model supports KPML, it is on by default. Dial rules are optional elements for SIP phones. Figure 7-7 shows the signaling interaction between a Type A SIP Phone and CUCM when no dial rules have been configured.

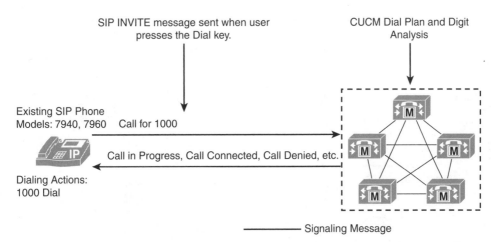

Figure 7-7   *Type A SIP Phone Signaling with No Dial rules Configured*

Type B phones and newer models support KPML and SIP dial rules. KPML is the default dialing behavior. However, if SIP dial rules are configured, KPML is disabled, and dial rules are used for call processing. In this case, the SIP phone provides local dial tone and processes dialed digits against the internal SIP dial rules before issuing a SIP INVITE message to CUCM.

Figure 7-8 illustrates signal processing for a Type B phone with dial rules configured. This process is the same for either Type A or Type B phones.

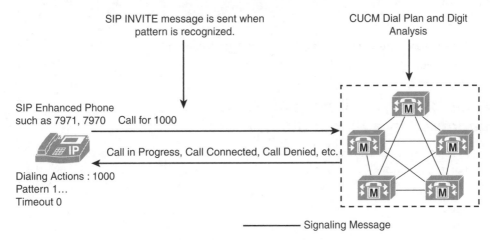

Figure 7-8   *Type B Phone Signaling with SIP Dial Rules Configured*

For Type B and newer phone models, KPML is the default signaling method. Figure 7-9 illustrates the use of SIP NOTIFY messages to convey each individual keypress from the phone to CUCM. For more information on this process, please refer to RFC 4730.

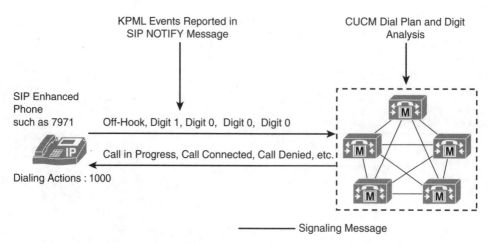

Figure 7-9 *KPML Signal Processing*

Trunks, such as SIP or H.323 trunks, and ISDN Primary Rate Interface (PRI) can be configured for overlap sending and receiving, allowing digits to be sent or received one by one. This may be required to be configured within countries that have variable length numbering plans.

> **Note**   Voice gateway and Cisco Unified Border Element (CUBE) dial plan is discussed in detail in Chapter 13, "Implementing Cisco IOS Voice Gateways and Cisco Unified Border Element."

In summary, CUCM supports both digit-by-digit dialing and en bloc dialing. The method used is dependent on the device and the protocol used.

Digit-by-Digit Analysis of Numbers Not Received In a Single Block

When CUCM does not receive all dialed digits at once (the en bloc addressing method is not used), then CUCM analyzes the digits as they are received. Figure 7-10 shows the matching logic utilized for digit analysis.

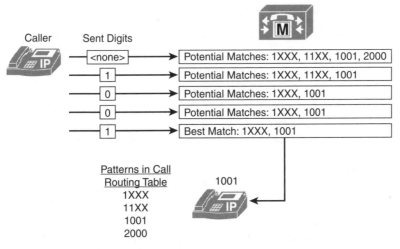

Figure 7-10 *Digit-by-Digit Analysis*

Be aware that if a phone sends dialed digits one by one, CUCM begins digit analysis immediately upon receiving the first digit. In fact, digit analysis starts one step earlier, when a phone indicates an off-hook state to CUCM. At that point, CUCM looks up a null string dialed number that matches all available call routing tables or may match a null string defined in a translation pattern in support of Private Line Automatic Ringdown (PLAR).

By analyzing each additional digit that is received, CUCM reduces the list of potential matches (that is, the call routing table entries that match the digits that have been received so far). After a single entry is matched, such as the directory number 1001 in Figure 7-10, the call is sent to the corresponding device.

Note CUCM does not always receive dialed digits one by one. SCCP phones support digit-by-digit dialing and can be configured to support en bloc dialing. SIP phones can use en bloc dialing to send the whole dialed string at once or can use KPML to send the string digit-by-digit. If digits are received en bloc, the whole received dial string is checked at once against the call routing table.

Variable-Length Patterns, Overlapping Patterns, and Urgent Priority

This section describes the postdial delay of variable-length patterns and overlapping patterns and explains how to solve this problem. The interdigit timer (T302 timer) plays a role in determining the length of time CUCM will wait to complete the call whenever multiple matching patterns contain a different number of matching digits.

Variable-Length Patterns and Interdigit Timeout

International destinations are usually configured by using the exclamation point (!) wildcard, which represents any quantity of digits (that is, variable-length patterns). For example, in North America, the route pattern 9.011! is typically configured for international calls. In most European countries, the same result is accomplished by using the 0.00! route pattern.

When matching a variable-length pattern, CUCM does not know when dialing is complete and waits for the T302 timer to expire (15 seconds by default) before processing the call. This postdial delay can be reduced or eliminated as follows:

■ Reduce the T302 timer (this timer is a Cisco CallManager service parameter) to allow earlier detection of the end of dialing. However, do not set this timer to less than 4 seconds, to prevent premature transmission of the call before the user finishes dialing.

■ Configure a second route pattern, followed by the pound sign (#) wildcard (for example, 9.011!# for North America or 0.00!# for Europe), and let users know that they can indicate end of dialing by terminating the number with the # key. This action is analogous to pressing the Send button on a cell phone.

> **Note**   The implementation of the interdigit timeout termination in CUCM is different from the implementation in Cisco IOS dial peers. In CUCM, the # is not only the instruction to stop digit collection but is also part of the dialed number. Therefore, if you use the # to avoid waiting for the expiration of the interdigit timeout, all variable-length route patterns must be configured twice (once with the # and once without). The IOS router assumes, by default, that a # at the end of a dial string is a terminating character. In IOS dial plan, it is not required to configure additional dial peers to support this character.

Overlaps and Interdigit Timeout

This section describes overlapping patterns and how they relate to the interdigit timeout.

A dial plan may include overlapping numbers. Overlaps occur when a pattern overlaps with another longer pattern or when there are two extensions with the same number in two different sites. In Figure 7-11, there are two overlaps: 141 overlaps with 1[2–4]XX and 131 overlaps with 1[2–4]XX and with 13!. By default, CUCM continues to collect digits as long as there are more potential matches in the dial plan.

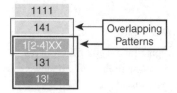

Figure 7-11   *Digit Overlap*

In Figure 7-11, a user dials 13115. CUCM interprets the number digit by digit as the user enters the digits on the keypad of the phone. After all received digits are analyzed, the only match is 13!. Although there is only a single matching pattern, CUCM must wait for additional digits, because the matched pattern is of variable length (the ! wildcard represents one or more digits). The call can be sent to the device that is associated with pattern 13! only after the interdigit timeout expires. In this scenario, you could lower the T302 timer or add a pattern 13!# to reduce or eliminate postdial delays.

If the user dials 131, the user also experiences a postdial delay. After these three digits are analyzed, there are two longer potential matches remaining (1[2–4]XX and 13!). CUCM detects that the end user finished dialing and that the longer matches are not applicable only after the interdigit timeout expires.

If the user dials 1415, the only matching pattern is 1[2–4]XX. This pattern does not include the ! wildcard, and CUCM does not have to wait for additional dialed digits. The call to 1415 can be routed immediately after receiving the fourth digit.

Urgent Priority

This section describes the function of the Urgent Priority parameter. Figure 7-12 shows the Urgent Priority option checked under the Route Pattern Configuration screen.

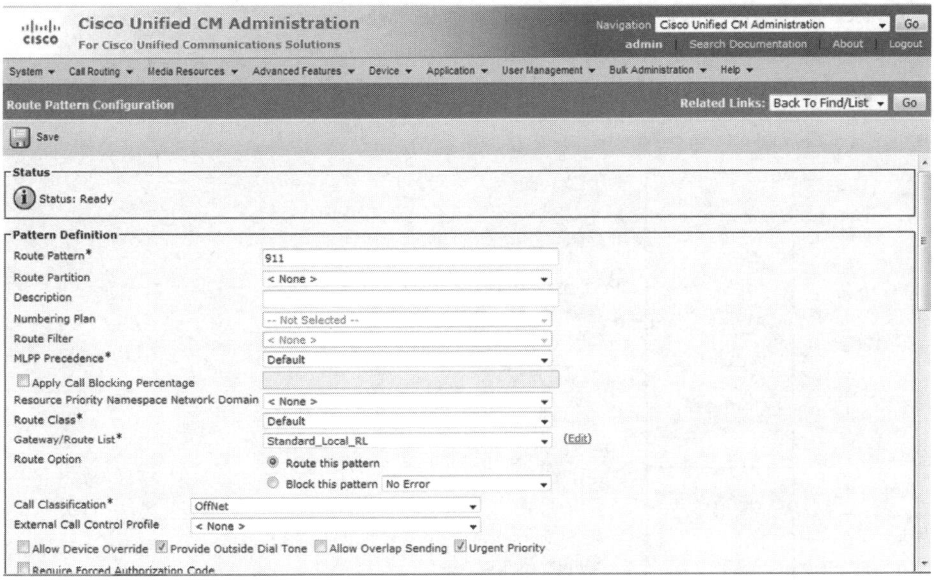

Figure 7-12 *Urgent Priority Checkbox*

Route patterns, translation patterns, and directory numbers have the Urgent Priority check box. The Urgent Priority check box can be used to force immediate routing of certain calls as soon as a match is detected, without waiting for the interdigit timer to expire when additional potential longer matches exist.

For example, in North America, if the patterns 9.911 and 9.[2–9]XXXXXX are configured and a user dials 9911, CUCM usually must wait for the interdigit timeout before routing the call, because further digits might cause the 9.[2–9]XXXXXX pattern to match. However, when urgent priority is enabled for the 9.911 route pattern, CUCM makes its routing decision as soon as the user has finished dialing 9911, without causing any postdial delay.

When you enable urgent priority, the specified route pattern is excluded from other, longer route pattern matches. If en bloc dialing is used and the provided number is longer than the urgent pattern, the urgent pattern is not considered.

Cisco Unified Communications Call Routing Logic

This section describes the call routing logic in CUCM.

Figure 7-13 illustrates the concept of digit matching for call handling. When a number is dialed, CUCM uses closest-match logic to select which pattern to match from among all the patterns in its call routing table.

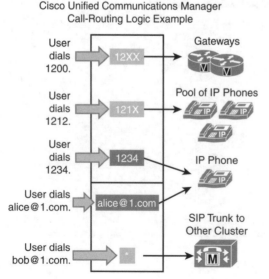

Figure 7-13   *Call Routing Logic*

In practice, when multiple potentially matching patterns are present, the destination pattern is chosen based on the following criteria:

■ The pattern matches the dialed string.

■ The pattern represents the smallest number of endpoints.

Note   Some entries of the call routing table can include wildcards. For example, an X in a numbered pattern represents one digit. If the exclamation point (!) is used in a numbered pattern, it stands for one or more digits.

Figure 7-13 shows an example in which the call routing table includes the numbered patterns 12XX, 121X, and 1234. The following examples explain the digit analysis and matching in CUCM based on Figure 7-13.

■ When a user dials the string 1234, CUCM compares the string to the patterns in its call routing table. In this case, there are two potentially matching patterns: 12XX and 1234. Both of these patterns match the dialed string, but 12XX matches a total of 100 numbers (from 1200 to 1299), whereas 1234 does not include any wildcard and therefore is one exact number. Based on closest-match logic, 1234 is selected as the destination of this call.

■ When a user dials the string 1210, then the pattern 121X is chosen, because out of the two potential matches, 121X and 12XX, 121X is the better match because it represents 10 numbers while 12XX represents 100 possible numbers.

■ When a user dials the URI alice@1.com, CUCM chooses the locally configured URI that is an exact match of the dialed URI.

■ When a user dials the URI bob@1.com, the only match is the SIP route pattern * (which stands for any URI). If there was a SIP route pattern *.1.com, then a call to bob@1.com would find a better match in the *.1.com SIP route pattern, because it is more specific than the * SIP route pattern.

Call Routing Components

As briefly explained in Chapter 6, "Overview of Dial Plan Design and Implementation in Cisco Unified Communications Manager," CUCM-based call routing has a few important elements. To recap, these elements are:

■ Route pattern

■ Route list

■ Route group

■ Gateways and trunks

Figure 7-14 gives an insight into the relationship between these call routing elements and the way these elements are configured in the CUCM.

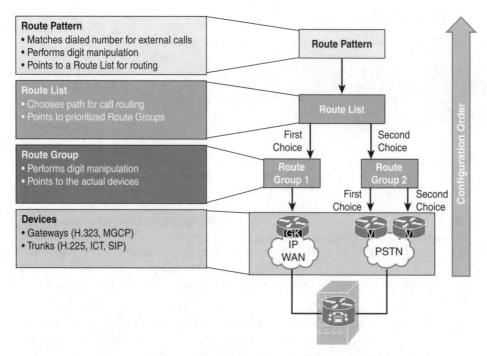

Figure 7-14   *CUCM Call Routing Elements Relationship and Hierarchy*

Note   The following sections flow top down (for example, the call flow from route pattern > route list > route group > gateway/trunk) for ease of understanding the call flowing from an endpoint to the PSTN/ITSP. However, in the real world the configuration sequence is bottom up; the gateway or trunk is defined first, then the route group(s) are defined, after which route list(s) are defined, and finally route pattern(s) are defined.

Before getting into the specific details of the call routing elements, the next section explains route plan report that is a comprehensive report of the various call routing and endpoint addressing elements in CUCM.

Route Plan Report

If you wish to get a comprehensive report containing the whole dial plan construct of CUCM, the route plan report is your single source of truth. It contains a listing of all the phone numbers, call park numbers, call pickup numbers, conference numbers (such as Meet-Me numbers), route patterns, and translation patterns in the system. The route plan report allows you to view either a partial or full list. You can accomplish this by selecting a route pattern, partition, route group, route list, call park number, call pickup number, conference number, or gateway. Figure 7-15 shows a route plan report illustrating the DNs, route patterns, translation patterns, and so on. To generate a route plan report, go to **Call Routing > Route Plan Report**.

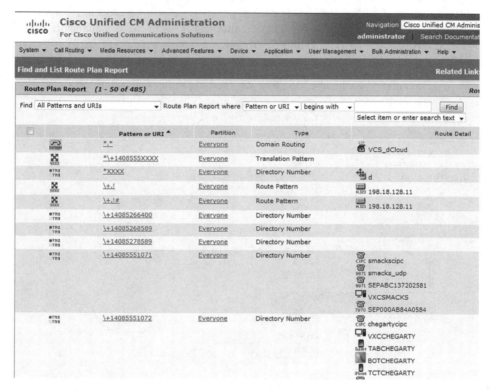

Figure 7-15 *CUCM Route Plan Report*

The route plan report can be saved as a comma-separated values (CSV) file that you can import into other applications (such as Microsoft Excel). To save the route plan report as CSV, click on the View in file option on top right corner.

Note The CSV file contains more detailed information than the web pages, including DNs for phones, route patterns, and translation patterns.

The following sections describe the call routing components of CUCM.

Route Pattern

CUCM does not know about any phone numbers external to CUCM. That's where the gateway endpoints and trunks allow CUCM to communicate with other systems using traditional TDM interfaces (FXO/FXS/T1-CAS/T1-PRI/E1-CAS/E1-PRI) or an IP-IP gateway such as CUBE; using H.323 or SIP as the communication protocols. A route pattern is a configured numeric pattern range that helps CUCM match a number not in its database and route the call outside of the Cisco Collaboration domain. After the route pattern is matched, the call is routed to the final destination.

Building on Figure 7-15, Figure 7-16 illustrates the call routing via route pattern.

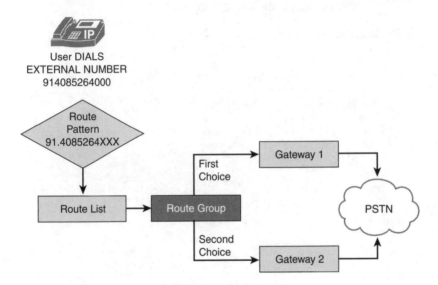

Figure 7-16   *Route Pattern–Based Call Routing*

As seen in Figure 7-16, a user dials 914085264000, which is not a number configured in CUCM database and therefore is a number outside of the enterprise network.

CUCM looks in its call routing database and finds the pattern that matches the dialed digits. When the closest match is found (that is, 4085264XXX), CUCM uses the route pattern to route the call out of the network via route pattern > route list > route group > gateway 1 or gateway 2 and to the PSTN.

Table 7-2 lists the various wildcard parameters that are supported in route patterns.

Table 7-2   *Route Pattern Wildcards*

Wildcard	Description
X	A single digit or character, such as 0–9, *, #
@	North American Numbering Plan (NANP) default

!	One or more digits (0–9, *, #)
[x–y]	Included range notation
[^x–y]	Excluded range notation
.	Digit discard instruction or DDI (Termination access code)
#	Terminates interdigit timeout
<wildcard>?	Matches zero or more occurrences of any digit that matches the previous wildcard
<wildcard>+	Matches one or more occurrences of any digit that matches the previous wildcard
\+	Matches the + sign as part of a number. (The \ denotes a delimiter that tells CUCM to process the + as its own character +, rather than the wildcard as previously shown.) The + is used for globalized E.164 call routing.

Note The @ wildcard is a special macro function that expands into a series of patterns representing the entire national numbering plan for a certain country. A route pattern of 9.@ will load a complex 166-route-pattern North American Numbering Plan (NANP) by default. CUCM can be configured to accept other national numbering plans.

Table 7-3 illustrates the various route patterns that can be matched using the wildcards described earlier.

Table 7-3 *Route Pattern Examples*

Route Pattern	Result
1234	One exact dialed number (that is, 1234)
1*1X	Matches dialed digits 1*10 to 1*19
12XX	Matches dialed digits 1200 to 1299, 12**, 12*#, 12#*, and 12##
13[25–8]6	Matches dialed digits 1326, 1356, 1366, 1376, and 1386
13[13–59]X	Matches dialed digits 1310–1319, 1330–9, 1340–9, 1350–9, or 1390–9
13[^3–9]6	Matches dialed digits 1306, 1316, 1326, 13*6, or 13#6
13!	Matches the string 13 followed by one or more digits
13!#	Matches the string 13 followed by one or more digits and then ended with a #
\+!	Matches a phone number starting with + and followed by one or more digits, as used by E.164 numbers

A route pattern can point to a device such as a gateway endpoint or a trunk; however, that will limit the availability of that device only to that specific route pattern. To be able to use device(s) among route patterns, it is important to have them assigned to route groups, which in turn get assigned to route lists, and route lists get assigned to route patterns.

Route patterns can be configured by browsing to **Call Routing > Route/Hunt > Route Group** and click **Add New**. Figure 7-17 shows the route pattern configuration to route calls to 4085264XXX numbers.

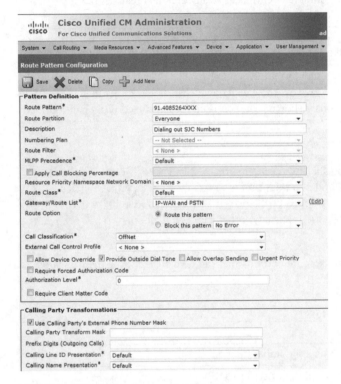

Figure 7-17   *Route Pattern Configuration*

Note that the Route List value IP-WAN and PSTN has been selected, and the Route this pattern radio button is selected. Furthermore, the Call Classification is OffNet and the Provide Outside Dial Tone checkbox is checked.

Digit manipulation can be carried out at Route Pattern or at the route group details level of the route list. These are covered later in the chapter.

Note   The end user can see the manipulated digits if you perform digit manipulation at the route-pattern level. If digit manipulation is done at the route list level, however, the end user will not see that on the phone. Any digit manipulation at the route list level completely overrides the setting at route pattern level.

Route Filters

When creating route patterns, you can use the @ wildcard to represent all the routes defined in the North American Numbering Plan (NANP). This is, however, undesirable in large implementations and where administrators want to exercise fine-grain controls.

Note   NANP includes high-expense patterns such as international dialing access and 900 (premium) numbers.

To control what can be dialed from CUCM while using the 9.@, route filters can come in handy. Route filters allow filtering unwanted calls and allow fine-grained control over outbound calls (while leveraging 9.@ route patterns). A number of preconfigured route filters are available in CUCM, as shown in Figure 7-18. These can be accessed by browsing to **Call Routing > Route Filter**.

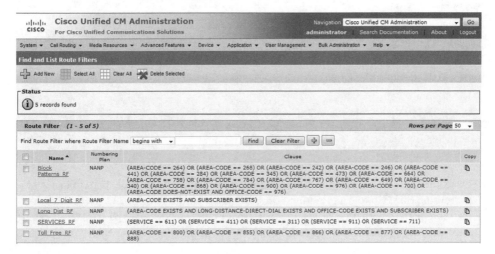

Figure 7-18   *CUCM Pre-Defined Route Filters*

You can design and configure route filters using a number of predefined clauses. Figure 7-19 illustrates the various clauses available.

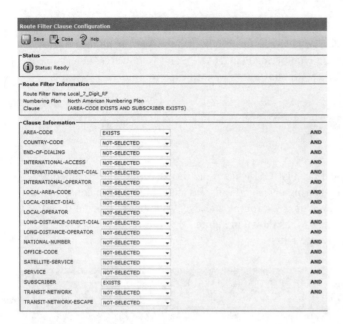

Figure 7-19 *Route Filter Clauses*

Note The clauses shown are for Route Filter Local_7_Digit_RF. These clauses, however, are available for all existing and newly defined route filters.

Once a route filter is defined, it must be applied to an appropriate route pattern using 9.@ for routing calls. Go to **Call Routing > Route/Hunt > Route Pattern** and select an existing route pattern with 9.@ as the target pattern (or create a new route pattern). Figure 7-20 illustrates the application of a preconfigured or new route filter for the NANP dial plan.

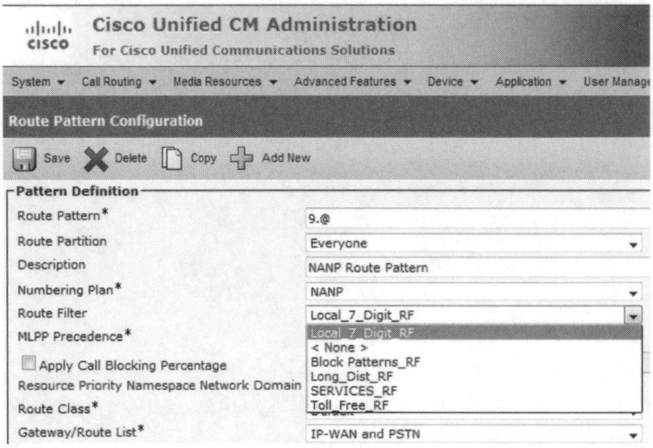

Figure 7-20 *Route Filter Application at Route Pattern*

Note that the numbering plan is set to NANP, which will be a greyed-out field if 9.@ is not the target route pattern.

The next section covers route lists.

Route List

A route list is a list of prioritized route groups. Route groups are always processed in a top-down prioritization. Figure 7-21 illustrates the concept of route lists.

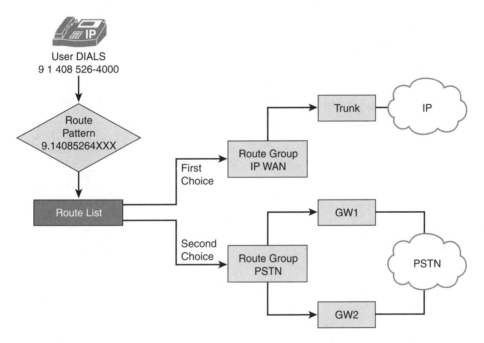

Figure 7-21   *Route List Overview*

As seen in Figure 7-13, when the user dials 914085264000, the call is routed via the route pattern 914085264XXX to the route list, which in turn routes the call to the prioritized list of route groups, with the first choice being the IP WAN route group and the second choice being PSTN route group. As the name signifies, the IP WAN route group routes calls over the IP trunk to the IP cloud (using ITSP or ICT), whereas the PSTN group routes the call to the traditional PSTN network via one or more gateways.

Figure 7-22 shows a route list configuration in which two route groups have been added to the route list example shown in Figure 7-21. To configure a route list, go to **Call Routing > Route/Hunt > Route List** and click **Add New.** The IP-WAN route group is listed first and has highest priority. If calls cannot be set up by using any trunk devices in the IP-WAN route group, the next route group in the list (PSTN) is used to route the call.

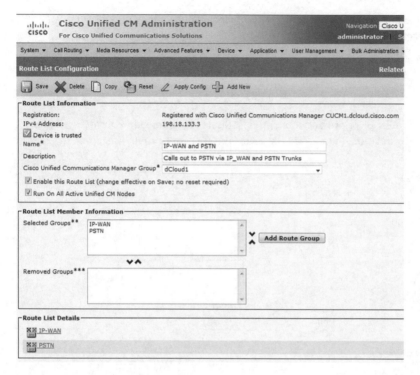

Figure 7-22   *Route List Configuration*

Route Group

A route group is a list of devices (gateways and trunks). A route group can be configured in two ways:

■ **Circular distribution:** Round robin

■ **Top-down distribution:** First entry in the list has the highest priority

The circular distribution is used for load-sharing scenarios, when it is desirable to have the two gateways/trunks used equally, for example, without any preference to one or the other. The top-down distribution is used to implement backup paths if the preferred path is unavailable. In other words, the first entry is always used for sending the calls out to the preferred gateway/trunk, and in case the gateway/trunk is unavailable, the secondary option is employed.

Note Digit manipulation in this model happens on the Route List configuration page, under the Route List Details for the selected route group in the route list. The gateways must have identical digit-manipulation requirements. It is recommended to put devices (gateways or trunks) that have a similar purpose into the same route group.

To configure a route group, go to **Call Routing > Route/Hunt > Route Group** and click **Add New**. Figure 7-23 shows the route group with IP-WAN trunks configured that is used by the route list defined in previous section.

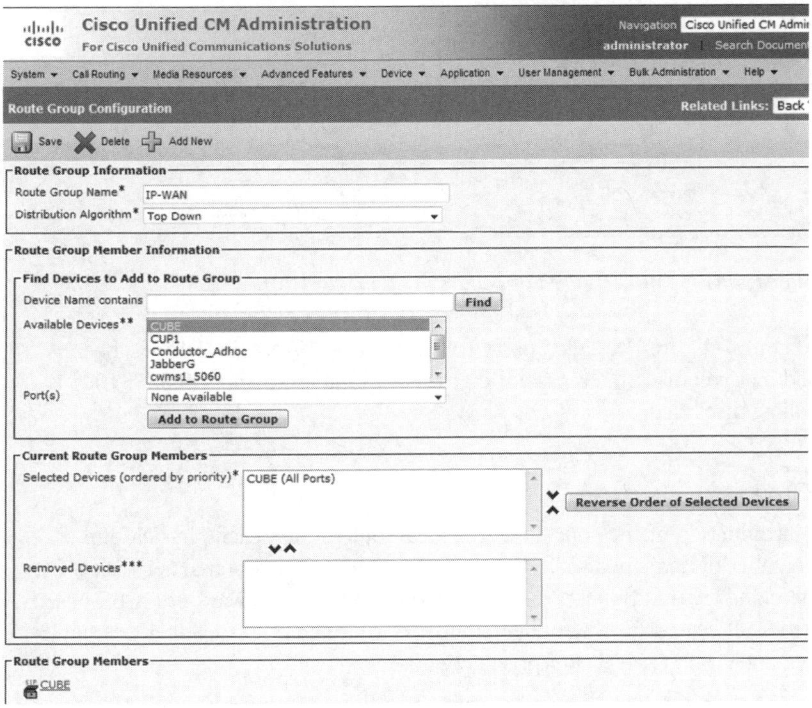

Figure 7-23 *Route Group Configuration*

Digit manipulation can be enabled at the route group level on the route list configuration page, under the route list details for the selected route group in the route list as shown in Figure 7-24.

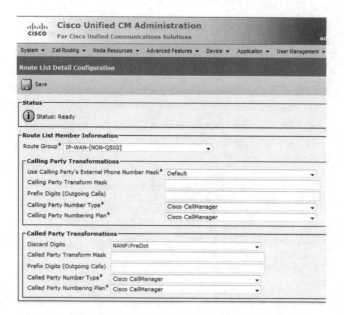

Figure 7-24 *Per Route Group Digit Manipulation Configuration*

As seen in Figure 7-24, for the called party transformation NANP: PreDot has been selected, and that will discard any predot digits. For example, when 9.14085551001 is dialed, 9 will be discarded.

Local Route Group

Before the introduction of the concept of the local route group, each physical site required a number of dedicated route groups for connecting the internal network with the PSTN world using traditional trunks terminating on voice gateways or CUBE-based SIP trunks to ITSP. The result was a huge number of routing entities leading to complex and sizable dial plans in typical enterprise networks.

Local route groups, however, enable decoupling the selection of a PSTN gateway or trunk for off-net dialing from the route patterns that are used to access the gateway. This greatly reduces the complexity and size of dial plans in CUCM and helps UC administrators manage the network in a better way. The Local Route Group Device Pool parameter was a new call routing element introduced with CUCM 7.0. The standard local route group is a new call routing element that appears in the list of available route groups that can be added to a route list. A route list can include this entry only one time. The local route group is selected by the inclusion in the device's device pool Local Route Group setting.

Note The Local Route Group parameter is set to <None> by default.

Route patterns that use the local route group are routed to the gateways that are associated with the local route group configured at the device pool level of the calling device. As a result, each site uses one global dial plan that points to a local route group. The device pool specifies a local gateway router at the site, and the call is routed to a local gateway.

For better understanding, as shown in Figure 7-25 the route pattern 9.1408555XXXX points to a route list that contains only the standard local route group.

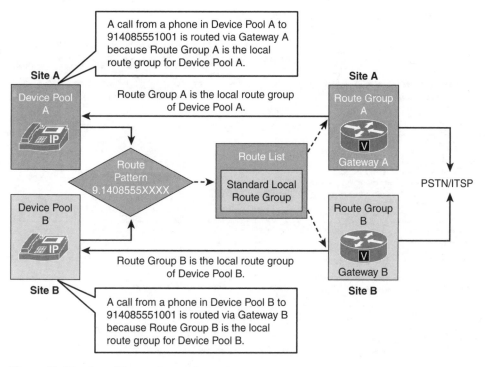

Figure 7-25 *Local Route Group Overview*

The breakdown of the example is as follows:

- Gateway A is associated with Route Group A, which is the local route group of Device Pool A at Site A.

- Gateway B is associated with Route Group B, which acts as the local route group to Device Pool B, at Site B.

- Gateway A is New York gateway, while Gateway B is the San Jose, CA, gateway.

Note It's always best to use a local gateway if one is available.

Now, when a phone that is associated with Device Pool A places a call to 914085551001, the standard local route group for this device pool is used to place the call to the PSTN from Gateway A. On the other hand, phones in Device Pool B will have their calls routed to Gateway B because of device pool B's configured local route group.

To configure a device pool to leverage Local Route Group, go to **System > Device Pool** and search for the device pool for which you want to setup a local route group. Figure 7-26 illustrates the selection of a route group from a list of available route groups under the **Standard Local Route Group** dropdown.

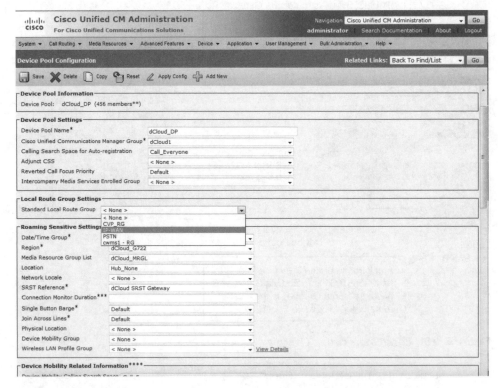

Figure 7-26   *Device Pool Standard Local Route Group Configuration*

Cisco Unified Communications Manager Based Digit Manipulation

The calls from any phone system need to be sent outside of an enterprise network so the users can communicate with a number of destinations. These destinations in turn might be located within the same site, different sites within the same organization, or other organization (such as partner organizations). The calls may be routed to locations within the same country or to different countries.

Completing various types of calls often requires dialing access codes or prefix numbers, or even the way the calls are presented to the carrier network (PSTN or ITSP). Cisco Unified Communications Manager (CUCM) has the capability to provide digit manipulation, which allows adding or removing digits to comply with a private or public numbering plan.

This section describes digit manipulation tools that allow a CUCM administrator to implement flexibility and transparency in the dial plan of the company by way of implementing external phone number masks, digit prefixing, digit stripping, transformation masks, translation patterns, and significant digits.

At large, three levels of digit-manipulation options are available for outbound calls:

- Digit manipulation configured on the route pattern that is used only when a route pattern points directly to a gateway and is not used if the route pattern is routed to the route list

- Digit manipulation configured at the route list detail level (application enforced at route group)

- Digit manipulation configured leveraging a transformation calling search space (CSS) on the gateway/trunk or device pool

Note   The details about transformation pattern and CSS are covered later in the chapter.

The next section gives an overview of digit manipulation in CUCM.

Digit Manipulation Overview

Digit manipulation in CUCM is used for multiple purposes:

- Digit manipulation is often used to change calling party numbers for caller ID purposes on outgoing PSTN calls

- Digit manipulation is also used to strip PSTN access codes before CUCM routes the calls to the gateway (PSTN).

- Digit manipulation is required for abbreviated dialing and to properly route inbound calls from the PSTN where an abbreviated internal dial plan exists.

- Digit manipulation is required to strip off PSTN access codes from the called party number before routing the call to the PSTN.

- Digit manipulation is used at times to change the calling party number from the abbreviated internal extension number to a full E.164 PSTN number to allow an easier redial (redialing by the called party) and for proper representation on the PSTN network.

Figure 7-27 gives an insight into the digit manipulation for call flows within an organization.

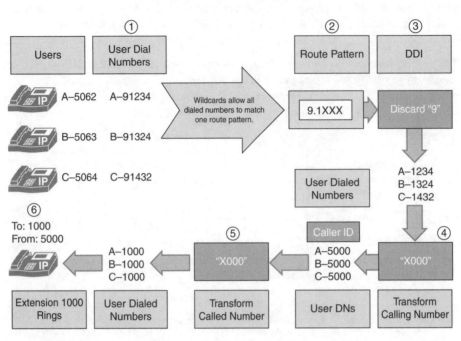

Figure 7-27   *CUCM-Based Digit Manipulation Overview*

Note   This is a typical example of how calls can be forced on net. For example, if the number belongs to an organization, the call may not be sent out to the PSTN but forced to be on net by manipulating digits, therefore saving toll charges. The user is never aware of the change, and for the user the whole experience remains transparent. Moreover, this example illustrates the use of various digit manipulation mechanisms at once. These are discussed in detail in the following sections.

In Figure 7-27, the following sequence of events occurs:

Step 1.   Users at extension (DN) 506[2-4] dial 91[2-4]XX. CUCM intercepts the call and realizes that it has a route pattern to match the dialed number, that is, 91XXX (closest match).

Step 2.   The call hits route pattern 9.1XXX (note the period (.) between 9 and 1)

Step 3.   The discard digit instruction (DDI) is set to discard 9 and keep 1XXX.

Step 4.   Within the route pattern, the calling number is transformed to X000, that is, taking the three most significant digits "as is" from the calling party and mapping the first digit, that is the least significant digit. Essentially any and all calling party numbers, for example 5062, 5063, and 5064, are changed to 5000.

Step 5.   Using the called party transformation mask, the least significant digit is taken "as is," while the three most significant digits are replaced by 0. Essentially, all calls to 1234, 1324, and 1432 are now changed to 1000.

Step 6.   DN 1000 is a local number configured in the CUCM database, and the extension rings, with the calling party DN as 5000.

The following sections describe the various digit manipulation methods.

External Phone Number Mask

The external phone number mask is leveraged in call routing to manipulate the internal directory number to digits that can be routed over the PSTN. The external phone number mask is configured on the DN configuration page in CUCM.

Additionally, the external phone number mask is available in the following entities:

■ Route pattern

■ Route list (via route group configuration as described earlier)

■ Translation pattern

■ Transformation pattern (Calling Party Transformation Pattern)

■ Hunt pilot

The external phone number mask is used for the following functions:

■ For automated alternate routing (AAR), the external phone number mask is used to change the internal dial plan into a PSTN-routable dial plan when rerouting intersite calls from the WAN to the PSTN (in case of WAN congestion).

> **Note**   The topic of AAR is covered in *Implementing Cisco IP Telephony and Video, Part 2.*

■ To change the display of the main phone number at the top of the LCD screen. A DN of 1001 with an external phone number mask of 408555XXXX would result in a displayed phone number of 4085551001.

■ To change the display of the caller ID for all calls in which the call classification is OffNet. The calling party number (caller ID) is changed to the full ten-digit DID phone number of the calling party.

Figure 7-28 depicts the External Phone Number Mask of +1408555XXXX for DN 4085551001. To configure an endpoint DN, go to **Device > Phone** and search for the endpoint for which you want to define the External Phone Number Mask.

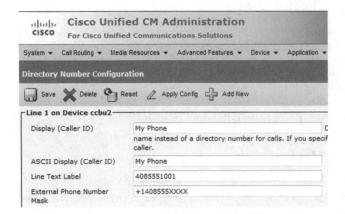

Figure 7-28   *External Phone Number Mask Definition on DN of an IP Phone*

Figure 7-29 illustrates the use of External Phone Number Mask in Route Pattern.

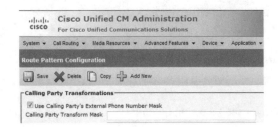

Figure 7-29   *Enabling Use of External Phone Number Mask on Route Pattern*

Note   A similar setup is applicable for Translation Patterns, Calling Party Transformation Pattern, and Hunt Pilot configuration where the check box must be checked for the call routing element to leverage the external phone number mask of the originating endpoint.

Significant Digits

For calls coming into a CUCM cluster from PSTN, the E.164 number may not make sense unless it is pruned to match the CUCM internal dial plan (unless the whole dial plan is based on E.164 notation). This is where the Significant Digits feature comes into play and instructs CUCM to analyze the configured number of digits (from right to left) of the called number for incoming calls received by a gateway or a trunk.

Setting the significant digits to four on a PSTN gateway instructs CUCM to ignore all but the last four digits of the called party number for routing incoming gateway or trunk calls. For example if an incoming call is destined for extension 1001 and the incoming number is an E.164 number such as 4085551001, setting the significant digits to four will strip all but last four digits (starting from right). Therefore, the resulting number will be 1001, which matches the inside extension as shown in Figure 7-30.

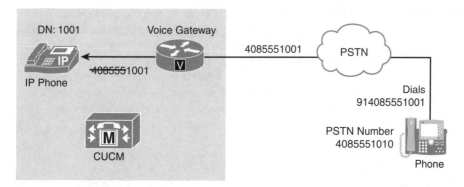

Figure 7-30 *Significant Digits Overview*

The Significant Digits feature is the easiest approach to convert incoming PSTN called numbers to an internal extension. However, the setting affects all calls received from the gateway. Moreover, the Significant Digits setting also cannot accommodate variable-length extension numbers on the internal network.

To set up the significant digits, go to **Device > Gateway (or Trunk)** and select the gateway (or trunk) for which this setting is to be configured. Under the Incoming Calls section, set the Significant Digits to a desired number for your internal dial plan, as shown in Figure 7-31.

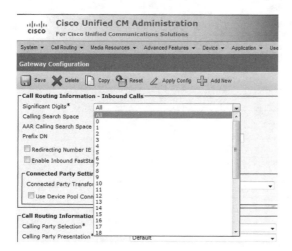

Figure 7-31 *Significant Digit Configuration at Gateway—Inbound Calls*

CUCM Digit Prefix and Stripping

More often than not, it's required that certain digits be prefixed to outbound calls or stripped from outbound calls for appropriate number presentation to the carrier. The Digit Prefix feature allows prefixing digits to a dialed number. Any digits that can be entered from a standard phone (0 through 9, *, and #) can be prepended to the calling or called party numbers. For example, while dialing a ten-digit number such as 4085551010, 91 may be required by the carrier to route the calls to long-distance numbers. This can be done by prefixing 91 so that the complete outbound number is in E.164 format (for example, 914085551010). Digit prefixing is available for either the calling or called party number and can be configured at the route pattern, route list, or translation pattern levels. Figure 7-32 illustrates the digit prefix instructions at the route pattern level. Similar configuration exists at the route list or translation pattern levels.

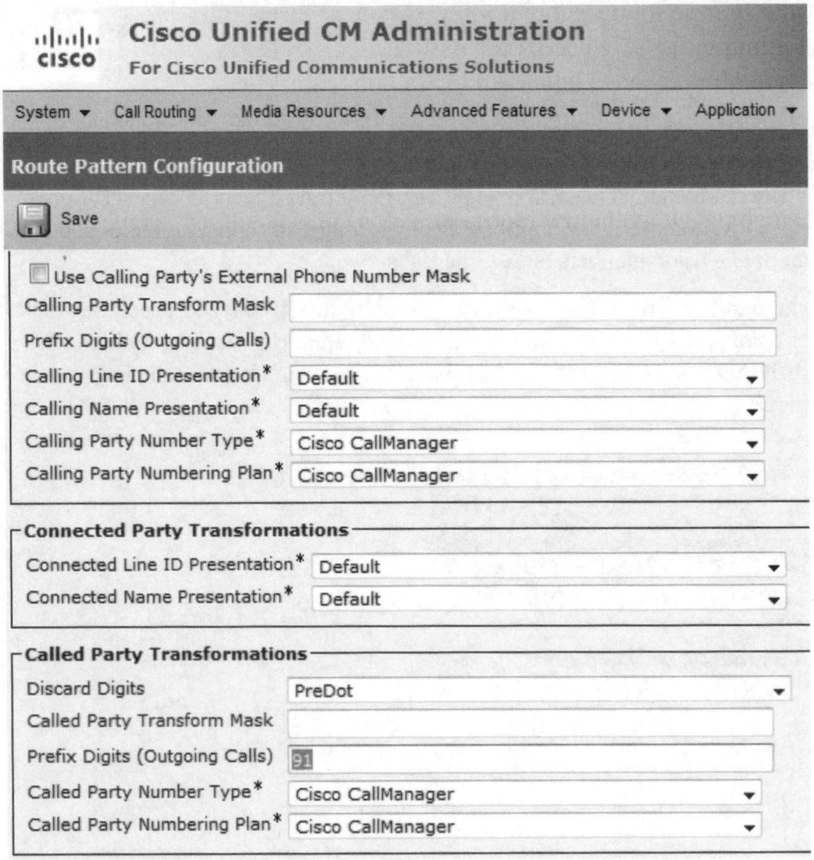

Figure 7-32   *Digit Prefixing at Route Pattern Level*

As depicted in Figure 7-33, the user at extension 1001 dials 4085551010, and because this number is not part of CUCM database, it needs to be routed to the PSTN domain. At the route pattern level, the number is matched and is prefixed by 91 before the dialed number is sent to the carrier network.

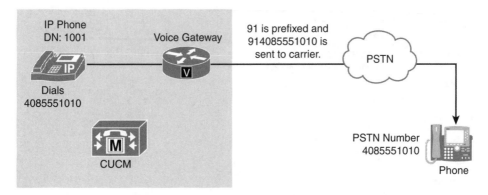

Figure 7-33 *Digit Prefix 91Added to Dialed Number*

Digit prefixing is the opposite of digit stripping or discard digits instruction (DDI). DDI removes parts of the dialed digit string before passing the number on to the next routing component or out to the PSTN. DDI removes a certain portion of the dialed string, such as the called party. As illustrated in Figure 7-34, DDI is set to discard 9 before the dialed number is sent to the carrier.

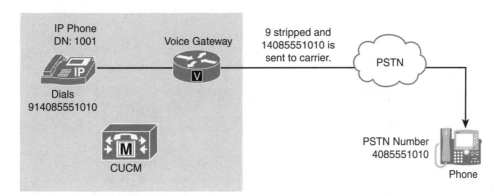

Figure 7-34 *DDI Instructions to Discard 9 from Dialed Number*

Digit stripping is configured in the Called Party Transformations section by selecting a Discard Digits setting from the drop-down menu, as shown in Figure 7-35.

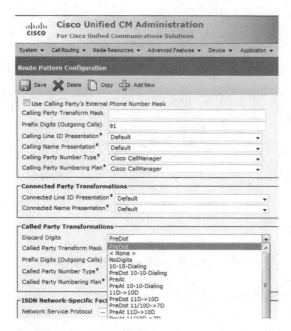

Figure 7-35   *DDI at Route Pattern Level*

Discard digit instructions can be configured at the route pattern and at the route group details level of the route list.

> **Note**   The PreAt, 11D/10D@7D, 11D@10D, IntlTollBypass, and 10-10-Dialing complex DDIs are not available unless the @ symbol is in the route pattern.

Before proceeding to digit manipulation methods, such as translation patterns and transformation patterns, let's try to understand the transformation masks. These are available at various levels within the call routing hierarchy—both for internal and external calls—and are key to transform calling party identity and/or called party identity.

Transformation Masks

More often than not, dialing transformations are required to modify either the calling party (initiator of the call) or the called party (destination of the call) number/digits. This is where transformation masks come in handy and allow the UC administrator to modify the calling number or automatic number identification (ANI) as well as adjust the called number or Dialed Number Identification System (DNIS).

As described earlier, digit translation in CUCM is possible through the transformation mask feature that can be found at various levels in CUCM, such as route pattern, route list details (route group), and translation pattern. The calling and called party transformation masks for calls outbound from an enterprise network can be assigned to route groups in the route list details or at route pattern level; that is applicable only when a route pattern is pointed directly to a gateway.

So, how do transformation masks work? Essentially, CUCM overlays the calling or called party number with the transformation mask so that the last character of the mask aligns with the last digit of the calling or called party number.

Note   Transformation masks operate much like significant digits in that the processing is always from right to left.

Now, there can be two situations:

1. A number is presented (calling or called party) and the transformation mask has X (acts as binary OR), so that the part of number matching the transformation mask passes as is.

2. The transformation mask has absolute numbers, in which case the number being transformed is replaced by the pattern matching the transformation mask.

Figure 7-36 gives an overview of transformation masks and the transformation operation.

Example 1

Dialed Number	**9.1 408 555 1010**
DDI Discard Pre-Dot	**1 408 555 1010**
Called Party Transformation Mask	**408 666 XXXX**
Resulting Dialed Number	**408 666 1010**

Example 2

Dialed Number	**9.1 408 445 1010**
DDI Discard Pre-Dot	**1 408 445 1010**
Called Party Transformation Mask	**XXXX XXXX 0000**
Resulting Dialed Number	**408 445 0000**

Figure 7-36   *Called Party Transformation Mask Examples*

As shown in Example 1 of Figure 7-36, the right-most four digits are passed "as is," whereas the rest of the number is changed from 408 555 to 408 666 (that is, number replacement). Subsequently in Example 2, while the first six digits (408 445) are kept "as is," the latter part or the most significant digits of the number are changed from 1010 to 0000.

> **Note**   If the number is longer than the mask, the mask adds extra digits to the original calling or called party pattern.

To configure transformation mask browse to the route pattern, route list detail (route group), or translation pattern via **Call Routing** menu and to configure the **Calling Party Transformation Mask** (under Calling Party Transformation) or **Called Party Transformation Mask** (under Called Party Transformation), enter data as shown in Figure 7-37.

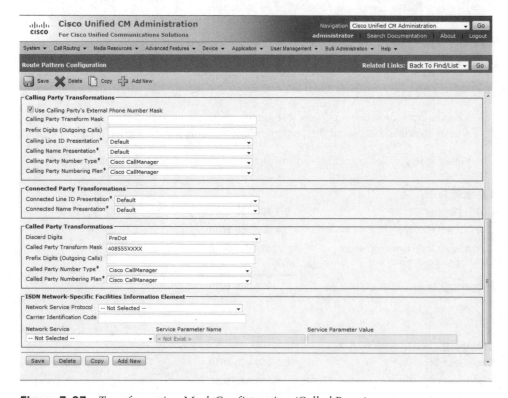

Figure 7-37   *Transformation Mask Configuration (Called Party)*

The next section describes translation patterns.

Translation Patterns

Translation patterns can be leveraged to manipulate digits before forwarding a call. A translation pattern is much like route pattern but with a difference; while a route pattern has access to external call routing elements, a translation pattern doesn't. In simpler terms, a route pattern is used to route calls outside of a CUCM cluster, whereas a translation pattern is used for routing calls within a CUCM cluster; thus there is post-digit manipulation. Also, both translation patterns and route patterns can be used to block patterns, but the default action is to attempt call routing.

Translation patterns use route pattern style matching and transformation mask-based digit manipulation. The pattern resulting after the translation pattern is applied is then rerouted by the system, thereby causing a second round of digit analysis. Eventually, the call is either routed to a device or blocked by CUCM.

Note   CUCM allows processing digits through translation patterns for only ten iterations to prevent call routing loops.

Figure 7-38 depicts a translation pattern to match 914085551XXX and transform the number into four-digit extension to keep the call on net. This is particularly useful when a range of numbers are owned by an organization and toll charges are to be avoided by keeping the calls on net (irrespective of user dialing behavior of four-digit or full E.164 number dialing).

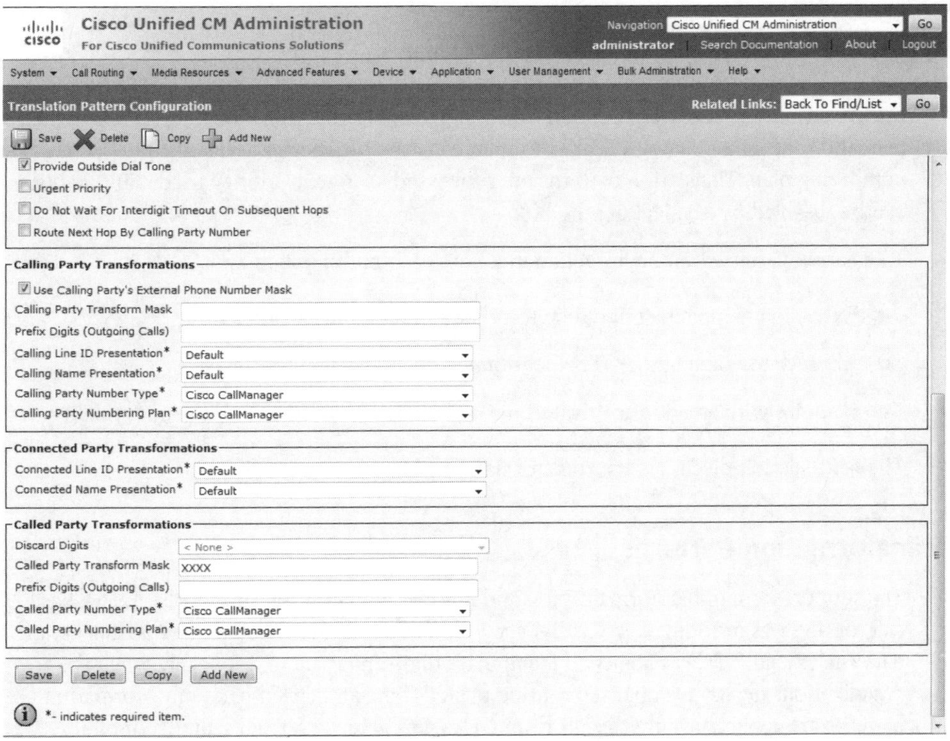

Figure 7-38   *Translation Pattern Configuration*

To configure a translation pattern, navigate to CUCM Administration, then go to **Call Routing > Translation Pattern**.

Figure 7-39 gives an insight into the call flow described earlier using the translation pattern.

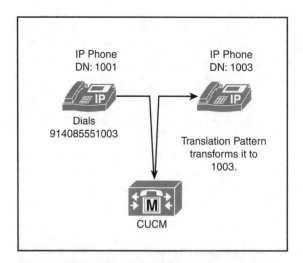

Figure 7-39 *Translation Pattern–Based Call Flow*

In case a translation pattern contains an @ sign, similar to a route pattern, a numbering plan and route filter can be selected to match certain number patterns of the selected numbering plan. Translation patterns are processed as urgent priority by default, and this can be disabled by unchecking the box.

Translation patterns can be leveraged in a host of situations such as:

- Extension mapping from public to private (internal) network

- Abbreviated dialing to PSTN locations

- Hotlines with a need for Private Line Automatic Ringdown (PLAR) functionality

The next section discusses the transformation patterns.

Transformation Patterns

The support for number normalization and number globalization support for E.164-based call routing was introduced in CUCM version 7.0. Calling and called party transformation patterns extend CUCM's ability to manipulate digits much more, especially when the organizations deploy a globalized routing plan. Calling and called party transformation patterns are applicable only to calls from CUCM to gateways, trunks, and endpoints (phones).

During digit analysis, CUCM treats transformation patterns similar to any other pattern in the call routing database (for example, a translation pattern or route pattern). Moreover, like any other calling search space (CSS), the calling and called transformation CSS can be used to restrict the patterns that are matched for the purpose of digit transformation. Calling and called party transformation CSSs can be applied in the phone, gateway, and device pool configuration locations of CUCM administration. Figure 7-40 shows the application of transformation CSS on an IP Phone.

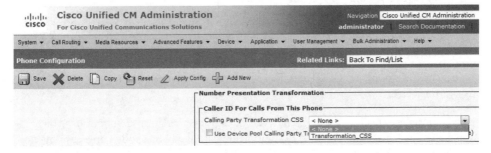

Figure 7-40   *Transformation CSS on IP Phone*

Figure 7-41 shows the option to select transformation CSS for calling or called party at the device pool level.

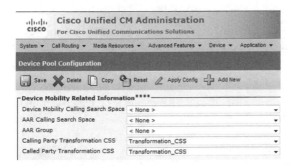

Figure 7-41   *Transformation CSS for Calling or Called Party at the Device Pool Level*

It is important to understand that instead of configuring an individual calling and called party transformation CSS at the device level, you can configure the devices to use calling and called party transformation CSSs configured at the device pool level. However, no transformation is performed if the device and associated device pool are not configured with a transformation CSS.

Note   Transformations patterns apply only to the outgoing call leg.

Calling and called party transformation patterns have the following key characteristics:

- Transformations are implemented in the global CUCM configuration.

- Calling and called party transformation patterns can be put into partitions, and access can be controlled tightly.

- Gateways and trunks can be configured with calling and called party transformation CSSs. Calling party transformations are supported on the Cisco IP phone, but called party transformations are not.

- The transformation CSS determines which transformation patterns are visible to the device.

It's important to realize that different levels of digit manipulation are not utilized all at once. For instance, only one level of digit manipulation will be applied on a case-by-case basis. Examples include:

- Any digit manipulation matches through a gateway or trunk transformation CSS results in all other digit manipulations being ignored.

- Digit manipulation settings on the route pattern take effect only when the route list details do not have any defined digit manipulations (as described earlier).

- A transformation CSS applied at the gateway/trunk or device pool will lead to the digit manipulations applied at the route pattern level to be skipped.

- In case a transformation calling search space (CSS) is configured on the device selected to route the call (or on that device's device pool), then transformations configured in the route pattern or route list are considered only if no match is found using the respective transformation CSS.

Note   The input to the transformation CSS always is the untransformed number before applying route pattern or route list transformations.

The following sections detail some examples of transformation patterns.

Note   DDI, digit prefixing, and other digit manipulation mechanisms are inherent to these use cases; however, they are not explicitly called out for ease of understanding.

Use Case 1

The user dials +14085551010 in partition A, and the number is modified from an 11-digit called party number in globalized number format (globalized dial plan) into a seven-digit called party number along with setting the numbering plan type to subscriber. Figure 7-42 gives an insight to the call flow.

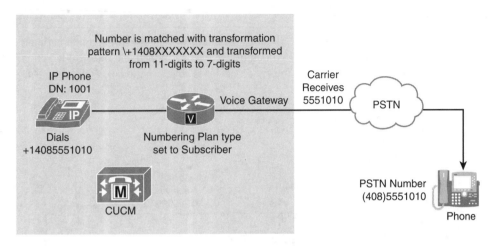

Figure 7-42 *Called Party Transformation Pattern Type Subscriber (Seven digits)*

Use Case 2

A user dials a +1XXXXXXXXXX globalized number. This pattern matches on all 11-digit patterns, beginning with the E.164 + character used to route international calls followed by a 1 and any ten digits. However, the pattern represents US area codes within a globalized route plan. As shown in Figure 7-43, the dialed number +14084451010 is matched and transformed on the gateway to 14084451010, with type national.

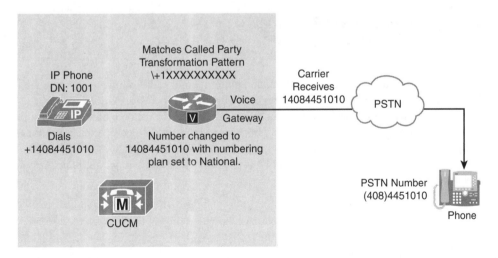

Figure 7-43 *Called Party Transformation Pattern Type National (11 digits)*

Use Case 3

A user dials +919999900000 which is a globalized number that is in turn an international number. The dialed number, +91999990000 (for India), is matched and transformed on the gateway with a prefix of 011 to indicate that this is an international call. Figure 7-44 depicts the call flow.

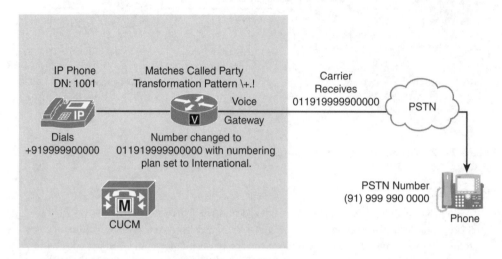

Figure 7-44 *Called Party Transformation Pattern Type International*

Note   Refer to *Implementing Cisco IP Telephony and Video Part 2* for a detailed discussion on globalized dial plans.

To configure a calling number transformation pattern, go to **Call Routing > Transformation > Transformation Pattern > Calling Party Transformation Pattern**. Figure 7-45 shows the configuration of a calling party transformation pattern. In this case, when a user set to use the external phone number mask (defined by the checkbox) dials and external number; the caller ID is transformed into 408445XXXX (keeping the last four digits "as is"). Finally, the caller ID is prefixed by 91 and sent with Calling Party Number Type as National.

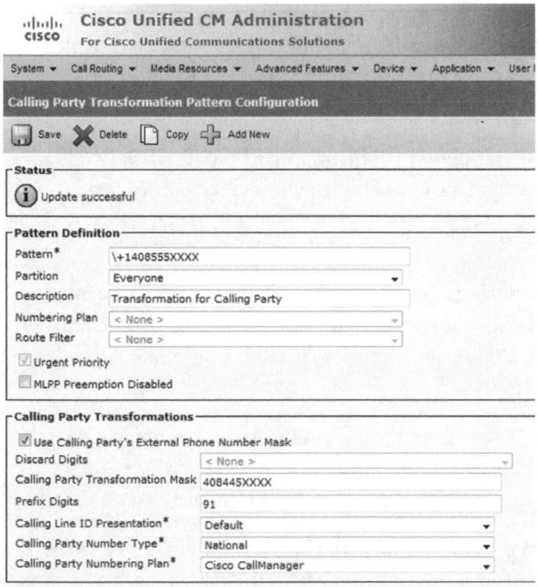

Figure 7-45 *Calling Party Transformation Pattern Configuration*

To configure a called party transformation pattern, go to **Call Routing > Transformation > Transformation Pattern > Called Party Transformation Pattern.** Figure 7-46 illustrates the configuration of a called party transformation pattern.

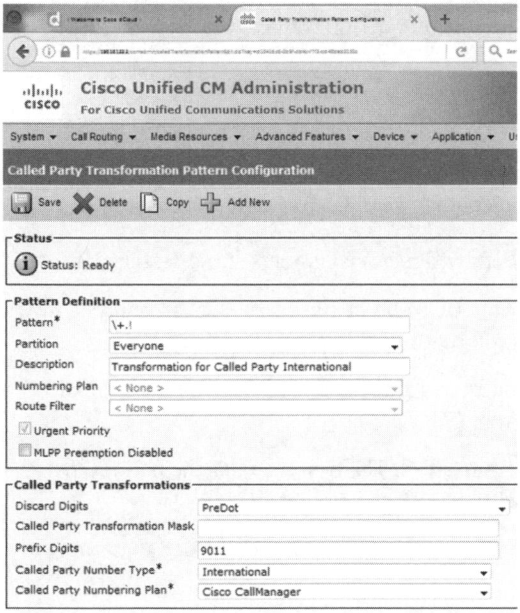

Figure 7-46 *Called Party Transformation Pattern Configuration*

In this case, when a user calls an international number, the transformation pattern \+.! is matched, and the called party number (such as +.919999908169) is subjected to the pre-dot digit discard mechanism, followed by the prefix 9011, and the Called Party Number Type is set as International.

To invoke a transformation pattern, the associated partition must be part of the transformation CSS at the device (gateway, trunk, or IP Phone) or device pool level.

Incoming transformation settings have the following characteristics:

■ Incoming calling and called party settings apply to calls received from gateways and trunks. They are not applicable to calls received from phones. In case of IP phones, the external phone number mask of directory numbers is used to globalize the calling party number from Cisco IP phones.

■ They allow the configuration of digit stripping, digit prefixes, and transformations to be applied to calling and called party numbers for calls inbound from trunks (another CUCM cluster or ITSP) and the PSTN to the CUCM cluster.

■ Different settings can be configured per number plan type (unknown, subscriber, national, and international) if the information is available in the call signaling.

■ Incoming calling and called party settings can be configured at the device, device pool, and/or global service parameter configuration levels in CUCM Administration.

Note H.225 trunks and H.323 gateways support incoming calling and called party settings based on numbering plan type, but Media Gateway Control Protocol (MGCP) gateways support only incoming calling party settings based on numbering plan type. Session Initiation Protocol (SIP) does not support numbering plan types.

Chapter Summary

The following list summarizes the key points that were discussed in this chapter:

■ In CUCM, endpoints can be identified by directory numbers and directory URIs.

■ Call routing is the procedure in which CUCM processes incoming call requests by looking up the dialed number in its call routing table.

■ Route patterns, route lists, route groups, and gateways/trunks form the essential elements for routing external calls from CUCM.

■ The best matching entry is used to route a call. The best match is the pattern that represents the fewest numbers.

■ When not all digits of a called number are received at once, the dialed digits are analyzed as they are received.

- In digit-by-digit analysis, overlapping patterns can cause post-dial delays. Configure shorter overlapping patterns as urgent so that they are processed immediately, even if longer overlapping patterns exist.

- Digit manipulation is useful in multiple ways—from keeping a call on net to presenting the right caller ID to ensuring that an incoming call hits the right destination.

- Multiple tools are available in CUCM for enabling and using digit manipulation for calling and called numbers, such as external phone number mask, discard digit instructions, translation patterns, transformation patterns, and so on.

- DDI and digit prefixes allow digit manipulation by discarding and adding digits to a number respectively.

- Significant digits allow defining the number of digits that should be considered when a number enters CUCM from the outside world (PSTN). This allows direct matching of the internal extension.

- Translation patterns are much like route patterns, expect that they allow call routing within a CUCM cluster. They're used for digit manipulation and enable passing a call up to 10 times within a translation pattern construct before the call can be sent to another call routing entity.

- Transformation patterns allow changing the calling party (ANI) or the called party (DNIS)

References

For additional information, refer to the following:

Cisco Systems, Inc. Cisco Collaboration System 10.x SRND, June 2014. http://www.cisco.com/c/en/us/td/docs/voice_ip_comm/cucm/srnd/collab10/collab10. html.

Review Questions

Use the questions here to review what you learned in this chapter. The correct answers are found in Appendix A, "Answers to the Review Questions."

1. What dial plan element is used to match the dialed digits for call routing to another cluster or the PSTN?

    a. Route pattern

    b. Route list

    c. Route group

    d. Gateway

    e. Trunk

2. What dial plan element is responsible for changing digits and sending the call for another dial plan lookup?

   a. Directory numbers

   b. Translation pattern

   c. Route pattern

   d. Hunt pilot

   e. Meet-me numbers

3. Which of the following wildcards represents a variable length number?

   a. @

   b. !

   c. X

   d. T

   e. #

4. Which of the following wildcards represent a single digit?

   a. @

   b. !

   c. X

   d. T

   e. #

   f. ( )

5. Which of the following wildcards represents the termination of the interdigit timeout?

   a. @

   b. !

   c. X

   d. T

   e. #

6. Which of the following two patterns does the route pattern 13[1349]X match?

   a. 13130

   b. 13199

   c. 1310

   d. 1349

7. What will happen when a user dials 90114912345 as en bloc dialing and CUCM matches the call to the route pattern 9.011!?

   a. The call will fail

   b. The call will route immediately after the dial button is pressed

   c. CUCM will wait for the # key press

   d. CUCM will wait for the T302 timer to expire

8. How should you configure the T302 timer?

   a. Disable the timer by setting the value to 0

   b. Leave the timer at its default value for best results

   c. Set the timer to a value of 1 to enable the timer

   d. Lower the value from the default to keep post-dial delay at an acceptable level

9. What happens when the urgent priority box is checked on a pattern?

   a. CUCM process the call right after the T302 timer expires

   b. CUCM allows all callers to dial this number

   c. CUCM does not wait for the T302 timer to expire but routes the call as soon as a pattern of the correct length is found

   d. CUCM sends the call as a 911 urgent call

10. Where is a URI configured?

    a. In the OTLD parameter

    b. In the directory number page

    c. Assigned via a translation pattern

    d. In the Application User details page

11. Which two patterns will match \+1.!?

    a. +1408551010

    b. +493534447890

    c. +14084451001

    d. A URI matching the DN of the dialed number

12. True or false? The ANI is the number called by the user.

    a. True

    b. False

13. A route filter can be provisioned to control the calls when using the @ sign in a pattern expression. At which place can a route filter be used?

    a. Route group

    b. Route list

    c. Route pattern

    d. Phone DN

14. What will be the result of matching a called number 4085556000 with the transformation mask 55588XXXXX?

    a. The resulting number will be 4085556000

    b. The resulting number will be 5558856000

    c. The resulting number will be 5558886000

    d. The resulting number will be 5555556000

15. A Cisco SCCP protocol–controlled phone supports which two dialing mechanisms?

    a. En bloc

    b. KPML

    c. Digit-by-digit

    d. Overlap send and receive

Chapter 8

Implementing Calling Privileges in Cisco Unified Communications Manager

Just as you don't want anyone and everyone entering or leaving your house or workplace, as a UC administrator you don't want people to make or receive calls to/from all various sources. As a UC administrator, you want to have a degree of control over what types of calls can be made using the enterprise telephony resources and who can make those calls. This is where calling privileges come in and the class of service required to implement those calling privileges. Calling privileges are an important dial plan component. They are used to implement class of service (CoS). Based on the calling device or line, access to some destinations is permitted, while access to others is not.

Chapter Objectives

This chapter describes the configuration tools that can be used to implement calling privileges and discusses different usage scenarios. Upon completing this chapter, you will be able to meet the following objectives:

- Describe calling privileges and their use.

- List the elements that are used to implement calling privileges.

- Describe partitions, CSSs, and their functions.

- Describe the considerations when implementing partitions and CSSs.

- List the required steps for implementing partitions and CSSs.

Calling Privileges Overview

This section describes calling privileges and their use.

Calling privileges are configured to control which call routing table entries are accessible from a particular endpoint (such as a phone, gateway, or trunk). The primary application of calling privileges is the implementation of class of service (CoS). CoS is typically used to control call charges by blocking access to costly service numbers and international calls for some or all users as defined by an organization's telephony policy. It is also used to protect the privacy of some users; for example, it may disallow direct calls to managers except through their assistants.

Calling privileges can also be used to implement special applications, such as routing calls to the same number in different ways based on different calling devices. In a multisite environment with public switched telephone network (PSTN) gateways at each site, PSTN route patterns may need be routed to the local PSTN gateway. Therefore, the same route patterns must exist multiple times (once per site in this example). Only the site-specific route patterns should be accessible by the devices at this site. A common example of this is to create 911 route patterns for each site that has local PSTN access. Each of these route patterns would be in a site-specific partition, and phones in a specific site are given access to only the local partition.

Another application that can use CoS is time-of-day routing, in which calls take different paths depending on when the call is placed.

> **Note**   This chapter addresses CoS in CUCM. For details on class of restriction (CoR) on Cisco IOS routers, refer to Chapter 13, "Implementing Cisco IOS Voice Gateways and Cisco Unified Border Element."

Calling-Privilege Implementation Overview

Many CoS implementations use a similar approach. Call types are often named after the calling functionality they represent, for example Long Distance or International. Calling classes group these call types to define a device's calling ability.

Table 8-1 shows the calling classes and their allowed destinations in a typical CoS implementation. These calling classes can then be assigned to devices or directory numbers (DNs).

Table 8-1   *Calling Privilege Example*

Calling Privilege Class (CoS)	Allowed Destinations
Internal	■ Internal
	■ Emergency
Local	■ Internal
	■ Emergency
	■ Local PSTN

Calling Privilege Class (CoS)	Allowed Destinations
Long Distance	■ Internal
	■ Emergency
	■ Local PSTN
	■ Long-distance PSTN
International	■ Internal
	■ Emergency
	■ Local PSTN
	■ Long-distance PSTN
	■ International
Premium	■ 1900 numbers

In Table 8-1, the class Internal allows only internal and emergency calls. The class Local adds permission for local PSTN calls. The class Long Distance also allows long-distance PSTN calls, and the class International enables international PSTN calls.

Table 8-1 presents common examples of the types of call classifications that might be configured. Additionally, other numbers that may be identified include toll-free numbers, as well as premium numbers that associate a charge for their usage.

Part of the dial plan design will identify what groupings of permissions are required. These typically differ company by company, but some common elements are present throughout. For example, lobby phones should have access to emergency numbers as well as internal numbers. They may have access to local numbers as well.

General staff should have access to emergency numbers, internal numbers, and local numbers. Often general staff will also have access to dial long-distance numbers.

Managers typically have access to dial all numbers, with the exception of premium numbers (1-900 numbers). Premium numbers should have a classification of their own so that access to these numbers can be denied. Typically these numbers are denied to all callers.

Toll-free numbers can have a classification of their own, and access to them might be permitted to specific staff, such as front desk operators.

Calling-Privileges Configuration Elements

This section describes the elements that are used to implement calling privileges as shown in Table 8-2.

Table 8-2 *Call Privilege Elements*

Calling Privileges Element	Characteristics
Partition	Group of numbers with similar reachability; for example staff partition which is assigned to all staff directory numbers.
Calling search space (CSS)	A list of partitions that are accessible to a particular device.
Time schedule and time period	Used to restrict certain partitions to be reachable only during specific times and days. The time schedule is applied to a partition. If no schedule is applied, that partition is available 24/7.

These elements are discussed in more details throughout this chapter.

Partitions and CSSs

This section describes partitions, calling search space, and their functions.

A partition is a tag or a label that is applied to a group of dialable patterns with identical accessibility. Partitions are assigned to call routing targets (that is, any entry of the call routing table), including the following:

- voicemail ports
- directory numbers
- URIs
- route patterns
- translation patterns
- Meet-Me conference numbers

When you apply a partition to a number or URI, you are effectively locking access to that number or URI. The only elements that can dial that number or URI are ones that have that partition in their CSS.

A CSS defines which partitions are accessible to a particular device. A device can call only those call routing table entries that are in partitions that are included in the CSS of the device.

CSSs are assigned to the sources of call routing requests, such as:

- Phones or directory numbers

- Translation patterns

- gateways

- trunks

- voicemail ports

- applications

A CSS is an ordered list of partitions. When a closest match number is found in a partition within the CSS, the system stops further analysis even when there might be another match in a lower partition.

Note   When you define a CSS containing a list of partitions, the system adds the <None> partition to the bottom of the list. This is not visible when you view the CSS, but it is important to understand that it is there. Therefore, a device can call any number associated with the visible partitions in their CSS, as well as any number that is still associated with the <None> partition.

Partition <None> and CSS <None>

This section describes what happens to entities that have not been assigned a partition or CSS.

By default, all entities that can be configured with a partition are in partition <None>, and all entities that can be configured with a CSS are assigned CSS <None>, which contains the <None> partition.

The source of a call routing request can always access the members of partition <None> (also called the null partition), regardless of the CSS of that call routing source.

Entities that do not have an assigned CSS (in other words, entities that use CSS <None>) can access only the call routing targets that are in partition <None>.

By default, if no partitions or CSSs are assigned, all entities are associated with the null partition and CSS <None>. Therefore, all calls are possible for all calling sources by default.

Analogy: Locks and Key Rings

Often, for discussion purposes, the analogy is made depicting a partition as a lock and a calling search space (CSS) as a key ring containing one or more keys to open the lock (match the callable partition). Figure 8-1 shows the interaction of configured partitions and CSSs, the null partition, and CSS <None>.

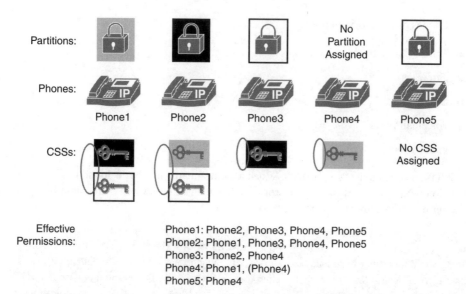

Figure 8-1   *Partition and CSS Logic*

The example shown in Figure 8-1 uses an analogy of locks and key rings. The locks represent partitions that the administrator applies to DNs; the key rings represent the CSSs that the administrator configures and applies to the phones.

In Figure 8-1, Phone1 DN is configured as a member of the blue partition, Phone2 DN is in the red partition, and Phone3 and Phone5 DNs are in the gold partition. Phone4 DN has not been assigned a partition. Following the analogy of locks and keys, there are three types of configured locks (blue, red, and gold) as well as the default lock <None>. Two of these locks are assigned to one phone each, and one of the locks is assigned to two phones. Phone4 is secured by the default lock since no other partition has been assigned.

The CSSs are represented as key rings. Phone1 has a key ring with red and gold keys. Phone2 has a key ring with blue and gold keys. Phone3 has a key ring with only a red key. Phone4 has a key ring with only a blue key, and Phone5 has the default key <None>.

As a result of this implementation of locks and keys, the following effective permissions apply:

- **Phone1:** Like all other phones, Phone1 has access to all devices that have the default lock (Phone4, in this example). In addition, Phone1 can unlock the red and gold locks because it has the appropriate keys. Therefore, Phone1 can access Phone2, Phone3, Phone4, and Phone5.

- **Phone2:** Like all other phones, Phone2 has access to all devices that have the default lock (Phone4). In addition, Phone2 can unlock the blue and gold locks because it has the appropriate keys. Therefore, Phone2 can access Phone1, Phone3, Phone4, and Phone5.

- **Phone3:** Like all other phones, Phone3 has access to all devices that have the default lock (Phone4). In addition, Phone3 can unlock the red lock because it has the appropriate key. Therefore, Phone3 can access Phone2 and Phone4.

- **Phone4:** Like all other phones, Phone4 has access to all devices that have the default lock (itself, in this example). In addition, it can unlock the blue lock because it has the appropriate key. Therefore, Phone4 can access Phone1 and itself, which is of no practical importance because Phone4 usually does not place a call to itself.

- **Phone5:** Like all other phones, Phone5 has access to all devices that have the default lock (Phone4). Phone5 cannot unlock any other locks because it does not have any keys other than the default <None> key. Therefore, Phone5 can access only Phone4.

To summarize the analogy that is in Figure 8-1: Partitions are like identical locks, which can be unlocked by the same key; CSSs are like key rings that include certain keys. If no lock (partition) is applied to a device, then all other devices can access that device. If only the default <None> CSS is present (no other CSS is configured), then only devices that have the default <None> lock can be accessed.

Partitions and CSS Example

A CSS can contain one or more partitions. However, quite often, it does not contain all the available partitions. Figure 8-2 shows an example of a CSS that contains the Chicago and San Jose partitions, but not the Atlanta partition.

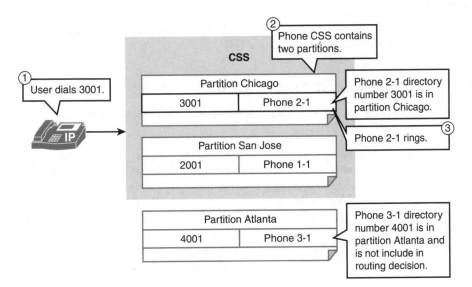

Figure 8-2 *Partitions and CSS Example*

In Figure 8-2, a phone has a CSS that contains two partitions, Chicago and San Jose. A third partition, Atlanta, exists but is not included in the CSS of the phone. These phone directory numbers are assigned to these partitions:

- Directory number 3001 (Phone 2-1) is assigned to the Chicago partition.

- Directory number 2001 (Phone 1-1) is assigned to the San Jose partition.

- Directory number 4001 (Phone 3-1) is assigned to the Atlanta partition.

The user places a call:

- The user dials 3001, which is the directory number of Phone 2-1.

- CUCM performs a call routing lookup of the number 3001 through the partitions that are configured in the CSS of the calling phone: Chicago and San Jose.

- CUCM finds a match in the Chicago partition, because the directory number 3001 of Phone 2-1 is assigned to this partition. Because no other matches exist, routing is complete, and Phone 2-1 rings.

Although Figure 8-2 shows partitions and CSS in the context of DNs, the same process would be applied to calls directed at URIs. Each configured URI can be assigned to a partition, and URIs that are learned through the Lightweight Directory Access Protocol (LDP) synchronization process are assigned to a default directory URI partition. This partition can be renamed or aliased to an existing partition and can be included in a device's CSS.

The call analysis process, from the perspective of call permissions, remains the same regardless of whether the target is a DN or a URI.

Partition and CSS Considerations

This section describes what needs to be considered when implementing partitions and CSSs.

A CSS is an ordered list of partitions. The partition that is listed first has higher priority than a partition that is listed later if equal matches are found. When CUCM performs a call routing lookup, all accessible entities are considered by best-match logic. Accessible entities include all targets that reside in a partition that is listed in the CSS of the calling phone and all targets that do not have an applied partition. Multiple identical entities can exist in the call routing table, but they must be in different partitions. One exception to this rule is phone directory numbers. When two or more devices share the same directory number within the same partition, the directory number is called a shared line.

In summary, the call routing table entry is chosen based on the following order:

1. The best match is chosen.

2. If multiple equally qualified matches exist, the order of the partition in the CSS of the calling device is the tie-breaker. In other words, if there is no single best match, the match that is found in the earlier listed partition in the device CSS is chosen.

Understanding Device CSS and Line CSS

This section describes the capability of IP phones to be configured with a device CSS and a line CSS, and how those CSSs interact with each other. Figure 8-3 shows the device and line CSS logic.

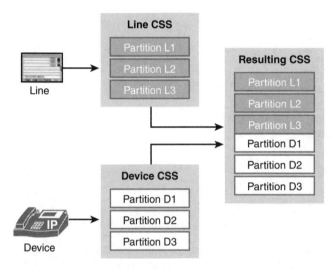

Figure 8-3   *Device and Line CSS*

On most sources of a call routing request, such as a trunk, gateway, or translation pattern, only one CSS can be configured. On IP phones, however, a CSS can be applied per line and once at the device level.

If both line and device CSSs are configured, the CSS of the line from which the call is placed is considered first. In other words, the line CSS partitions are concatenated (but preferred) with the partitions of the device CSS. The result, from a processing perspective, is one composite CSS containing the line-level CSS partitions at the top and the phone-level CSS partitions at the bottom.

Note   On computer telephony integration (CTI) ports, the line CSS and the device CSS are placed in reverse order. The partitions of the device CSS are placed before the partitions of the line CSS.

Example—IP Phone Line CSS and Device CSS Interaction

When both line-level and device-level CSSs are present, the line-level partitions will be preferred if there are multiple best-match entries. Figure 8-4 provides an example of an IP phone that is configured with a line CSS and a device CSS.

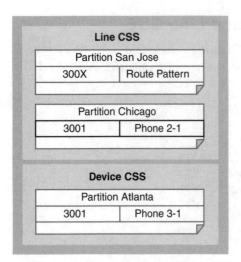

Figure 8-4   *Line and Device CSS Example*

In Figure 8-4, the line CSS of the calling phone includes the San Jose and Chicago partitions, and the device CSS of the calling phone includes the Atlanta partition.

Route pattern 300X is in the San Jose partition, directory number 3001 is used at Phone 2-1 in the Chicago partition, and the same directory number (3001) is used at Phone 3-1 in the Atlanta partition.

If the calling phone dials 3001, CUCM interprets the dialed digits and searches for the closest match. Because the two directory number entries (3001) in the call routing table are more specific (a complete match) than the route pattern (300X, which represents 10 numbers), the route pattern is not a candidate for the final routing decision. Out of the two equally matched directory numbers, the number of Phone 2-1 is used to extend the call because it is in the partition that is listed first in the line CSS.

Figure 8-4 illustrates that the line CSS has higher priority than the device CSS. If the line CSS and device CSS were reversed, the call would be sent to Phone 3-1.

Note   Although route pattern 300X matches the dialed number and is listed in the first partition, it is not used to route the call in the example in Figure 8-4. The first priority for the call routing decision is the best match. The order of partitions is important only if multiple best matches exist.

Note A common misunderstanding is that the first matching pattern that is found (regardless of the quality of the match) when searching through the partitions in the CSS is used for call routing. If this scenario were true, then subsequent partitions of the CSS would be looked at only if no match was found in the earlier partitions. However, all partitions are immediately considered for best-match logic. The partition order is relevant only if multiple best matches exist.

A line-device approach can be used to lock down access to certain number patterns by defining blocking CSS at the line level (with partitions pointing to blocking route patterns) followed by allowing CSS at the device level (with partitions that allow access to specific destinations). This allows for fine-tuned access to certain destinations whether the phone is used by a desk worker, a mobile worker with a device profile (extension mobility login), or in a device roaming scenario using device mobility.

Partition and CSS Configuration

This section lists the required steps for partition and CSS implementation.

The configuration of partitions includes the following steps:

Step 1. Create partitions.

Step 2. Assign partitions to dialable patterns, such as directory numbers, route patterns, or translation patterns.

The configuration of CSSs includes the following steps:

Step 1. Create CSSs.

Step 2. Add partitions, in the desired order, into each newly created CSS.

Step 3. Assign CSSs to entities that can request lookups to the call routing table to route a call. Examples of such entities are phones and phone lines, trunks, gateways, and translation patterns.

When configuring partitions and CSSs, you want to be cognizant of the order in which you apply the elements. Generate partitions first, because they have to exist before creating the CSS. However, if you create and apply the partition before you create and apply the CSS, you are in fact locking access to all numbers until the CSS is applied. A better approach is to perform the steps in the following order:

Step 1. Create partitions

Step 2. Create CSSs

Step 3. Apply CSSs

Step 4. Apply partitions

The net effect of this configuration order is that you distribute the keys before you apply the locks. Therefore, all numbers are reachable during the process until the partitions are applied, at which time the correct permissions will be in place.

Note   A translation pattern is used in both roles. The pattern is a dialable pattern in the call-routing table (that is, the target of a call-routing request). If matched, the pattern invokes a new call-routing request for the translated pattern. The partition at the translation pattern specifies who can match the pattern (the partition is required in the CSS of the calling device). The CSS at the translation pattern specifies the entries of the call routing table that the translation pattern can see for its call routing request, when trying to find the translated pattern in the call routing table.

Chapter Summary

The following list summarizes the key points that were discussed in this chapter:

- Calling privileges are used to implement class of service or special applications that require calls to be treated differently depending on the caller.

- Partitions and CSSs are the two most important elements of calling privilege implementation.

- Partitions are applied to groups of called numbers with identical reachability characteristics.

- CSSs are ordered lists of partitions to which the assignee of the CSS has access.

- The order of partitions within a CSS is relevant for call routing.

- The implementation of calling privileges includes the configuration of partitions and CSSs and their assignment to patterns and devices such as lines, phones, trunks, and gateways.

References

For additional information, refer to the following:

Cisco Systems, Inc. *Cisco Unified Communications Manager Administration Guide, Release 10.0(1)*, June 2014. http://www.cisco.com/c/en/us/td/docs/voice_ip_comm/cucm/admin/10_0_1/ccmcfg/CUCM_BK_C95ABA82_00_admin-guide-100.html.

Cisco Systems, Inc. *Cisco Unified Communications Manager System Guide, Release 10.0(1)*, June 2014. http://www.cisco.com/c/en/us/td/docs/voice_ip_comm/cucm/admin/10_0_1/ccmsys/CUCM_BK_SE5FCFB6_00_cucm-system-guide-100.html.

Cisco Systems, Inc. *Cisco Collaboration System 10.x SRND*, June 2014. http://www.cisco.com/c/en/us/td/docs/voice_ip_comm/cucm/srnd/collab10/collab10.html.

Review Questions

Use the questions here to review what you learned in this chapter. The correct answers are found in Appendix A, "Answers to the Review Questions."

1. Which two of the following represent CoS elements? (Choose two.)

    a. Directory numbers

    b. Partitions

    c. Calling search spaces

    d. Route patterns

    e. Translation patterns

2. What can be assigned to either a DN or a phone to provide calling privileges?

    a. Route group

    b. Partition

    c. Calling search space

    d. Route list

3. What element locks access to a DN when applied?

    a. Route group

    b. Partition

    c. Calling search space

    d. Route list

4. How does CUCM process CSSs when a CSS is applied at both the phone level and at the line level?

    a. Phone-level CSS is ignored if line-level CSS is present.

    b. Line-level CSS is ignored if phone-level CSS is present.

    c. Phone-level CSS is processed first, followed by line-level CSS.

    d. Line-level CSS is processed first, followed by phone-level CSS.

5. Partitions are not applied to which of the following elements?

    a. Directory numbers

    b. Translation patterns

    c. Route patterns

    d. SIP trunks

    e. Voicemail ports

6. CSSs are not applied to which of the following elements?

   a. Route patterns

   b. Translation patterns

   c. Directory numbers

   d. Meet-Me numbers

7. In which order is call routing processed with respect to CSSs?

   a. First partition match in the CSS

   b. Closest match, then first partition in concatenated CSS

   c. Closest match at line-level CSS, then first partition at line-level CSS

   d. Closest match at phone-level CSS, then closest match at line-level CSS

8. Which devices can call numbers in the <None> partition?

   a. Any device

   b. Only devices that have the <None> CSS

   c. Only devices that also have the <None> partition

   d. Only devices that do not have a CSS assigned

9. Which numbers can be called by a device with the <None> CSS?

   a. Any number

   b. No number

   c. Any number with the <None> CSS assigned to it

   d. Any number with the <None> partition assigned to it

10. Which should be the last configuration step when configuring partitions and CSSs?

    a. Create partitions

    b. Create CSSs

    c. Apply partitions

    d. Apply CSSs

Chapter 9

Implementing Call Coverage in Cisco Unified Communications Manager

Many businesses have various sales or service support departments that work as groups to process inbound calls from customers. These businesses typically require several phone lines and a way to make the lines work together so that if one representative is busy or unavailable, the call rolls over to other members of the group until it is answered or forwarded to an auto-attendant or voicemail. Call hunting is the mechanism that helps manage inbound calls and ensure that they are handled accordingly. This chapter demonstrates how call coverage can be achieved in many ways, as required and defined by the needs of an organization.

Chapter Objectives

This chapter describes how to implement call hunting, call queuing, and lists other call coverage features such as Call Forward, Shared Lines, and Call Pickup. Upon completing this chapter, you will be able to meet the following objectives:

- Describe call coverage options in Cisco Unified Communications Manager
- Describe how call hunting works in Cisco Unified Communications Manager
- Describe call hunting scenarios in Cisco Unified Communications Manager
- Describe how call queuing works in Cisco Unified Communications Manager
- Describe the steps that are involved in call hunting and call queuing configuration

Call Coverage Overview

Call coverage is an essential part of the Cisco Collaboration network dial plan and ensures that all incoming calls are answered as required or mandated by business processes. Call coverage can be defined into two major categories:

- Call coverage features for an individual user
- Call hunting

Call coverage for an individual user allows the user to decide how to manage incoming calls to their line. For example, John can set up his desk phone (line) to forward all incoming calls to his mobile phone while he is away from his desk. This doesn't affect any other phone/directory number (DN), as the changes made to John's phone line are very specific. Moreover, some call coverage features for individual users can be implemented by the users themselves, while some require the administrator to configure the same.

In contrast to call coverage for individual users, call hunting is a system configuration and can only be implemented by the administrator. For example, when you call your telephone service provider, you're greeted by the interactive voice recognition (IVR) system, after which the call is sent to a live agent (provided you choose that option). Now, the call treatment depends on whether agents are assisting other customers or are available to take your call; accordingly the call may be queued until an agent is available to answer the call, or it may get rolled over from one agent's line to next agent's until an agent is able to answer the call. Eventually, if all agents are busy and the call cannot be answered, CUCM can be programmed to send the call to a voicemail box.

The sections that follow describe the various call coverage features and their implementation.

Call Coverage Features for Individual Users

The following call coverage features can be implemented for individual users in a Cisco Collaboration environment:

- **Call Forward:** If the called phone does not answer the call, the call is forwarded to another phone or voicemail as configured. Call Forward can be further categorized into one of the following:
  - Call Forward All (CFA)
  - Call Forward Busy (CFB)
  - Call Forward No Answer (CFNA)
  - Call Forward Unregistered (CFUR)
  - Call Forward No Coverage (CFNC)
  - Forward on CTI failure.

Note   Out of these, CFA, CFB, and CFNA are the only user-configurable options. These features are explained in following section.

- **Shared lines:** A shared line is a directory number (DN) that is assigned to more than one device in the same cluster within the same partition, allowing the call to be accepted on more than one phone at same time. On a call to a shared line, all the phones associated with it ring together.

- **Call Pickup:** Call Pickup allows a call that is ringing on a phone to be picked up at another phone within same pickup group. The user must press the PickUp and Answer soft keys to pick up the call. The user gets connected to the incoming call that has been ringing the longest.

- **Group Call Pickup (GPickUp):** Group Call Pickup allows users to pick up incoming calls in another Call Pickup group. The user must press the GPickUp soft key, dial the group number of another pickup group, and answer the call to make the connection.

- **Directed Call Pickup:** Directed Call Pickup allows users to pick up a ringing call on a DN directly by pressing the GPickUp soft key and entering the directory number of the device that is ringing. The user must press the GPickUp soft key, dial the DN of the ringing phone, and answer the call that will now ring on the user phone to make the connection.

- **Other Pickup (OPickUp):** Other Group Pickup allows users to pick up incoming calls in a group that is associated with their own pickup group. When more than one associated group exists, the priority of answering calls for the associated group goes from the first associated group to the last associated group. The user must press the soft keys OPickUp and Answer to make the call connection.

- **Call Park:** CUCM offers a Call Park feature that enables a user to place a call on hold on one phone (extension) and retrieve the same call from a different phone (extension). Call Park places the call on hold and parks it on a virtual directory number (DN) chosen automatically from a range of call park numbers predefined by the administrator. Once a call is parked, a number is displayed to users that they can dial from a different phone (both phones should be registered with same CUCM cluster) so they can retrieve the call.

- **Directed Call Park:** This feature is similar to call park with a major difference: the user-preferred number can be defined so that the call will be parked on this number every time. The user transfers a call to the directed call park number by pressing the Transfer soft key and then entering the directed call park number (a retrieval number that the user already knows).

Call Forward

Call forwarding is an important call coverage operation, because it allows both the user and system administrator to set up simple yet powerful call routing functions. The various call forwarding options can be enabled on a per line or DN basis and applied to a physical phone and device profile, whichever is active at the time. Figure 9-1 shows the various call forwarding options available on a physical phone and a device profile's line.

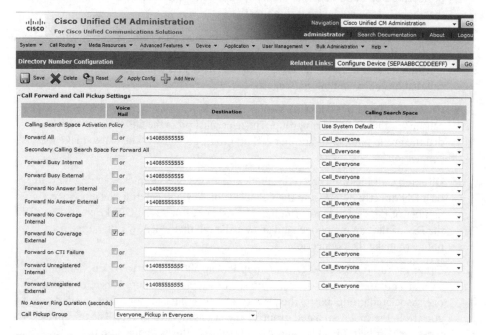

Figure 9-1   *Call Forward Options on a Physical Phone Line/Device Profile Line*

As seen in Figure 9-1, the various call forward options available are CFA, CFB (internal/external), CFNA (internal/external), CFNC (internal/external), Forward on CTI Failure, and Forward Unregistered (internal/external). Also, note that this line/DN is part of the Everyone_Pickup group.

> **Note**   Call Pickup, Group Call Pickup/Directed Group Call Pickup, and Other Pickup all depend on the relationship between the Call Pickup Groups and their assignment to the line/DN of the device/device profile, as explained later in this section.

Call Forward All (CFA) can be set up by the individual user either on the phone itself using the **CfwdALL** soft key or via the CUCM end user Self Care portal accessible via **http://<server address>/ucmuser**. Users can set up the line/DN to forward all their calls to a particular number (for example, their mobile number) where they can be reached. They can choose their device and configure the **call forward, call busy,** or **call no answer** settings to any number they want an internal or external call forwarded to, as shown in Figure 9-2.

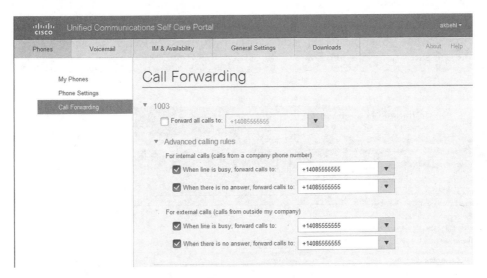

Figure 9-2 *UCMUser Self Care Portal Call Forward Options*

As seen in Figure 9-2, if the user unchecks the **Forward all calls** to option, the options under **Advanced calling rules** for Call Forward Busy and Call Forward No Answer are available (for both internal and external calls). However, if the user checks the **Forward all calls** to option, the other options are greyed out. As described earlier, Call Forward All (CFA), Call Forward No Answer (CFNA), and Call Forward Busy (CFB) are options available for the user to set up via the UCMUser self-care portal. CFA can be set up from the Telephony User Interface (TUI) using the CFwdAll soft key.

Call Forward Unregistered (CUFR), Call Forward No Coverage (CFNC), and Forward on CTI Failure are options limited to the UC administrator only.

Call Pickup

As discussed earlier, Call Pickup allows calls to be picked up by members of the same or a different group (based on the configuration) so that users can answer calls on behalf of their colleagues. For instance, user A and user B are part of same call pickup group Everyone_Pickup. When a call lands on user A's phone and user A is not available, user B can press the CallPickup soft key on his/her phone, followed by the Answer soft key, to pick up the call on user B's phone without ever going to user A's phone. This feature is most useful in a group where people can answer calls on someone's behalf and connect with the customer/caller.

An extension to call pickup is Group Call Pickup, Directed Group Call Pickup, and Other Group Pickup. These have been discussed earlier. Figure 9-3 depicts the soft keys required for enabling Call Pickup, Group Call Pickup (and Directed Group Call Pickup), and Other Pickup.

Note   Directed Group Call Pickup is an extension of Group Call Pickup, and there is no dedicated soft key for this function.

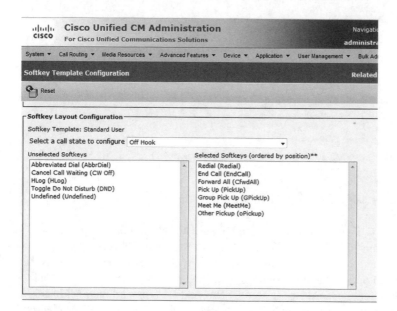

Figure 9-3   *Call Pickup, Group Call Pickup, and Other Pickup Soft Keys*

Call Pickup Groups define the relationship within and outside of a group for the functions described earlier. To configure a Call Pickup Group, follow these steps.

Step 1.   Go to **Call Routing > Call Pickup Group.** Click **Add New.**

Step 2.   Define **Call Pickup Group Name, Call Pickup Group Number** (that can be called by other group members for Group Call Pickup, Directed Group Call Pickup, or Other Pickup), provide a **Description,** and (optionally) assign the Call Pickup Group to a **Partition** as depicted in Figure 9-4.

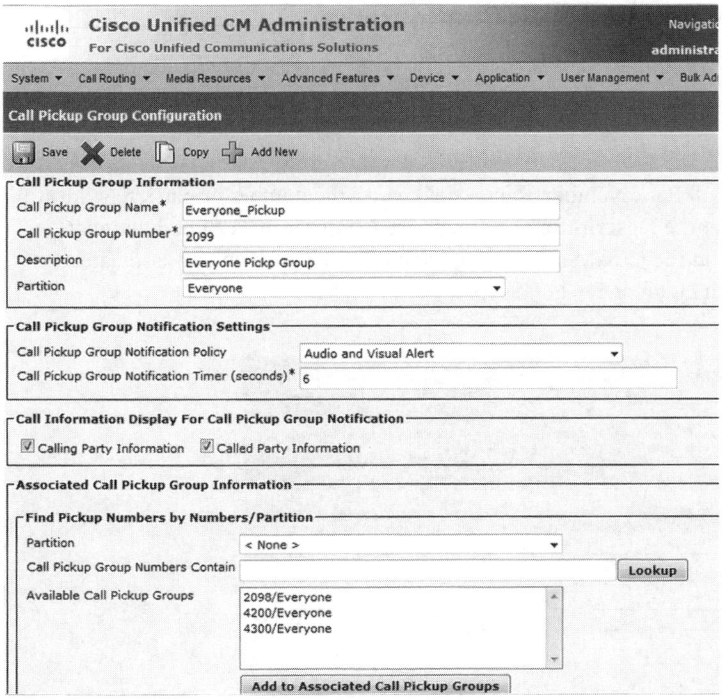

Figure 9-4 *Call Pickup Group Configuration*

Note   If a Call Pickup Group number is assigned to a partition, only those phones that can dial numbers in that partition can use the Call Pickup group. Select None if you wish to give every phone access to the Call Pickup Group.

Step 3.   Define the **Call Pickup Group Notification Settings** to display **Audio** or **Visual** or both **Audio and Visual Alert** notification when a user in the Call Pickup Group receives a call.

Step 4.   Subsequently define **Call Information Display For Call Pickup Group Notification** to display the identification of the calling party and/or called party. This setting can be toggled only if Call Pickup Group Notification is set to Audio or Visual or Audio and Visual Alert.

Step 5.   To group together the Call Pickup Groups in the same partition, search them by defining the partition and add the member to the group. Click **Save**.

Note   Appropriate phone templates must be assigned a call pickup or group pickup button so the phone with those templates can leverage the call pickup feature.

The next section covers Call Park.

Call Park and Directed Call Park Configuration

To configure Call Park, follow these steps:

Step 1.   Go to **CUCM Administration GUI > Call Routing > Call Park**. Click **Add New**.

Step 2.   In the **Call Park Number/Range** field, enter the number or pattern (wildcard) and enter the **Description** (optional), **Partition** for this call park number/range, and the CUCM server with which the call park will be associated, as shown in Figure 9-5. Click **Save**.

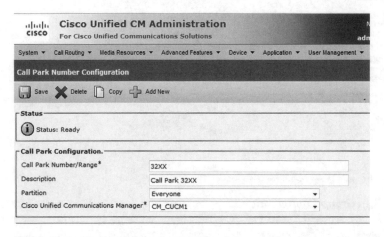

Figure 9-5   *Call Park Configuration*

To configure Directed Call Park, follow these steps:

Step 1.   Go to **Call Routing > Call Directed Park**. Click **Add New**.

Step 2.   Enter the number/pattern in the **Number** field. Enter the **Description** (optional) and **Partition** details as shown in Figure 9-6.

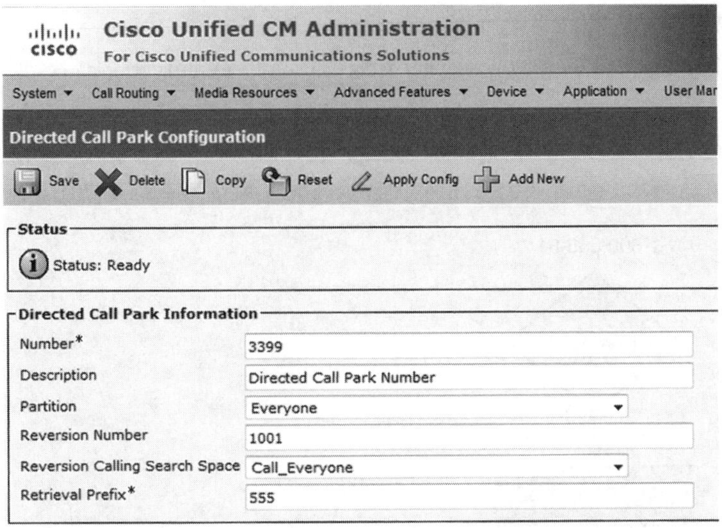

Figure 9-6   *Directed Call Park Configuration*

Step 3.   In **Reversion Number** field, enter an extension to which the parked call should be forwarded if it is not retrieved. Subsequently select a **Reversion Calling Search Space**.

Step 4.   Enter the **Retrieval Prefix** that will be dialed by the user, followed by the number to retrieve the call. Click **Save**.

The next section covers Call Hunting, which is required for complex call coverage scenarios.

Call Hunting

Call hunting is another complex and flexible feature that provides call coverage. Call hunting is based on a pilot number that, if called directly or used as a Call Forward target, allows hunting through multiple line groups. Several hunting algorithms exist, ranging from a round-robin selection of group members to a broadcast option that rings all members of a line group. This feature is limited to configuration by UC administrator.

When the result of call hunting is that all agents are on a call, callers can be put on hold and in a queue. This feature is known as call queuing. Call queuing allows hunt pilot callers to be held in a queue while they wait for an agent to become available. It enables customers to provide a professional call coverage solution without the need to deploy a Cisco Unified Contact Center product if they do not need the rich features of a contact center solution.

Call Hunting Overview

This section describes how call hunting works in Cisco Unified Communications Manager (CUCM).

The CUCM call hunting implementation comprises the following components, as shown in Figure 9-7.

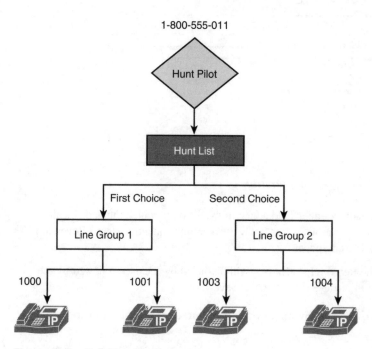

Figure 9-7 *Call Hunting Process*

As seen in Figure 9-7, Call Hunting works top-down in a pyramid format (that is, **Hunt Pilot > Hunt List > Line Group > DNs**). The following sections explain Call Hunting in detail.

Hunt Pilots

Hunt pilots are dialable patterns, similar to route patterns and directory numbers, in the call routing table. The hunt pilot points directly to a hunt list. As seen in Figure 9-7, 18005550111 is the hunt pilot. Hunt lists point to line groups, which then point to endpoints. A hunt pilot can be called directly, providing a single number to start the call routing flow. In addition, IP phones can be configured to forward received calls to the hunt pilot as a method of providing call coverage.

A call within the hunting process ignores the forwarding configuration of line-group members. This means that if the hunting algorithm rings a phone and the call is not answered, the Call Forward No Answer (CFNA) setting of that phone is ignored.

The hunting algorithm goes on to the next line-group member. Similar to a route pattern, at hunt pilot, digit manipulation can be configured to transform the calling, connected, and called party's number/name before the call is passed on to hunt list(s). Figure 9-8 illustrates a hunt pilot configuration.

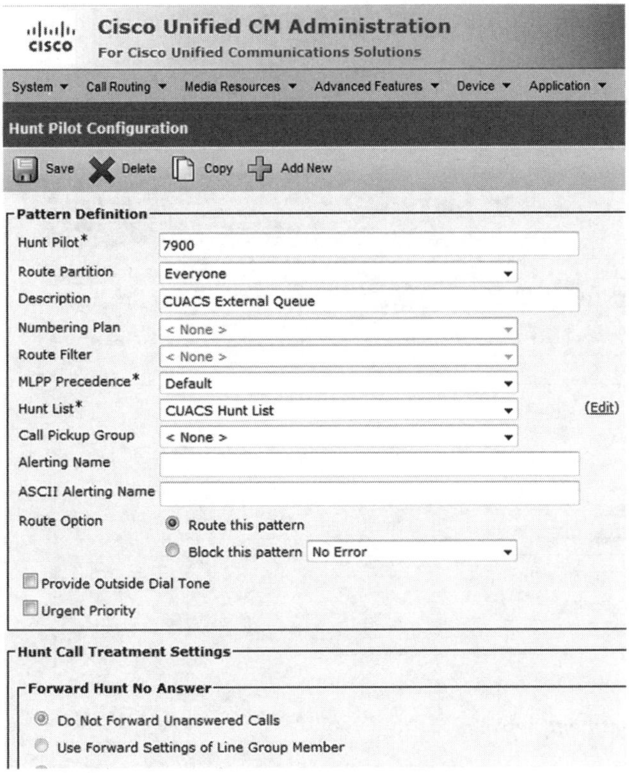

Figure 9-8 *Hunt Pilot Overview*

Note   It is important to understand that just like any DN, a hunt pilot can be assigned to a partition and is only dialable by a DN or incoming (gateway) trunk if the device/trunk has the appropriate CSS.

Calls can be redirected to a final destination when the hunting fails because of one or both of these reasons:

■ All hunting options have been exhausted, and the call still is not answered.

■ A maximum hunt timer that is configured at the hunt pilot has expired.

The call redirection is configured in the Hunt Call Treatment Settings section of the Hunt Pilot Configuration page, and the destination for this redirect can be any of these options:

■ No call redirection

■ Using Call Forward No Answer (CFNA) or Call Forward Busy (CFB) settings of the line member.

■ A specific destination that is configured globally at the hunt pilot, as shown in Figure 9-9

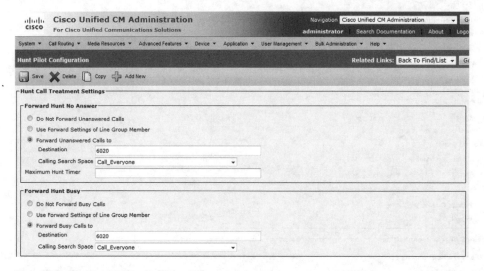

Figure 9-9   *Hunt Pilot Call Treatment Settings*

Note   The Maximum Hunt Timer value is by default 1800 seconds or 30 minutes. It can, however, be set between 1 to 3600 seconds

It is important to understand that a hunt pilot can either be set to use **Hunt Call Treatment Settings** or **Queuing.** Call queuing is discussed later in this chapter.

If call hunting fails because all the hunting options are exhausted or a timeout period expires, the call can be sent to a personalized destination for the person who was originally called. For example, if you set the Forward No Coverage field in the Directory Number Configuration page to a voicemail number, the call is sent to the voice mailbox of that person if hunting fails.

These considerations apply to calls that are processed by hunt pilots:

- Call Pickup and Group Call Pickup are not supported on calls that a hunt pilot distributes.

- A member of the line group cannot pick up a hunt pilot call that is offered to another member in the line group, even if both members belong to the same Call Pickup group. The hunt pilot can distribute calls to any of its line group members, regardless of the calling privileges implementation at the line-group member. If line-group members are configured with a partition, the hunt pilot overcomes all partitions and calling search space (CSS) restrictions.

Hunt Lists

Hunt lists are assigned to hunt pilots and act as a bridge between the hunt pilot and lines/ DNs. A hunt list is an ordered list of line groups that are used for call coverage. Hunt lists have the following characteristics:

- Multiple hunt pilots can point to the same hunt list.

- Multiple hunt lists can contain the same line group.

- A hunt list is a prioritized list of line groups; line groups are hunted in the order of their configuration in the hunt list.

- A hunt list does not perform digit manipulation.

Figure 9-10 gives an overview of a hunt list.

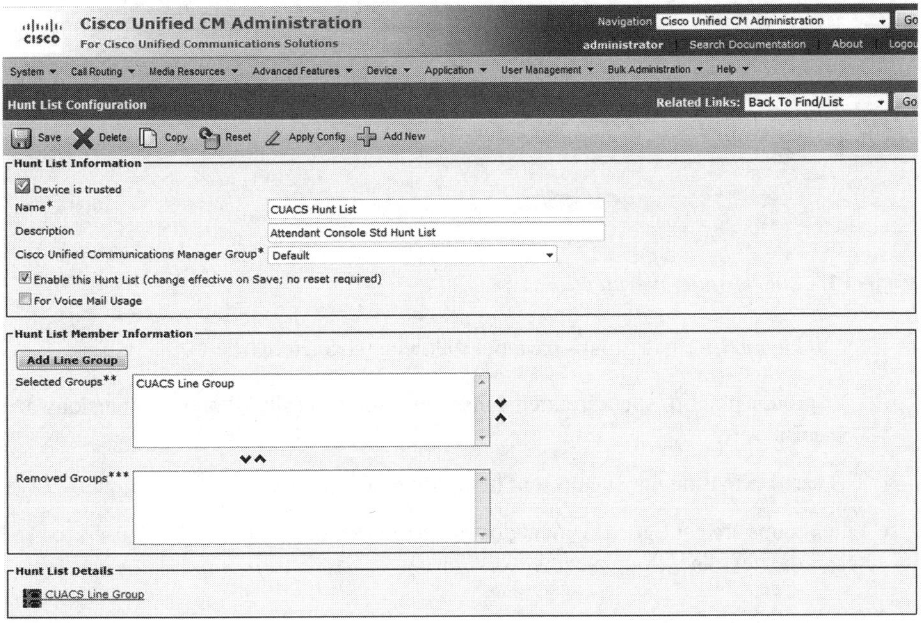

Figure 9-10 *Hunt List Overview*

> **Note**   A hunt list can be compared with a route list that acts as a bridge between route pattern and route group(s).

Line Groups

Line groups are analogous to route groups. Line groups contain the line(s)/DN(s) to which a call should be directed, following **hunt pilot > hunt list > line group > DN** logic. Line groups are assigned to hunt lists. A hunt list can have one or more line groups. At the line group, hunt options and distribution algorithms can be specified to define how call hunting should be performed for the members of a line group. Line groups control the order in which a call is distributed to the members of the line group. Figure 9-11 gives an overview of the line group.

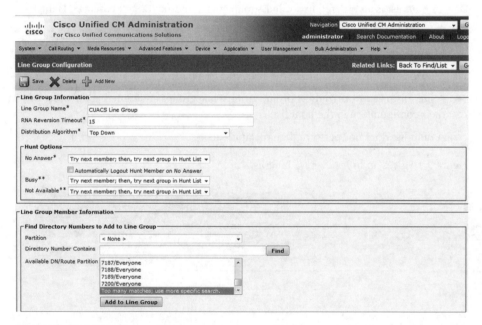

Figure 9-11   *Line Group Overview*

As seen in Figure 9-11, line groups have the following characteristics:

- Line groups point to specific extensions, which are typically IP phone extensions or voicemail ports.

- The same extension may be present in multiple line groups.

- Line groups are configured with a global distribution algorithm, which is used to select the next line-group member for hunting.

- Line groups are configured with a hunt option, which describes how hunting should be continued after trying the first member of the line group. The hunt option is configured per hunt-failure event: no answer, busy, and not available.

- The Ring No Answer Reversion (RNAR) timeout specifies how long the hunting algorithm rings a member of the line group before proceeding to hunt the next line according to the Line Group No Answer hunt-option setting.

Numbers (DN) or ports (voicemail ports) can be assigned to line groups. Line group members are the endpoints that a line group can access.

Line groups can be set to use the following distribution algorithms:

- **Top down:** distributes a call to idle or available members starting from the first idle or available member of a line group to the last idle or available member.

- **Circular:** distributes a call to idle or available members starting from the (n+1)th member of a line group, where the nth member is the next sequential member in the list who is either idle or busy.

- **Longest ideal:** distributes a call to idle members, starting from the longest idle member to the least idle member.

- **Broadcast:** distributes a call to all idle/available members simultaneously.

Note   Computer telephony integration (CTI) ports and CTI route points cannot be added to a line group. Therefore, calls cannot be distributed to endpoints that are controlled through CTI applications.

Call Hunting Operation

This section describes the operation of call hunting.

As seen in Figure 9-12, two line groups are configured: Agents (containing directory numbers 2001 and 2002) and Operators (containing directory numbers 2101 and 2102). The line groups are assigned to the Helpdesk hunt list. A hunt pilot, also named Helpdesk, with the pattern 2222 is configured to use the Helpdesk hunt list for call coverage.

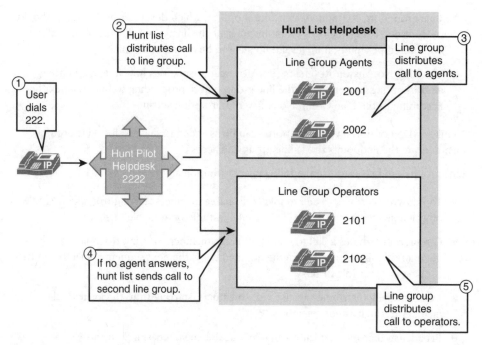

Figure 9-12 *Call Hunting Logic*

The following high-level steps describe how this hunt pilot processes calls:

Step 1. A user dials 2222, matching the hunt pilot number. The hunt pilot sends the call to the Helpdesk hunt list.

Step 2. The hunt list picks the first line group, Agents.

Step 3. The line group distributes the call to the assigned agent directory numbers.

Step 4. If no agent answers, the hunt list sends the call to the second line group, Operators.

Step 5. The Operators line group distributes the call to the operator directory numbers.

Call Hunting Flow

Call hunting flow is the process by which a call proceeds through a hunting algorithm. Figure 9-13 illustrates the call hunting flow in CUCM call hunting configuration.

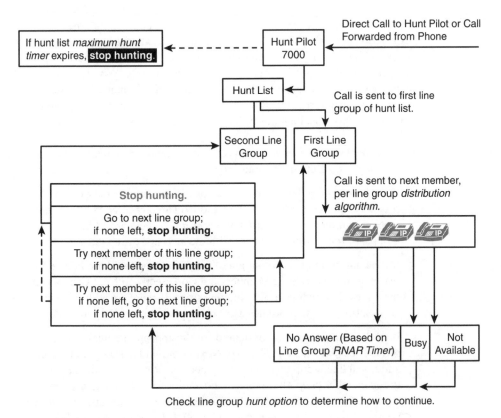

Figure 9-13 *Call Hunting Flow*

The call hunting flow in a CUCM call hunting configuration is as follows:

Step 1.   A direct call is placed to the hunt pilot number, or a call is forwarded from a phone to the hunt pilot number.

Step 2.   The hunt pilot that is configured with the appropriate hunt pilot number starts the maximum hunt timer to monitor the overall hunting time. If the timer expires, hunting stops. The hunt pilot is associated with a hunt list.

Step 3.   The hunt list that is associated with the hunt pilot sends the call to the next line group that is configured in the hunt list (starting with the first line group).

Step 4.   The line group sends the call to the next line-group member, based on the distribution algorithm that is configured for the line group. The possible distribution methods as discussed earlier are as follows:

- Top-down

- Circular

- Longest idle time

- Broadcast

Step 5.   If the line-group member (or members, in case of broadcast) that the distribution algorithm selects does not answer the call, the hunt option specifies how hunting should continue. The hunt option is configured independently, per hunt failure reason, for the line group. Possible hunt failure reasons are no answer, busy, and not available. In hunt failures that result in no answer, the RNAR timer that is configured for the line group has expired. The possible hunt failure behaviors and options are detailed here:

- If the hunt option that is configured for the appropriate hunt failure reason is Stop Hunting, hunting stops.

- If the hunt option that is configured for the appropriate hunt failure reason is Skip Remaining Members and Go Directly to Next Group, and there are no more line groups, hunting stops. If there are additional line groups, to the process continues with the next line group (Step 4).

- If the hunt option that is configured for the appropriate hunt failure reason is Skip Remaining Members and Go Directly to Next Group, and there are no more line groups, hunting stops. If there are additional line groups, the process continues with the next line group (Step 4).

- If the hunt option that is configured for the appropriate hunt failure reason is Try Next Member Then Try Next Group in Hunt List, and there are additional line-group members, the process continues with the next line-group member (Step 4). If there are no additional line-group members, the next line group is used. If there are additional line groups, the process continues with the next line group (Step 4). If there are no more line groups, hunting stops.

Figure 9-14 illustrates the termination of the call hunting process.

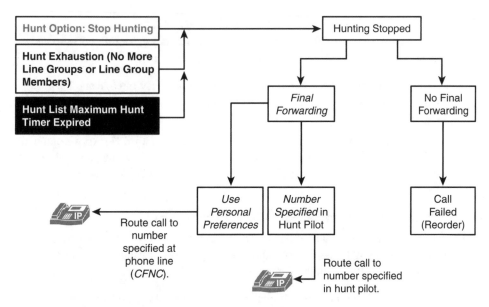

Figure 9-14 *Call Hunting Stopped*

When hunting stops, it may be due to one or more of the following:

- Stop Hunting is the hunt option that was applied after a call was not accepted by the last attempted line-group member.

- After hunting attempted the last line-group member, there were no other line-group members or other line groups to be used. This reason is known as hunt exhaustion.

- The maximum hunt timer that is configured for the hunt pilot expired.

The process then continues:

Step 6.   Review the hunt pilot configuration for its final forwarding settings. If the hunt pilot is not configured for final forwarding, the call fails and a reorder tone is played.

Step 7.   Review the final forwarding destination settings that are configured for the hunt pilot. If a final forwarding number is specified for the hunt pilot, the call is rerouted to the specified number.

Call Coverage Scenarios (with and without Hunting)

This section describes call hunting scenarios in CUCM, including examples and related questions and answers to help you comprehend the topic of call hunting.

Example 1: Internal and External Forwarding (No Hunting)

User A at directory number 3000 has the following configuration for Call Forward and Call Pickup Settings on the Directory Number Configuration page:

- **Call Forward Busy:** CFB is determined by the Forward Busy Internal and Forward Busy External settings. CFB forwards incoming internal and external calls to 3001 when 3000 is busy.

- **Call Forward No Answer:** CFNA is determined by the Forward No Answer Internal and Forward No Answer External settings. CFNA forwards incoming internal calls to 3001 and external incoming calls to 303 555-0111 when 3000 does not answer.

Example 2: Internal and External Forwarding (with Hunting)

Alternatively, forwarding to a hunting construct is another option. In this case, user A at directory number 3000 has the configuration for Call Forward and Call Pickup Settings on the Directory Number Configuration page:

- **Call Forward Busy:** Incoming internal calls are forwarded to 3001, and external calls are forwarded to hunt pilot 7000 when 3000 is busy.

- **Call Forward No Answer:** Incoming internal calls are forwarded to 3001, and external incoming calls are forwarded to hunt pilot 7000 when 3000 does not answer.

Assume that hunt pilot 7000 is associated with hunt list ABC and has four hunt parties (lines/DNs) that are distributed over Line Group 1 and Line Group 2. Hunt pilot 7000 has no final forwarding fields provisioned (default).

> **Question:** Which behavior results when an internal caller calls 3000 and user 3000 is busy?

> **Answer:** The call forwards to line 3001.

> **Question:** Which behavior results when an external caller calls 3000 and user 3000 does not answer?

> **Answer:** The call forwards to hunt pilot 7000, which causes hunting to lines 3001, 3002, 4001, and 4002. If one of the hunt parties answers, the caller is connected to that party. If no hunt party answers, then regardless of the reason, the caller receives a reorder tone (or an equivalent announcement).

Example 3: Internal and External Forwarding with Hunting

This section describes another example of call hunting configuration.

The Forward Hunt No Answer field for hunt pilot 7000 is set to destination 3002, but all Forward Hunt Busy fields are empty.

Question: Which behavior results when an external caller calls 3000 and user 3000 does not answer?

Answer: The call forwards to hunt pilot 7000, which causes hunting to lines 3001, 3002, 4001, and 4002. If one of the hunt parties answers, the caller is connected to that party.

If all hunt parties are busy, the caller receives a reorder tone (or an equivalent announcement).

If at least one hunt party is alerted (rings), the call forwards to 3002, because 3002 is the value that is configured for the Forward Hunt No Answer field.

Question: What if user 3000 is busy when an external call arrives?

Answer: In this case, the same results occur because user 3000 forwards external calls to hunt pilot 7000 for both busy and no-answer conditions.

Example 4: Internal and External Forwarding with Hunting

This section shows an example that extends the call hunting process by amending some of its forwarding options.

Question: Which behavior results when an external caller calls 3000 and user 3000 does not answer?

Answer: The call forwards to hunt pilot 7000, which causes hunting to lines 3001, 3002, 4001, and 4002.

If one of the hunt parties answers, the caller is connected to that party. If at least one party is alerted, hunting exhausts because there was no answer, and the call forwards to 3002.

If all hunt parties are busy, the call forwards to the Forward No Coverage External setting of the original called party (user 3000). In this case, the call forwards to the hunt pilot 303 555-0111.

Question: What if user 3000 is busy when an external call arrives?

Answer: In this case, the results are the same, because user 3000 forwards external calls to hunt pilot 7000 for both busy and no-answer conditions.

Note   If the hunt pilot is configured to use personal preferences but the corresponding Forward No Coverage field is not set on the phone, the call fails. This configuration results in the same behavior as when there is no final forwarding setting on the hunt pilot.

Example 5: Using the Maximum Hunt Timer While Hunting

This section shows an example in which the maximum hunt timer expires.

The RNAR timer for a line group determines how long hunting rings a hunt party before moving to the next party in its list (assuming that the customer did not select the broadcast algorithm). This timer has a default value of 10 seconds.

> **Question:** In the case of four hunt parties, how long will it take before hunting exhausts?

> **Answer:** It will take 40 seconds before hunting exhausts (10 seconds RNAR * 4 hunt members).

Assume that the maximum hunt timer for hunt pilot 7000 is set to 25 seconds. The call must be answered within this time. In this example, the hunt timer is 2.5 times the RNAR timer, which is 10 seconds.

Call Hunting Configuration

Follow these steps to configure call hunting in CUCM:

Step 1.   Go to **Call Routing > Route Hunt > Line Group**. Click **Add New**. Create a line group: define a name for the line group, add members, and configure the distribution algorithm and hunt options as shown in Figure 9-15.

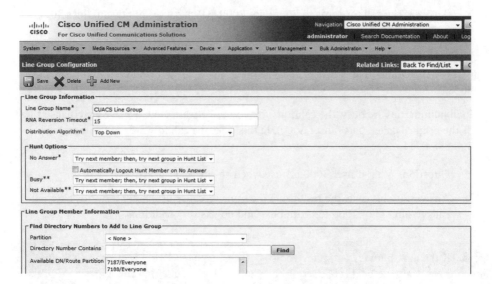

Figure 9-15   *Line Group Configuration*

Step 2.   Go to **Call Routing > Route Hunt > Hunt List**. Click **Add New**. Create a hunt list by defining the name, adding description, selecting the

CUCM group, and adding the line group created in Step 1 to this hunt list as depicted in Figure 9-16. Make sure that the Enable this Hunt List checkbox is checked.

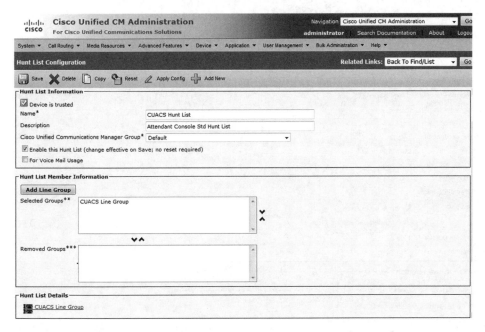

Figure 9-16   *Hunt List Configuration*

Step 3.   Go to **Call Routing** > **Route Hunt** > **Hunt Pilot**. Click **Add New**. Create the hunt pilot by defining the hunt pilot number and partition, and associate the hunt list created in previous step with the hunt pilot as shown in Figure 9-17. Ensure that Route Option is set to Route This Pattern and the Hunt Forward Settings or Queuing is set up appropriately. Also, if digit manipulation is required, be sure to set up the Called, Connected, or Calling transformations.

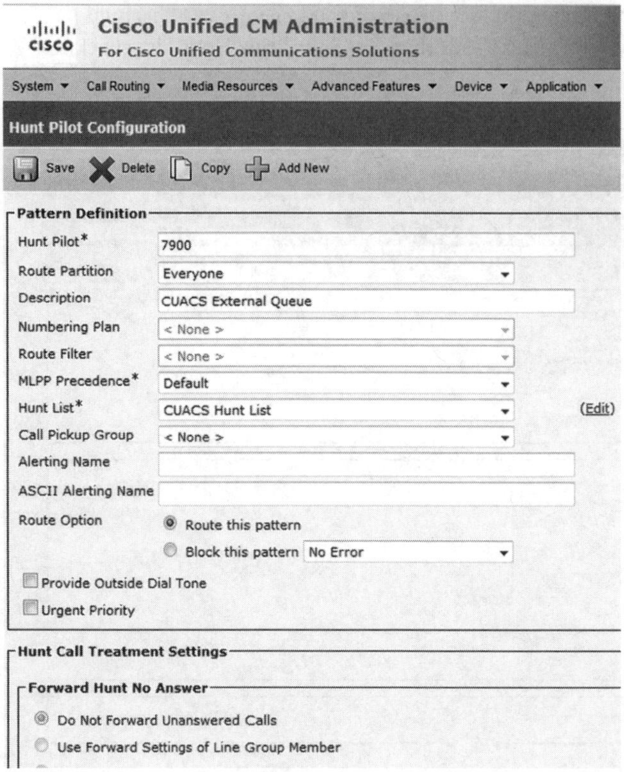

Figure 9-17   *Hunt Pilot Configuration*

Step 4.   If the hunt pilot is set up to use the **Hunt Call Treatment Settings** of line members, configure call coverage settings on phone lines. Click **Save**.

Note   Use concise and descriptive names for line groups and hunt lists. The Companyname-Location-Group format usually provides a sufficient level of detail and is short enough to enable you to quickly and easily identify a line group. For example, CiscoDallasAA1 might identify a Cisco Access Analog line group for the Cisco office in Dallas.

Call Queuing

As discussed earlier in this chapter, call queuing allows hunt pilot callers to be held in a queue while they wait for an agent to become available. Call queuing is based on the existing call distribution capabilities that are provided by hunt lists and hunt pilots. It enables calls to a hunt pilot to be redirected to a queue if all agents that are associated with the hunt pilot are busy or do not answer.

Note   When none of the members of the hunt pilot are available or are unregistered at the time of the call, you can set up an alternate number field through the "When no hunt members are logged in or registered" settings in the hunt pilot configuration, so the calls can be routed to a desired extension/number.

Agents can be part of multiple hunt pilots in which queuing is enabled.

Note   In call queuing, a line group member may be referred to as an agent. However, call queuing does not support an agent desktop application, routing based on agent skills, or similar contact center features. Moreover, the Hunt Login/Logout (HLOG) soft key enables users to login to the Hunt Pilot they are a part of and join the queue.

When an agent does not answer an offered call, the agent is automatically logged out of the hunt group. This action also applies to shared line appearances. The autologout occurs after expiration of the RNAR timer.

When an agent becomes idle, the following process occurs:

1. CUCM checks all queues to which the agent is currently subscribed for waiting callers.

2. Out of these queued callers, the caller that has been waiting the longest is routed to the agent.

Note   An agent becomes idle after logging into a hunt group or after finishing a call.

Call queuing supports two different announcement types:

- **Initial announcement:** This announcement is played once at the beginning of the call. It can be configured to be played before or after the call is queued.

- **Periodic announcement:** This announcement is played at a configurable interval while the call is held in the queue.

CUCM has preinstalled announcements in US English, but custom announcements can be uploaded. Uploading custom announcements is similar to uploading custom music on hold (MOH) audio files.

Announcements are configured at the MOH Audio Source configuration page. The announcement to be played is chosen by referring to an MOH Audio Source at the hunt pilot configuration page.

Configure an agent phone with the Queue Status IP phone feature button. If pressed, this feature button provides information about the hunt pilot number, the number of queued calls, and the longest waiting time.

For call queuing to work over SIP trunks, Provisional Response ACKnowledgement (PRACK) must be enabled on the SIP trunk.

Call Queuing is an Additional Option after Hunting Stops

Figure 9-18 illustrates the modified part of the call hunting process when call queuing is enabled.

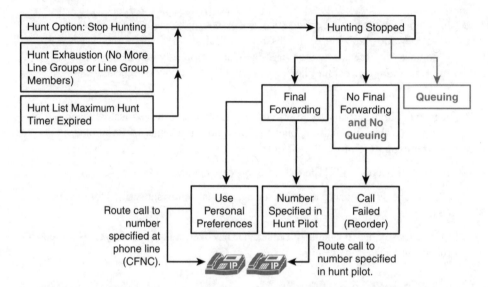

Figure 9-18   *Call Queuing is an Additional Option after Hunting Stops*

The actual hunting process can stop because of hunt exhaustion, expiration of the hunt list maximum hunt timer, or the presence of a configured stophunting condition.

Queuing can be enabled as another option for management of calls once CUCM stops hunting. The other two previously existing options (attempt final forwarding to a configured number or disconnect the call) are still configurable, but they are mutually exclusive. In other words, only one option can be chosen per hunt pilot.

Call Queuing Process

Call queuing is the process in which calls are held before being forwarded to be answered or sent to an alternate destination, such as voicemail. Figure 9-19 illustrates the process of managing calls that are queued based on the hunt pilot configuration.

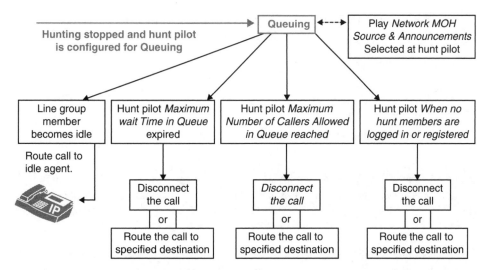

Figure 9-19 *Call Queuing Logic*

> **Note** Hunt pilot–based call queuing is a basic call queuing mechanism. Cisco offers Cisco Unified Enterprise Attendant Console (CUEAC), Cisco Unified Contact Center Express (UCCX), and Cisco Unified Contact Center Enterprise (UCCE) for advance call queuing and scripting. The details regarding these products are out of the scope of this text. To learn more about these products, please visit www.cisco.com

When a caller is to be placed into a queue, CUCM first checks if any hunt members are logged in or registered. If no hunt members are logged in or registered, the caller is not put into the queue of the called hunt pilot.

Then CUCM checks whether the queue of the hunt pilot is already full. The Maximum Number of Callers Allowed in Queue hunt pilot configuration setting is used to decide whether the new caller can be added to the queue.

If both checks are passed successfully, the caller is added to the queue. A timer is started that monitors the time that this caller spends in the queue. If the queued call cannot be delivered to an agent before expiration of the configured Maximum Wait Time in Queue, the call is removed from the queue at expiration of the timer.

If a call is not queued at all or is removed from the queue, a final call management option must be configured. A call is not queued if no agents are logged in or registered or if the maximum number of queued calls is reached. A call is removed from the queue at the expiration of the maximum wait timer. The default is to disconnect the call.

The default can be changed independently according to the individual scenario by specifying a secondary destination to which the call should be routed. This secondary destination is similar to the final forwarding configuration at the hunt pilot when call queuing is not enabled. A secondary destination can be one of the following:

■ directory number

■ voicemail number

■ shared line

■ another hunt pilot (with or without queuing enabled)

Note   Be aware that sending the call to another queuing-enabled hunt pilot can result in long queuing times. This situation is especially important when cascading multiple hunt pilots.

The Maximum Number of Callers Allowed in Queue parameter is configurable from 1 to 100. The default is 32. The Maximum Wait Time in Queue is configurable from 0 to 3600 seconds. The default is 900. Each value is configurable per hunt pilot.

Call queuing supports the playing of announcements once at the beginning of a call and periodically while a call is held in a queue.

Call Queuing Configuration

The steps to configure hunt pilot, hunt list, and line groups are similar to the steps for call hunting configuration covered earlier.

For call queuing, proceed with the following steps:

Step 1.   In the Hunt Pilot configuration, instead of Hunt Call Treatment Settings chose Queuing by checking the check box labeled Queue Calls.

Step 2.   Configure queuing options such as **Network Hold MOH Source & Announcements, Maximum Number of Callers Allowed in Queue, Maximum Wait Time in Queue,** and **When no hunt member answer, are logged in, or registered** as shown in Figure 9-20. Click **Save.**

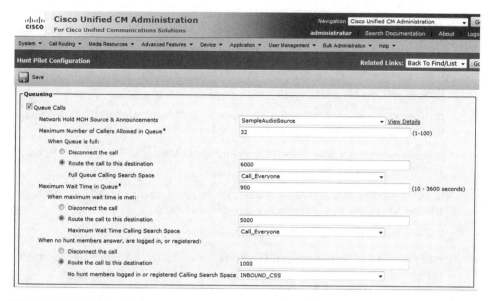

Figure 9-20 *Call Queuing Configuration*

Step 3.   If required, upload custom announcements and configure MOH audio source with announcements

Chapter Summary

The following list summarizes the key points that were discussed in this chapter:

■ CUCM offers several features for call coverage, including Call Forward, shared lines, Call Pickup, Group Call Pickup, Other Pickup, Call Hunting, and Call Queuing.

■ Call hunting options are configured per line group and specify how to continue hunting when the selected line-group member does not answer

■ Distribution algorithms, also configured per line group, specify how to select a line-group member

■ During hunting, the hunt option, distribution algorithm, RNAR timeout, maximum hunt timer, and final forwarding settings are considered in the hunt logic

■ Call hunting implementation includes the configuration of hunt pilots, hunt lists, and line groups

■ Call queuing queues calls and plays announcements when call hunting does not find an ideal line group member to pick up the call

References

For additional information, refer to the following:

Cisco Systems, Inc. Cisco Unified Communications Manager Administration Guide, Release 10.0(1), June 2014.

http://www.cisco.com/c/en/us/td/docs/voice_ip_comm/cucm/admin/10_0_1/ccmcfg/CUCM_BK_C95ABA82_00_admin-guide-100.html.

Cisco Systems, Inc. Cisco Unified Communications Manager System Guide, Release 10.0(1), June 2014.

http://www.cisco.com/c/en/us/td/docs/voice_ip_comm/cucm/admin/10_0_1/ccmsys/CUCM_BK_SE5FCFB6_00_cucm-system-guide-100.html.

Cisco Systems, Inc. Cisco Collaboration System 10.x SRND, June 2014.

http://www.cisco.com/c/en/us/td/docs/voice_ip_comm/cucm/srnd/collab10/collab10.html.

Review Questions

Use the questions here to review what you learned in this chapter. The correct answers are found in Appendix A, "Answers to the Review Questions."

1. Which of the following is not a call forwarding option that can be configured at the directory number of a phone?

   a. Call Forward Queue Exhaustion

   b. Call Forward All

   c. Call Forward Busy

   d. Call Forward No Coverage

2. What is the easiest way for an end-user to configure phone settings, such as call forward options?

   a. Using Self-Care portal

   b. Asking UC administrator to make changes on the user's behalf

   c. Making changes on CUCM Administration GUI

   d. The end-user cannot configure any Call Forward settings

3. What two mechanisms will allow multiple phones to ring at the same time? (Choose two.)

   a. Shared lines

   b. Hunt group

c. Route pattern

d. Route list

4. Which feature allows a call to be picked up on another phone in the same department?

a. Shared line

b. Call pickup

c. Call hunting

d. Group pickup

5. Which feature allows a call to be picked up on another phone in a different department?

a. Shared line

b. Call pickup

c. Call hunting

d. Group pickup

6. If no agents are logged into a hunt pilot, how will the call be processed by CUCM?

a. The call can be redirected to a predefined number on hunt pilot.

b. The call will be dropped.

c. The call will be queued and the user will stay for 3600 seconds before CUCM drops the call.

d. The call will always be sent to voicemail of the hunt pilot.

7. Which component of call hunting does a hunt pilot point to?

a. Line group

b. Line group members

c. Telephony call dispatcher

d. Hunt list

8. Which component of call hunting does a hunt list point to?

a. Line group

b. Line group members

c. Telephony call dispatcher

d. Hunt list

9. Which call forwarding option is used when calls forwarded to the hunt pilot exhaust (final forwarding)?

   a. CFA

   b. CFB

   c. CFNB

   d. CFNC

   e. CFUR

10. Which line group distribution mechanism routes calls in a round-robin fashion between all the members of the line group?

    a. Broadcast

    b. Top down

    c. Circular

    d. Longest idle

Chapter 10

Implementing Media Resources in Cisco Unified Communications Manager

Cisco Collaboration network leverages fundamental communication protocols, and one of these protocols is Real-Time Transport Protocol (RTP). RTP is the media-bearing protocol in any IP-enabled communications network and can be leveraged to offer a number of functions to users such as conferencing and music on hold. These features need certain media resources to function properly.

This chapter describes available hardware and software media resources and discusses how they are configured in Cisco Unified Communications Manager (CUCM) to provide features such as conferencing, transcoding, media termination, and music/video on hold. It also explains how to perform access control to media resources using media resource groups and media resource group lists and the function of trusted relay points (TRPs).

Chapter Objectives

Upon completing this chapter, you will be able to meet the following objectives:

- Describe various media resources and their functions

- Describe how CUCM supports media resources

- Describe audio and video conferencing

- Configure conferencing media resources

- Describe and configure music and video on hold (MOH and VOH)

- Describe annunciator

- Describe trusted relay point (TRP)

- Describe media resource management

Media Resources

A media resource can be defined as a software- or hardware-based entity that performs media-processing functions on the voice/video streams to which it is connected.

Cisco Collaboration network (CUCM, voice gateways, media servers/blades) offer the following media resources for a rich end-user experience:

- Conferencing
  - Audio
  - Video
- Transcoding
- MTP (media termination point)
- Annunciator
- MOH (music on hold)
- VOH (video on hold)
- TRP (trusted relay point)

CUCM offers software-based media resources. The Cisco IP Voice Media Streaming Application Service (IPVMS) runs in the background as a process and provides the following media resource functions:

- Audio conference bridge (G.711 only)
- MTP
- Annunciator
- MOH

> **Note**   Cisco IPVMS service needs to be manually activated from Feature Services under CUCM Serviceability.

The following media resources cannot be provided directly by CUCM and require dedicated hardware or software products:

- Video conference bridge
- Transcoder
- VOH
- TRP

Note   CUCM supports software media resources and media resources that can be defined as an instance of an actual hardware resource as a function of IPVMS. For example, CUCM offers software conference bridge and annunciator as a native service and resource by virtue of IPVMS, whereas it offers VOH and Transcoder as a defined entity in IPVMS for an external resource such as Cisco MediaSense and Cisco IOS router's DSP resources respectively.

Not all of the media resources described are needed in every deployment. Software resources are provided by native CUCM and IOS services, whereas hardware features are provided by Digital Signal Processors (DSP). The DSP resources are hardware modules in the gateway router or switch such as Packet Voice DSP Module (PVDM) modules. The software resources are controlled by the Cisco IP Voice Media Streaming Application Service running on CUCM.

Note   All hardware resource limitations are well documented in the media resource chapter of the document *Solution Reference Network Design Guidance* (SRND) available online at www.cisco.com/go/srnd. It is a best practice to use the Cisco DSP Calculator, which you can find at www.cisco.com/go/dspcalculator. The Cisco DSP Calculator requires Cisco.com membership access.

Media Resource Support

As described earlier in this chapter, CUCM offers software-based media resources. You must start the IP Voice Media Streaming Application Service to activate the following media resources:

- Audio conferencing (G.711 only)

- MTP

- Annunciator

- Video on hold (VOH)

- Music on hold (MOH)

Note   As a best practice, while designing a CUCM cluster ensure that you consider the number of concurrent conference, MTP, Annunciator, and MOH sessions when possible. Running IPVMS on a call processing CUCM can be detrimental and is not recommended in medium to large enterprise networks. Implementing a dedicated CUCM for MOH server and other media functions is recommended. Whenever possible, try to leverage hardware media resources for handling complex codecs.

The following media resources are available only in hardware:

- Transcoding

- Conferencing TRP

- Voice termination

Note The voice-termination function is needed when an incoming or outgoing Time Division Multiplex (TDM) call is terminated on a gateway. This is not a specific media resource function; however PVDM-based DSPs are needed to convert TDM to IP and vice versa. The TDM leg is terminated by the Cisco IOS router's DSP and has to perform decoding, coding, packetization, and depacketization functions.

Hardware resources can be used to offer multi-codec conferencing in addition to the G.711-only conferencing CUCM offers. Transcoding can only be performed in hardware as it involves multiple codecs.

Conferencing

The following section discusses the audio conferencing media resources.

Audio Conferencing

CUCM supports two types of conference calls—Ad Hoc conference and Meet-Me conference. As the name suggests, the Ad Hoc conference can be initiated by either of two parties already on a voice call. Meet-Me, on the other hand, requires the initiating party to start a conference call by pressing the Meet-Me soft key, and other participants can join by dialing a predetermined Meet-Me number. Each Meet-Me conference can host up to 16 participants, and each conference call requires a unique Meet-Me number.

Skinny Call Control Protocol (also known as Skinny Client Control Protocol or SCCP) is used to set up and tear down calls between hardware media resources and CUCM. All audio streams from any endpoint are always terminated by the media resource involved in the call. There is no direct IP phone to IP phone audio stream with media resources involved in the call flow.

To clarify further, if user A calls user B, a direct RTP stream is established between the two phones/endpoints, with signaling going to CUCM. No part of RTP is associated with CUCM except when MOH is played to the party on hold. In contrast to the above scenario, if user A decides to initiate a conference with user B and user C, a dedicated media resource (CUCM-based or hardware-DSP-based) is required, and all three phones/endpoints will get their RTP latched to this media resource. There is no direct RTP stream(s) between the three parties in conference.

As seen in Figure 10-1, there are three different audio streams, one from the public switched telephone network (PSTN) phone and the other two from VoIP audio streams using Real-Time Transport Protocol on the network.

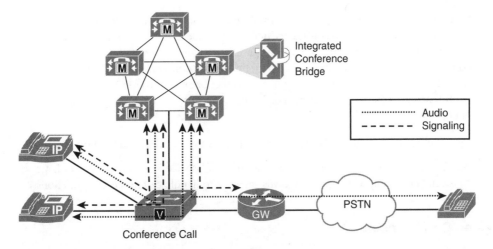

Figure 10-1 *CUCM-Based Audio Conferencing Overview*

Note A software conference bridge is created automatically when IPVMS service is activated on a CUCM server.

Signaling messages are exchanged between IP phones and CUCM, between conference bridge(s) and CUCM, and between gateways and CUCM.

RTP bearer traffic streams are sent from the IP phones and the voice gateway to the conference bridge resource mixing the audio. The conference resource mixes the audio streams and sends back a unique audio stream to the IP phones and the voice gateway. The audio stream must subtract the audio stream of the person receiving the audio stream so that no echo is heard. Some conference devices, because of processing limitations, mix only the three loudest talkers.

Note In this scenario, the voice gateway is acting as TDM termination endpoint for the PSTN phone and at the same time as an endpoint to send/receive the RTP stream from the conference bridge.

Signaling messages (control traffic) are exchanged among the IP phones, CUCM, and the conferencing resource (if a hardware resource or a version of Cisco Unified MeetingPlace is used). Cisco Unified MeetingPlace is not covered in this book.

> **Note**   The Cisco Press book *Voice and Video Conferencing Fundamentals* is an excellent resource for a more thorough understanding of audio conferencing and videoconferencing.

CUCM does not distinguish between software- and hardware-based conference bridges when it processes a conference allocation request. Allocation of conferencing resources is covered in further detail later in this chapter. The number of individual conferences and maximum number of participants per conference vary based on the resource in use. In a large deployment, it is recommended to use hardware conferencing resources, as software conferencing resources have the following limitations:

- CUCM-based software conferencing resources support only the G.711 codec.

- These conferencing resources make use of CUCM's CPU and memory, so a large number of calls will impact CUCM's capacity to handle call processing functions.

Video Conferencing

Similar to an audio conference bridge, a video conference bridge joins multiple participants into a single video call. Video conferencing resources can be hardware or software based. The Cisco IP Voice Media Streaming Application Service does not support video conferences. Cisco TelePresence MCUs, Cisco TelePresence Server, and Cisco IOS-based DSPs are media resources that can support video conferencing. CUCM, along with other components (for example, Cisco TelePresence Conductor, MCU, or TelePresence Management Suite), supports a number of video conferences such as:

- **Ad Hoc or Instant conference:** A point-to-point call hosted on CUCM, escalating to a three-party call hosted on a conference bridge.

- **Meet-Me or Rendezvous conference:** These types of conferences are also referred to as static or permanent conferences. In a Meet-Me conference, the conference host shares the address with other users, who can dial in to that address at any time, which allows users to join a call without previous scheduling.

- **Scheduled conferences:** As the name suggests, a conference can be booked via Cisco TelePresence Management Suite (TMS) and/or integration using Cisco TMS with a definite start and end time as well as a predefined set of participants.

> **Note**   For more details on various video conferencing solutions based on Cisco TelePresence MSE 8000 series and Cisco TelePresence servers, refer to Chapter 11, "Cisco Video Conferencing."

Media streams exist between each conference participant and the conference bridge. Signaling messages are exchanged between conference participants and CUCM and between the video conference bridge and CUCM. The following are some enterprise grade video conferencing solutions:

- The Cisco TelePresence MSE 8000 Series, Cisco TelePresence MCU 5300 Series, and Cisco TelePresence Server use SIP to communicate with CUCM.

- Cisco IOS routers leverage PVDM3 DSPs (with Cisco IOS Software Release 15.1.4M and later releases) and use SCCP to communicate with CUCM.

The number of individual video conferences and the maximum number of participants per conference and type of the conference that the resource can support can be different, depending on the resource.

For example, the video portion of the conference can operate in one of three meeting experience modes, depending on the conferencing device:

- **Full-screen voice activation (Cisco TelePresence Server and Cisco TelePresence MCU):** The active participant is shown in a full screen while the other participants appear as a picture-in-picture overlaid along the bottom of the display.

- **Continuous presence (Cisco TelePresence Server and Cisco TelePresence MCU):** Also known as Active presence, this provides a view of multiple participants on a single display.

In addition, video conferencing can use any of the following methods to select the dominant speaker:

- Voice activation mode

- Manual selection of the dominant speaker

- Automatic participant list cycling

Cisco IOS-Based Conference Bridges

An alternative to the built-in software conference bridge on CUCM is the Cisco IOS router–based hardware conference bridge. The IOS conference bridge is based on Packet Voice DSP module, generation 2 (PVDM2) or Packet Voice DSP module, or generation 3 (PVDM3) modules. They can provide audio (both PVDM 2 and PVDM 3) and video (only with PVDM3) conferencing services. The number of the concurrent conferences and conference participants depends on the DSP resources available on the IOS router.

Cisco IOS hardware audio conference bridges support mixed mode audio conferences. This means that participants can use different codecs (multi-codec). The Cisco IOS conference bridge can also provide transcoding as needed. Just like a software audio conference bridge, the Cisco IOS–based hardware audio conference must be configured as a conference media resource in CUCM, be registered with CUCM call processing nodes, and be controlled by the Cisco Media Resource Manager (MRM). The capabilities (including the supported codecs and the maximum number of participants) of the conference bridge are configured at the Cisco IOS router.

Three types of Cisco IOS video and audio conference bridges exist in a Cisco Collaboration network:

- Homogeneous video conference bridge

- Heterogeneous video conference bridge

- Guaranteed audio video conference bridge

Cisco IOS Homogeneous Video Conference Bridges

This section describes the hardware-based homogeneous audio and video conference bridge that is provided by Cisco IOS routers with PVDM3 modules.

> **Note**   Cisco Integrated Service Router (ISR) G2 routers running Cisco IOS 15.1(4) M or later can act as IOS-based hardware conference bridges that support Ad Hoc and Meet-Me audio and video conferencing. PVDM3 modules must be installed on the router to enable it as a video conference bridge.

The homogeneous video conference bridge specifies the IOS-based conference bridge type that supports homogeneous video conferencing. A homogeneous video conference is a conference in which all participants use the same video format. All the endpoints must support the same video format, and the conference bridge sends the same data stream format to all the video participants. If the conference bridge is not configured to support the video format of an endpoint, the caller on that phone connects to the conference as an audio-only participant.

Cisco IOS Heterogeneous Video Conference Bridge

This section describes the hardware-based heterogeneous audio and video conference bridge that is provided by Cisco IOS routers with PVDM3 modules.

As the name suggests, the Cisco IOS Heterogeneous Video Conference Bridge specifies the IOS-based conference bridge type that supports heterogeneous video conferences, which unlike the homogeneous bridge, allows support for the conference participants to connect to the conference bridge with different video formats.

In heterogeneous conferences, transcoding and transsizing features are required to convert the signals between the various formats. The following DSP are able to complete this function:

- PVDM3-128

- PVDM3-192

- PVDM3-256

Note   Cisco IOS Heterogeneous Video Conference cannot be configured on the IOS router without an appropriate PVDM installed on the router.

While a Cisco IOS Heterogeneous Video Conference supports video switching and video transcoding, it uses a large amount of DSP resources for this operation. The number of supported conference participants and conferences depends on the number of concurrent sessions required and type of codecs to be supported by the heterogeneous video conference.

At the start of the conference, the phones negotiate the video format, and phones with the same video format are grouped into the same video capability class. Phones supporting a different video format are grouped into a different video capability class. The router dynamically converts multiple data streams as needed for the different video capability classes to communicate.

Cisco Guaranteed Audio Video Conference Bridge

This section describes the hardware-based audio guaranteed conference bridge that is provided by Cisco IOS routers with PVDM3 modules.

A Cisco Guaranteed Audio Video Conference Bridge is similar to a homogeneous video conference bridge, but DSP resources are only reserved for audio connections.

If you have limited DSP resources, this configuration ensures that participants are able to join the conference, as you can reserve the DSP resources just for audio. Video service cannot be guaranteed and is provided as a best-effort service. If DSP resources are available when the conference is initiated, video connections are established. Otherwise, the callers are connected to the conference as audio participants. When participants connect to a conference with video, the same codec must be used. No video transcoding is supported for this type of conference bridge.

Conference Bridge Configuration

A CUCM-based software conference bridge is automatically created on the server where IPVMS is activated. A software conference bridge is shown in Figure 10-2.

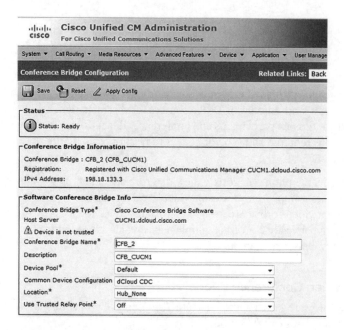

Figure 10-2 *CUCM-Based Software Conference Bridge*

CUCM-based hardware conference bridge configuration requires CUCM configuration and Cisco IOS router configuration. Follow these steps to configure a hardware conference bridge:

Step 1. Go to **Tools** > **Service Activation**. After choosing the server on which IPVMS will run, select the Cisco IP Voice Media Streaming App check box and click **Save** to activate the service.

Step 2. The Cisco IPVMS parameters can be fine-tuned to meet the deployment requirements. These are accessible through CUCM Administration by choosing **System** > **Service Parameters**. The following two conference bridge service parameters are available:

- **Call Count:** This parameter specifies the maximum number of conference participants that the conference bridge will support. The configurable range is 0 to 256, and the default is 48.

- **Run Flag:** This parameter determines whether the conference bridge functionality of the Cisco IPVMS is enabled. The default is True.

Step 3. Go to **Media Resources** > **Conference Bridge**. Click **Add New**.

Step 4. Select **Conference Bridge Type** as **Cisco IOS Enhanced Conference Bridge**. For **Conference Bridge Name**, enter the name matching associated DSP Profile name in Cisco IOS router as shown in Figure 10-3.

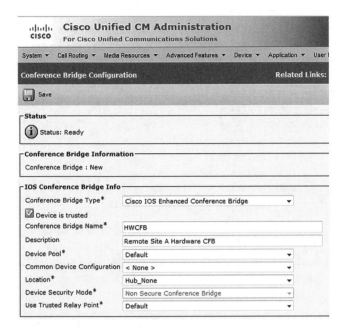

Figure 10-3 *CUCM-Based Hardware (IOS Enhanced) Conference Bridge*

Step 5.   Enter other optional and required fields such as **Description, Device Pool, Common Device Configuration, Location, Device Security Mode** (which must match the security mode on the IOS router), and **Use Trusted Relay Point** (default None). Click **Save**.

Note For more information on security aspects of media resources and CUCM, refer to the Cisco Press book *Securing Cisco IP Telephony Networks*.

A Cisco IOS router configuration to support hardware conferencing is shown in Example 10-1.

Example 10-1 *Cisco IOS Hardware Conference Bridge Configuration*

```
CFBRouter(config)# voice-card 0
CFBRouter(config-voicecard)# dsp services dspfarm
!
CFBRouter(config)# sccp local GigabitEthernet0/0
CFBRouter(config)# sccp ccm 198.18.133.3 identifier 1 priority 1 version 7.0+
CFBRouter(config)# sccp
!
CFBRouter(config)# sccp ccm group 1
CFBRouter(config-sccp-ccm)# bind interface GigabitEthernet0/1
```

```
CFBRouter(config-sccp-ccm)# associate ccm 1 priority 1
CFBRouter(config-sccp-ccm)# associate profile 1 register HWCFB
CFBRouter(config-sccp-ccm)# switchback method graceful
!
CFBRouter(config)# dspfarm profile 1 conference
CFBRouter(config-dspfarm-profile)# codec g711ulaw
CFBRouter(config-dspfarm-profile)# codec g711alaw
CFBRouter(config-dspfarm-profile)# codec g729ar8
CFBRouter(config-dspfarm-profile)# codec g729abr8
CFBRouter(config-dspfarm-profile)# codec g729r8
CFBRouter(config-dspfarm-profile)# codec g729br8
CFBRouter(config-dspfarm-profile)# maximum conference-participants 20
CFBRouter(config-dspfarm-profile)# maximum sessions 20
CFBRouter(config-dspfarm-profile)# associate application SCCP
CFBRouter(config-dspfarm-profile)# no shut
```

Each command is explained in Table 10-1.

Table 10-1 *Cisco IOS Media Resource Configuration Commands*

Command	Description
dspfarm (DSP farm)	To enable DSP farm service, use the **dspfarm** command in global configuration mode. The DSP farm service is disabled by default.
dsp services dspfarm	To enable DSP farm services for a particular voice network module, use the **dsp services dspfarm** command.
sccp local	To select the local interface that SCCP applications (transcoding and conferencing) use to register with CUCM, use the **sccp local** command in global configuration mode.
sccp ccm	To add a CUCM server to the list of available servers and set various parameters, including IP address or Domain Name System (DNS) name, port number, and version number, use the **sccp ccm** command in global configuration mode.
sccp	To enable the SCCP protocol and its related applications (transcoding and conferencing), use the **sccp** command in global configuration mode.
sccp ccm group	To create a CUCM group and enter SCCP CUCM configuration mode, use the **sccp ccm group** command in global configuration mode.
associate ccm	To associate a CUCM with a CUCM group and establish its priority within the group, use the **associate ccm** command in SCCP CUCM configuration mode.

associate profile	To associate a DSP farm profile with a CUCM group, use the **associate profile** command in SCCP CUCM configuration mode.
dspfarm profile	To enter DSP farm profile configuration mode and define a profile for DSP farm services, use the **dspfarm profile** command in global configuration mode.
codec	To specify call density and codec complexity based on a particular codec standard, use the **codec** command in DSP interface DSP farm configuration mode.
associate application sccp	To associate SCCP to the DSP farm profile, use the **associate application sccp** command in DSP farm profile configuration mode.
maximum sessions (DSP farm profile)	To specify the maximum number of sessions that are supported by the profile, use the **maximum sessions** command in DSP farm profile configuration mode.
no shutdown	If you fail to use the **no shutdown** command, the DSP farm profile will display in the gateway but fail to operate.

To verify the Cisco IOS media resource configuration, use the **show** commands, as demonstrated in Example 10-2.

Example 10-2 *Verifying Cisco IOS Conference Bridge Configuration*

```
CFBRouter# show sccp
SCCP Admin State: UP<Anchor0>
Gateway IP Address: 10.1.1.101, Port Number: 2000
IP Precedence: 5
User Masked Codec list: None
Call Manager: 198.18.133.3, Port Number: 2000<Anchor2>
Conferencing Oper State: ACTIVE - Cause Code: NONE
Active Call Manager: 198.18.133.3, Port Number: 2000
TCP Link Status: CONNECTED, Profile Identifier: 1
<output omitted for brevity>
!
CFBRouter# show sccp ccm group 1
CCM Group Identifier: 1
<output omitted for brevity>
Associated CCM Id: 1, Priority in this CCM Group: 1
Associated Profile: 1, Registration Name: HWCFB
Registration Retries: 3, Registration Timeout: 10 sec
Keepalive Retries: 3, Keepalive Timeout: 30 sec
CCM Connect Retries: 3, CCM Connect Interval: 10 sec
Switchover Method: GRACEFUL,Switchback Method: GRACEFUL_GUARD
<output omitted for brevity>
!
```

```
CFBRouter# show dspfarm profile 1
Dspfarm Profile Configuration
Profile ID = 1, Service = CONFERENCING, Resource ID = 1<Anchor10> <Anchor11>
Profile Description :
Profile Admin State : UP
Profile Operation State : ACTIVE
<output omitted for brevity>
Codec Configuration
Codec : g711ulaw, Maximum Packetization Period : 30 , Transcoder: Not Required
Codec : g711alaw, Maximum Packetization Period : 30 , Transcoder: Not Required
Codec : g729ar8, Maximum Packetization Period : 60 , Transcoder: Not Required
Codec : g729abr8, Maximum Packetization Period : 60 , Transcoder: Not Required
Codec : g729r8, Maximum Packetization Period : 60 , Transcoder: Not Required
Codec : g729br8, Maximum Packetization Period : 60 , Transcoder: Not Required
```

Various CUCM service parameters can be fine-tuned to meet the deployment or organization's requirements and include the following:

- **Suppress Music on Hold to Conference Bridge:** This parameter determines whether MOH plays to a conference when a conference participant places the conference on hold. The default is True.

- **Drop Ad Hoc Conference:** This parameter determines how an Ad Hoc conference terminates. This is an important toll-fraud prevention setting, because inside facilitators can set up a conference call to expensive international numbers and then drop out of the call. Valid values are as follows:

  - **Never (default):** The conference remains active after the conference controller and all on-net parties hang up. This default setting could result in potential toll fraud.

  - **When Conference Controller Leaves:** Terminate the conference when the conference controller hangs up.

  - **When No On-Net Parties Remain in the Conference:** Terminate the conference when there are no on-net parties remaining in the conference. This distinction is important because the conference controller might have to drop out of the call, but other business partners on the call should continue the conference. The When Conference Controller Leaves option hangs up the call when the conference controller leaves the conference.

Note   For more information on security aspect of media resources and CUCM security, refer to the Cisco Press book *Securing Cisco IP Telephony Networks*.

- **Advanced Ad Hoc Conference Enabled:** This parameter determines whether advanced Ad Hoc conference features are enabled. These features include the ability for conference participants other than the conference controller to add new participants to an existing Ad Hoc conference (conference chaining), the ability for any conference participant who is not a controller to drop other participants from the conference through the ConfList and RmLstC soft keys, and whether Ad Hoc conferences can be linked using features such as conference, join, direct transfer, and transfer.

- **Nonlinear Ad Hoc Conference Linking Enabled:** This parameter determines whether more than two Ad Hoc conferences can be linked directly to an Ad Hoc conference in a nonlinear fashion. Nonlinear conference linking occurs when three or more Ad Hoc conferences are linked directly to one other Ad Hoc conference. Linear conference linking occurs when one or two Ad Hoc conferences are linked directly to one other Ad Hoc conference.

- **Maximum Ad Hoc Conference:** This parameter specifies the maximum number of participants who are allowed in a single Ad Hoc conference. The value of this field depends on the capabilities of the software/hardware conference bridge.

- **Maximum Meet-Me Conference Unicast:** This parameter specifies the maximum number of participants that are allowed in a single Meet-Me conference. The value of this field depends on the capabilities of the software/hardware conference bridge. A software conference bridge is capable of conferencing up to 128 participants. When a conference is created, the system automatically reserves a minimum of three streams, so specifying a value less than three allows a maximum of three participants. The range is 1 to 128. The default is 4.

Meet-Me Conference Configuration

Follow these steps to configure Meet-Me conference settings.

Step 1. Go to **CUCM Administration GUI > Call Routing > Meet-Me Number/ Pattern**. Click **Add New**.

Step 2. Enter the number/pattern to be used as a Meet-Me number.

Step 3. Provide the information required for **Description, Partition,** and **Maximum Security Level.**

- Choose **Authenticated** to block participants with nonsecure phones from joining the conference.

- Choose **Encrypted** to block participants with authenticated or nonsecure phones from joining the conference.

- Choose **Non Secure** to allow all participants to join the conference.

- Click **Save.**

Note   Meet-Me bridges do not offer any security, scheduling, or name-confirmation features. Security and scheduling features are offered by the Cisco MeetingPlace and Cisco MeetingPlace Express products. The conference controller could be given access to the ConfList soft key, which will allow the controller to view the conference participants by caller ID information. The conference controller can individually remove users, but does not have access to the users' line state information.

Transcoding

At times it is required to have one codec converted to another; for example G.729 calls traversing over WAN from remote site may be converted to G.711 at the data center so that the interactive voice response (IVR) system such as Cisco Unified Contact Center Express (UCCX) can record the calls. A transcoder converts an incoming RTP stream using one audio codec into an outgoing RTP stream that uses a different audio codec. The transcoder in Figure 10-4 is implemented using DSP resources in the Cisco router and is used to convert between G.711 and G.729 codecs.

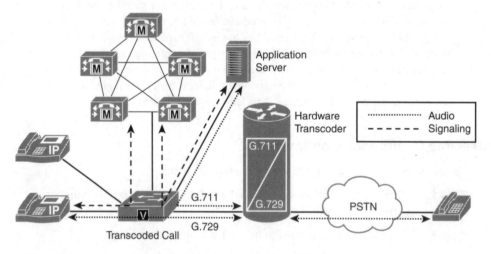

Figure 10-4   *Cisco IOS Route– Based Transcoding Overview*

Transcoders are necessary when audio streams are using compressed audio codes (G.729 or Internet Low Bandwidth Codec [iLBC]), but the resource they are attempting to use accepts only G.711 calls. iLBC operates at 15.2 kbps. Most Cisco Unity/Cisco Unity Connection voicemail deployments use the G.711 audio codec for voicemail storage to guarantee high quality. Moreover, certain devices and legacy products may not support complex/lossy codecs such as G.729, and the incoming RTP stream must be converted to G.711.

Audio streams (RTP bearer channels) are set up between the telephony devices and the transcoder. Signaling messages are exchanged between the telephony devices and CUCM and between the transcoder resource and CUCM. DSP resources are required to perform transcoding. Those DSP resources are located in Cisco routers and switches.

Transcoder Configuration

Similar to conference bridge configuration, a transcoder also needs to be configured on both CUCM and the Cisco IOS router. To configure a transcoder on CUCM, follow these steps.

Step 1.   Go to **CUCM Administration > Media Resources > Transcoder.** Click **Add New.**

Step 2.   For **Transcoder Type,** select **Cisco Conference Enhanced IOS Media Termination Point** and enter a name matching the DSP profile configuration in the IOS router as shown in Figure 10-5. Enter other required details, such as Device Pool and Common Device Configuration. Click **Save.**

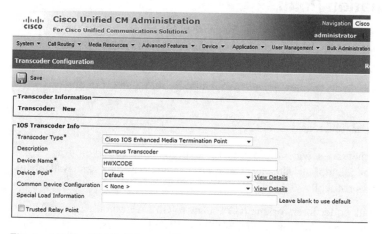

Figure 10-5   *CUCM Transcoder Configuration*

Example 10-3 explains the configuration for enabling transcoding resources on an IOS gateway (building on Example 10-1 for conferencing).

Example 10-3   *Cisco IOS Transcoding Configuration*

```
CFBRouter(config)# sccp ccm group 1
CFBRouter(config-sccp-ccm)# bind interface GigabitEthernet0/1
CFBRouter(config-sccp-ccm)# associate ccm 1 priority 1
CFBRouter(config-sccp-ccm)# associate profile 2 register HWXCODE
CFBRouter(config-sccp-ccm)# switchback method graceful
!
```

```
CFBRouter(config)# dspfarm profile 2 transcode
CFBRouter(config-dspfarm-profile)# codec g711ulaw
CFBRouter(config-dspfarm-profile)# codec g711alaw
CFBRouter(config-dspfarm-profile)# codec g729ar8
CFBRouter(config-dspfarm-profile)# codec g729abr8
CFBRouter(config-dspfarm-profile)# maximum sessions 20
CFBRouter(config-dspfarm-profile)# associate application SCCP
CFBRouter(config-dspfarm-profile)# no shut
```

As can be seen, the major changes between Example 10-1 and Example 10-3 are that the associate profile number is different (conferencing uses 1 and transcoding is using 2), the dspfarm profile number is set to 2 for transcoding (whereas it was 1 for conferencing), and the dspfarm profile is set for transcoding.

The next section describes Cisco Media Termination Point.

Media Termination Point

A Media Termination Point (MTP) is a software process that runs as part of the Cisco IPVMS service on CUCM. Like conference bridges, MTPs can also be software or hardware devices.

An MTP bridges two media streams and allows them to be set up and torn down independently.

MTPs serve two major functions:

■ Provide supplementary services (hold, transfer, conferencing, and so on) for an H.323 version 1 endpoint/gateway. These supplementary services are available in H.323 version 2 protocol.

■ Provide SIP trunk codec interworking (G.711ulaw to G.711alaw and vice versa) as well as conversion of DTMF tones from SCCP to SIP and vice versa.

Note   A software MTP is created automatically when IPVMS service is activated on a CUCM server.

Audio streams exist between telephony devices and the MTP resource. Signaling messages are exchanged between the telephony devices and CUCM. Figure 10-6 illustrates a hardware-based MTP.

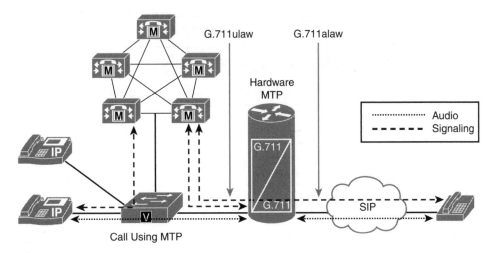

Figure 10-6   *Cisco IOS Router–based Media Termination Point Overview*

As depicted in Figure 10-6, the IT service provider (ITSP) is using G.711alaw for the
SIP trunks, while G.711ulaw is being used in the enterprise setup. To interwork between
the two differing codecs and characteristic call legs, MTP can intercept the call and
provide the necessary codec and feature interworking.

Media Termination Point Configuration

Software MTPs are created when the IPVMS service is activated on a CUCM
server. For a software MTP, the only configuration required is to change the device
pool. To change the MTP's device pool, go to **Media Resources** > **MTP** and select the
MTP for which device pool is to be changed. Choose the appropriate device pool
and click **Save**.

A hardware MTP, on the other hand, requires configuration on CUCM and Cisco IOS
router. To configure a hardware MTP on CUCM, follow these steps.

Step 1.   Go to **Media Resources** > MTP and click **Add New**.

Step 2.   Configure a media termination point (MTP) similar to the one shown in
Figure 10-7. Set the **Media Termination Point Type** as **Cisco IOS Enhanced
Software Media Termination Point,** provide the **Media Termination Point
Name** and **Description** (optional), and select a **Device Pool.** Click **Save**.

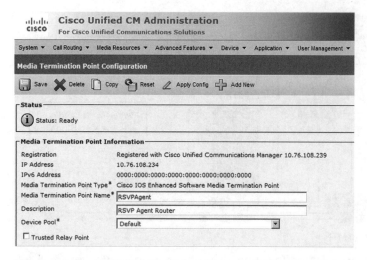

Figure 10-7 *CUCM Media Termination Point Configuration*

The next step is to configure the IOS gateway to provide MTP resources.

Note   In this case, the IOS gateway is also configured to be an RSVPAgent for RSVP QoS.

As seen in Example 10-4, the profile number is unique to MTP resources (1 was for conference and 2 for transcoding) and the **dspfarm** profile is set for type **mtp** with the profile number as 3.

Example 10-4 *IOS MTP (RSVP) Configuration*

```
CFBRouter(config)# sccp ccm group 1
CFBRouter(config-sccp-ccm)# associate ccm 1 priority 1
CFBRouter(config-sccp-ccm)# associate ccm 2 priority 2
CFBRouter(config-sccp-ccm)# associate profile 3 register RSVPAgent
!
CFBRouter(config)# dspfarm profile 3 mtp
CFBRouter(config-dspfarm-profile)# codec pass-through
CFBRouter(config-dspfarm-profile)# rsvp
CFBRouter(config-dspfarm-profile)# maximum sessions software 20
CFBRouter(config-dspfarm-profile)# associate application SCCP
CFBRouter(config-dspfarm-profile)# no shut
```

Annunciator

An annunciator is a function of the Cisco IP Voice Media Streaming Application Service that provides the capability to stream spoken messages or various call-progress tones from the CUCM system to a user. Annunciator plays recorded announcements to devices on the occurrence of specific events, such as a user dialing an invalid number. An annunciator is automatically created when IPVMS service is activated on one or more nodes in a cluster. The annunciator can send multiple one-way RTP streams to devices such as Cisco Unified IP Phones or gateways, using SCCP messages to set up the RTP stream. Tones and announcements are predefined by the system. The announcements support localization and can also be customized by replacing the appropriate Windows Audio Volume (WAV) file. The annunciator supports G.711 a-law, G.711 mu-law, G.729, and Cisco wideband audio codecs without transcoding resources.

Signaling messages are exchanged between telephony devices and CUCM. The audio stream is one-way, from the annunciator to the telephony device. The annunciator is a software component of CUCM as shown in Figure 10-8.

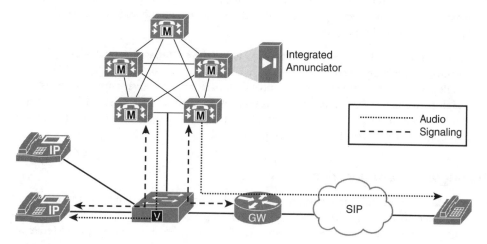

Figure 10-8 *Annunciator Overview*

The annunciator service is responsible for the following features:

- **Cisco Multilevel Precedence and Preemption (MLPP):** This feature has streaming messages that it plays in response to the following call-failure conditions:

  - Unable to preempt because of an existing higher-precedence call.

  - A precedence (prioritization) access limitation was reached.

  - The attempted precedence level was unauthorized.

  - The called number is not equipped for preemption or call waiting.

- **Integration through SIP trunk:** SIP endpoints can generate and send tones in-band in the RTP stream, but SCCP cannot. An annunciator is used with an MTP to generate or accept dual-tone multifrequency (DTMF) tones when integrating with a SIP endpoint.

- **Cisco IOS gateways and intercluster trunks:** These devices require support for call-progress tone (ringback tone).

- **System messages:** During the following call-failure conditions, the system plays a streaming message to the end user:

  - A dialed number that the system cannot recognize

  - A call that is not routed because of a service disruption

  - A number that is busy and not configured for preemption or call waiting

- **Conferencing:** During a conference call, the system plays a barge-in tone to announce that a participant has joined or left the bridge.

The annunciator is configured to support 48 simultaneous streams by default. The maximum recommended is 48 for an annunciator running on the same server with the CUCM service (call processing).

If the server has only 10-Mbps connectivity, lower the setting to 24 simultaneous streams. A standalone server without the CUCM service supports up to 255 simultaneous announcement streams, and a high-performance server with dual CPUs and a high-performance disk system supports up to 400 streams. Multiple standalone servers can be added to support the required number of streams. The maximum streams are configured in the Cisco IPVMS service parameters.

Annunciator Configuration

In order to set up an annunciator, no specific configuration is needed except to change the device pool to a specific device pool, for example changing a device pool to campus-DP that contains all media resources. To change the device pool, go to **Media Resources** > **Annunciator** and select the annunciator for which the device pool is to be changed. Choose the appropriate device pool and click **Save**.

Music on Hold

The music on hold (MOH) feature is part of the Cisco IP Voice Media Streaming Application (IPVMS) service running on CUCM. It provides music to callers when their calls are placed on hold or a supplementary service is initiated. Supplementary services include (but are not limited to) the following: transfer, park, and conference. When a supplementary service is initiated, the call is temporarily put on hold before the function is completed. Implementing MOH is relatively simple but requires a basic understanding of the following:

- IP unicast and multicast traffic

- MOH call flows

- Configuration options/requirements

- Server behavior

Audio streams are setup between telephony devices and the MOH server. Signaling messages are exchanged between telephony devices and CUCM. Figure 10-9 illustrates the MOH operation of CUCM.

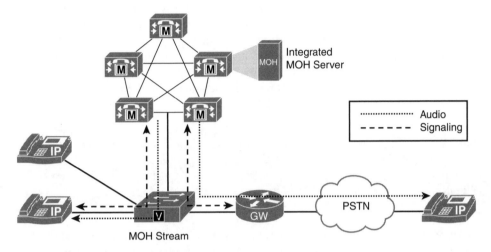

Figure 10-9   *Music on Hold Overview*

As seen in Figure 10-9, the PSTN caller gets MOH when the IP phone user keeps the call on hold.

The MOH feature has two main requirements:

- A MOH server must provide the MOH audio stream source(s).

- CUCM must be configured to use the MOH streams provided by the MOH server when a call is placed on hold.

The IPVMS MOH feature enables users to place on-net and off-net callers on hold with music instead of the default "on hold tone." The MOH source makes music available to any on-net or off-net device placed on hold. On-net devices include Cisco IP phones and applications placed on hold. Off-net users include those connected through Media Gateway Control Protocol (MGCP), SIP, and H.323 gateways. The MOH feature is also available for plain old telephone service (POTS) phones connected to the Cisco IP network through Foreign Exchange Station (FXS) ports.

It is also possible to configure multicast MOH streaming to leverage external media servers providing media streams. CUCM Express and Cisco Unified Survivable Remote Site Telephony (SRST) gateways can be configured as media streaming servers for MOH, too. The CUCME and SRST router–based resources provide MOH by streaming one audio file stored in the router's flash memory or a fixed audio source connected through an optional ear and mouth (E&M) hardware interface. Detailed information about this feature is available in the *CUCM Solution Reference Network Designs* (SRND) guide at Cisco.com.

The basic operation of MOH in a Cisco Collaboration environment consists of a holding party and a held party. The holding party is the endpoint placing a call on hold, and the held party is the endpoint placed on hold, receiving MOH.

The MOH stream that an endpoint receives is determined by a combination of the user hold audio source identifier of the device placing the endpoint on hold (holding party) and the configured prioritized list of MOH resources of the endpoint placed on hold (held party). The user hold audio source configured for the holding party determines the audio file to be streamed when the holding party puts a call on hold. The held party's list of MOH resources determines the server from which the held party will receive the MOH stream.

Note   When multiple MOH servers are active in your network, make sure that all the configured MOH files are available on all MOH servers. Also, ensure that the clusterwide parameters under Service Parameter configuration in the CUCM for MOH are set for multiple codecs and not only G.711.

CUCM ships with a default MOH audio file. For MOH audio source, additional audio files can be added to the MOH server. Endpoints/devices can be configured to play different audio files as required. An MOH audio source file can be assigned as user hold audio source and/or network hold audio source to the phones. If an audio source file is defined at device level, it overrides the device pool audio source preference. To upload an MOH audio file (the file must first be uploaded to the CUCM that is functioning as the MOH server), go to **CUCM Administration GUI > Media Resources > Music on Hold Audio Source Files**, click **Add New > Upload File**, and select an audio file you wish to upload as an MOH file and click **Upload**.

Unicast and Multicast Music on Hold

The CUCM MOH server supports multicast and unicast for MOH streaming. The advantage of using multicast over unicast for MOH streaming is that it saves bandwidth and reduces the load on the MOH server, especially for remote sites and offices that connect to a main (campus) site over the WAN. Saving bandwidth is not usually an issue for campus LAN environments, but reducing load on the MOH server is always a big consideration. Reducing the number of media streams is especially advantageous when the MOH server is located on the same server as call processing. It is advisable to scope MOH traffic to the local site so that MOH does not consume excessive WAN bandwidth. There are various ways of implementing multicast scoping and unicast filtering on the data network.

MOH files using audio codecs (G.711 mu-law, G.711 a-law, Cisco wideband, and G.729) are generated by CUCM when files with a .wav extension are uploaded to the MOH server. The recommended format for audio source files includes the following specifications:

- 16-bit PCM WAV file

- Stereo or mono

- Sample rates of 48, 32, 16, or 8 kHz

> **Note**   CUCM version 10.x does not support USB or sound card for fixed audio source, as it's a virtual appliance running on Cisco UCS (or a supported third-party blade server) on VMware as hypervisor.

A unicast MOH stream is a point-to-point, one-way audio RTP stream between the server and one endpoint device. Unicast MOH uses a separate source stream for each connection. As more endpoint devices receive MOH, the number of MOH streams increases. If 100 devices are on hold, 100 independent streams of RTP traffic are generated over the network between the server and the endpoints receiving the MOH. The number of streams can potentially have a negative effect on network throughput. Unicast MOH is useful in networks where multicast is not enabled or where devices are not capable of multicast; with it an administrator can still take advantage of the MOH feature. Figure 10-10 illustrates the unicast MOH process.

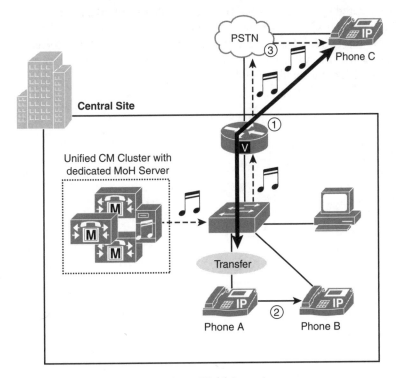

Figure 10-10   *Unicast Music on Hold Overview*

As seen in Figure 10-10, Phone A and Phone C are on call. The user at Phone A decides to transfer the call to Phone B. When the user presses the Transfer soft key and attempts to transfer the call to Phone B, Phone C gets MOH from the dedicated MOH server in the CUCM cluster.

Multicast MOH streams are point-to-multipoint, one-way audio RTP streams between the MOH server and the multicast group IP address. Multicast MOH conserves system resources and bandwidth because it enables multiple users to use the same audio source stream to provide MOH. If 100 devices were simultaneously on hold, a single multicast RTP stream could be replicated over the network to all 100 resources. Bandwidth and server processor utilization are greatly reduced. It is recommended to use a multicast IP address of 239.1.1.1 through 239.255.255.254 because these multicast addresses are implicitly scoped by the router because the IP packets are generated with a time-to-live (TTL) value of 2. Each data router decrements the TTL value by 1. When a TTL of 0 is reached, the packet is not forwarded by a router. A TTL of 0 has a drop operation.

Multicast MOH is based on MOH capabilities of the Cisco IOS router's feature Cisco Unified SRST (working in standby or fallback mode). To leverage this feature, the Cisco IOS SRST gateway/router is configured for multicast MOH and continuously sends a MOH stream that to the endpoints appears as though a multicast MOH stream has been generated by the CUCM MOH server. In other words, the router sits as a proxy for MOH between CUCM and the endpoints, as the logical next hop for endpoints to receive MOH from. This is done by configuring the CUCM MOH server for multicast MOH and setting the max-hops value in the MOH server configuration to 1. Figure 10-11 describes the multicast MOH process.

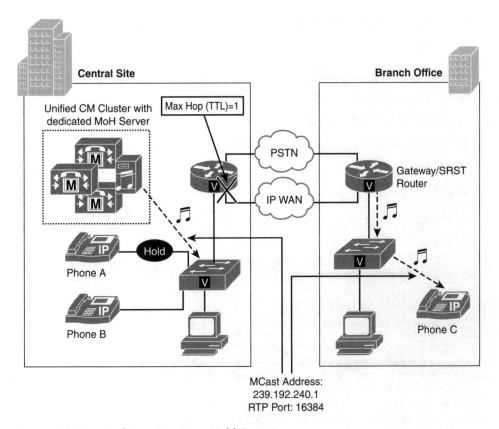

Figure 10-11   *Multicast Music on Hold Overview*

To understand the multicast MOH process depicted in Figure 10-11, it is important
to understand the role of the CUCM MOH server, the remote site voice gateway/SRST
router, and the campus router. When Phone A (campus site) puts Phone C (remote
site) on hold, the following steps occur:

Step 1.   The CUCM MOH server and (SRST) voice gateway located at the remote
site are set up to use the same multicast address and port number for
their streams as shown in Figure 10-11.

Step 2.   The MOH packets generated by CUCM MOH server at the campus site are
dropped by the campus router as the TTL exceeds the hops.

Step 3.   The remote site voice (SRST) gateway continuously generates a
multicast MOH stream so that the IP phones get this stream, which appears
to be coming from the CUCM MOH server.

Unicast and Multicast MOH Configuration

Unicast MOH is enabled by default in CUCM when IPVMS is activated on a server. Assign the MOH server to a media resource group (MRG) and allocate the MRG to a media resource group list (MRGL), which is then assigned to either device pool or the device (IP phone) itself.

Enabling multicast MOH includes the following steps:

Step 1. Configuring the CUCM MOH server at the main site

Step 2. Configuring the campus router

Step 3. Configuring the voice gateway at the remote site

To configure CUCM for supporting multicast MOH, follow these steps.

Step 1. Go to **CUCM Administration GUI** > **Media Resources** > **Music on Hold Audio Source** and select the audio source you are enabling for multicast. Ensure that the **Allow Multicast** check box is checked, as shown in Figure 10-12.

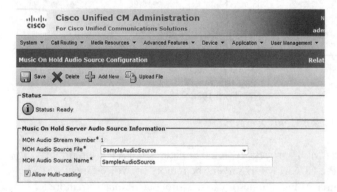

Figure 10-12 *Multicast Music on Hold Audio Source Configuration*

Note The MOH audio sources are identified by a MOH audio stream number from 1 to 51. Up to 50 prerecorded sources and one live audio source are available per CUCM cluster. In the Music On Hold Audio Source Configuration window, select the MOH audio stream number of the audio source that you want to configure.

Step 2. Go to **Media Resources** > **Music on Mold Server** and under **Multi-cast Audio Source Information** check the checkbox **Enable Multi-cast Audio Sources on this MOH server** as shown in Figure 10-13. Subsequently, set the multicast-base IP and port (these must match the remote site's router multicast configuration under call-manager-fallback). Set up the increment multicast on port basis or IP address basis and set the maximum hops for the audio source to 1. Click **Save**.

Note   Multicast increment on port or IP address basis has a rationale to it, and to understand the implications in detail refer to the next section. You can also refer to the book *Implementing Cisco IP Telephony and Video, Part 2.*

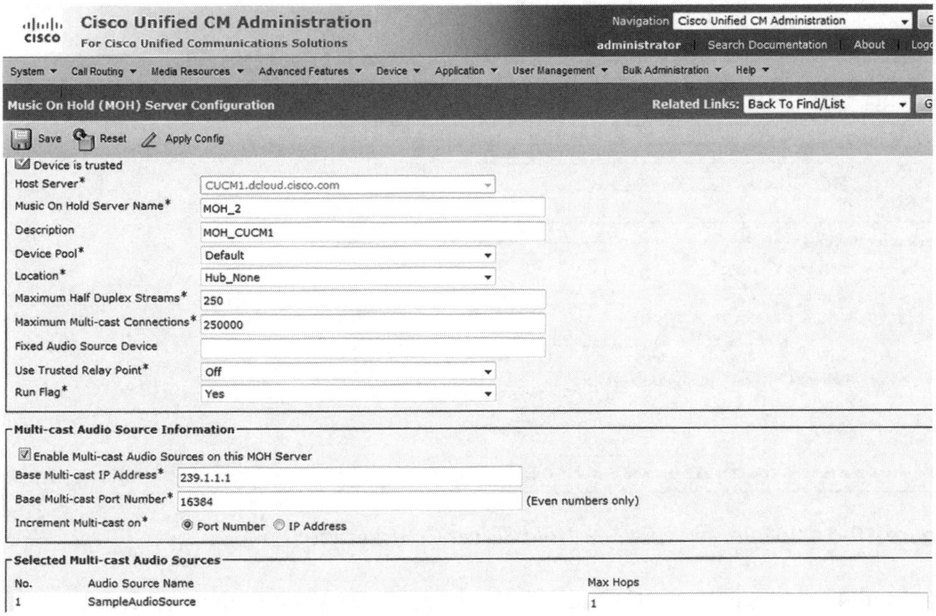

Figure 10-13   *Multicast Music on Hold Server Configuration*

Step 3.   Assign the MOH server to a media resource group (MRG) by browsing to **Media Resources > Media Resource Group** as shown in Figure 10-14. The following list of CUCM service parameters and the associated defaults are related to MOH:

- Suppress MOH to Conference Bridge (True)

- Default Network Hold MOH Audio Source ID (1)

- Default User Hold MOH Audio Source ID (1)

- Duplex Streaming Enabled (False)

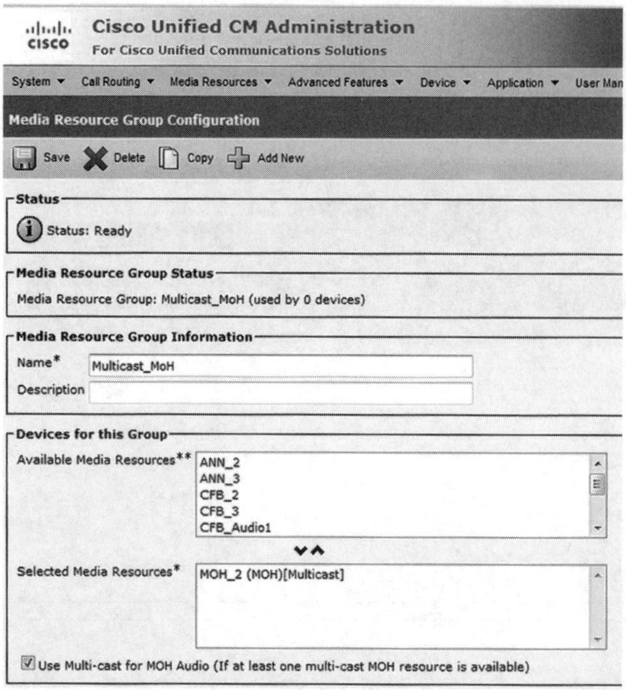

Figure 10-14 *Multicast Music on Hold Server Configuration*

Step 4.   Assign the MRG to an MRGL by going to **Media Resources > Media Resource Group List** and assigning the MRGL to a device pool.

Next, the main site router must be configured to drop any MOH multicast packets that are destined to a remote site, traversing the WAN (considering that TTL was set to 1 in CUCM by setting max hop). Example 10-5 illustrates the configuration of the campus router.

Example 10-5 *Configuration for Campus IOS Router to Drop Multicast Packets*

```
Campus-Site(config)# ip access-list extended MOH
Campus-Site(config-ext-nacl)# deny ip any host 239.1.1.10 range 16384 16484
Campus-Site(config-ext-nacl)# permit ip any any
!
Campus-Site(config)# interface GigabitEthernet 0/0
Campus-Site(config-if)# ip access-group MOH out
Campus-Site(config)# no ip pim sparse-mode
```

Finally, the remote site IOS router needs to be configured to generate multicast stream for locally connected IP phones. The configuration for the remote site router is covered in Example 10-6.

Example 10-6   *Configuration for Remote Site IOS Router to Support Multicast*

```
Remote-Site(config)# ip multicast-routing
!
Remote-Site(config)# interface GigabitEthernet 0/0
Remote-Site(config-if)# description WAN
Remote-Site(config-if)# ip address 10.1.1.1 255.255.255.0
Remote-Site(config-if)# ip pim sparse-dense-mode
!
Remote-Site(config)# interface GigabitEthernet 0/1
Remote-Site(config-if)# description Local Site Phones
Remote-Site(config-if)# ip address 10.1.2.1 255.255.255.0
Remote-Site(config-if)# ip pim sparse-dense-mode
!
Remote-Site(config)# ccm-manager music-on-hold
!
Remote-Site(config)# interface loopback 1
Remote-Site(config-if)# ip address 10.86.108.82 255.255.255.255
!
Remote-Site(config)# call-manager-fallback
Remote-Site(config-cm-fallback)# ip source-address 10.86.108.82 port 2000
Remote-Site(config-cm-fallback)# moh music-on-hold.au
Remote-Site(config-cm-fallback)# multicast moh 239.1.1.1 port 16384 route
  10.86.108.82 198.18.133.3
```

The commands used in Examples 10-6 are explained in Table 10-2.

Table 10-2   *Cisco IOS Multicast MOH Configuration Commands*

Command	Description
ip multicast-routing	Enables multicast routing support.
ip pim sparse-dense-mode	Enables PIM to operate in sparse or dense mode, depending on the multicast group. This command should be enabled on all ingress/egress interfaces, from/to CUCM and IP phones,
ccm-manager music-on-hold	Enables MOH.
call-manager-fallback	Defines the fallback configuration to be used when the router is in SRST mode.
moh <filename>	Defines the file to be used for MOH. A router can have multiple audio files; however, one file can be used for multicast MOH.
multicast moh	Defines the multicast MOH parameters, such as base IP, port number, and route to reach CUCM MOH server.

Multicast MOH IP Address and Port Considerations

The CUCM MOH server can stream multiple multicast MOH files. This implies that a base multicast IP must be specified, followed by a port. Also, the decision of choosing IP address versus port increment must be made. To better understand the implication of IP address or port increment, consider the following points:

- For each audio source enabled for multicast, four streams are enabled for the increment (one per codec):

    - G.711 mu-law

    - G.711 a-law

    - G.729

    - Wideband

- When incrementing on IP address, each stream consumes one IP address, which implies that each audio source requires four IP addresses.

Note   It is recommended to increment multicast on IP address instead of on port number so each stream has a unique IP assigned to it, for this helps avoid any firewall-induced network saturation (which can be a result of increasing the number of ports per IP beyond a usual limit).

- When incrementing on ports, two ports are reserved for each audio stream: one for RTP and the other for the Real-Time Transport Control Protocol (RTCP). Hence, each stream consumes two ports, which further implies that it is two ports per codec and a total of eight ports per audio stream.

Video on Hold

Video on hold (VOH) is a new feature available in CUCM 10.x that works together with Cisco MediaSense. CUCM allows video streams to be sent to a caller while the call is placed on hold. The Cisco Media Sense server can stream audio and video content to a video endpoint when directed by CUCM. Cisco MediaSense can store and stream audio and video content with CUCM as call control and uses SIP as the signal protocol. Cisco MediaSense is capable of providing high-definition video content at 1080p and 720p, or lower resolutions such as 360p. Signaling messages are exchanged between video endpoints and CUCM and between the media content server and CUCM. Figure 10-15 illustrates the VOH component of CUCM.

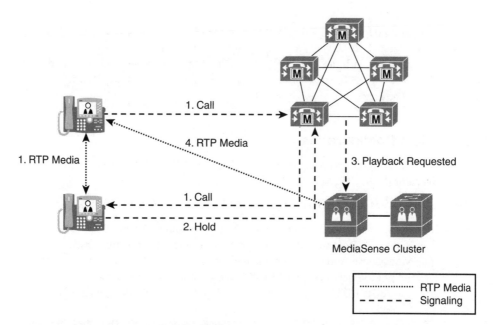

Figure 10-15 *Video on Hold Overview*

As seen in Figure 10-15, RTP media is established between the two video endpoints. The following is the sequence of events for VOH.

Step 1. One video endpoint keeps the other on hold, with the user deciding to put the other party on hold, and the video stream from Cisco MediaSense is played back to the requesting endpoint.

Step 2. CUCM forwards the VOH request to Cisco MediaSense. The MediaSense server starts video playback to the video endpoint on hold.

VOH is the primary video function for CUCM integration with MediaSense. However, MediaSense can also be leveraged with other Cisco Collaboration applications, such as:

- Video Greetings/Video Messaging in Unity Connection

- Video in queue for callers while they wait for Video-enabled Agent or Expert with Remote Expert Solution

- Using existing CUCM—MediaSense integration with video enabled call-center agents (UCCX and UCCE).

> **Note** Video on hold supports load balancing by redistributing video playbacks across multiple Cisco MediaSense servers. For load balancing, the Cisco MediaSense server sends a 302 Redirect message with the IP address of the new MediaSense server. In return, the CUCM reroutes the call to the new Cisco MediaSense server based on the IP address in the 302 Redirect message.

Video on Hold Configuration

Configuring VOH requires configuration on CUCM and Cisco MediaSense. The following steps detail CUCM configuration for VOH:

Step 1. Go to **Media Resources > Video on Hold Server**. Click **Add New**.

Step 2. Define a new **Video on Hold Server** by providing a **Name, Description** (optional), **Default Video Content Identifier** (needs to match Cisco MediaSense Audio file as explained later), and the **SIP Trunk** created for integration between CUCM and Cisco MediaSense, as illustrated in Figure 10-16. The associated SIP Trunk parameters are defined/displayed.

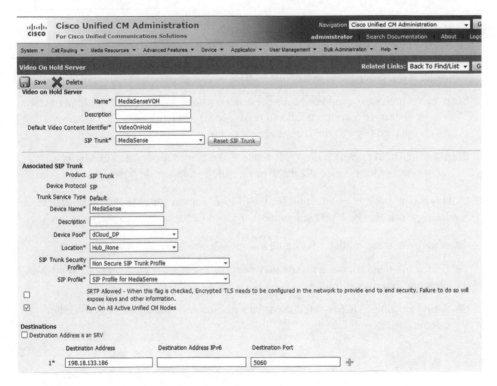

Figure 10-16 *CUCM VOH Server Configuration*

Note   Ensure that the **Run On All Active Unified CM Nodes** checkbox is checked.

Step 3.   Define the Cisco MediaSense IP Address/SRV. In this case the IP address is defined with SIP port 5060. Click **Save**.

Step 4.   Assign the newly created VOH server to a MRG and the MRG to a MRGL. Assign the MRGL to a SIP trunk that will be used by the video endpoints.

To configure Cisco MediaSense, follow these steps.

Step 1.   Go to **Cisco MediaSense Administration GUI > Administration > Unified CM Configuration** and ensure that the relevant CUCM server(s) are defined as AXL Service Provider and Call Control Service Provider as shown in Figure 10-17. Click **Save**.

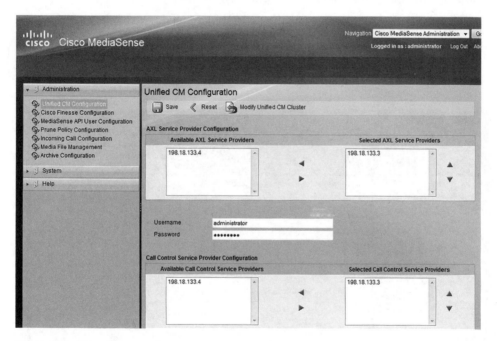

Figure 10-17   *Cisco MediaSense CUCM Configuration*

Step 2.   Go to **Administration > Media File Management**. Here you can upload new VOH files that can be played to video endpoints on hold. The video file in this case is **VideoOnHold** as shown in Figure 10-18.

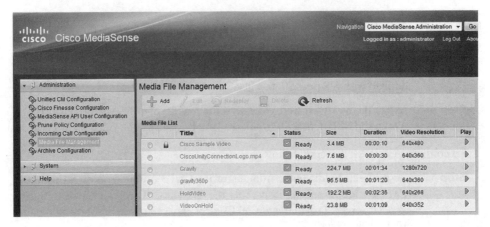

Figure 10-18 *Cisco MediaSense VOH File Configuration*

Step 3.   Browse to **Administration > Incoming Call Configuration**. As defined
           earlier (the **Default Video Content Identifier** in Step 2 of CUCM VOH
           configuration), the VideoOnHold file will be used for calls put on hold.
           Figure 10-19 illustrates the Incoming Call Configuration.

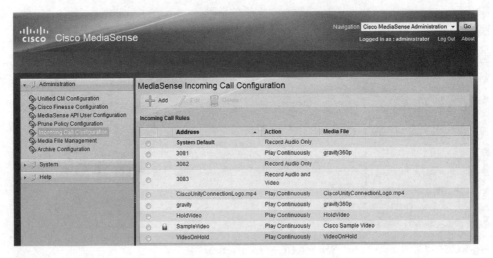

Figure 10-19 *Cisco MediaSense Incoming Call Configuration*

At this time the configuration of VOH is complete, and the endpoints with access to
VOH resource can play the VOH file to the party on hold.

Trusted Relay Point

A Trusted Relay Point (TRP) is a device that can be inserted into a media stream to act as a control point for that stream. It may be used to provide further processing on that stream or as a method to ensure that the stream follows a specific path. There are two components of the TRP functionality: the logic utilized by CUCM to invoke the TRP and the actual device that is invoked as the anchor point of the call. The TRP functionality can invoke an MTP device to act as that anchor point, as shown in Figure 10-20.

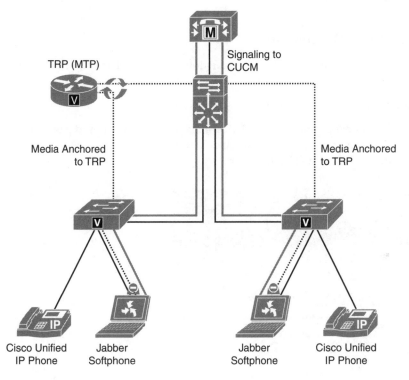

Figure 10-20   *Trusted Relay Point—Anchored Call Flow*

As seen in Figure 10-20, a TRP is introduced between the Jabber Softphone clients so that the media is anchored to the IOS voice gateway and calls can be forced to traverse from data to voice VLAN so that QoS policies or (IOS) firewall traversal policies can be enforced.

CUCM allows locally configured phones to be designed to invoke a TRP for any call to or from that phone.

Use cases for TRPs include QoS enforcement at the anchor point, firewall traversal, and inter-VRF communication. An example of using TRP is utilizing the TRP as an anchor point for media streams in a redundant data center with firewall redundancy.

For example, when redundant data centers are involved in a call, it is necessary to ensure that the call setup signaling passes though the same application layer gateway that the corresponding RTP stream is going to use. If the signaling and media take different paths, a UDP pinhole is not opened. The solution might be a TRP. Subscribers in each data center can invoke TRPs that provide anchoring of the media and ensure that the media streams flow through the appropriate firewall. The TRP provides an IP address that enables a specific host route for media that can ensure the same routing path as the call signaling. This method is used to ensure that signaling and media pass via the same firewall, thus solving the issue.

Trusted Relay Point Configuration

Configuration of TRP is similar to MTP configuration, with CUCM and IOS router configuration to support MTP.

To configure a TRP on CUCM, follow these steps:

Step 1. Go to **Media Resources** > **Media Termination Point**. Click **Add New**. Define an MTP and enable TRP by checking the **Trusted Relay Point** checkbox as shown in Figure 10-21. Click **Save**.

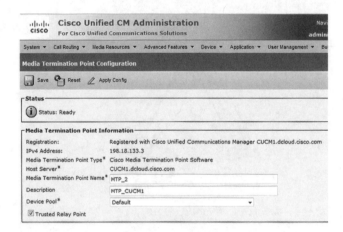

Figure 10-21 *Trusted Relay Point Configuration*

Step 2. Assign the MTP to a MRG and the MRG to a MRGL. Subsequently, assign the MRGL either to a device pool (so that this TRP is available to all IP phones using it) or on a device-by-device basis.

Step 3. Go to **Device** > **Phone** and select the phone(s) for which TRP is required. Scroll down on the phone settings page and set up **Use Trusted Relay Point** to **On**, as depicted in Figure 10-22. Click **Save**, followed by **Apply Config**.

The IOS router configuration for MTP remains the same as Example 10-4 (except that **rsvp** will not be used under the **dspfarm** configuration) as shown in Figure 10-22.

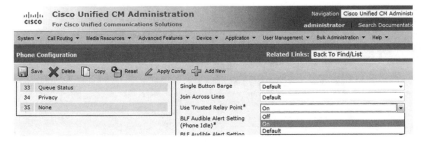

Figure 10-22   *Trusted Relay Point Enablement on Phone*

Media Resource Management

Once various media resources are defined, they need to be managed and assigned to the intended devices/endpoints/device pools. Media resource management is accomplished by creating media resource groups (MRG) and media resource group lists (MRGL). Media resources are assigned to MRGs, whereas MRGs are assigned to MRGLs.

All media resources are located in a null media resource group by default (and are accessible by all devices). Usage of media resources is load balanced among all existing devices.

> **Note**   Hardware resources should be preferred in the selection algorithm, based on their enhanced capabilities (multiple audio codec support) and the reduction of load on the CUCM.

The media resource manager (MRM) controls and manages the media resources within a cluster. MRM service enhances CUCM features by making it easier for CUCM to control access to transcoder, annunciator, conferencing, MTP, VOH, and MOH resources.

Media resource groups (MRG) define logical groupings of media sources. They create a logical collection of them and are normally arranged to service a geographical location.

Media resource group lists (MRGL) specify a list of prioritized MRGs. An application can select required media resources from the available resources according to the priority order that is defined in the MRGL. MRGLs are assigned to devices or device pools providing hierarchical processing order of media resources. MRGLs are analogous to route lists, whereas MRGs are equivalent to route groups.

Media Resource Group and Media Resource Group List Configuration

This section describes the configuration of media resource group and media resource group list as shown in the following steps:

Step 1.   To add a MRG, navigate to **Media Resources > Media Resource Group**. Click **Add New**. At the Media Resource Group Configuration window, enter a name and description for the MRG and add the desired media resources to the MRG. An example MRG is shown in Figure 10-23.

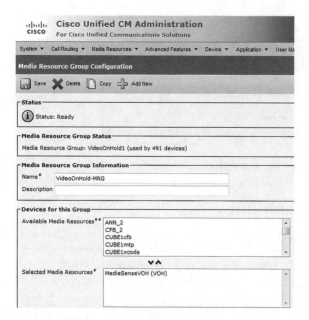

Figure 10-23 *MRG Configuration*

Note It is strongly recommended to have a MRG per resource type and site. This helps segregating resources based on physical/logical site(s) and containing a specific type of resource per MRG, for example, conference bridges in one MRG, MOH in another MRG, and so on.

Step 2. To add a MRGL, navigate to **Media Resources > Media Resource Group List**. At the Media Resource Group List Configuration window, enter a name for the MRGL and add the desired MRG(s) to the MRGL. An example MRGL is depicted in Figure 10-24.

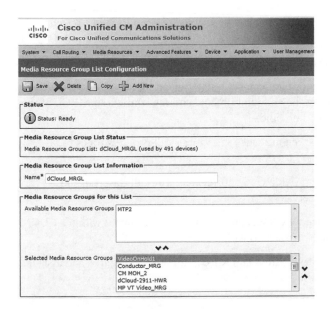

Figure 10-24 *MRGL Configuration*

Note Because the order of MRGs within an MRGL specifies the priorities of the MRG, it is important to list the MRGs in the desired order: for example, choosing that hardware conference bridges should be used before software conference bridges.

Step 3. MRGLs can be assigned to devices (phones, trunks, or gateways) or to device pools. If the device pool associated with the phone has a different MRGL, the phone configuration overrides the device pool inheritance.

Chapter Summary

The following list summarizes the key points that were discussed in this chapter:

- Media resources are required for voice termination (voice gateway, IP-TDM), audio conferencing, transcoding, MTP, annunciator, MOH, VOH, and Trusted Relay Point (TRP).

- There are no direct endpoint-to-endpoint RTP streams if a media resource is involved.

- Only hardware-based conference bridges support mixed-mode conferences, with participants using different codecs. CUCM-based conferencing only supports G.711.

- The Cisco IPVMS service on CUCM must be enabled to support media resource capabilities.

- A maximum of 51 unique audio sources can be configured in a cluster.

- The MOH stream that an endpoint receives is determined by the user hold audio source of the device placing the endpoint on hold and the configured MRGL of the endpoint/device pool placed on hold.

- The annunciator streams spoken messages and various call-progress tones to endpoints.

- Trusted Relay Points (TRP) provide QoS enforcement, firewall traversal, and inter-VRF communication services.

- The Media Resource Manager (MRM) controls the media resources within a CUCM cluster. The media resources are shared within a cluster.

- To limit media resource access, MRGs and MRGLs must be configured and assigned at device pool or device level.

Review Questions

Use the questions here to review what you learned in this chapter. The correct answers are found in Appendix A, "Answers to the Review Questions."

1. Which of the following media resources acts as a codec translator?

   a. Transcoder

   b. Software conference bridge

   c. Annunciator

   d. Music on hold

2. Which of the following media resources requires hardware (digital signal processors or DSP) media resources?

   a. Conference bridge

   b. Music on hold

   c. Transcoding

   d. Annunciator

3. Which device protocol is used to signal video media resources (for example, VOH)?

   a. SCCP

   b. H.323

c. SIP

d. MGCP

4. Which two scenarios require a Media Termination Point? (Choose two.)

a. Mixed-mode audio conference

b. RFC 2833 on Type A phone

c. RFC 2833 on Type B phone

d. Supplementary services on H.323 Version 1 endpoint

e. Supplementary services on H.323 Version 2 endpoint

5. Which audio codec is supported in software conferencing?

a. iLBC

b. G.729

c. G.722

d. G.711

6. What are the three types of video conferencing supported by CUCM? (Choose three.)

a. Ad-Hoc

b. Rendezvous

c. Co-resident

d. Scheduled

7. What are two types of valid audio conferences? (Choose two.)

a. Reservationless

b. Ad Hoc

c. Scheduled

d. Meet-Me

e. Broadcast

8. Which network technology limits the processor utilization of music on hold on CUCM?

a. Multicast

b. Broadcast

c. Unicast

d. Anycast

9. Which multicast IP address is used for local multicast?

    a. 255.255.255.255

    b. 239.1.1.1

    c. 225.1.1.1

    d. 235.1.1.1

10. Which of the following is not a function of a Trusted Relay Point?

    a. Audio codec conversion

    b. Firewall traversal

    c. QoS enforcement

    d. VRF communication

Chapter 11

Cisco Video Conferencing

Cisco offers a range of video conferencing solutions for small, medium, and large enterprises. These solutions offer state-of-the-art video conferencing that enables the mobile workforce, customers, and remote offices to be connected. This in turn improves real-time decision making and provides an in-person experience that is immersive and pervasive.

The Telepresence server and MSE 8000 Series provide high-density, high-performance conferencing services. This chapter presents an overview of these platforms and describes their architecture, capabilities, and available features.

Chapter Objectives

Upon completing this chapter, you will be able to meet the following objectives:

- Describe the features and capabilities of the Cisco TelePresence MSE 8000 Series.

- Describe the Cisco TelePresence MSE 8000 feature blades.

- Describe the capabilities of the feature blades.

- Explain how to enable access the Cisco TelePresence MSE 8000 feature blades.

- Describe how to integrate Cisco TelePresence Server with Cisco Unified Communications Manager (CUCM).

- Describe the integration options of Cisco TelePresence conferencing resources with Cisco Unified Communications Manager (CUCM) when using Cisco TelePresence Conductor.

Cisco TelePresence MSE 8000 Overview

The Cisco TelePresence MSE 8000 series is a highly scalable and flexible chassis-based platform for high-definition video conferencing and voice communication. This platform is a powerful, fault-tolerant solution designed for the mission-critical communication needs of large enterprises. The Cisco TelePresence MSE 8000 series chassis can support up to ten blades and two fan trays. The first slot is reserved for the Cisco Supervisor MSE 8050 blade, while the other nine slots can be used for Cisco TelePresence MCU media blades or other Cisco TelePresence MSE 8000 series service blades. Figure 11-1 gives an overview of the Cisco TelePresence MSE 8000 series chassis.

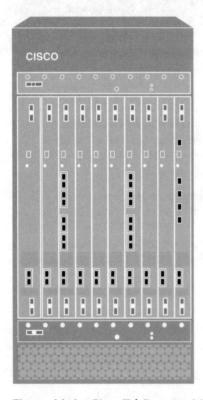

Figure 11-1   *Cisco TelePresence MSE 8000 Series Chassis*

The Cisco TelePresence MSE 8000 is ideal for the large-scale communication needs of sizeable enterprises and service providers that require a scalable high-availability and high-performance conferencing solution. Cisco TelePresence MSE 8000 offers the following functionalities:

■ Multipoint Control Unit (MCU)

■ Cisco TelePresence Server

■ ISDN and serial gateways

Cisco Supervisor MSE 8050 blade occupies the first slot on the Cisco MSE 8000 series chassis. Cisco TelePresence Server is available as an MSE 8710 blade for the Cisco TelePresence MSE 8000 series chassis. This option is suitable for organizations that already have a Cisco TelePresence MSE 8000 or need greater video conferencing capacity. Cisco TelePresence MCU MSE 8510 Media 2 Blade offers the MCU functionality and supports up to 80 Standard Definition (SD) video ports or 20 full High Definition (HD) video ports.

A fully equipped Cisco TelePresence MSE 8000 has the following capabilities:

- Up to 180 high-definition 1080p conference ports

- Up to 720 standard-definition conference ports

- Up to 72 ISDN Primary Rate Interface (PRI) instances

- Up to 144 serial ports

- Up to 216 high-definition (720p30) conference ports

Note   The listed capabilities are the maximum capabilities and are available when the Cisco TelePresence MSE 8000 chassis is full and no redundancy is provided.

Additional features of the Cisco TelePresence MSE 8000 include the following:

- More than 1 Gbps of conferencing bandwidth

- Support of a wide range of protocols, including H.323, Session Initiation Protocol (SIP), and H.320 Integrated Services Digital Network (ISDN)

- Support of Advanced Encryption Standard (AES) encryption

- Support of Cisco TelePresence Multiway, analogous to CUCM Ad Hoc conferencing

Cisco TelePresence MSE 8000 Features

The Cisco TelePresence MSE 8000 chassis offers the following features:

- High-definition conferencing and gateway capabilities

- Ten hot-swappable option slots (one supervisor blade and up to nine feature blades)

- Active environmental monitoring

- Support for integration with Cisco TelePresence Management Suite (TMS)

- Support for integration with Cisco Video Communication Server (VCS)

- Support for integration with Cisco Unified Communications Manager (CUCM)

- Multiple and interchangeable functions, including media and gateway blades

The following feature blades are available for the Cisco TelePresence MSE 8000 series chassis:

- **Cisco Supervisor MSE 8050:** for system management and configuration

- **Cisco TelePresence Server MSE 8710:** provides high-definition Cisco TelePresence Server

- **Cisco TelePresence MCU MSE 8510:** provides high-definition Cisco TelePresence MCU

- **Cisco TelePresence ISDN GW MSE 8321:** Interconnects ISDN networks with IP-based video conferencing solutions

- **Cisco TelePresence Serial GW MSE 8330:** Interconnects serial-based networks with IP-based video conferencing solutions

Depending on the blades, some feature blades can be grouped into a cluster on the Cisco TelePresence MSE 8000. The maximum number of feature blades per cluster differs per feature blade. The sections that follow discuss the various feature blades and their key characteristics.

Cisco TelePresence Server MSE 8710 Feature Blade

The Cisco TelePresence Server MSE 8710 blade is a high-definition-capable Cisco TelePresence Server that has the same interface as a Cisco TelePresence Server 7010. The Cisco TelePresence Server MSE 8710 and its setup in a Cisco Collaboration environment is shown in Figure 11-2.

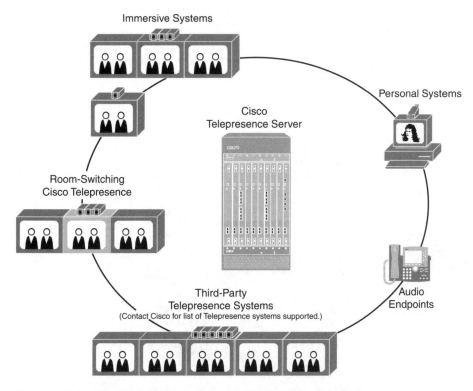

Figure 11-2   *Cisco TelePresence Server MSE 8710 Feature Blade*

The Cisco TelePresence Server MSE 8710 blade supports two management modes—locally or remotely managed. When an external device like Cisco TelePresence Conductor controls the MSE 8710 blade, the remotely managed mode is used. In remotely managed mode, most of the configuration resides at the external device.

The capacity of the blade depends on the management mode:

- **Locally managed mode:** This management mode supports 12 full high-definition (1080p30) participants or 24 high-definition (720p30) participants.

- **Remotely managed mode:** This management mode supports 12 full high-definition (1080p30) participants, 24 high-definition (720p30) participants, 48 standard-definition (480p30) participants, or 97 low-definition (360p) participants

Note   Non-HD ports are only available in remotely managed mode, where Cisco TelePresence Conductor controls the Cisco TelePresence Server MSE 8710 blade.

You can group up to four 8710 blades in a cluster, resulting in a maximum of 48 full high-definition participants, 96 high-definition participants, or 192 standard-definition participants per cluster. The total number of participants per cluster is limited to 200. The maximum number of participants per conference is limited to 104.

Cisco TelePresence MCU MSE 8510 Feature Blade

The Cisco TelePresence MCU MSE 8510 blade is a high-definition multimedia Cisco TelePresence Multiparty Conferencing Unit (MCU). Figure 11-3 illustrates an MCU MSE 8510 in a Cisco video conferencing setup.

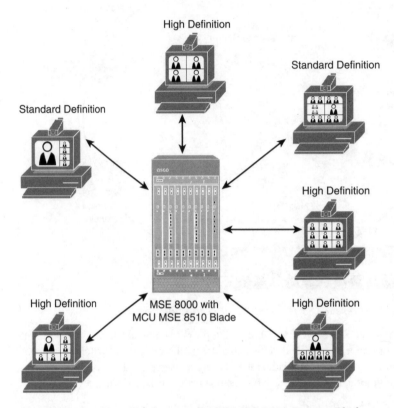

Figure 11-3 *Cisco TelePresence MCU MSE 8510 Feature Blade*

When locally managed, the TelePresence MCU MSE 8510 can be configured in one of the following modes:

- HD mode, which supports 20 video ports with full high-definition (1080p30) or high-definition (720p60) and 20 audio-only ports.

- SD mode (448p30), which supports 80 video ports.

The mode configuration is a system-wide setting. The whole blade can only be in one mode or the other. If the blade is in HD mode, then each endpoint receives the highest quality that the endpoint supports (up to 1080p30), but regardless of the quality that is actually used, one of the 20 high-definition ports is consumed in HD mode. This situation applies to standard-definition participants, to participants that are only capable of low resolution (360p), and to audio-only participants.

Because of this limitation, a single audio-only conference with 20 participants occupies a full Cisco TelePresence MSE 8510 MCU blade when the multipoint control unit is in HD mode. If you want to support endpoints with different capabilities in a more efficient way, use Cisco TelePresence Conductor for remotely managed mode, which allows better resource utilization of Cisco TelePresence MCUs.

Up to three Cisco TelePresence MCU MSE 8510 blades can be grouped into a cluster that provides 60 high-definition ports and 60 audio-only ports or 240 standard-definition ports per cluster. When nine blades are in a Cisco TelePresence MCU MSE 8000 chassis, up to 180 high-definition and 180 audio-only ports or up to 720 standard-definition ports are available.

If you need more than 60 participants in a single conference, you can cascade two conferences that reside on different clusters. Cascading means that one conference must call the other conference (by its conference number).

Cisco TelePresence ISDN MSE 8321 Feature Blade

The Cisco TelePresence ISDN GW MSE 8321 is a high-capacity and scalable blade. It provides seamless integration between IP and ISDN networks with feature transparency offering high-definition video conferencing for organizations using ISDN. Figure 11-4 shows the Cisco TelePresence ISDN MSE 8321 Feature Blade in action.

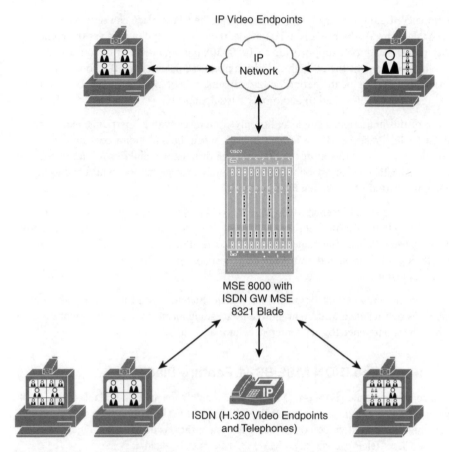

Figure 11-4 *Cisco TelePresence ISDN MSE 8321 Feature Blade*

The Cisco TelePresence ISDN MSE 8321 feature blade has following features:

- H.239 for presentation-sharing capabilities

- Video resolutions up to high definition 720p at 30fps

- Support for up to 8 PRI ISDN ports in a single blade and up to 72 PRI ISDN ports in a single chassis

- Support for up to 240 voice calls at 64 Kbps per blade and up to 120 video calls at 128 Kbps per blade

- Bandwidth per call from 56 Kbps to 2 Mbps

Note A maximum of eight Cisco TelePresence ISDN GW MSE 8321 blades can be supported in one Cisco TelePresence MSE 8000 chassis. The remaining ninth slot can be used by any other feature blade.

Cisco TelePresence Serial MSE 8330 Feature Blade

Cisco TelePresence Serial MSE 8330 allows transparent integration between IP and serial video conferencing networks. This blade is highly scalable, offering feature transparency and powerful dial-plan capabilities. It allows organizations using networks attached through serial interfaces leverage the benefits from IP-based HD video conferencing solutions. Figure 11-5 shows a Cisco TelePresence Serial MSE 8330 Feature Blade as broker between the serial and IP networks.

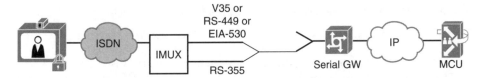

Figure 11-5   *Cisco TelePresence Serial MSE 8330 Feature Blade*

The Cisco TelePresence Serial MSE 8330 feature blade has following key characteristics:

- Offers video resolutions up to HD 720p at 30 fps

- Supports up to 16 serial ports in a single blade and up to 144 serial ports in a single chassis

- Supports up to 16 video calls at 1920 kbps each, per blade

- Supports bandwidth per call from 56 to 1920 kbps

The next section describes Cisco TelePresence MSE 8000 configuration.

Cisco TelePresence MSE 8000 Feature Blade Configuration

This section explains how to enable access to Cisco TelePresence MSE 8000 feature blades. After you install the Cisco TelePresence MSE 8000 Series chassis and supervisor blade, you can configure the other feature blades in the chassis by using the supervisor web interface.

To access the web interface, follow these steps:

Step 1.   Navigate to *http://<IP address of the supervisor module>.*

Step 2.   Log into the system with a valid administrator username and password.

Step 3.   From the navigation pane, click the **Hardware** tab. The Blades window is displayed, which lists the available feature blades.

Step 4.   In the Type column, configure the IP address of the applicable feature blade.

Step 5.   Click the IP address of a feature blade to connect to the user interface of the feature blade. The user interface of the feature blade depends on the type of feature blade (Cisco TelePresence Server or Cisco TelePresence MCU user interface).

Cisco Telepresence Server

The Cisco TelePresence Server is a transcoding device that offers flexible video, audio, and content-sharing capabilities for multiparty videoconferencing. The Cisco TelePresence Server can be integrated with the following video call control platforms:

- CUCM

- Cisco TelePresence Video Communication Server (VCS)

The integration can be either direct or via Cisco TelePresence Conductor.

The following is a list of supported platforms for the Cisco TelePresence Server:

- The Cisco TelePresence Server on Virtual Machine runs on the Cisco Unified Communications System or third-party specification-based server platforms. This option offers a virtualized solution.

- The Cisco TelePresence Server on Cisco Multiparty Media 310 and Cisco Multiparty Media 320 is an entry-level appliance solution that can be stacked for more capacity.

- The Cisco TelePresence Server on Cisco TelePresence Server MSE 8710 is a chassis-based platform that is ideal for large enterprises and service providers that require a high-availability and highly scalable solution. The Cisco TelePresence Server 7010 is a standalone appliance with the same characteristics.

- The Cisco TelePresence Server can also run on the Cisco TelePresence MCU MSE 8510 and on the Cisco TelePresence MCU 5300 Series platforms, with the appropriate license upgrade. These platforms usually run the Cisco TelePresence MCU application but can be changed to using the Cisco TelePresence Server application.

Note Feature support varies per platform.

Cisco TelePresence Server Licensing

This section describes the two license models available for Cisco TelePresence Server.

Table 11-1 shows the differences between Cisco Personal Multiparty and a screen license model.

Table 11-1 *Properties of Cisco TelePresence Server Models*

Feature and Function	Personal Multiparty	Screen License Model
Tied to a named host	Yes	No
Minimum order	25 Host Licenses	None
Restricted conference size	3 + 1 Ports	Limited
Number of conference IDs per named host	1	Limited
Requirement that host be present in the conference	Yes	Configurable
Maximum resolution	720p30 (HD)	1080p30 (Full HD)
Support for ad hoc escalation from CUCM	Yes	Yes
Conductor load balancing	User based licensing only	Support for port or user based licensing

Cisco Personal Multiparty is available within the Cisco Unified Workspace Licensing Professional package. For each license selected, one named host is entitled to provide multiparty meetings with up to three more parties, using a personalized contact address.

In the screen license model for the TPS 7010, one license enables one 1080p30 screen plus content sharing or two 720p30 screens plus content sharing. The maximum Cisco TelePresence Server capacity is achieved with 12 screen licenses. Twelve screen licenses support twelve 1080p30, twenty-four 720p30, forty-eight 480p30, or ninety-seven 360p30 screens.

Cisco TelePresence Server Features

Cisco TelePresence Server offers the features shown in Table 11-2.

Table 11-2 *Cisco TelePresence Server Features*

Feature	Function/Benefit
Cisco TelePresence ActivePresence.	Supports a full-screen immersive view of the primary speakers with an overlay of others in the call. It is designed to maximize the large-scale immersive experience and is available on all ports
Cisco TelePresence ActiveControl	Allows the participant lists and control conferences and layouts to be seen by the conference participant.

(Continued)

Table 11-2 *Continued*

Feature	Function/Benefit
Integration with Cisco TelePresence Management Suite	Manages conference booking, scheduling, and resources.
Integration with Cisco TelePresence Conductor	Supports Ad Hoc conferences for CUCM, remotely managed mode for Cisco TelePresence Server, and optimized conferencing.
The Cisco TelePresence Server on Cisco MSE 8710 or Cisco TelePresence Server 7010	Manages platforms locally while all other versions can be run only in remotely managed mode by Cisco TelePresence Conductor.
Cisco ClearPath	Provides improved media resilience in lossy networks for better video performance.
Cisco TelePresence ClearVision technology	Provides resolution enhancement by up to four times, enabling less-powerful PCs and video-conferencing endpoints to participate in calls at higher definitions.

Options for Integrating Cisco TelePresence Server with Cisco Unified Communications Manager

This section describes the options for integrating Cisco TelePresence Server with CUCM.

A Cisco TelePresence Server cannot be configured as a hardware conference bridge in CUCM. Therefore, the only way to support Ad Hoc and Meet-Me conferences on Cisco TelePresence Server is to control the Cisco TelePresence Server via Cisco TelePresence Conductor. Cisco TelePresence Conductor must be added as a hardware conference bridge media resource in such a scenario.

Rendezvous conferences can be supported directly by the Cisco TelePresence Server or via Cisco TelePresence Conductor. However, not all Cisco TelePresence Server platforms can be integrated with CUCM for rendezvous conferencing. For example, a virtualized Cisco TelePresence Server cannot be directly integrated with CUCM for rendezvous conferencing.

A Cisco TelePresence Server is in locally managed mode when it interacts directly with CUCM to support rendezvous conferences. Rendezvous conferences can also be provided via Cisco TelePresence Conductor in remotely managed mode. Ad Hoc and Meet-Me conferences are only supported in remotely managed mode.

These Cisco TelePresence Servers are supported by Cisco TelePresence Conductor:

- Cisco TelePresence Server 7010 version 3.0(2.46) or later version

- Cisco TelePresence Server MSE 8710 version 3.0(2.46) or later version

- Cisco TelePresence Server version 3.1 or later version on Virtual Machine

- Cisco TelePresence Server version 3.1 on Multiparty Media 310/320

> **Note**   Cisco TelePresence Server must be in locally managed mode to integrate directly with CUCM.

Rendezvous Call Flow with the Cisco TelePresence Server

This section shows the call flow when a rendezvous conference is initiated in an environment where the Cisco TelePresence Server is directly integrated with CUCM.

The following steps describe the call flow for rendezvous conferences.

Step 1.   An endpoint dials a rendezvous conference number.

Step 2.   CUCM matches a route pattern that points to a route list or an SIP trunk that refers to the Cisco TelePresence Server.

Step 3.   CUCM routes the call to the Cisco TelePresence Server via an SIP trunk.

Step 4.   The Cisco TelePresence Server matches the called number to a conference numeric ID.

Step 5.   The Cisco TelePresence Server starts the conference.

Step 6.   The Cisco TelePresence Server accepts the call that was received from CUCM.

Integrating Cisco TelePresence Server and Cisco Unified Communications Manager (CUCM)

This section describes how to integrate a Cisco TelePresence Server with CUCM. The Cisco TelePresence Server must be in locally managed mode to integrate directly with CUCM.

A Cisco TelePresence Server can be integrated with CUCM to support rendezvous video conferencing. Rendezvous conferences are supported only when a Cisco TelePresence Server is directly integrated with CUCM. Rendezvous conferences require a route pattern and an SIP trunk to be configured in CUCM. Ad Hoc and Meet-Me conferences are not supported when a Cisco TelePresence Server is directly integrated with CUCM. Scheduled conferences can be managed via Cisco TelePresence Management Suite (TMS) or directly through the Cisco TelePresence Server user interface.

> **Note**   A Cisco TelePresence Server that is used for scheduled conferences should not be used for rendezvous conferences in order to guarantee port availability for scheduled calls. Deploy separate, dedicated Cisco TelePresence Servers if you want to provide both scheduled conferences and rendezvous conferences.

Cisco TelePresence Server Configuration

The following steps show the Cisco TelePresence Server configuration:

Step 1.   Log into the web page of the Cisco TelePresence Server as an administrator and go to **Network > DNS**. Configure the DNS settings.

Step 2.   Go to **Network > Services** and check the Services. Enable Hypertext Transfer Protocol Secure (**HTTPS**) and disable **SIP (UDP)**, as shown in Figure 11-6.

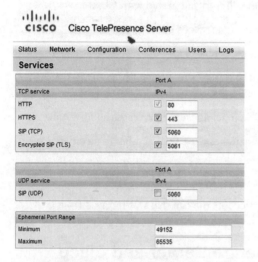

Figure 11-6   *Cisco TelePresence Server Services Configuration*

Note   To avoid longer delays in the detection of unresponsive peers, it is highly recommended to use SIP over Transmission Control Protocol (TCP) instead of SIP over User Datagram Protocol (UDP).

Step 3.   Choose **Configuration > Time** and configure the (NTP) Host with the IP address of the NTP server. Ensure that the network time is synced.

Step 4.   Choose **Configuration > SIP Settings** and click **Use Trunk** in the **Outbound Call Configuration** drop-down list. Enter the IP address of the CUCM in the **Outbound Address**. In the **Outbound Domain** field, enter the CUCM hostname or IP address that is configured in CUCM (under **CUCM Administration GUI > System > Server**) as shown in Figure 11-7.

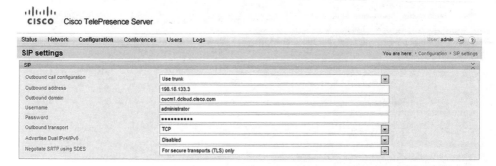

Figure 11-7 *Cisco TelePresence Server SIP Settings*

Step 5.   Proceed to **Conferences > Add New Conference**. Enter the conference name in the **Name** and the **ID** in the Numeric ID fields respectively.

> **Note**   The numeric ID must match the conference number that is dialed by the endpoint and then sent from the CUCM to the Cisco TelePresence Server via the SIP trunk.

Cisco Unified Communications Manager Configuration

This section describes CUCM configuration for integration with a Cisco TelePresence Server.

The following steps describe CUCM configuration for integration with a Cisco TelePresence Server.

Step 1.   Go to the CUCM Administration GUI, go to **Device > Trunk**, and create an SIP trunk. Enter the **Device Name** and click the **device pool** in the Device Pool drop-down list.

> **Note**   If you want to selectively choose nodes of a CUCM cluster, apply the corresponding Unified CM Group to the SIP trunk via the device pool. If you want to use all nodes of the cluster, check the **Run On All Active Unified CM Nodes** check box.

Step 2.   Under **SIP Information > Destination Address**, enter the IP address as shown in Figure 11-8 and set:

- **SIP Trunk Security Profile** as Non Secure SIP Trunk Profile
- **SIP Profile** as Standard SIP Profile for TelePresence Conferencing

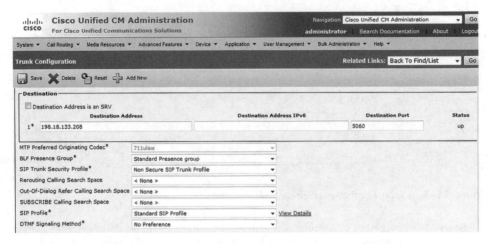

Figure 11-8 *CUCM TelePresence Server SIP Trunk Settings*

Step 3.   To route rendezvous calls to Cisco TelePresence, a route pattern is required. Go to **Call Routing > Route/Hunt > Route Pattern** and create a route pattern that points to the SIP trunk configured in Step 2. In the Route Pattern field, enter the route pattern that matches the pattern that is configured as the conference numeric ID at the Cisco TelePresence Server.

Note · If you do not want to allow all devices to call the rendezvous conference number, apply a partition to the route pattern and then implement calling search spaces (CSSs) as needed.

Cisco TelePresence Conductor

Cisco TelePresence Server and Cisco TelePresence MCU are high-performance and scalable conferencing resources, but they do have some limitations regarding consolidated management, optimal license utilization, and integration support with CUCM. Cisco TelePresence Conductor is a platform that solves these issues by simplifying and enhancing management of Cisco TelePresence conferencing resources. Figure 11-9 gives an overview of Cisco TelePresence Conductor and its place in the Cisco Collaboration network.

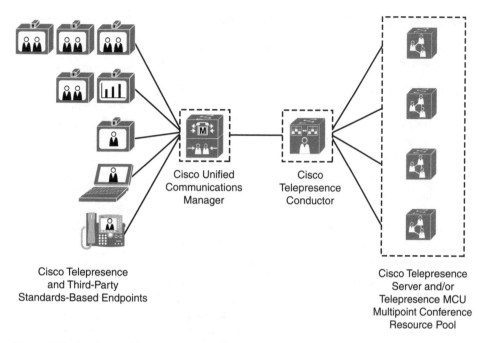

Figure 11-9   *Cisco TelePresence Conductor Overview*

As seen in Figure 11-9, Cisco TelePresence Conductor simplifies multiparty video communications by orchestrating the different resources that are needed for each conference. Cisco TelePresence Conductor simplifies and enhances conference resource management, and makes conferences easy to join and administer. It uses knowledge of all available conferencing resources and their capabilities to help ensure dynamic and intelligent conference placement and optimum resource usage.

The Cisco TelePresence Conductor works with the following video call control platforms:

- CUCM

- Cisco VCS

Cisco TelePresence Conductor is available as a dedicated appliance and as a virtualized application that runs on Cisco Unified Computing System (Cisco UCS) platforms or third-party server platforms. The appliance has four 10/100/1000 BASE-TX Ethernet ports, and one RS-232 console port. Each Cisco TelePresence Conductor supports up to 30 Cisco TelePresence MCUs or Cisco TelePresence Servers for up to 2400 calls. For even greater resilience, up to three Cisco TelePresence Conductors can be stacked in a cluster.

Cisco TelePresence Conductor Licensing

Three types of licenses are supported on Cisco Telepresence Conductor. Depending on the deployment size, the following license options are available:

- **Cisco TelePresence Conductor Essentials:** Cisco TelePresence Conductor software can be downloaded as a virtualized application and installed without a license key in a limited-capacity mode. This license option enables conference resource orchestration for a single, standalone Cisco TelePresence Server or Cisco TelePresence MCU.

- **Cisco TelePresence Conductor Select:** For small to medium-sized deployments, a license key is available that enables support for up to 50 concurrent calls. This license option enables conference resource orchestration for more than one Cisco TelePresence Server and Cisco TelePresence MCU. Two medium-sized Cisco TelePresence Conductor virtual machines supporting up to 50 concurrent call sessions can be configured as a cluster to provide resilience.

- **Cisco TelePresence Conductor:** For larger deployments, a full-capacity version of Cisco TelePresence Conductor is required. Up to 2400 concurrent calls or up to 30 Cisco TelePresence Servers or Cisco TelePresence MCUs are supported by one full-capacity Cisco TelePresence Conductor appliance or cluster. Up to three full-capacity Cisco TelePresence Conductors can be clustered to provide resilience.

Note   The version of Cisco TelePresence Conductor is determined by the installed license keys (option keys and release keys).

Table 11-3 gives an overview of Cisco TelePresence Conductor licensing options.

Table 11-3   *Cisco TelePresence Conductor License Options*

	Conductor Essentials	**Conductor Select**	**Conductor**
Deployment size	Small	Small to medium	Medium to large
Number of conference bridges	1 (standalone)	30	30
Concurrent call sessions	Number of calls supported by the conference bridge	50	2400
Clustering	No	Yes	Yes
Access to TAC	No	Yes	Yes
Deployment option	VM only	VM only	VM and appliance

Cisco TelePresence Conductor Features

This section describes the features of Cisco TelePresence Conductor. Table 11-4 illustrates the main features that are provided by Cisco TelePresence Conductor.

Table 11-4 *Features and Benefits of Cisco TelePresence Conductor*

Features	Description
Conference bridge support.	Supports Cisco TelePresence Server and Cisco TelePresence MCU.
Conference virtualization	Dynamically selects the most appropriate Cisco TelePresence conferencing resources for each new conference.
Resource management	Provides intelligent resource orchestration and load balancing.
Customizable templates	Handles different demands and service entitlements of conference attendees by providing customizable templates that define the exact characteristics of a conference and are tailored for the participants.
Conference personalization	Helps ensure that the conferencing experience is tailored to meet the personal preferences of each user for settings such as layout and PINs.
Support for rendezvous conferences	Supports rendezvous conferences with additional options and modes: ■ **Meeting:** There is just one type of participant, and all participants are given the same priority. ■ **Lecture:** There are two types of participants with different priority levels. Each participant type has a different alias to dial into the conference. ■ **Role configuration for conference attendees:** Roles include chairperson, guest, and participant.
Support for Ad Hoc and Meet-Me conferences	Can be configured as a hardware conference bridge in CUCM media resource configuration. In contrast to rendezvous conferences, media resource groups and media resource group lists apply to such a conference. No route pattern is required for Ad Hoc and Meet-Me conferences in CUCM.

Options for Integrating Cisco TelePresence Conferencing Resources

This section describes the options for integrating Cisco TelePresence conferencing resources and CUCM when using Cisco TelePresence Conductor.

A Cisco TelePresence MCU can be configured as a hardware conference bridge in CUCM to support Ad Hoc and Meet-Me conferences. In this scenario, the Cisco TelePresence MCU is seen as a CUCM media resource. No route pattern is required.

The same implementation option can be achieved by configuring Cisco TelePresence Conductor as the hardware conference bridge media resource in CUCM and then associating the Cisco TelePresence MCU with Cisco TelePresence Conductor. The advantages of such a configuration include centralized management of Cisco TelePresence MCUs and more efficient license utilization.

CUCM can use a Cisco TelePresence MCU for rendezvous conferences. From the CUCM perspective, a rendezvous conference is not a conference, but calls that are placed to the conference number of the rendezvous conference are routed like any other call. No media resource is configured in CUCM, but a route pattern and an SIP trunk are required. The SIP trunk points directly to the Cisco TelePresence MCU or to the Cisco TelePresence Conductor, which then controls the Cisco TelePresence MCU.

A Cisco TelePresence MCU is in locally managed mode when it interacts directly with CUCM. The Cisco TelePresence MCU interacts directly with CUCM as a hardware conference bridge media resource to support CUCM Ad Hoc and Meet-Me conferences or as an SIP peer to support rendezvous conferences.

A Cisco TelePresence MCU is in remotely managed mode when it is controlled by Cisco TelePresence Conductor. In such a deployment, the Cisco TelePresence MCU does not directly communicate with CUCM.

When CUCM is not integrated with Cisco TelePresence Conductor, separate Cisco TelePresence MCUs are required to support Ad Hoc, Meet-Me, and rendezvous conferences. When CUCM is integrated with Cisco TelePresence Conductor, requests for Ad Hoc, Meet-Me, and rendezvous conferences are received by the Cisco TelePresence Conductor and can be passed on to a single Cisco TelePresence MCU.

The following Cisco TelePresence MCUs are supported by Cisco TelePresence Conductor:

- Cisco TelePresence MCU 4200 Series version 4.2 or later version

- Cisco TelePresence MCU 4500 Series version 4.2 or later version

- Cisco TelePresence MCU 5300 Series version 4.3(2.17) or later version

- Cisco TelePresence MCU MSE 8420 version 4.2 or later version

- Cisco TelePresence MCU MSE 8510 version 4.2 or later version

Ad Hoc and Rendezvous Call Flows with Cisco TelePresence Conductor

The following sections describe the Ad Hoc conference and rendezvous conference call flows when Cisco TelePresence Conductor is integrated with Cisco TelePresence and CUCM.

Ad Hoc or Meet-Me Call Flow with Cisco TelePresence Conductor

This section describes the call flows when an Ad Hoc or Meet-Me conference is set up via Cisco TelePresence Conductor, and is illustrated in the following steps.

Step 1.   Once a call from one endpoint to another is connected, the caller or called party can tap the Add+ button and call a third endpoint, followed by tapping the Merge or Join button to connect all parties

Step 2.   Alternatively, an endpoint can join a Meet-Me conference by using join function.

Step 3.   While the conference is being requested, CUCM checks the Media Resource Group List (MRGL) of the endpoint that initiates the conference and allocates Cisco TelePresence Conductor as the media resource for the conference.

Step 4.   CUCM sends a request for a conference bridge to the Cisco TelePresence Conductor via the SIP trunk.

Step 5.   Cisco TelePresence Conductor accepts the request and creates a conference.

Step 6.   The call is routed to the allocated conference bridge, and an Instant Meeting is established.

In Cisco TelePresence Conductor, the conference is allocated as shown in the following steps:

Step 1.   Cisco TelePresence Conductor uses a conference template to obtain parameters that will be applied to the conference. In the conference template, the service preference is also configured.

Step 2.   The configured service preference is used to select a conference bridge pool based on configured priorities.

Step 3.   The selected conference bridge pool is used to search for a conference bridge.

Step 4.   The first available conference bridge of the pool is used to create the conference.

Rendezvous Call Flow with Cisco TelePresence Conductor

This section describes the call flow when a rendezvous conference is set up via Cisco TelePresence Conductor. The call flow is as follows:

Step 1. An endpoint dials a rendezvous conference number.

Step 2. CUCM matches a route pattern, which refers to an SIP trunk. The SIP trunk points to Cisco TelePresence Conductor.

Step 3. CUCM routes the call to the Cisco TelePresence Conductor via an SIP trunk.

Step 4. Cisco TelePresence Conductor matches the called number to a conference alias and creates a conference.

Step 5. The call is routed to the conference bridge.

In Cisco TelePresence Conductor, the conference is allocated as shown in the following steps:

Step 1. Cisco TelePresence Conductor matches the called number to a configured conference alias pattern.

Step 2. Cisco TelePresence Conductor uses the parameters of a conference template to create a conference.

Step 3. The service preference that is configured in the conference template is used to select a conference bridge pool based on the configured priorities.

Step 4. The conference bridge pool is used to select an available conference bridge for the conference.

Step 5. The conference is created on the selected conference bridge.

Note   The conference template can contain auto-dialed participants that are automatically added to the conference. This ability is often used when conference recording is needed for a particular rendezvous conference.

You can confirm that Conductor is able to dynamically create a new permanent meeting. While in the call, go to the Conductor and login as administrator. Proceed to **Status > Conferences**. Expand the meeting and observe the information available in Conductor.

Alternatively, you can also view the conference details via Cisco TelePresence Server. Go to the Cisco TelePresence Server GUI and log in as administrator. Go to **Conferences > Conferences** and click on the **active meeting**. Click **Expand all** to see live screenshots of the send and receive video streams.

Integrating Cisco TelePresence Conductor and Cisco Unified Communications Manager

This section covers integration of the Cisco TelePresence Server, TelePresence Conductor, and CUCM to support Ad Hoc and rendezvous conferencing.

Cisco TelePresence Server Configuration

This section covers the configuration of Cisco TelePresence Server for integration with Cisco TelePresence Conductor.

Step 1. For the TelePresence Conductor to communicate with the TelePresence Server, it uses credentials for a user account that has administrator rights. Go to Cisco TelePresence GUI and go to **Users > Add new user** and click **New**. Add a user with **API access** as shown in Figure 11-10.

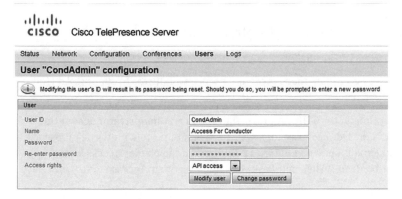

Figure 11-10 *Cisco TelePresence Server User Configuration*

Step 2. Go to **Network > Services**. Check the box next to 443 and and click **Apply changes**.

Step 3. Go to **Configuration > SIP settings** and configure **Outbound address** as address for Conductor, **Outbound domain**, and **Outbound Transport** as TLS as shown in Figure 11-11. Click Apply changes.

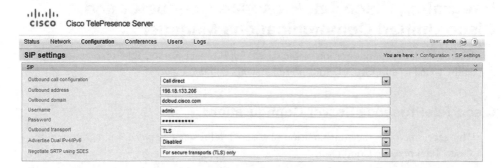

Figure 11-11 *Cisco TelePresence SIP Settings*

At this time, the Cisco TelePresence Server is configured for integration with Cisco TelePresence Conductor. The next section describes Cisco TelePresence Conductor configuration for integration with the Cisco TelePresence Server and CUCM.

Cisco TelePresence Conductor Configuration

This section describes Cisco TelePresence Conductor configuration.

Follow these steps to configure the Cisco TelePresence Conductor to support Ad Hoc and rendezvous conferences.

Step 1.   Go to Conductor GUI and proceed to **Users > Administrator accounts.** Click **New.** Define a user for CUCM to communicate with the TelePresence Conductor as shown in Figure 11-12. Provide the **Name, Access level** (must be Read-Write), and **Password,** then set **Web Access** to **No.** Click **Save.**

Figure 11-12 *Cisco TelePresence Conductor User Configuration*

Step 2.   Set up the system DNS and NTP by browsing **to System > DNS** and **System > Time** respectively. Ensure that Network Time is synchronized.

Step 3.   Conductor needs additional IP addresses that will be associated with the Ad Hoc (instant meeting) and rendezvous (permanent meeting) conferences.

To configure the second and third Network Interface Cards (NICs), go to **System > IP** and under **Additional address for LAN 1** click **New**. Provide second and third IP addresses as shown in Figure 11-13.

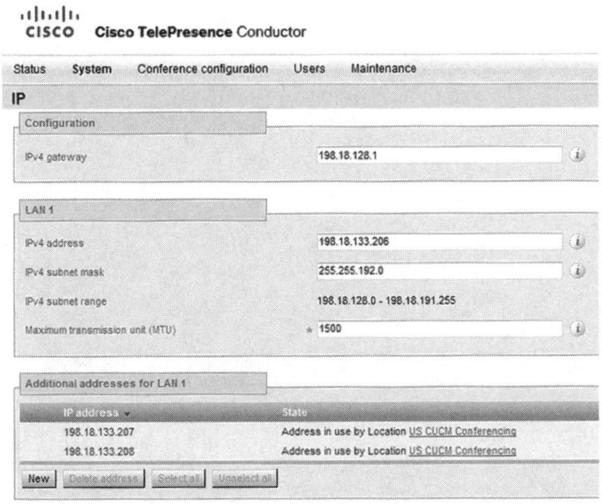

Figure 11-13   *IP Address Allocation for Ad Hoc and Rendezvous Conferences*

Step 4.   Go to **Conference configuration > Conference bridge pools** and click **New**. Define the **Pool name** and set the **Conference bridge type** as TelePresence Server, as shown in Figure 11-14. Click **Create pool**.

Figure 11-14   *Conference Bridge Pool Configuration*

Step 5.   Click **Create conference bridge** to add the conference bridge to the newly created TelePresence Server's bridge pool as illustrated in Figure 11-15. Click **Create conference bridge**.

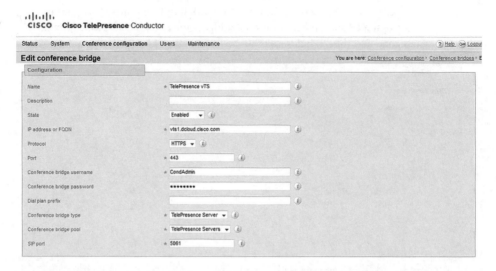

Figure 11-15 *Conference Bridge Configuration*

Note   Once the conference bridge is defined, ensure that under pool section in the Status column it shows up as Active. For example, the conference bridge TelePresence vTS is listed as Active, as shown in Figure 11-14 in Step 4.

> **Step 7.**   Go to **Conference configuration > Service Preferences** and click **New**. Provide **Service Preference name**, **Description**, and **Conference bridge type** (set as TelePresence) as shown in Figure 11-16. Click **Add Service Preference**. Under Pool name, choose TelePresence Servers and click **Add selected pool**. Click **Save**.

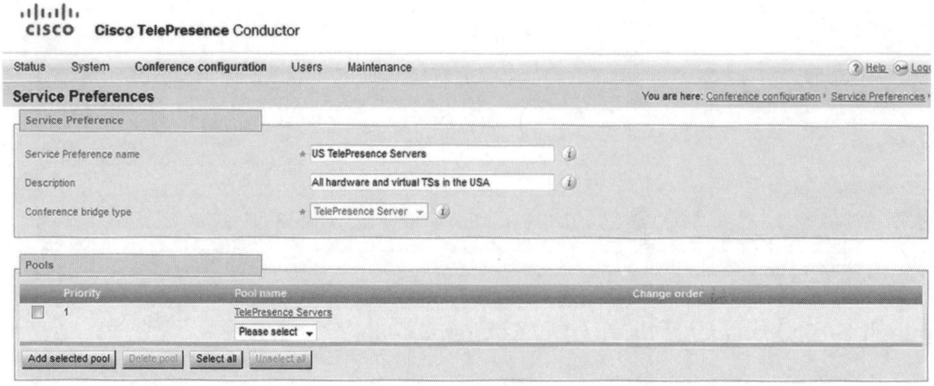

Figure 11-16 *Service Preference Configuration*

Step 8.   Templates are required to define conference configuration parameters. To create an instant meeting template, go to **Conference Configuration > Conference templates** and click **New**. As shown in Figure 11-17, enter the **Name, Service preference,** and **Content quality details**. Click **Create conference template**. Click **New**.

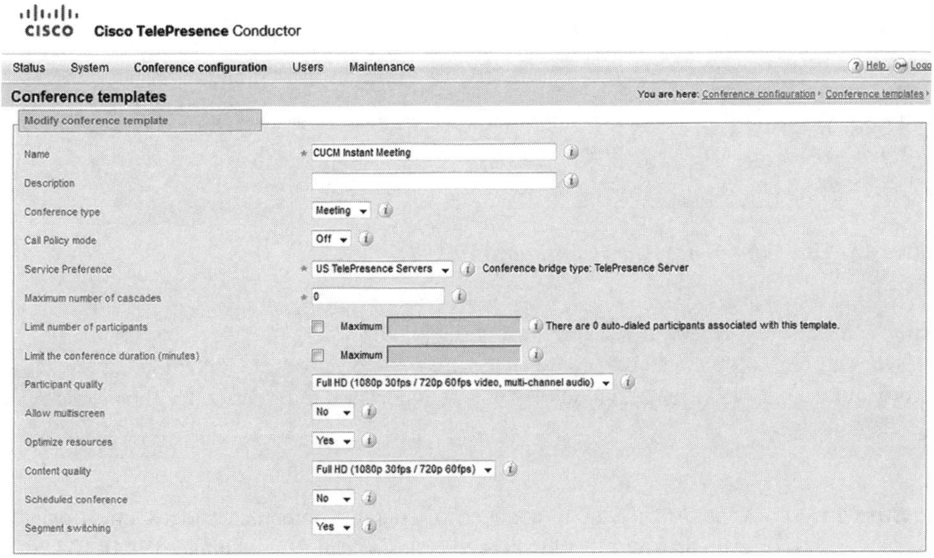

Figure 11-17   *Conference Template Configuration*

Step 9.   To add a permanent conference template, click **Create conference template**. As in Step 8, define the various parameters. Define the rendezvous conference so it can be recognized by a distinctive name, for example, CUCM Rendezvous Conference.

Step 10.   To invoke a conference template, a conference alias is required. The conference alias can be a string, SIP URI, or a DN, dialed by the endpoint to get to the conference. Go to **Conference configuration > Conference aliases** and click **New**. Provide the **Name, Description, Incoming Alias (must use regex), Conference name,** and **Conference template** as shown in Figure 11-18. Click **Save**.

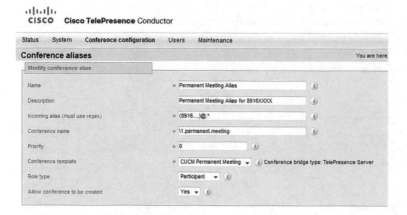

Figure 11-18   *Conference Alias Configuration*

Note   In an instant meeting escalation, using the join button on the video endpoint escalates a point to point call to a conference with three or more attendees; the conference alias is not used. CUCM tells Conductor the conference alias information for the instant meeting.

Step 11.   Locations are needed to connect to separate conference bridges. Locations correlate different IP addresses to types of calls; for example, 198.18.133.207 was used for Ad Hoc conferences and 192.18.133.208 for rendezvous conferences. To create a location, go to **Conference configuration > Locations** and click **New**. Provide information for **Location name, Description, Conference type** (should be set to Both), **Ad hoc IP address (local), Template, Rendezvous IP Address (local),** and **Trunk IP address** as shown in Figure 11-19. Click **Add location**.

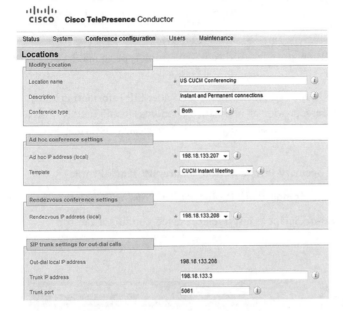

Figure 11-19 *Conference Location Configuration*

Step 12. Go to **Conference configuration > Conference bridge pools**, and then click the **TelePresence Servers** link. Select the **Location** that was defined in Step 11. Click **Save**.

Note   This links the bridge pools to the location for Conductor autodial participants.

This completes the Cisco TelePresence Conductor configuration. The next section addresses CUCM configuration for supporting Ad Hoc and rendezvous video conferencing calls.

CUCM Configuration

CUCM can be configured to use one or more SIP trunks to Cisco TelePresence Conductor so different trunks can be used for rendezvous (permanent meeting) and for Ad Hoc (instant meeting) conferences.

Note   Using one or more trunks, CUCM can receive or place voice, video, and encrypted calls; exchange real-time event information; and communicate in other ways with call control servers and other external servers.

Follow these steps to configure CUCM to support Ad Hoc and rendezvous conferences.

> **Note**   These steps are common for Ad Hoc and rendezvous conferencing trunks.

Step 1.   Go to **Device > Trunk** and click **Add New**. The trunk type should be **SIP**; click **Next**.

Step 2.   Provide a **Device Name** and **Device Pool**, and under **SIP Information > Destination Address**, provide an alternative IP address (configured for LAN 1 in previous section for Ad Hoc/rendezvous conferences), as shown in Figure 11-20:

■ Set **SIP Trunk Security Profile** as **Non Secure SIP Trunk Profile**

■ Set **SIP Profile** as **Standard SIP Profile for TelePresence Conferencing**

■ Set **Normalization Script** as **cisco-telepresence-conductor-interop**

Click **Save**.

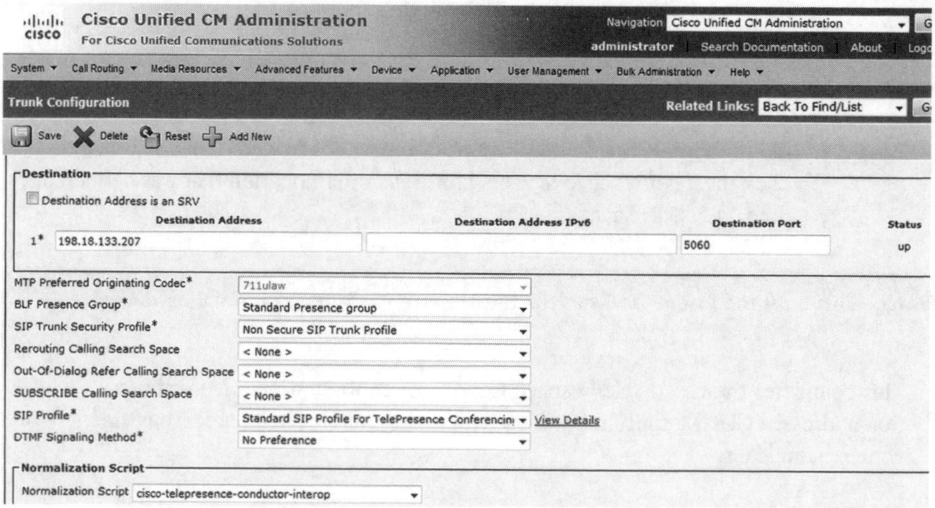

Figure 11-20   *CUCM to TelePresence Conductor SIP Trunk*

Step 3.   Define a route pattern for rendezvous (permanent meetings) conferences. Go to **Call Routing > Route/Hunt > Route Pattern**, and then click **Add New**. Enter the **Route Pattern** (for example, 8916XXXX), and for **Gateway/Route List** choose the Rendezvous SIP Trunk configured in Step 2.

Step 4.   Go to **Media Resources > Conference Bridge** and click **Add New**. Enter the **Conference Bridge Type** as Cisco TelePresence Conductor, **Conference Bridge Name**, **SIP Trunk**, **Username**, and **Password** as shown in Figure 11-21. Click **Save**.

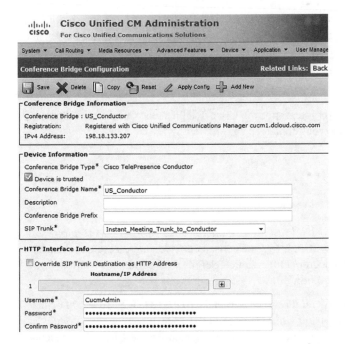

Figure 11-21 *CUCM TelePresence Conductor Conference Resource Configuration*

Step 5.   Go to **Media Resources > Media Resource Group** and create an MRG with
the Cisco TelePresence Conductor defined in the previous step. Finally, go
to **Media Resources > Media Resource Group List** to create an MRGL, and
add the MRG to it. This MRGL can be assigned to device pool or to the video
endpoints.

At this time, Ad Hoc and rendezvous meetings can be established from video endpoints.

Chapter Summary

The following list summarizes the key points discussed in this chapter:

- Cisco has a wide portfolio to support video conferencing. This includes the Cisco
  TelePresence MSE 8000 series (with feature blades), Cisco TelePresence Server with
  native CUCM integration, Cisco TelePresence Conductor integrated with CUCM
  and Cisco TelePresence Server, and Cisco TelePresence Management Server–based
  conferencing.

- The Cisco TelePresence MSE 8000 series offers enterprise-grade video conferencing
  and options to enterprises with and without IP capabilities.

- Cisco TelePresence Server is a scalable platform that offers both Ad Hoc (with Cisco
  TelePresence Conductor) and rendezvous conferencing.

- Cisco TelePresence Conductor is an enterprise-grade video conferencing solution that works with Cisco TelePresence Server, Cisco Video Communication Server, and CUCM.

- Cisco TelePresence Server direct integration with CUCM supports only rendezvous conferencing.

- Cisco TelePresence Server integration via Cisco TelePresence Conductor supports both Ad Hoc and rendezvous conferencing.

References

For additional information, refer to the following:

Cisco Systems, Inc. *Cisco TelePresence Conductor with Unified CM Deployment Guide, Release XC2.3 & 10.0*, http://www.cisco.com/c/dam/en/us/td/docs/telepresence/infrastructure/conductor/config_guide/TelePresence-Conductor-Unified-CM-Deployment-Guide-XC2-3.pdf.

Cisco Systems, Inc. *Cisco TelePresence Server 7010 and MSE 8710 V3.0 Locally Managed Mode Deployment Guide*, September 2014.http://www.cisco.com/c/dam/en/us/td/docs/telepresence/infrastructure/ts/deployment_guide/Cisco_TelePresence_Server_Deployment_Guide.pdf.

Cisco Systems, Inc. Configuring Video Conferences and Video Transcoding, September 2014.http://www.cisco.com/c/en/us/td/docs/voice_ip_comm/cucme/feature/guide/Video-trans-conf.pdf.

Cisco Systems, Inc. Cisco Collaboration Systems 10.x Solution Reference Network Designs (SRND), May 2014. http://www.cisco.com/c/en/us/td/docs/voice_ip_comm/cucm/srnd/collab10/collab10.html

Review Questions

Use the questions here to review what you learned in this chapter. The correct answers are found in Appendix A, "Answers to the Review Questions."

1. Which of the following blades offers Full HD conferencing for up to 20 participants resources and acts as a codec translator?

   a. 8510

   b. 8710

   c. Conductor

   d. 310

2. Which of the following is the maximum number of HD multipoint participants supported by the MSE 8000?

   a. 100

   b. 96

   c. 700

   d. 180

3. What is the highest support bandwidth of the MSE 8000?

   a. 10 Mbps

   b. 100 Mbps

   c. 1 Gbps

   d. 10 Gbps

4. Which feature provides greater resiliency in a lossy network?

   a. Cisco ClearPath

   b. Cisco ClearVision

   c. Enhanced QoS

   d. ActiveControl

   e. Conductor Remote Management

5. Which of the following is required between CUCM and the TelePresence Server?

   a. IP tunnel

   b. MGCP gateway

   c. H.323 gateway

   d. SIP trunk

6. True or false? The Cisco TelePresence Server can run in a virtual machine.

   a. True

   b. False

7. How many calls can a Cisco TelePresence Conductor support?

   a. 4000

   b. 2400

   c. 800

   d. 1024

   e. 720

8. To set characteristics of the call layout, switching and presentation modes, which of the following should be applied?

   a. Layout guides

   b. Templates

   c. Lecture sets

   d. Conference configuration sets

9. True or false? Rendezvous calls are viewed as conferences to CUCM.

   a. True

   b. False

10. A rendezvous call is pointed to what resource by CUCM in the call routing process?

   a. H.323 gateway

   b. Device pool

   c. Translation pattern

   d. Route pattern

Chapter 12

Quality of Service in Cisco Collaboration Solutions

Cisco Collaboration solutions enable users to leverage the power of true collaborative network with voice, video, data, and associated services available on same network. However, when voice and video are converged with data, it is essential to understand the impact of such a mix: that is, the impact on quality of voice/video communications. Voice and video streams are real time and need to be treated differentially compared to data. This is where quality of service (QoS) helps prioritize real-time traffic and overcome a number of traffic flow issues.

Chapter Objectives

Upon completing this chapter, you will be able to meet the following objectives:

- Describe the requirements for quality of service by identifying issues affecting packet networks carrying voice and video traffic.

- Describe the need for quality of service in converged networks.

- Describe the quality of service requirements for voice and video traffic.

- Describe classification and marking.

- Describe the DiffServ model.

- Describe queuing.

- Describe traffic policing and shaping.

- Describe Medianet for video QoS.

- Describe voice and video traffic bandwidth calculation.

An Introduction to Converged Networks

Before the convergence of data and real-time traffic, the focus was on connectivity. With voice and data flows coming together into the network and data trying to utilize as much bandwidth as possible at any given time, voice packets are impacted.

> **Note**   Data traffic is bursty by nature, whereas voice traffic can be consistent (audio) or bursty (video).

Data protocols that were developed as networks proliferated have adapted to the bursty nature of data networks, and brief network congestion is survivable for many types of traffic streams. For example, when you retrieve email, a delay of a few seconds is generally not noticeable. Even a delay of minutes is annoying but not unexpected, and depending on the infrastructure between the endpoints and email servers, is generally not viewed as a critical failure. Furthermore, if a data stream loses a few packets, because of TCP-based connectivity the lost packets can be retransmitted.

On the other hand, as applications such as voice and video became more common, separate networks were built to accommodate the differing traffic flows. Because each application had different traffic characteristics and requirements, network designers deployed nonintegrated networks, such as a data network, and an ISDN network for video traffic. Converged networks bring the traffic together, sharing the same network infrastructure to carry the various data flows.

With the prevalence of converged networks, the demand for quality of service mechanisms is readily apparent as voice and video traffic cannot tolerate delay, jitter and packet loss as they traverse the network. Without these QoS measures, voice and video traffic drops packets, and conversations become useless. There has been an expectation when picking up a phone to have a clear and uninterrupted conversation, and as video conferencing has gained adoption, the same expectation is applied.

Data packets on the other hand, are typically large and can survive delays and drops. It is possible to retransmit part of a dropped data file, but it is not feasible to retransmit a part of a voice or video conversation. Therefore, data traffic is often shaped and set to a lower priority through QoS mechanisms. Since the access for data or voice packets is on a first-come, first-served basis, depending on the number of users, applications, and data or voice flows accessing the network at any given time; voice is susceptible to delay, packet loss, and other issues.

Even a brief network outage on a converged network can seriously disrupt business operations. With inadequate preparation of the network, voice transmission can be choppy to unintelligible. Gaps in speech or video frames are particularly troublesome and noticeable. Silence for audio, and dropped packet frames in video are frustrating to users, and in certain applications cause issues such as in voice-mail systems, where silence is a problem.

Quality of Service Overview

The role and goal of quality of service (QoS) is to provide better and more predictable network service with dedicated bandwidth, controlled jitter and latency, and improved loss characteristics as required by the applications and traffic types. QoS achieves these goals by providing tools for managing network congestion, shaping network traffic, using network segments more efficiently, and setting traffic policies across the network.

Note   QoS is not a substitute for bandwidth. If the network is congested, packets will be dropped. QoS allows for the control of traffic that must be dropped or delayed, and how and when traffic is handled during congestion.

Voice and video over IP traffic (VoIP) consists of two parts: media/bearer traffic and signaling traffic. Media traffic is based on Real-Time Transport Protocol (RTP), which runs on top of User Datagram Protocol (UDP). Signaling traffic is based on a number of protocols, such as Session Initiation Protocol (SIP), Skinny Client Control Protocol (SCCP), H.323 protocol, and Media Gateway Control Protocol (MGCP), and is TCP/UDP based. When an RTP packet is lost, recreating or retransmitting it is neither possible nor worthwhile. As the name suggests, RTP works in real time and is not worth restoring, since missing packets will not make sense when they arrive out of order (not in correct sequence) during a live conversation.

In today's converged networks where voice, video, and data coexist, it is important to treat voice and video traffic differently from data traffic, which is mostly TCP-based and is easily retransmitted without loss of quality. Quality of service (QoS) enables network administrators to leverage tools for providing special treatment for delay- and time-sensitive traffic such as voice. The network infrastructure must provide classification, policing, and scheduling services for multiple traffic classes.

A QoS policy is a network-wide definition of the specific levels of QoS that are assigned to different classes of network traffic. In a converged network, having a QoS policy is as important as having a security policy. A QoS policy is a definition of the QoS levels that are assigned across a network.

Three basic steps are involved in implementing QoS on a network:

Step 1.   Identify traffic and its requirements: Study the network to determine the type of traffic that is running on the network, and then determine the QoS requirements for the different types of traffic.

Step 2.   Group the traffic into classes with similar QoS requirements: As an example of these groupings, the voice and video traffic flows are put into dedicated classes with guaranteed bandwidth, and all of the data traffic is put into a best-effort class.

Step 3.   Define QoS policies to meet the QoS requirements for each traffic class: Voice traffic is given top priority and is always transmitted first. The video traffic is transmitted after voice but before the best-effort traffic, which is transmitted only when no other traffic is present.

Voice Quality Impacting Factors

This section explains the various factors that impair the quality of communications on converged networks. Voice and video quality is affected by the following three QoS factors:

- **Latency (delay):** The unwarranted delay in time required for a packet to traverse the network from source to destination

- **Jitter (delay variation):** Irregular time intervals in the arrival of packets

- **Packet loss:** Packets lost in transit from source to destination due to network congestion, link flapping, or other reasons

Figure 12-1 depicts the three factors discussed.

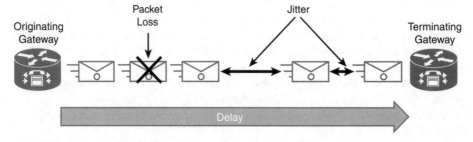

Figure 12-1   *Latency, Packet Loss, and Jitter*

Latency (delay) can cause degradation in voice quality. Latency should be kept under 150 ms of one-way or 300 ms round-trip time (RTT) for end-to-end (from mouth to ear) delay to ensures user satisfaction.

Jitter buffers are used to ascertain that variable delays are converted to constant delays. Adaptive jitter buffers can help overcome jitter issues by dynamically tuning the jitter buffer size to the lowest acceptable value.

Many sources of delay are introduced both during packet creation and transit from source to destination, as outlined in Table 12-1. Moreover, the delay can be either a fixed delay or a variable delay, depending on where it is introduced. Fixed delay adds to overall delay introduced from source to destination. Variable delay is a function of queues and buffers.

Table 12-1   *Sources of Delay During Voice Packet Formation and Transit*

Delay Type	Description
Coder delay	The time taken by a digital signal processor (DSP) to compress a block of pulse code modulated (PCM) samples. This is a fixed delay function for a certain endpoint with a certain codec.
Packetization delay	The time it takes to put a payload (encoded voice) into a voice packet and encapsulate it within IP, UDP, and RTP headers. It's a fixed delay function.

Queuing delay	The delay experienced as a frame is queued, waiting to be transmitted on a link. It's a variable delay function because the amount of delay depends on link speed and current traffic conditions.
Serialization delay	The time taken to put a frame on the wire from a network interface. It's a fixed delay function.
Propagation delay	The time taken for a bit to traverse a network link (from one end to the other). This is a fixed delay.
De-jitter delay	The delay experienced as a result of a de-jitter buffer on a receiving device (such as a Cisco IOS router) that eliminates any jitter between packets before they are sent out to their destination. It's a fixed delay function.

Voice and Video Traffic Characteristics and QoS Requirements

This section describes the traffic characteristics and various requirements for voice and video QoS.

Audio traffic has the following key characteristics:

- Bandwidth: Constant bitrate (smooth) with small footprint (small packet size)

- Loss sensitive

- Delay sensitive

Video traffic has following key characteristics:

- Bandwidth: Variable bitrate (bursty) with medium/large footprint

- Loss sensitive

- Delay sensitive

Figure 12-2 depicts the audio vs. video traffic relation between bandwidth and time.

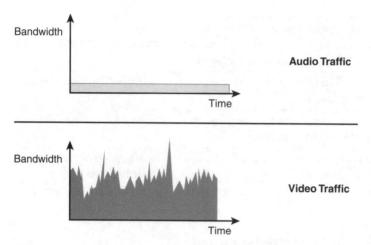

Figure 12-2 *Voice Audio and Video Traffic Characteristics*

Voice (Bearer) Traffic

The following list summarizes the key QoS requirements and recommendations for voice (bearer) traffic:

- Voice traffic should be marked to DSCP EF (46) per the QoS baseline and RFC 3246.

- Packet loss should be no more than 1 percent.

- One-way latency (mouth to ear) should be no more than 150 ms.

- Average one-way jitter should be targeted to be under 30 ms.

- A range of 21 to 320 kbps of guaranteed priority bandwidth is required per call (depending on the sampling rate, the VoIP codec, and Layer 2 media overhead).

- 150 bps + Layer 2 overhead guaranteed bandwidth should be provided for voice-control traffic per call.

Video (Bearer) Traffic

Video traffic can be categorized into three broad categories:

- Interactive/IP telephony video (videoconferencing)

- Streaming video (unicast or multicast)

- Immersive video (TelePresence)

Note CUCM supports different DSCP markings for immersive video traffic and videoconferencing (IP video telephony) traffic. By default, CUCM has preconfigured the recommended DSCP values for immersive video calls at CS4 and for IP video telephony calls at AF41.

When provisioning for interactive video (video conferencing) traffic, the following guidelines are recommended:

■ Interactive video traffic should be marked to DSCP AF41

■ Loss should be no more than 1 percent.

■ One-way latency should be no more than 150 ms.

■ Jitter should be no more than 30 ms.

■ Excess videoconferencing traffic can be marked down by a policer to AF42 or AF43.

■ Assign interactive video to either a preferential queue or a lower priority queue.

When provisioning QoS for streaming video traffic, follow these guidelines:

■ Streaming video (whether unicast or multicast) should be marked to DSCP AF31.

■ Loss should be no more than 5 percent.

■ Latency should be no more than 4 to 5 seconds (depending on the video application's buffering capabilities).

■ There are no significant jitter requirements.

■ Guaranteed bandwidth (CBWFQ) requirements depend on the encoding format and rate of the video stream.

■ Streaming video applications (unicast or multicast), apart from known sources in an organization, may be marked as Scavenger—DSCP CS1, implemented in the Scavenger traffic class and assigned a minimal bandwidth (CBWFQ) percentage. For example, video from YouTube may be treated this way.

Note   Streaming video applications have more tolerant QoS requirements, as they are not delay sensitive (the video can take several seconds to buffer) and are largely not sensitive to jitter (because of application buffering). However, streaming video might contain valuable content, such as e-learning applications or multicast company meetings, in which case it requires service guarantees.

Call Signaling Traffic

Call signaling traffic originally was marked to DSCP AF31. As defined in RFC 2597, for the assured forwarding classes, flows could be subject to markdown and aggressive dropping of marked-down values. Progressively, the DSCP marking has been changed to CS3 in-line with the QoS baseline marking recommendation for call signaling as defined in RFC 2474. The traffic flows are not subject to aggressive markdown and dropping in this DSCP class. The call signaling traffic protocols, such as SCCP, SIP, MGCP, and H.323, should be marked as DSCP CS3 (or legacy value of DSCP AF31 for backward compatibility).

The next section discusses the QoS deployment architectures.

QoS Implementation Overview

QoS can be implemented via Integrated Services (IntServ) or Differentiated Services (DiffServ) architectures. The IntServ architecture provides QoS by assuring treatment for a specific traffic flow. For example, IntServ has Resource Reservation Protocol (RSVP) as a QoS mechanism where each router on the path for packet transmission is informed of the upcoming packet stream and bandwidth is guaranteed in an end-to-end fashion before a call is setup between the calling and called endpoints.

The DiffServ architecture, on the other hand, differentiates/classifies various types of traffic and provides several levels of service based on that classification. Unlike IntServ, DiffServ labels packets with a particular priority marking that can be referenced by other network devices/applications and hence classified in various traffic classes to be treated accordingly.

To help deploy QoS for Collaboration (and converged) networks, Cisco provides a QoS toolkit composed of the following tools:

- Classification and marking

- Traffic policing

- Queuing

- Traffic shaping

Figure 12-3 illustrates the QoS order of operation at a high level.

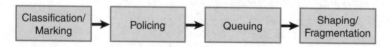

Figure 12-3   *QoS Order of Operation*

QoS operation largely depends on QoS policies provisioned in a network. It starts with classification and marking, followed by policing and queuing, and finally shaping and fragmentation. It is essential to plan and deploy end-to-end QoS in LAN, WAN, and virtualized environments to ensure that voice and video quality is acceptable. The sections that follow discuss QoS tools and their application.

Classification and Marking

Classification is the process by which Cisco Collaboration infrastructure devices and applications identify packets or frames and sort traffic into different classes. Before getting into the specifics of classification and marking, it is important to understand the trust boundary concept as well as concepts behind trusted, conditionally trusted, and untrusted devices.

Trust Boundary

Classification is based on various criteria, such as IP address or protocol and port. Moreover, packet or frame (Layer 3 or Layer 2) classification and marking can be carried out based on whether a device is trusted or untrusted (that is, the source of packets/frames; for example, a Cisco Unified IP Phone would be trusted). A device can be defined as a trusted or conditionally trusted device if it can mark or remark packets and can correctly classify traffic. If a device doesn't mark traffic and cannot classify it appropriately according to the network requirements, it is an untrusted entity. Figure 12-4 gives an overview of trusted vs. conditionally trusted vs. untrusted devices in a Cisco Collaboration solution.

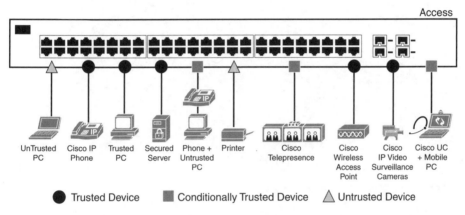

Figure 12-4 *Trusted vs. Conditionally Trusted vs. Untrusted Devices at Access Layer*

As seen in Figure 12-4, various entities connect to the access layer switch, with the following categories of devices:

- **Trusted devices:** Devices such as Cisco Unified IP Phones, Cisco Wireless Access Points, and Cisco IP Video Surveillance cameras.

- **Conditionally Trusted Devices:** PCs connected (daisy-chained) to IP Phones, PCs running soft clients such as Jabber, and Cisco TelePresence screens.

- **Untrusted Devices:** User-owned laptops and network printers.

Although it's normal to think of bandwidth as being infinitely available within a LAN, it is important to configure LAN switches to ensure that voice and video traffic receive the required QoS treatment. This further helps marking and classifying traffic closest to the source so that the data center and WAN edge devices trust the marking from the user access layer: Cisco Unified IP Phones, TelePresence endpoints, and so on. It is important to establish a trust boundary to classify and mark traffic as close to its source as possible. This is where a trust boundary must be defined.

QoS Trust Boundary

When deploying QoS, a trust boundary must be defined so that the QoS marking(s) can be trusted from the devices connected at that boundary. The definition of a trust boundary depends on what types of devices are connected at the access layer in a LAN and their trust level (as defined in previous section).

The trust boundary is critical when trusting or untrusting traffic flows. An optimal trust boundary is closer to the source of data. Figure 12-5 illustrates the concept of establishing a viable trust boundary in a typical Cisco Core, Distribution, and Access network.

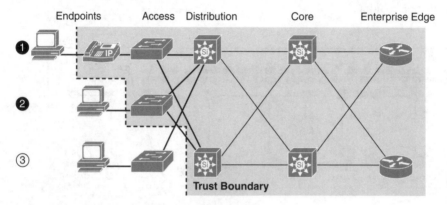

Figure 12-5   *Trusted Boundary Definition*

As seen in Figure 12-4, **1** and **2** are optimal trust boundaries, because these are closest to the source. On the other hand, **3** is a suboptimal choice to trust incoming flow from a device.

Because Cisco Unified IP Phones can exchange CDP messages with the Cisco switch, the switch can extend trust to the IP phones and trust traffic received from the IP phones. The Cisco IP phones can re-mark any traffic received from a connected PC on the PC port to class of service (CoS) 0. This process is illustrated in the following steps:

Note   CoS or Layer 2 QoS marking is described in the next section.

Step 1.   The switch and Cisco Unified IP Phone exchange CDP messages.

Step 2.   The switch extends the trust boundary to the IP phone.

Step 3.   The IP phone sets CoS to 5 for phone-sourced media traffic and to 3 for phone-sourced signaling traffic. Additionally, the IP phone sets CoS to 0 for traffic from the PC port.

Step 4.   The switch trusts CoS values from the IP phone (if the switch port is configured to trust the connected IP phone) and maps CoS to DSCP for output queuing. The result is CoS 5 = DSCP EF and CoS 3 = DSCP AF31/CS3.

The command to configure trust boundary and CoS/DSCP values up to or beyond an IP Phone is **mls qos trust**. The possible QoS trust policies for ports connected to conditionally trusted Cisco Unified IP Phones are listed in Table 12-2.

Table 12-2 *Switch CoS Trust Policies*

QoS Trust Policy	Description
mls qos trust cos	The switch trusts the CoS value of all frames entering an interface.
mls qos trust cos pass-through	The switch does not overwrite the CoS value.
mls qos trust dscp	The switch trusts the DSCP value of the packets entering an interface.
mls qos trust device cisco-phone	The switch trusts all CoS values that it receives from a Cisco Unified IP Phone.
switchport priority extend cos	The switch overwrites the CoS value of Ethernet frames received from the computer connected to the PC port of the Cisco Unified IP Phone.
switchport priority extend trust	The switch trusts all CoS values on the Ethernet frames receive from the computer connected to the PC port of the Cisco Unified IP Phone.

Figure 12-6 gives an overview of trusted, conditionally trusted, and untrusted configurations.

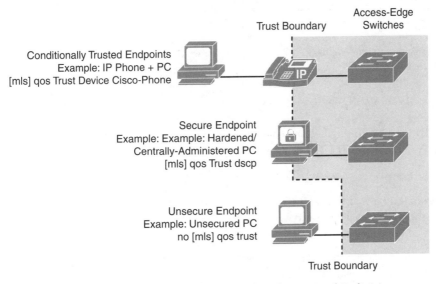

Figure 12-6 *Trusted, Conditionally Trusted, and Untrusted Definition*

Based on the defined trust boundary and configuration on the device/switch, traffic (packets/frames) can be identified based on classification criteria and can be marked according to a policy so that other network devices and applications will recognize these packets/frames and treat them as per the QoS policy being applied.

Note   Traffic can be marked using fields within packets and frames at Layer 3 and Layer 2 respectively.

At Layer 3, the type of service (ToS) or Differentiated Services (DS) fields in an IP header can be used for marking. At Layer 2, the 802.1p (user priority field) in the IEEE 802.1Q tag can be used for marking traffic. Subsequent sections explain the CoS and ToS markings. The next sections explain the concept of Layer 2 or CoS and Layer 3 or ToS (IP precedence/DSCP) markings.

Layer 2 Marking (CoS)

Class of service (CoS) markings are applied to frames (Layer 2 or data link layer) that transit an 802.1Q trunk. An IEEE 802.1Q tag consists of Tag Protocol ID (TPID) and Tag Control Information (TCI) fields. Figure 12-7 depicts the Layer 2 frame with IEEE 802.1Q tag.

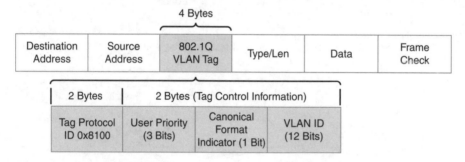

Figure 12-7   *IEEE 802.1Q Tag-based CoS Marking*

The TPID field is a 2-byte field and contains a fixed value of 0×8100 that indicates a tagged (802.1Q) frame. The TCI field is a 2-byte field that contains three subfields:

- **User Priority:** A 3-bit field used to reflect the QoS priority of the frame.

- **Canonical Format Indicator (CFI):** A 1-bit field that indicates whether the type of information that a frame is carries is in a canonical (Ethernet) or noncanonical (Token Ring) format.

- **VLAN ID:** A 12-bit field that indicates the VLAN from which the frame originated. CoS markings leverage the 3 bits from the User Priority field from within the TCI field in a 802.1Q tagged frame. Because CoS markings use 3 bits, CoS values range from 0 through 7, with values 6 and 7 being reserved, as shown in Table 12-3 that summarizes the various CoS values.

Table 12-3 *CoS Values*

CoS	Description
7	Reserved
6	Reserved
5	Voice bearer
4	Video conferencing
3	Call signaling
2	High priority
1	Medium priority
0	Best effort

As seen in Table 12-3, the markings use the three 802.1p priority bits and allow a Layer 2 Ethernet trunk frame to be marked with eight different levels of priority, values 0 to 7. The three bits allow for eight levels of classification, permitting a direct correspondence with IPv4 IP precedence ToS values as discussed in next section.

Layer 3 Marking (ToS)

At Layer 3 (network layer), packet marking can be accomplished using the ToS byte in an IPv4 header. Two predominant types of marking mechanisms leverage the ToS byte: IP Precedence and Differentiated Services Code Point (DSCP).

IP Precedence uses the three precedence bits in the IPv4 header's ToS (type of service) field to specify class of service for each IP packet (IETF RFC 1122). The most significant three bits on the IPv4 ToS field provide up to eight distinct classes, of which six are used for classifying services and the remaining two are reserved. On the edge of the network, IP Precedence is assigned by the client device or the router, so that each subsequent network element can provide services based on the determined policy or the SLA.

> **Note** IP Precedence is an old approach and has been successively replaced by DSCP for marking IP packets.

IP Precedence uses the 3 leftmost bits in the ToS byte. With 3 bits to use, IP Precedence values can range from 0 to 7, with 6 and 7 reserved. The fields in the ToS byte are as follows:

- **(IP) Precedence:** A 3-bit field used to specify the relative priority or importance of a packet.

- **Type of Service (ToS):** A 4-bit field that defines how the network should make trade-offs between throughput, delay, reliability, and cost.

- **MBZ:** Must be zero.

Figure 12-8 shows the ToS byte structure.

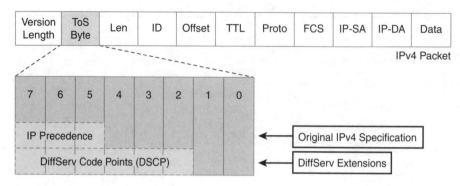

Figure 12-8   *ToS Byte Overview*

Figure 12-9 gives an insight into the IP Precedence bits (0–2), ToS bits (3–6), and MBZ bit.

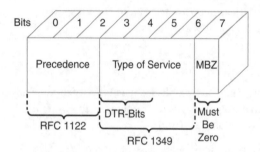

Figure 12-9   *IP Precedence, ToS, and MBZ Bits Overview*

Table 12-4 summarizes the various IP Precedence values.

Table 12-4   *IP Precedence Values (and Mapping to CoS)*

IP Precedence Value	Description	CoS
111 (7)	Network control (highest priority)	7
110 (6)	Internetwork control	6
101 (5)	Critical (RTP—Audio)	5
100 (4)	Flash override (Video)	4
011 (3)	Flash (signaling)	3
010 (2)	Immediate	2
001 (1)	Priority	1
000 (0)	Routine/best effort	0

DSCP uses the six bits in the IPv4 header to specify class of service for each IP packet (IETF RFC 2474). The 6 leftmost bits from the ToS byte in an IPv4 header form the DiffServ (DS) field. With 6 bits, DSCP has up to 64 DSCP values (0 to 63) that are assigned to various classes of traffic. The Internet Engineering Task Force (IETF) recommends selective DSCP values to maintain relative levels of priority. These selective values are called per-hop behaviors (PHB) and determine how packets are treated at each hop along the path from the source to the destination. On the network edge, the IP DSCP is assigned by the client device or the router, so that each subsequent network element can provide services based on the determined policy or the SLA.

The subfields in the DS byte are as follows:

- **DSCP:** A 6-bit field used to specify the DSCP value (and therefore PHB) of a packet.

- **CU:** Currently unused.

Figure 12-10 gives an overview of DSCP bits and CU bits.

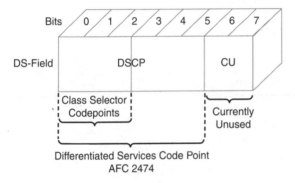

Figure 12-10 *DSCP and CU Bits Overview*

Figure 12-11 illustrates the relationship between the ToS byte, IP Precedence, and DSCP fields.

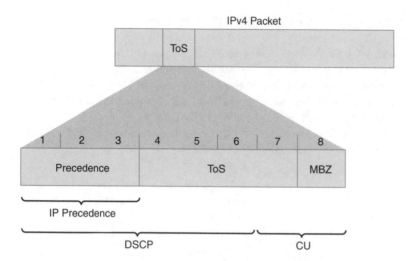

Figure 12-11 *IPv4 ToS Byte IP Precedence and DSCP Overview*

Table 12-5 shows the relationship between DSCP and IP Precedence values.

Table 12-5 *DSCP to IP Precedence Value Relationship*

Traffic Type	IP Precedence (Decimal)	DSCP (Binary)
Network control	7	111XXX
Internetwork control	6	110XXX
Critical	5	101110
Class 4	4	100XXX
Class 3	3	011XXX
Class 2	2	010XXX
Class 1	1	001XXX
Standard	0	000000

Note The Class Selector code points are of the form "xxx000." The first three bits are the IP Precedence bits. Each IP Precedence value can be mapped into a DiffServ class. CS0 (Default) equals IP Precedence 0, CS1 IP Precedence 1, and so on. In case a packet is received from a non-DiffServ-aware router that understands IP precedence markings, the DiffServ router can still understand the encoding as a Class Selector code point.

When configuring a router to mark or recognize a DSCP value, decimal numbers or the name of a specific DSCP value can be used. The four different DiffServ PHBs are as follows:

- **Assured forwarding (AF):** Specifies four AF PHBs grouped into four classes. When using AF, the first 3 bits of the DS field define the queuing class (1 to 4), and next 2 bits define the drop probability (1 to 3). The 6th bit is always zero. AF therefore has 12 classes to it and provides assurance of a packet as long as it doesn't exceed the subscribed rate.

- **Best effort (BE):** Specified when all 6 bits of the DS field are 0; that is, the packet doesn't need any specific QoS treatment or doesn't meet the requirements of any of the other defined classes. BE is also known as default PHB.

- **Class Selector (CS):** Used for backward compatibility with network devices and applications that use IP Precedence. When using this PHB, the last 3 bits of the DSCP field are 0.

- **Expedited forwarding (EF):** States a low-delay, low-loss, and low-jitter QoS treatment with guaranteed bandwidth.

Cisco recommends applying classification/marking applicable to all types of traffic, including voice and video media, call signaling traffic, and different data traffic flows. This set of recommendations is called the Cisco QoS baseline. Table 12-6 gives an insight into these service classes.

Table 12-6 *Service Classes Based on Cisco QoS Baseline for Voice, Video, and Data*

Network Service/Application	Classification/Service Class
Network control traffic for switches and routers	CS6 (DSCP 48)
IP voice media traffic (with LLQ)	EF (DSCP 46)
Broadcast video	CS5 (DSCP 40)
Multimedia conferencing	AF41 (DSCP 34)
Real-time interactive	CS4 (DSCP 32)
Multimedia streaming	AF31 (DSCP 26)
Voice and video signaling traffic (SIP, H.323, MGCP, SCCP)	CS3 (DSCP 24)
Low latency data	AF21 (DSCP 18)
Operation, administration, and maintenance (OAM) data	CS2 (DSCP 16)
High throughput data	AF11 (DSCP 10)
Low priority data	CS1 (DSCP 8)
Best effort	BE (DSCP 0)

Leading Practices for Classification and Marking for Video Traffic

In addition to the previously discussed QoS requirements for video traffic, the following are best practices associated with interactive video:

- Interactive video traffic should be marked to DSCP AF41.

- Excess videoconferencing traffic can be marked down (policing) to AF42 or AF43.

- Streaming video should be marked to DSCP CS4 (for both unicast and multicast streams).

- Non-business-oriented streaming video applications, such as entertainment video content, may be marked as Scavenger class DSCP CS1.

Queuing

Beginning with classification and marking, a packet needs to be treated according to the QoS policy. QoS tools such as policing or queuing can make forwarding or dropping decisions based on these markings. Queuing is a congestion management tool. It ensures that during temporary periods of congestion traffic (packets) is buffered, prioritized, and, if required, reordered before being transmitted to the destination.

A number of queuing tools are available in Cisco IOS and are listed in Table 12-7.

Table 12-7 *Cisco Queuing Toolset*

Queuing Tool	Description
First-In, First-Out (FIFO)	A default queuing mechanism for interfaces with speeds greater than 2.048 Mbps. As the name suggests, the packets are treated as they arrive, and no reordering is done.
Priority Queuing (PQ)	A legacy queuing method with four queues, where higher-priority queues must be emptied before forwarding traffic from lower-priority queues.
Custom Queuing (CQ)	A legacy queuing method that entertains up to 16 queues in a round-robin (RR) cycle, emptying a prespecified number of bytes from each queue during each iteration.
Weighted Fair Queuing (WFQ)	A flow-based algorithm, derived from Fair Queuing (FQ), and a default queuing method for low-speed interfaces. WFQ makes forwarding decisions based on a packet's size and Layer 3 priority marking.
IP RTP priority	A legacy queuing method that creates a strict PQ for voice traffic for a range of UDP destination ports, with other packets treated with the WFQ method.

Low-latency queuing (LLQ)	The queuing method created specifically for voice and video traffic. LLQ allows traffic to be categorized in up to 64 different classes, with different amounts of bandwidth or priority treatment for these classes.
Class-Based Weighted Fair Queuing (CBWFQ)	Similar to LLQ, but without the PQ mechanism.

Figure 12-12 shows LLQ and other Class-Based Weighted Fair Queues implemented on Cisco IOS router.

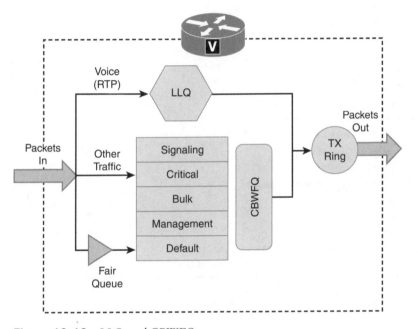

Figure 12-12 *LLQ and CBWFQ*

Cisco recommends CBWFQ or LLQ methodologies for queuing with current versions of Cisco IOS in Cisco Collaboration networks. Example 12-1 illustrates the Modular Quality of Service (MQC) approach to LLQ.

Example 12-1   *MQC Approach to LLQ*

```
Router(config)# class-map match-any RTP-Audio
Router(config-cmap)# match ip dscp ef
Router(config-cmap)# match ip precedence 5
!
Router(config)# class-map match-any RTP-Video
Router(config-cmap)# match ip dscp cs4
Router(config-cmap)# match ip dscp af41
Router(config-cmap)# match ip precedence 4
!
Router(config)# class-map match-any Signaling
Router(config-cmap)# match ip dscp cs3
Router(config-cmap)# match ip dscp af31
!
Router(config)# policy-map Voice-Priority
Router(config-pmap)# class RTP-Audio
Router(config-pmap-c)# priority percent 20
Router(config-pmap-c)# class RTP-Video
Router(config-pmap-c)# priority percent 10
Router(config-pmap-c)# class Signaling
Router(config-pmap-c)# bandwidth 128
Router(config-pmap-c)# class class-default
Router(config-pmap-c)# fair-queue
!
Router(config)# interface serial 0/0
Router(config-if)# ip address 10.10.1.250 255.255.255.0
Router(config-if)# service-policy output Voice-Priority
```

Table 12-8 describes the commands used in Example 12-1.

Table 12-8   *MQC Commands*

Command	Description
class-map	Defines the class map to be used to match the traffic ingress to the router. The two major settings are **match-any** (Boolean OR) or **match-all** (Boolean AND) although there are multiple other options, such as **match protocol**, **match ip**, **match access-group**, and so on.
ip dscp	Allows matching a traffic flow to a DSCP value based on marking from the device or switch port.
ip precedence	Allows matching a traffic flow to an IP Precedence value based on marking from the device or switch port.

policy-map	Defines the policy map that is used to define values and thresholds for class map(s). The policy map brings together one or more classes and is applied to an outbound or inbound interface to match traffic and apply QoS policies.
priority	Defines the priority for certain classes of traffic (EF, CS5, CS3) and specifies the amount of bandwidth allocated to the priority queue (which defines both the guaranteed minimum as well as the policed maximum)
bandwidth	Specifies a minimum bandwidth guarantee to a traffic class during traffic congestion.
service-policy	Applies the policy map to an interface. A service policy can be applied in an output or input direction (outbound and inbound respectively).

In Example 12-1, **match-any** commands are used to match RTP audio (DSCP EF and IP Precedence 5) and video (DSCP CS4 and IP Precedence 4) traffic. Signaling traffic is matched by matching DSCP values AF31 and CS3. Voice audio is given priority treatment (guaranteed 20 percent of the link's bandwidth), whereas video traffic is given 10 percent of the link bandwidth as priority guaranteed bandwidth. Signaling traffic is given up to 128 kbps of guaranteed bandwidth, and the remaining traffic is treated by class default via fair queuing method (that is, this traffic is entertained only when the priority queues have first been serviced up to their assigned bandwidth).

The next section discusses traffic policing and shaping mechanisms.

Traffic Policing and Shaping

Traffic policing and shaping help regulate bandwidth usage by limiting the amount of traffic. Policing limits traffic rates by dropping, remarking, or transmitting traffic if the traffic conforms to a policy. Policing can occur within a network or at the network edge (towards the WAN).

Shaping, on the other hand, involves regulating excessive traffic rates by delaying (buffering) traffic. Shaping usually occurs at the edge of a network and can be applied to an interface in an output direction. Because traffic policing limits traffic transmission by dropping packets, it is more suitable for high-speed links such as LAN or Multiprotocol Label Switching (MPLS) links. Traffic shaping is more suitable for lower-speed links such as Multilink PPP (MLP) and Frame Relay, as it buffers excess traffic.

Both policing and shaping configurations can specify a committed information rate (CIR), committed burst (Bc), and excess burst (Be). Both shaping and policing rely on token-bucket algorithms in which tokens influence how much traffic can be sent, with each token allowing either 1 bit or 1 byte to be sent. There are three types of class-based policers that can be configured using the MQC:

■ **Single-rate two-color policer:** A single token bucket is used, and traffic either conforms to or exceeds the configured rate. Actions can be stated for traffic that conforms or exceeds the specified rate.

■ **Single-rate three-color policer:** Two token buckets are used, with tokens periodically added to the first bucket, and any overflowing tokens going to the second bucket as shown in Figure 12-13. Actions can be stated for traffic that conforms, exceeds, or violates the specified rate.

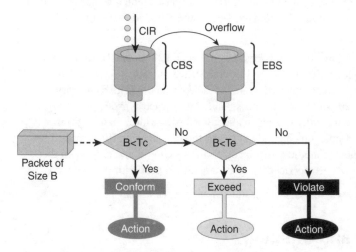

Figure 12-13 *Single-Rate Three-Color Policer*

Note   CBS is Committed Burst Size, EBS is Excess Burst Size, Tc is Token Count for CBS, and Te is Token Count for EBS.

■ **Two-rate three-color policer (RFC 2698):** Comparable to the single-rate three-color policer, the difference is that tokens are periodically added to both buckets, as shown in Figure 12-14. Actions can be stated for traffic that conforms, exceeds, or violates the specified rate.

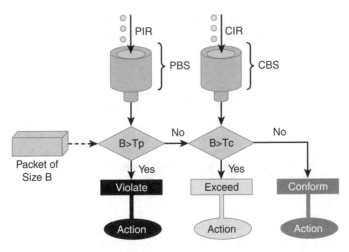

Figure 12-14   *Two-Rate Three-Color Policer*

Note   PIR is Peak Information Rate, CBS is Committed Burst Size, PBS is Peak Burst Size, Tp is Token count for PBS, and Tc is Token Count for CBS.

Example 12-2 illustrates a single-rate three-color policer using the MQC in which the traffic conforming to the policy is marked DSCP AF21. The traffic exceeding the policy-defined rate is marked DSCP AF11, and the traffic violating the exceed action is dropped.

Example 12-2   *Traffic Policer Configuration*

```
Router(config)# class-map HTTP-Secure
Router(config-cmap)# match protocol secure-http
!
Router(config)# policy-map HTTPS
Router(config-pmap)# class HTTP-Secure
Router(config-pmap-c)# police cir 512000 bc 64000 be 64000 conform-action set-dscp-
  transmit af21 exceed-action set-dscp-transmit af11 violate-action drop
!
Router(config)# interface FastEthernet 0/0
Router(config-if)# service-policy output HTTPS
```

Traffic shaping uses a token-bucket system to determine whether to transmit, delay, or drop new packets. The following entities form the basis of traffic shaping (CIR, Bc, Tc):

■ With the token-bucket system, each interface has a committed information rate (CIR), which is the rate at which the interface can transmit packets for an interval of time, or in token-bucket theory, the rate at which the tokens are added to the bucket.

- The sustained burst rate (Bc) defines the maximum number of tokens that the bucket can contain at a given interval. When a packet arrives at an interface, it takes a token from the bucket.

- When a packet is transmitted, the token is released, and after the time interval (Tc), the token is returned to the bucket. If the bucket is empty, any new packets arriving at that interface are queued until the time interval has elapsed and the tokens have been replenished.

Note   Traffic shaping buffers the traffic to a certain bitrate, and then policing drops the traffic when it exceeds a certain bitrate.

Traffic shaping can be applied to a number of different Layer 2 technologies, such as Ethernet, ATM, High-Level Data Link Control (HDLC), PPP (ISDN and dialup interfaces are not supported), and Frame Relay.

Note   With the exception of Frame Relay, all of these technologies support Generic Traffic Shaping (GTS).

Traffic shaping is recommended by Cisco under the following conditions:

- There is a mismatch between link speeds at a central site and remote sites (that is, the central site link speed is greater than that of the remote sites).

- The aggregate link speed at remote sites is greater than that at the central site.

Example 12-3 illustrates GTS-based traffic shaping.

Example 12-3   *GTS-Based Traffic Shaping*

```
Router(config)# interface Serial0/1
Router(config-if)# ip address 10.10.10.51 255.255.255.0
Router(config-if)# traffic-shape rate 256000 32000 32000 1000
!
Router# show traffic-shape

Interface   Se0/1
        Access Target    Byte    Sustain    Excess    Interval  Increment Adapt
VC      List   Rate      Limit   bits/int   bits/int  (ms)      (bytes)   Active
-              256000    8000    32000      32000     125       4000      -
```

In Example 12-3, traffic shaping is used to limit the rate on all traffic on interface serial0/1 to 256 kbps. This limit is imposed by delaying any traffic over 32 kb/interval; the interval of time used to shape traffic is 125 ms. So, in this case, during each 125-ms interval, interface serial0/1 can transmit up to 32 kb. Any amount of traffic that exceeds the 32 kb limit during that interval is queued until the next interval.

Traffic shaping can also leverage the MQC framework, and when configuring MQC-based shaping, traffic can be shaped to either average or peak. If shape average is specified, traffic is sent at the CIR, with bursting of Be bits per timing interval enabled. If shape peak is specified, traffic is forwarded at the peak rate.

Example 12-4 shows the configuration of class-based Frame Relay traffic shaping for HTTPS traffic at least 256 kbps but no more than 512 kbps.

Example 12-4 *Frame Relay Traffic Shaping*

```
Router(config)# class-map HTTP-Secure
Router(config-cmap)# match protocol secure-http
!
Router(config)# policy-map HTTPS
Router(config-pmap)# class HTTP-Secure
Router(config-pmap-c)# shape average 512000
Router(config-pmap-c)# bandwidth 256
!
Router(config)# map-class frame-relay FRFMAP
Router(config-map-class)# service-policy output HTTPS
Router(config-map-class)# frame-relay fragment 640
!
Router(config)# interface serial 0/0
Router(config-if)# frame-relay traffic-shaping
!
Router(config-if)# interface serial 0/0.1 point-to-point
Router(config-subif)# ip address 10.10.1.250 255.255.255.0
Router(config-subif)# frame-relay interface-dlci 100
Router(config-fr-dlci)# class FRFMAP
```

Medianet

To facilitate anywhere, anytime immersive or pervasive video, the underlying network needs to be tuned accordingly. Since video traffic is bursty and unpredictable, fine-tuning an existing network infrastructure for video traffic can be challenging.

Medianet is the architecture for successful deployment of multiple media and collaboration applications with special focus on video. It requires Media Services Interface (MSI)–equipped products and features in both smart endpoints/applications and smart network infrastructure, as shown in Figure 12-15. However, Medianet does not require an entirely end-to-end network with Medianet enabled in every hop.

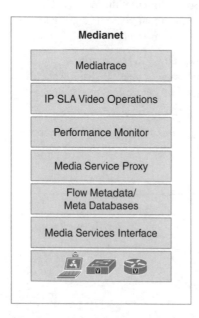

Figure 12-15   *Medianet Architecture*

Medianet components are explained in Table 12-9.

Table 12-9   *Cisco Medianet Components*

Medianet Component	Description
Mediatrace	A Medianet component that helps discover Layer 2 and Layer 3 devices along the flow path and can provide information ranging from device-specific, such as CPU or memory, to interface-specific, such as input interface speed, to flow-specific, such as DSCP values or jitter. Mediatrace collects information from network nodes along the traffic flow path and presents this information for easy analysis. Infrastructure devices such as routers must have Mediatrace enabled for discovery and information sharing. It leverages RSVP as the transport protocol.
IP Service Level Agreement Video Operation (IP SLA VO)	A readiness assessment tool for gauging a network's capacity to carry rich-media traffic. It is used for network-based IP-SLA for synthetic traffic generation, pre-deployment assessment, pre-event testing, and post-event troubleshooting and measurements. It allows tracking video-critical statistics using the network, where each element becomes a "probe."

Performance Monitor	A Cisco tool that discovers and validates RTP traffic on a hop-by-hop basis. It is used to determine jitter, packet loss, and multiplexed media streams. Performance Monitor also recognizes TCP flows and IP constant bit rate (CBR) traffic. For TCP, Performance Monitor reports on round-trip time (RTT) and packet loss, whereas for IP CBR traffic, Performance Monitor reports packet loss and media rate variation (MRV). It also helps isolate faults in the network quickly because of its ability to discover and report on a per-hop basis.
Media Services Proxy (MSP)	Provides a subset of Medianet services on behalf of non-Cisco and legacy endpoints. The primary function of MSP is to evolve Medianet from Cisco only to include third-party endpoints by leveraging standards-based signaling protocols such as SIP and H.323. This enables a Medianet-enabled network to learn about the characteristics of endpoints and applications from legacy systems or third-party devices. MSP should be positioned at the user (access) edge and resource (enterprise) edge.
Flow metadata/ meta databases	Enables the application to convey information about itself to the underlying network via MSI-enabled endpoints as well as MSP- or NBAR-enabled infrastructure on behalf of non-MSI endpoints (such as smart phones and tablets). This information comprises flow metadata and builds meta databases. Different metadata identifies different media flows. It uses RSVP as the transport protocol. Metadata can be enabled at MSI-compliant endpoints, routers with NBAR, and soft clients.
Media Services Interface (MSI)	A software package that resides on the endpoints. MSI comes with multiple APIs to enable endpoints and media applications to take advantage of the Medianet services. MIS enables a media application to identify itself and its media flow to the network. MSI also enables network management to have better visibility into the application and its media flow. For PCs, MSI is available for download from Cisco.com as MSI.msi and runs as a Windows service. MSI service is shared by all MSI-aware applications, such as WebEx and Jabber for Windows.

Medianet QoS Classes of Service

Multiple endpoints and applications can leverage Medianet. However, each group of devices, endpoints, and media applications has unique traffic patterns and service level requirements that necessitate a dedicated QoS class to meet that service level. RFC 4594 presents configuration guidelines for DiffServ service classes to meet specific business requirements. Table 12-10 describes the various network applications and respective QoS (DiffServ) service classes.

Table 12-10 *Medianet Service Classes, Based on Cisco QoS Recommendation*

Network Service/ Application	Description	Service Class (DSCP)	Queuing and Dropping
VoIP telephony	For VoIP telephony media/bearer traffic. Applicable to RTP streams leveraging various codecs such as G.711 and G.729.	EF	PQ
Broadcast video	For broadcast TV or live events. Applicable to live video traffic from Cisco Digital Media System (DMS) streams to desktops, Cisco IP Video Surveillance, or live Cisco Enterprise TV (ETV) streams.	CS5	Optional PQ
Real-time interactive	For high-definition interactive video applications, including voice and video content such as Cisco TelePresence.	CS4	Optional PQ
Multimedia conferencing	For desktop software–based multimedia collaboration applications such as Cisco Unified Personal Communicator and Cisco Unified Video Advantage. It focuses primarily on voice and video components of these applications.	AF4	Bandwidth queue + WRED
Multimedia streaming	For video-on-demand (VoD) streaming video flows. Applicable to applications such as Cisco Digital Media System VoD streams.	AF3	Bandwidth queue + WRED
Network control	For network control plane traffic such as routing protocols (for example, EIGRP, OSPF, BGP, HSRP).	CS6	Bandwidth queue
Voice/video signaling	For voice and video signaling traffic that supports IP voice and video telephony. Applicable to signaling protocols such as SCCP, SIP, H.323, and MGCP.	CS3	Bandwidth queue
Ops, admin, management (OAM)	For network operations, administration, and management traffic, such as SSH and SNMP.	CS2	Bandwidth queue
Transactional data	For interactive data applications such as Enterprise Resource Planning (ERP) and Customer Relationship Management (CRM) applications.	AF2	Bandwidth queue + DSCP WRED

Bulk data	For noninteractive data applications such as email, FTP/SFTP transfers, backup operations, and so on.	AF1	Bandwidth Queue + DSCP WRED
Best effort	Acts as the default class for applications that do not require a specific level of service and can be assigned to this class.	DF	Default Queue + RED
Scavenger	For low-priority data and non-business-related traffic, such as P2P and gaming-oriented applications.	CS1	Minimum Bandwidth Queue

Voice and Video Bandwidth Calculations

This section describes the bandwidth calculations for voice and video traffic, as well as Layer 2 overhead considerations.

Bandwidth Calculations for Voice Calls

This section gives insight to calculation of bandwidth for voice (audio) calls.

To calculate bandwidth requirements for voice traffic, you must have the following information:

- choice of codec
- packetization interval

A key factor to consider is that payload size is comparable to header size. The more packets you have and the shorter the packetization time, the more overhead you will have.

In Table 12-11, the bandwidth requirements per codec are shown. The bandwidth shown in the table as is required per call does not take into account Layer 2 overhead.

Note If Layer 2 overhead is taken into account, total overhead is even higher. In addition, this formula does not consider the effect of any link-efficiency tools.

Table 12-11 *Voice Codec Bandwidth Requirements*

Codec	Packetization Period	Voice Payload	Packets Per Second (PPS)	Bandwidth Per Call
G.711	20 ms	160 bytes	50	91.56 kbps
G.729	20 ms	20 bytes	50	31.2 kbps
iLBC	20 ms	38 bytes	50	38.4 kbps
G.722	20 ms	160 bytes	50	87.2 kbps

The formula to calculate the bandwidth per call is:

```
Bandwidth per call = (Voice Payload + L3 OH + L2 OH) X PPS X 8bits/byte
Where, L3 = Layer 3, L2 = Layer 2, OH = Overhead, PPS = Packets Per Second
```

Bandwidth Calculations for Video Calls

This section describes how to perform bandwidth calculations for video traffic when implementing QoS in the network.

Deciding bandwidth requirements for voice traffic is relatively straightforward. Once you specify the codec, the required bandwidth and the quality of that compressed signal are automatically defined. The quality of the compressed signal is the width of the frequency spectrum of the encoded voice signal.

Calculations are different for video codecs. Resolution and frame rate calculations are based on endpoint capabilities, and at times, user selection criteria are based on the desired call quality. In addition, video conferencing traffic utilizes optimum definition profiles. There are three categories of optimum definition profiles:

- High

- Medium

- Normal

The profiles are defined based on the quality of the image gathered by the camera and the quality of lighting available. The profiles set bandwidth utilization, with the best lighting and camera requiring less bandwidth for the image. Out of the three profiles, High is typically utilized for dedicated videoconference rooms, with excellent lighting and a high quality camera, and saves up 50% of the bandwidth compared to Normal. Medium is used for stable, well-lit areas with decent quality cameras and saves approximately 25% of the bandwidth compared to Normal, which is used for poorly lit environments.

Optimal resolution profiles provide a good demonstration of how much the system can compress video input. With perfect lighting conditions and predefined bandwidth, higher resolution and higher frame rates are possible. Table 12-12 shows that with perfect lighting conditions, it is possible to achieve resolution of 720 lines and 60 frames with 1152 kbps of bandwidth. If the input signal is not as good—perhaps the lighting conditions are not ideal—the codec lowers either the frame rate (from 60 fps to 30 fps) or the resolution (from 720 lines to 576) to fit the video into same bandwidth pipe.

Table 12-12 *Video Profile Bandwidth*

Optimum Definition Profile	Frame Rate	Resolution				
		W288p30	**W448p30**	**W576p30**	**720p30**	**1080p30**
Normal	30 fps	256 kbps	512 kbps	768 kbps	1152 kbps	2560 kbps
	60 fps	128 kbps	512 kbps	1152 kbps	1472 kbps	2240 kbps
Medium	30 fps	128 kbps	256 kbps	512 kbps	1152 kbps	1920 kbps
	60 fps	128 kbps	384 kbps	512 kbps	768 kbps	1152 kbps
High	30 fps	128 kbps	256 kbps	512 kbps	768 kbps	1472 kbps
	60 fps	128 kbps	384 kbps	768 kbps	1152 kbps	1920 kbps

When encoding and transmitting video, there is a trade-off between high resolution and a high frame rate. Sports events, like a basketball game or a car race, look better with a higher frame rate, while a business meeting is better at a higher resolution over motion.

Bandwidth Calculations for Layer 2 Overhead

This section describes Layer 2 overhead details that are related to bandwidth calculations.

Most typical Layer 2 technologies and their associated overhead are described in the following list. Consider these overheads when calculating bandwidth requirements for a single VoIP call.

- **802.3 Ethernet:** 14+4 bytes

- **802.1Q Ethernet:** 4 additional bytes

- **Frame Relay:** 6 bytes (9 bytes with LFI (link fragmentation and interleaving))

- **PPP:** 6-9 bytes

Note Data-link transport protocols use various preambles, frame headers, flags, cyclic redundancy check (CRC), Asynchronous Transfer Mode (ATM) cell padding, and other things that influence bandwidth calculations. Therefore, the header can vary.

In Table 12-13, the Layer 2 overhead requirements per codec and per PPS amount are shown.

Table 12-13 *Layer 2 Overhead Requirements*

Codec	Packets Per Second	Voice Over 801.Q	Voice Over Frame Relay with LFI	Voice Over MLPPP
G.711	50	93 kbps	84 kbps	86 kbps
G.711	33	83 kbps	77 kbps	78 kbps
G.729	50	37 kbps	28 kbps	30 kbps
G.729	33	27 kbps	21 kbps	22 kbps

Table 12-13 shows the bandwidth requirements, including Layer 3 and Layer 2 overhead, for the G.711 and G.729 audio codecs at 50 and 33 PPS.

The sample calculation below uses the formula that was previously mentioned. The example shows how to calculate the required bandwidth for a single G.711 call, when the call is transported over Ethernet with 801.Q VLAN framing at 50 packets per second (pps) and 20-ms packetization period:

$$\text{BW Per Call} = (160 + 40 + 32) \times 50 \times 8 \text{ bits/byte} = 93 \text{ kbps}$$

where:

- 160 bytes is the G.711 payload collected over 20 ms.

- 40 bytes is the Layer 3 + overhead (IP, UDP, RTP headers).

- 20 bytes is the Layer 2 overhead for 801.Q Ethernet.

- 50 pps is the sampling rate.

- 8 bits per byte is used to convert byte values into bits for the final bits-per-second result, which is 93 kbps.

Use the same approach when calculating the required bandwidth for other codecs and Layer 2 technologies.

Chapter Summary

The following list summarizes the key points that were discussed in this chapter:

- Cisco Collaboration solutions offer multiple applications for both audio and video over a converged network.

- Converged networks must take into account delay, jitter, and packet loss to provide adequate service and reliability to voice and video traffic.

- Cisco offers a QoS toolkit that can be leveraged for implementing end-to-end QoS.

- Classification and marking is the first step in performing QoS and can be conducted at Layer 2 (CoS) and Layer 3 (ToS).

- DSCP (with PHB) and IP Precedence are interoperable and are the most commonly used DiffServ methods in Collaboration networks for Layer 3 QoS.

- Traffic policing offers various mechanisms to sort, remark, or discard traffic based on defined conditions.

- Traffic shaping allows shaping traffic to confirm to an interface's logical/physical maximum transfer limit, thereby controlling the flow of traffic to remote site.

- Medianet offers a comprehensive suite of applications/components to fine-tune a Cisco Collaboration network for supporting video pertinent QoS for broadcast, streaming, IP telephony, and immersive calls.

- Voice and video call bandwidth calculation is influenced by Layer 2, Layer 3, compression and security technologies that impose overhead.

- Video bandwidth calculations are based on resolution profiles, and bandwidth can be largely affected by lighting and camera quality.

References

For additional information, refer to the following:

Cisco Systems, Inc. Cisco Collaboration Systems 10.x Solution Reference Network Designs (SRND), May 2014.

http://www.cisco.com/c/en/us/td/docs/voice_ip_comm/cucm/srnd/collab10/collab10.html

Cisco QoS DocWiki

http://docwiki.cisco.com/wiki/Quality_of_Service_Networking

Enterprise Media QoS

http://www.cisco.com/c/en/us/td/docs/solutions/Enterprise/WAN_and_MAN/QoS_SRND_40/QoSIntro_40.html#77037

Review Questions

Use the questions here to review what you learned in this chapter. The correct answers are found in Appendix A, "Answers to the Review Questions."

1. Which of the following is not a QoS configuration?

   a. Compress the data and headers.

   b. Drop low-priority packets early.

   c. Increase the bandwidth of the link.

   d. Incorporate advanced queuing technologies.

   e. Reduce link MTU size.

2. Which two features characterize converged network traffic? (Choose two.)

   a. No low-speed links

   b. Time-sensitive packets

   c. Network protocol mix

   d. Intolerance of brief outages

   e. Bursty small packet flow

3. Which of the following voice codecs utilizes the least amount of bandwidth?

   a. G.722

   b. G.711

   c. G.729

   d. iLBC

4. Which statement is the least applicable for the definition of a QoS policy?

   a. User-validated

   b. Networkwide

   c. Time-based

   d. Ports that are opened on firewalls

   e. Different classes of network traffic

5. Which of the following are the most common values for packets per second for voice traffic? (Choose two.)

   a. 50 pps

   b. 88 pps

c. 72 pps

d. 33 pps

6. True or false? Layer 2 overhead doubles the bandwidth required for a voice packet.

   a. True

   b. False

7. Which of the following profiles utilizes the most bandwidth?

   a. High

   b. Normal

   c. Medium

   d. iBLC

8. Medianet is used primarily for which type of traffic in Cisco Collaboration network?

   a. Video traffic

   b. Signaling traffic

   c. Audio traffic

   d. WebEx traffic

9. True or false? IP Precedence is a Layer 3 QoS mechanism.

   a. True

   b. False

10. True or false? SIP Trunks using TCP as protocol from CUCM are insensitive to latency and delay.

    a. True

    b. False

11. Which element binds a QoS policy to a physical or logical interface on IOS router?

    a. Policy map

    b. Class map

    c. Service policy

    d. GTS

Implementing Cisco IOS Voice Gateways and Cisco Unified Border Element

Cisco Collaboration network leverages Internetwork Operating System (IOS) voice gateways to (inter)connect different networks (e.g. PSTN to IP and vice versa) and different protocols (e.g. SIP to H.323). A Cisco IOS voice gateway is the fundamental block of Cisco Collaboration network and offers various functions; from most trivial to more complex. An IOS voice gateway can be configured as a Public Switched Telephone Network (PSTN) termination endpoint or can be configured as Session Border Controller (Cisco Unified Border Element [CUBE]) to broker two or more heterogeneous (varied features or protocols) networks.

Chapter Objectives

This chapter describes the functions and features of Cisco IOS voice gateways and CUBE. Upon completing this chapter, you will be able to meet the following objectives:

- Describe Cisco IOS gateway protocols

- Describe and Configure Cisco IOS Digital Voice Ports

- Describe and Configure IOS dial plan

- Describe Cisco Unified Border Element (CUBE) and its features

- Configure Cisco Unified Border Element (CUBE)

Cisco IOS Gateway Voice Signaling Protocols

Cisco IOS gateway supports a number of voice-signaling protocols such as:

- Cisco Media Gateway Control Protocol (MGCP)

- Session Initiation Protocol (SIP)

- H.323

Note   Cisco IOS gateways and VG2XX, 3XX support Skinny Client Control protocol (SCCP) as well as signaling. This is primarily for collaboration services such as conference bridge, transcoder, and media termination point (MTP).

Before understanding how the Cisco IOS voice gateway functions, it is imperative to recognize the various protocols that are used by the IOS voice gateway (and CUBE). The following sections explain these protocols and the relevant call flows.

Media Gateway Control Protocol

Cisco Media Gateway Control Protocol (MGCP) is an implementation of the MGCP architecture for controlling media gateways on IP networks connected to the plain old telephone service (POTS). MGCP is defined in RFC 3435 and is a text-based master/slave protocol, with a call-control agent (e.g. CUCM) as master and a controlled IOS gateway port as slave. Figure 13-1 illustrates Cisco MGCP gateway functionality in a Cisco Collaboration environment.

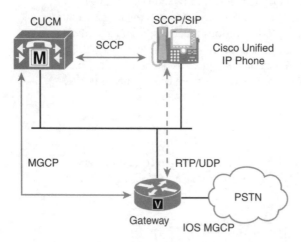

Figure 13-1   *MGCP Gateway in Cisco Collaboration Network*

As seen in Figure 13-1 the IOS gateway running MGCP protocol is interconnecting the IP network to PSTN network. Cisco Unified Communications Manager (CUCM) and IOS voice gateway establish an MGCP connection whereas CUCM and user endpoint (IP Phone) establish a SIP or skinny client control protocol (SCCP) connection. While the signaling flow is between gateway and CUCM, and endpoint (IP Phone) and CUCM; the media (RTP) stream is established directly between the endpoint and IOS voice gateway.

MGCP uses session description protocol (SDP) for specifying and negotiating the media streams. MGCP leverages user datagram protocol (UDP) port 2427 for control traffic and transport control protocol (TCP) port 2428 for backhaul (explained later in this section). MGCP allows centralization of dial plan (due to its master/slave nature) as the dial plan intelligence is with CUCM. The MGCP architecture defines MGCP Media Gateway Control (MGC) and Media Gateway (MG). MGC is a call-control agent such as CUCM and has the call-control intelligence (dial plan and signaling backhauled to call control) and controls MGs analog (FXS/FXO) or digital (T1-PRI/T1-CAS) ports/trunks.

MGCP architecture defines nine call states, defined in Table 13-1.

Table 13-1 *MGCP Call States*

MGCP Call State	Description
CreateConnection (CRCX)	Command from a call-control agent to an MGCP-controlled gateway for creating a new connection between two MGCP endpoints. The connection creation is based on parameters such as codec, allowable bandwidth, gain control, silence suppression, and so on.
ModifyConnection (MDCX)	Command from a call-control agent to an MGCP-controlled gateway that modifies the parameters associated with an existing connection.
DeleteConnection (DLCX)	Bidirectional command that is used by a call-control agent to inform the gateway that it should terminate a connection. A gateway can also send this command to indicate that a connection needs to be terminated. The gateway also sends statistics associated with the connection when contacting the call-control agent.
EndpointConfiguration (EPCF)	Configuration command from a call-control agent to an MGCP-controlled gateway. It configures the gateway with the Bearer Information, i.e., to specify whether audio calls will be encoded using mu-law or a-law.
NotificationRequest (RQNT)	Command from a call-control agent to an MGCP-controlled gateway to instruct the gateway to inform the call-control agent when specific events such as on-hook/off-hook actions or dual tone multi-frequency (DTMF) tones occur on a specified endpoint.
AuditEndpoint (AUEP)	Command from a call-control agent to an MGCP-controlled gateway to audit the status of an endpoint (port), such as bearer information, signal status, and event status.
AuditConnection (AUCX)	Command from a call-control agent to an MGCP-controlled gateway to discover the status of a connection, such as connection mode, call ID, and connection parameters.

(Continued)

Table 13-1 *Continued*

MGCP Call State	Description
Notify (NTFY)	Command from a gateway to a call-control agent to inform the call-control agent when requested events occur such as on-hook/off-hook and digit reception.
RestartInProgress (RSIP)	Command from a gateway to a call-control agent to inform the call-control agent that the gateway is taking an endpoint or group of endpoints out of service or returning an endpoint or group of endpoints to service. There are three types of restart: Restart (endpoint in service), Graceful (wait until call clearing), and Forced (endpoint out of service).

MGCP also uses certain return codes that reflect different events occurring on the gateway and, accordingly, enables the gateway to update the call-control agent. The types of MGCP return codes defined in RFC 3661 are as follows:

- **000:** Response acknowledgment message

- **1XX:** Transaction execution-related messages

- **2XX:** Transaction successful messages

- **4XX:** Transient error messages

- **5XX:** Permanent error messages

MGCP messages are sent on UDP port 2427, and TCP port 2428 is used to exchange keep-alive packets between an MGCP-controlled gateway and CUCM. This allows for MGCP PRI/BRI backhaul between an MGCP gateway and CUCM wherein the backhaul is used to transport ISDN Q.931 (D channel signaling) information from the gateway to CUCM. This allows CUCM to recognize the status of ISDN Layer 3 for the port/endpoint/trunk being controlled on the MGCP gateway.

Note: When MGCP backhaul interface is configured, Q921 (Layer 2 of ISDN PRI Circuit) is terminated on the MGCP gateway (endpoint) whereas the Q931 (Layer 3 of ISDN PRI circuit) signal is sent to CUCM. This reduces the administrative effort of configuring the call-routing intelligence at one place i.e. in the call agent or CUCM.

By default, MGCP gateways leverage a Call Manager Group (CMG—a list of CUCM servers in preferred order) for call survivability. This implies that in case the communication between an MGCP gateway and the primary (active) CUCM server that setup the calls is lost, the call continues over the gateway. Meanwhile, a message on the IP Phone's screen displays "CM Down, Features Disabled." At this point, the supplementary services including call hold, park, transfer, and conference will not work. Moreover, new calls to the MGCP gateway will not work until the MGCP gateway re-registers with the backup call–processing server(s) such as a secondary or tertiary CUCM server in the Call Manager group.

MGCP Gateway Call Flow

An MGCP gateway registers to its preferred CUCM server as defined in CUCM Group and on the gateway. Figure 13-2 illustrates the MGCP call flow between a CUCM server and MGCP endpoints registered to it.

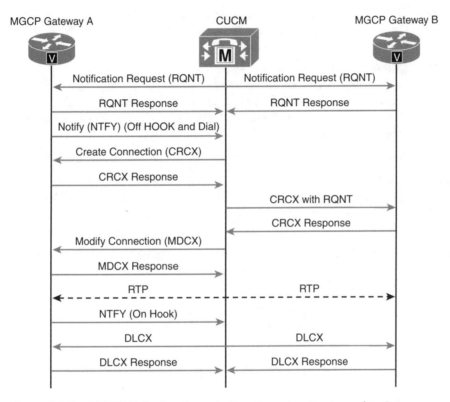

Figure 13-2 *MGCP Call Flow between Two Gateways Registered to Same CUCM Server*

The following events occur during the MGCP call flow illustrated in Figure 13-2:

Step 1.   The call-control agent (CUCM) sends a notification request (RQNT) to each gateway. The request instructs the gateways to wait for an off-hook transition (event). When the off-hook transition event occurs, the call-control agent instructs the gateways to supply a dial tone (signal).

Step 2.   The gateways respond to the request (RQNT). The gateways and the call-control agent wait for a triggering event.

Step 3.   An endpoint/user on Gateway A goes off-hook. Gateway A sends a notify (NTFY) to CUCM, and CUCM in turn provides a dial tone to the endpoint.

Step 4.   As the user at the endpoint on Gateway A enters the digits, the gateway sends a notify (NTFY) to CUCM to advise that a requested event has occurred, followed by identifying the endpoint and the event (that is, the dialed digits).

Step 5.   CUCM does digit analysis and, after confirming that a call is possible based on the dialed digits, instructs Gateway A to create a connection (CRCX) with its endpoint (port/trunk).

Step 6.   The gateway responds with a session description if it is able to accommodate the connection. The session description identifies (at least) an IP address and UDP port for use in a subsequent RTP session.

Step 7.   CUCM sends a connection request to Gateway B. In the request, CUCM provides the session description obtained from Gateway A. CUCM also sends a notification request that instructs Gateway B about the signals and events that it should now consider relevant, such as ringing and the endpoint's off-hook transition.

Step 8.   Gateway B responds to the request with its session description to CUCM.

Step 9.   CUCM relays the session description received from Gateway B to Gateway A in a modify connection request (MDCX). This request might contain an encapsulated notify request that describes the relevant signals and events at this stage of the call setup. Gateway A responds to the request.

Step 10.   Now that Gateway A and Gateway B have the required session descriptions to establish the RTP session, they open an RTP stream over prenegotiated (CUCM relayed) IP addresses and UDP ports.

Step 11.   The endpoint/user on Gateway A terminates the call and goes on-hook. CUCM requested a notification of such an event, so Gateway A notifies CUCM.

Step 12.   CUCM sends a delete connection (DLCX) request to each gateway so the session can be terminated.

Step 13.   The gateways delete the connection and respond to CUCM.

MGCP Gateway and CUCM Configuration

This section addresses the configuration of an MGCP gateway and relevant configuration on CUCM.

To add an MGCP gateway in CUCM, follow these steps:

Step 1.   Go to the CUCM Administration page and choose **Device > Gateway**.

Step 2.   Click **Add New**.

Step 3.   From the Gateway Type drop-down menu, choose the MGCP gateway type that you want to add, followed by MGCP as the protocol.

Step 4.   Enter the gateway Domain Name (such as 3945E.mynetwork.local, which must match the configured name and domain on the IOS gateway), enter a description, and select the appropriate CUCM Group as shown in Figure 13-3.

Figure 13-3   *CUCM MGCP Gateway Configuration*

Step 5.   Configure the Slot/VIC/Endpoint. Click **Save**.

Step 6.   Select the subunit (depending on the router model number) and configure the same.

Example 13-1 shows the MGCP configuration on an IOS voice gateway.

Example 13-1   *MGCP Gateway Configuration*

```
MGCPRouter(config)# ccm-manager fallback-mgcp
MGCPRouter(config)# ccm-manager switchback graceful
MGCPRouter(config)# ccm-manager redundant-host 198.18.133.7
MGCPRouter(config)# ccm-manager music-on-hold
MGCPRouter(config)# ccm-manager mgcp
!
MGCPRouter(config)# mgcp
MGCPRouter(config)# mgcp call-agent 198.18.133.3  2427 service-type mgcp version 0.1
MGCPRouter(config)# mgcp dtmf-relay voip codec all mode out-of-band
```

```
MGCPRouter(config)# mgcp bind control source-interface loopback 0
MGCPRouter(config)# mgcp bind media source-interface loopback 0
MGCPRouter(config)# mgcp dtmf-relay codec all mode out-of-band
!
MGCPRouter(config)# dial-peer voice 9999 pots
MGCPRouter(config-dial-peer)# service mgcpapp
MGCPRouter(config-dial-peer)# port 0/0/1:23
```

Table 13-2 describes the various commands used in Example 13-1.

Table 13-2   *Cisco IOS Gateway MGCP Commands*

Command	Description
ccm-manager fallback-mgcp	Enables CUCM fallback when a CUCM server is unavailable.
ccm-manager switchback graceful	Enables graceful switchback from one CUCM server to another in case of a CUCM server failure.
ccm-manager redundant-host	Defines redundant host(s), i.e., CUCM servers for the MGCP gateway to connect with when primary CUCM server is down or connection with it is lost.
ccm-manager music-on-hold	Enables Music on Hold (MOH).
mgcp call-agent	Defines call-control agent(s) for the MGCP gateway.
mgcp bind control source-interface	Binds signaling to the desired interface (physical, logical, or loopback).
mgcp bind media source-interface	Binds signaling to the desired interface (physical, logical, or loopback).
mgcp dtmf-relay codec	Defines DTMF-related parameters.
mgcpapp	Associates a dial peer with the MGCP application.

The next section describes Session Initiation Protocol (SIP).

Session Initiation Protocol

Session Initiation Protocol (SIP) is an IETF standards-based signaling protocol used for multimedia (voice and video) communications. SIP is an application-layer protocol and can leverage TCP or UDP for transmission. It is a text-based protocol much alike Hypertext Transfer Protocol (HTTP).

Note SIP also offer TLS for signaling, known as Secure SIP (SIPS). While SIP uses TCP/UDP port 5060; SIPS uses TCP port 5061. For more information regarding SIPS and secure SIP trunks, refer to Securing Cisco IP Telephony Networks.

Analogous to MGCP, SIP uses SDP for negotiating media types and formats, such as audio and video codecs, transport protocol parameters, ports, and so on. SIP, however, unlike MGCP, works in a peer-peer relationship. SDP operates in an offer-answer approach such that the session-initiating endpoint (UA) specifies desired session parameters (such as supported codecs), and the receiving endpoint (UA) replies with matching session parameters. Each resource in a SIP network is identified by a Uniform Resource Identifier (URI). A typical SIP URI is in the following format: sip:*username*:*password*@*host*:*port*. Figure 13-4 depicts a SIP gateway setup in a Cisco Collaboration network.

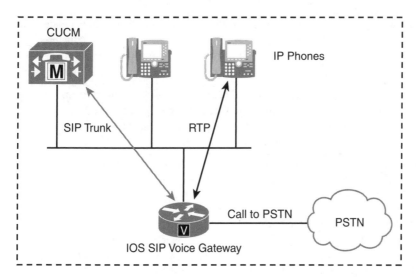

Figure 13-4 *SIP Gateway in a Cisco Collaboration Network*

SIP sends DTMF digits in-band. However, it can use out-of-band DTMF as well. In a SIP session, DTMF can be transported as:

- KeyPad Markup Language (KPML)
- Unsolicited Notify (UN)
- Network Termination Equipment (NTE) (RFC 2833).

KPML and UN are out-of-band DTMF transportation mechanisms, whereas NTE is an in-band mechanism for DTMF delivery. KPML and NTE are standards based, whereas UN is a nonstandard protocol.

A SIP network includes many entities for establishing, terminating, and managing SIP sessions, as listed and described in Table 13-3.

Table 13-3   *SIP Network Components*

Network Element	Description
SIP user agent (UA)	Manages send and receive SIP messages and manages a session. A SIP endpoint can act as both a user agent client (UAC) and a user agent server (UAS).
SIP user agent client (UAC)	Initiates and sends requests and gets a response from a SIP UAS or SIP proxy server. UAC, however, is a logical role and lasts only for the duration of a SIP transaction.
SIP user agent server (UAS)	Responds to SIP requests by accepting, rejecting, or redirecting the request. Analogous to UAC, UAS is also a logical role that lasts only for the duration of a SIP transaction.
SIP proxy server	Provides routing, enforces policies, provides features, and authenticates and authorizes users.
SIP redirect server	UAS server that provides address translation and that generates 3XX (redirection) responses to requests it receives, thereby directing the client to contact an alternate set of URIs. It allows SIP proxy servers to redirect invites to external domains as well.
SIP registrar server	A SIP endpoint that accepts REGISTER requests from SIP UAs and places the information received in those requests into a location service for the domain it handles. This allows users to register their current locations.
SIP back-to-back user agent (B2BUA)	Receives requests from UAs. However, it generates a new request on their path to the destination.

There are two SIP message types: request and response. A request message is sent by a client to a server and is used to invoke certain methods (functions). A response message is sent by a server to a client in answer to the request and indicates the status of the request received. Table 13-4 lists the methods available for SIP requests.

Table 13-4   *SIP Request Methods*

Method	Description
INVITE	Used by a UA to initiate a session with a UAC. When this arrives at a UAS, the UAS processes it and sends a suitable type of response message.
REGISTER	Method used by a UA to indicate its current IP address and the URI for which it would like to receive calls to register its contact information. Cisco SIP phones send their MAC addresses and register their lines with the primary CUCM using REGISTER messages.
ACK	Confirms reliable message exchange and is sent in reply to a final response message from a server.

BYE	Terminates a session between users.
CANCEL	Terminates a pending request (a request for which a final response has not yet been received).
OPTIONS	Requests information about the capabilities of a caller, without setting up a call.
Provisional Response Acknowledgement (PRACK)	Adds an acknowledgment system to the Provisional response (1XX). PRACK is sent in response to a Provisional response.

Table 13-5 lists the types of SIP responses.

Table 13-5 *SIP Responses*

SIP Response	Description
Provisional (1XX)	Indicates that a request has been received and is being processed. It is informational in nature.
Success (2XX)	Indicates success (the action was successfully received, understood, and accepted).
Redirection (3XX)	Indicates that further action needs to be taken by the sender to complete the request, perhaps in case of a redirection in response to a UA by SIP proxy.
Redirection (4XX)	Indicates client failure to in response to or to comply with a request.
Server Error (5XX)	Indicates a server's failure to fulfill a valid request by client.
Global Failure (6XX)	Indicates a global failure and that the request cannot be fulfilled at any server.

SIP supports early offer (EO) and delayed offer (DO) for capability negotiation. In case of an early offer, the SDP message is sent from the calling party to the called party in the initial INVITE message. The called party responds with the negotiated capability in the 200 OK to the calling party. In case of delayed offer, the called party sends the SDP message in the 200 OK message to the calling party. The calling party responds with the negotiated parameter in the ACK message to the called party. SIP also supports early media and delayed media for media channel negotiation. In the case of early media, the media between the called and calling party is established before the session establishment. The called party sends 183 instead of 180 and allows the calling party to establish a bearer channel between the two. With delayed media, the media is established once the SIP session negotiation is complete.

Cisco IOS gateways support call survivability that leverage the SIP trunk to CUCM cluster. The device pool of the CUCM SIP trunk configuration (configuration is covered in next section) offers the ability to the IOS gateway to leverage the call manager group and offer graceful switchover to next call processing server if the connection with active CUCM is lost.

SIP Gateway Call Flow

Figure 13-5 depicts a SIP call flow between Gateway A (UAC) and Gateway B (UAS).

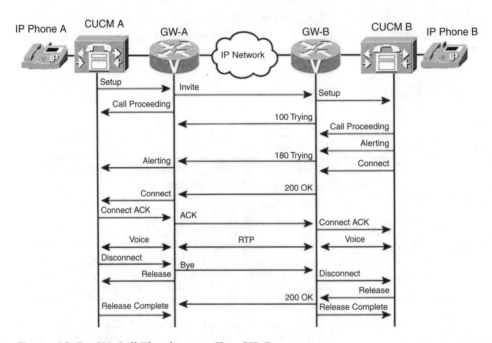

Figure 13-5   *SIP Call Flow between Two SIP Gateways*

In Figure 13-5, IP phone A initiates a call to IP phone B. After IP phone A initiates the call, the call flow proceeds as follows.

Step 1.   Phone A dials the DN of Phone B. After digit analysis, CUCM A sends a call setup signal to GW-A, which then sends a SIP INVITE message to GW-B. This INVITE contains SDP information for capabilities negotiation. In the meanwhile, GW-A also sends a call proceeding message to CUCM A.

Step 2.   GW-B exchanges call setup message with CUCM B and sends SIP responses 100 (trying) and 180 (ringing) to GW-A.

Step 3.   When the IP Phone B picks up the call, CUCM B sends a connect message to GW-B, which then forwards a SIP 200 (OK) response to GW-A. This OK response contains SDP information with the capabilities that both IP phones support.

Step 4.   GW-A delivers a connect message to CUCM A. When CUCM A acknowledges that with a connect ACK, GW-A sends a SIP ACK message to GW-B.

Step 5.   GW-B sends a connect acknowledgement to CUCM B, and the call is active. At this point, normal voice streams exist between the two IP phones and the gateways.

Step 6.   When IP phone A hangs up the phone, CUCM A sends a call disconnect message to GW-A. GW-A then sends a SIP BYE message to GW-B and a release message to the CUCM A. CUCM A in turn responds with a release complete message.

Step 7.   GW-B sends a call disconnect message to CUCM B, which responds with a release message.

Step 8.   GW-B forwards a SIP 200 (OK) response to GW-A and a release complete message to CUCM B. The call is concluded.

SIP Gateway Configuration

To configure a SIP gateway for communication with CUCM, a SIP trunk is required.

Note   A SIP gateway does not register with a call-control agent like an MGCP gateway.

The following steps show how to add a SIP trunk in CUCM.

Step 1.   Go to the CUCM Administration page and choose **Device > Trunk**. Click **Add New**.

Step 2.   From the Trunk Type menu, choose **SIP Trunk**. From the Device Protocol menu, choose **SIP**.

Step 3.   Enter the **Device Name, Description, Device Pool,** and other parameters as shown in Figure 13-6.

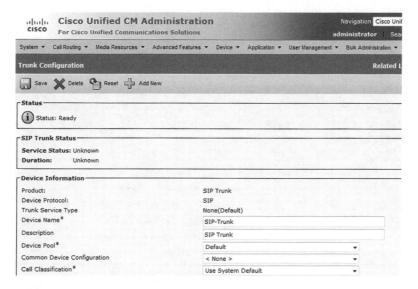

Figure 13-6   *SIP Trunk Configuration*

Step 4.   In the **SIP Information** section, you can add either an IP address for the SIP router or a DNS Service (SRV) record as shown in Figure 13-7. After entering the other mandatory parameters, click **Save**.

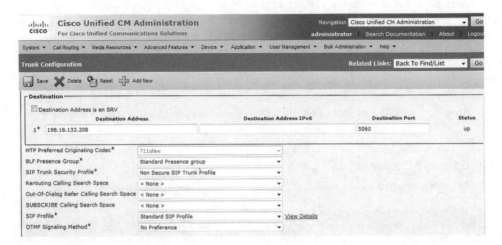

Figure 13-7   *SIP Trunk—Destination Configuration*

Example 13-2 shows the configuration of the SIP gateway.

Note   The configuration includes support for early offer.

Example 13-2   *SIP Gateway Configuration*

```
SIPRouter(config)# interface loopback 0
SIPRouter(config-if)# ip address 198.18.133.208 255.255.255.0
!
SIPRouter(config)# voice service voip
SIPRouter(conf-voi-serv)# sip
SIPRouter(conf-serv-sip)# session transport tcp
SIPRouter(conf-serv-sip)# bind control source-interface loopback 0
SIPRouter(conf-serv-sip)# bind media source-interface loopback 0
SIPRouter(conf-serv-sip)# early-offer forced
!
SIPRouter(config)# dial-peer voice 10 voip
SIPRouter(config-dial-peer)# session protocol sipv2
SIPRouter(config-dial-peer)# session target ipv4:198.18.133.3
SIPRouter(config-dial-peer)# destination-pattern 1...$
SIPRouter(config-dial-peer)# dtmf-relay rtp-nte sip-notify
SIPRouter(config-dial-peer)# codec g711ulaw
```

Table 13-6 describes the various commands used in Example 13-2.

Table 13-6   *Cisco IOS Gateway SIP Commands*

Command	Description
voice service voip	Defines the voice service parameters (in this case for SIP).
session transport tcp	Enables transport over TCP for SIP trunk to CUCM.
bind control source-interface	Binds signaling to the desired interface (in this case loopback 0).
bind media source-interface	Binds media to the desired interface (in this case loopback 0).
early-offer forced	Enables forced early-offer for sending SDP in initial INVITE.
session protocol sipv2	Defines the session protocol as SIP to be used on VOIP dial-peer.
dtmf-relay rtp-nte sip-notify	Specifies the use of RFC 2833 in-band DTMF relay as first priority and out-of-band DTMF relay using the SIP notify method, second priority.

The next section describes H.323 protocol.

H.323 Protocol (Suite)

H.323 is a suite of protocols, codecs, and standards and was developed by ITU as a framework for interactive multimedia communications. An H.323 gateway is a device that can interface with the public switched telephone network (PSTN), IP networks, call-control agents, H.323 gatekeepers, H.323 endpoints, and so on. Figure 13-8 shows the placement of an H.323 gateway in a Cisco Collaboration network.

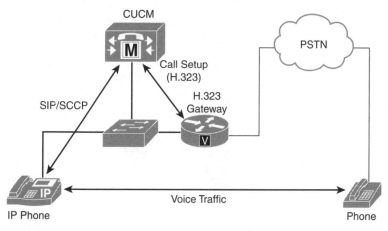

Figure 13-8   *H.323 Gateway in a Cisco Collaboration Network*

The following are key protocols in H.323 suite.

- **H.225:** Also known as H.255.0, H.225 is a call-control and signaling protocol used to establish, control, and terminate calls between H.323 endpoints.

- **H.245:** A control channel protocol to transmit nontelephone signals such as information related to capabilities, jitter management, and flow control, establish logical channels for the transmission of media, and so on. In certain cases, H.245 can be tunneled within H.225.

- **H.225 RAS (Registration, Admission, and Status):** Used for communication between H.323 endpoints (such as CUCM) and gatekeeper or gatekeeper-to-peer gatekeeper communication. RAS has a number of messages for registration, admission, and status, most of which have a response type of confirm or reject.

- **H.235:** Provides security within the H.323 suite for both signaling and media.

- **H.239:** A standard for multiple video channels within a single H.323 session. H.239 enables dual streams for use in videoconferencing, one for live video and the other for presentation/still images.

- **H.450:** This series of protocols describes various supplementary services such as call transfer, call hold, and so on.

- H.460: This series of protocols defines optional extensions that may be implemented by an endpoint or a gatekeeper Network Address Translation (NAT)/firewall (FW) traversal.

Table 13-7 lists the H.225 call signaling messages.

Table 13-7   *H.225 Signaling Messages*

Call Signaling Message	Description
Setup	Sent by the H.323 gateway to initiate an H.323 session.
Setup Acknowledge	Sent by the destination device to the initiating device.
Call Proceeding	Sent by the destination endpoint to indicate that it has received all the information and is trying to reach out to the called endpoint.
Connect	Sent by the destination endpoint to the calling endpoint to indicate that the call has been accepted/answered.
Alerting	Sent by the destination endpoint to the originating endpoint to indicate that the called phone is ringing.
Information	Used to send additional information for a call. For example, when using overlap sending, each digit is sent one at a time in an information message.
Release Complete	Sent by a device to indicate the call's release.

Progress	Sent by an H.323 gateway to indicate a call's progress. You typically see progress messages when internetworking with a non-ISDN network because audio cut-through must be treated differently in this case.
Status	Used to respond to an unknown call signaling message or to a status inquiry message.
Status Inquiry	Used to request call status. Normally the device receiving this message responds with a status message indicating the current call state for the specific call reference.
Notify	Used to notify a device of a change that has occurred in the call.

H.323 Call Flow

This section gives an insight to H.323 gateway-based call flow. Figure 13-9 gives an overview of the call flow.

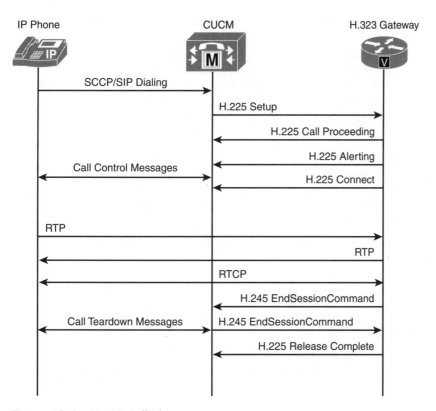

Figure 13-9   *H.323 Call Flow*

The following steps describe the call flow:

Step 1.   When an IP phone initiates a call (using SCCP or SIP protocol with CUCM), CUCM sends an H.225 setup message that instructs the gateway to initiate a call to the destination (PSTN) phone.

Step 2.   The gateway initiates the call setup to the PSTN and at same time sends an H.225 Call Proceeding message to CUCM.

Step 3.   As the ISDN Alerting information comes in to the H.323 gateway from the PSTN switch, it informs CUCM about the state of the call such that CUCM can instruct the IP phone to play back the call proceeding tone.

Step 4.   When the called party on the PSTN phone picks up the call and the H.323 gateway receives a Connect message from the PSTN switch, the H.323 gateway forwards that message as an H.225 message to CUCM to establish the call.

Step 5.   RTP stream is established between the IP phone and the H.323 gateway.

Step 6.   When the user at the IP phone hangs up, CUCM sends an H.225 Release Complete message to the H.323 gateway to terminate the call.

Similar to SIP protocol, H.323 gateways can initiate an H.323 session in two ways: fast-start and slow-start. Fast-start (also known as *fast connect*; available in H.323 version 2) allows the media channels to be operational before the CONNECT message is sent. Essentially, H.245 is still negotiated later. However, the actual media channels can be established by tunneling H.245 within H.225 messages. Slow-start implementations on other hand require that the media channels wait until after the CONNECT message to negotiate IP addresses, ports, and codecs. In slow start, many H.245 messages are exchanged over a separate TCP connection.

H.323 gateways by default do not support call preservation and need additional configuration to support the same to be configured. This can be achieved by an enabled call preservation feature by configuring **call preserve** under voice service voip > h323. Additionally, on CUCM enable call preservation for H.323 gateways by browsing to **Service > Service Parameters > Cisco Unified CallManager > Advanced** and setting the clusterwide parameters for **Device-H.323 > "Allow Peer to Preserve H.323 Calls"** parameter to True.

H.323 Gateway and CUCM Configuration

An H.323 gateway must be defined in CUCM. To add an H.323 gateway in CUCM, follow these steps:

Note   Unlike an MGCP gateway, an H.323 gateway does not register with CUCM.

Step 1.   Go to the **CUCM Administration** page and choose **Device > Gateway**. Click **Add New**.

Step 2.   From the Gateway Type drop-down menu, choose **H.323 Gateway**.

Step 3. Enter the **Device Name** (IP address or DNS name of the gateway), **Description**, **Device Pool**, and other parameters as shown in Figure 13-10. Click **Save**.

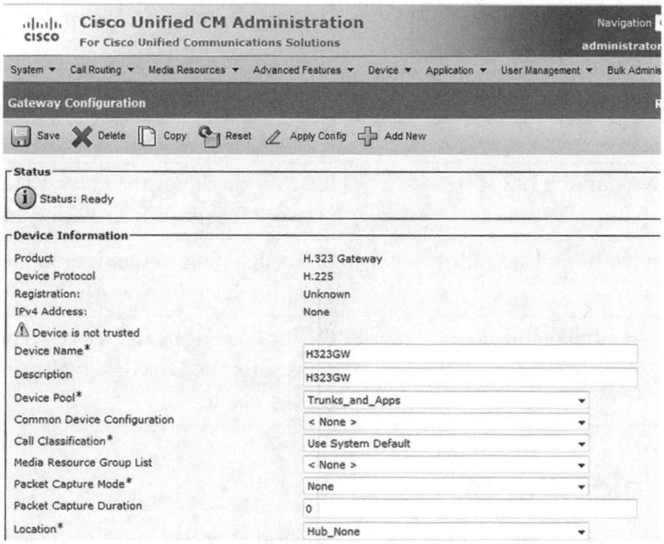

Figure 13-10 *CUCM H.323 Gateway Configuration*

To configure an H.323 gateway to communicate with a call-control agent such as CUCM, the gateway can be configured as shown in Example 13-3.

Example 13-3 *H.323 Gateway Configuration*

```
H323Router(config)# voice service voip
H323Router(conf-voi-serv)# h323
H323Router(conf-serv-h323)# ccm-compatible
H323Router(conf-serv-h323)# call start fast
!
H323Router(config)# interface loopback 0
H323Router(config-if)# ip address 198.18.133.208 255.255.255.0
H323Router(config-if)# h323-gateway voip interface
H323Router(config-if)# h323-gateway voip h323-id H323Router
H323Router(config-if)# h323-gateway voip bind srcaddr 198.18.133.208
!
H323router(config)# dial-peer voice 100 voip
H323router(config-dial-peer)# destination-pattern 1...$
H323router(config-dial-peer)# session target ipv4:198.18.133.13
H323router(config-dial-peer)# dtmf-relay h245-alphanumeric
H323router(config-dial-peer)# codec g711ulaw
H323router(config-dial-peer)# no vad
```

Table 13-8 describes the various commands used in Example 13-3.

Table 13-8 *Cisco IOS Gateway H.323 Commands*

Command	Description
voice service voip	Defines the voice service parameters (in this case for H.323).
ccm-compatible	Enables CUCM compatible signaling.
call start fast	Enables fast-start.
h323-gateway voip id h323-id	Identify the ID of the gateway in an H.323 network (used for RAS with Gatekeepers).
h323-gateway voip bind srcaddr	Binds signaling to the desired interface (in this case loopback 0).
dtmf-relay h245-alphanumeric	Defines out-of-band DTMF relay mechanism that transports the DTMF signals using H.245 (media channel).

Digital Voice Ports

Digital interfaces/ports connect the POTS world to the IP world and leverage digitization of signaling and audio transmissions. Digitization of voice has many benefits, including quality improvement, more channels to transmit voice, and overall lower cost of operation. Digital interfaces/circuits come in many flavors, such as T1, E1, Basic Rate Interface (BRI), Primary Rate Interface (PRI), and so on. These ports are available as modules that fit in an IOS router card/slot (on the chassis) as shown in Figure 13-11.

Figure 13-11 *Cisco MFT VWIC interface card with Two Flex T1/E1 ports*

The following is an overview of the various digital voice ports available in the Cisco Collaboration network.

- **T1:** Uses time division multiplexing (TDM) to transmit digital data over 24 voice channels using channel-associated signaling (CAS)

- **E1:** Uses time division multiplexing TDM to transmit digital data over 32 timeslots including 30 voice channels, 1 framing channel, and 1 signaling channel

- **ISDN:** A circuit-switched telephone network system designed to allow digital transmission of voice and data over ordinary telephone copper wires. ISDN has the following implementations.

  - **BRI:** Total bandwidth is 128 kb/s; across 2 B channels and 1 D channel

  - **T1 PRI:** Total bandwidth is 1.5 Mb/s; across 23 B channels and 1 D channel

  - **E1 PRI:** Total bandwidth is 2.044 Mb/s; across 30 B and 2 D channels

Table 13-9 gives insight into the various interface types.

Table 13-9 *Cisco Digital Voice Port Characteristics*

	BRI	**T1 PRI**	**E1 PRI**
B Channels	2 × 64 kb/s	23 × 64 kb/s	30 × 64 kb/s
D Channels	1 × 16 kb/s	1 × 64 kb/s	1 × 64 kb/s
Framing	16 kb/s	8 kb/s	64 kb/s
Total Data Rate	160 kb/s	1.544 Mb/s	2.048 Mb/s
Framing	NT, TE frame	SF, ESF	Multiframe
Line Coding	2B1Q or 4B3T	AMI or B8ZS	HDB3

The following sections describe the features and configuration of the digital voice ports.

Integrated Services Digital Network

Integrated services digital network (ISDN) is a circuit-switched telephone network system designed to allow digital transmission of voice and data over conventional telephone copper wires. ISDN is an ITU-T standard protocol that is defined by various network layers such as:

- **ISDN Q.911:** a physical layer protocol, equivalent to the physical layer of the Open Systems Interconnection (OSI) model.

- **ISDN Q.921:** At Layer 2, ISDN signaling is provided by the Link Access Procedure on the D (signaling) channel (LAPD), as specified in ITU-T Q.921. Terminal endpoint identifier (TEI) identifies end devices and can either be statically configured at the end device or dynamically allocated by the PSTN.

■ **ISDN Q.931:** ISDN call-control signaling and access to services is specified by ITU-T Q.931, which allows call setup, maintenance, and teardown. Q.931 supports user-to-user, circuit-switched, and packet-switched connections in addition to several call establishment, termination, and information messages.

ISDN leverages common channel signaling (CCS). Channel-associated signaling (CAS) on the other hand is the other flavor of digital signaling used for signaling between PBXs and traditional telephony. Following sections describe the two signaling methods and associated digital voice port implementations.

Common Channel Signaling

Common channel signaling (CCS) allows voice, video, and data to be sent over separate channels (media over B channels whereas signaling over D channels). The signaling data is sent over a (dedicated) single D (data) channel used by all B (bearer) channels.

> **Note**   B, or bearer, channels are media channels in which actual information travels whereas the D, or data channel, is the control channel that describes the signaling aspect pertinent to the B channels.

There are two ISDN (CCS) interface types:

■ **Basic Rate Interface (BRI):** Provides two 64-kbps bearer channels and a 16-kbps signaling channel, also known as 2B+D. A BRI interface has an aggregate bit rate of 144 kbps.

■ **Primary Rate Interface (PRI):** Provides 23 (T1) or 30 (E1) channels each with 64-kbps bearer channels and a single 64-kbps signaling channel, also known as 23B+D or 30B+D. A T1 has an aggregate bit rate of 1.544 mbps, whereas an E1 has a bit rate of 2.048 mbps

Figure 13-12 illustrates ISDN BRI interface.

Figure 13-12   *ISDN BRI Interface*

Example 13-4 illustrates the BRI interface configuration.

Example 13-4 *BRI Interface Configuration*

```
BRIRouter(config)# network-clock-participate wic 0
!
BRIRouter(config)# interface bri 0/0
BRIRouter(config-if)# no ip address
BRIRouter(config-if)# isdn switch-type basic-net3
BRIRouter(config-if)# isdn incoming-voice voice
BRIRouter(config-if)# isdn protocol-emulate user
BRIRouter(config-if)# no shutdown
```

Table 13-10 describes the various commands used in Example 13-4.

Table 13-10 *Cisco IOS Gateway BRI Commands*

Command	Description
network-clock participate wic	Enables the ports on a specified network module or Voice/WAN interface card (VWIC) to use the network clock.
interface bri <slot number>	Defines the BRI interface number for specified slot number.
isdn switch-type	Defines ISDN switch type. For BRI options are basic-net3 and basic-qsig.
isdn incoming-voice voice	Enables the port to treat incoming ISDN voice calls as voice calls.
isdn protocol-emulate user	Configures (Layer 1) port mode emulation as a slave. (protocol-emulate network defines switch/master side).
no shutdown	Enables BRI port

Figure 13-13 illustrates ISDN T1 PRI interface.

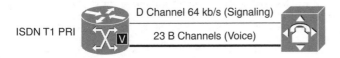

ISDN T1 PRI — D Channel 64 kb/s (Signaling) — 23 B Channels (Voice)

Figure 13-13 *T1 PRI Interface*

Example 13-5 illustrates the T1 PRI interface configuration.

Example 13-5   *T1 PRI Interface Configuration*

```
PRIRouter(config)# card type t1 0 0
!
PRIRouter(config)# voice-card 1
PRIRouter(config-voicecard)# codec complexity medium
!
PRIRouter(config)# controller t1 0/0
PRIRouter(config-controller)# clock source line
PRIRouter(config-controller)# cablelength long 0db
PRIRouter(config-controller)# framing esf
PRIRouter(config-controller)# linecode b8zs
PRIRouter(config-controller)# pri-group timeslots 1-23
!
PRIRouter(config)# interface Serial 0/0:23
PRIRouter(config-if)# no ip address
PRIRouter(config-if)# isdn switch-type primary-ni
PRIRouter(config-if)# isdn incoming-voice voice
PRIRouter(config-if)# isdn-bchan-number-order descending
PRIRouter(config-if)# isdn protocol-emulate user
PRIRouter(config-if)# no shutdown
```

Table 13-11 describes the various commands used in Example 13-5.

Table 13-11   *Cisco IOS Gateway T1 PRI Commands*

Command	Description
card type t1 <slot subslot >	Sets the card type to T1.
voice-card 1	Enters voice card interface configuration mode.
codec complexity medium	Specifies the codec complexity. The available options are flex—up to 16 calls, high—up to 6 voice calls, or medium—up to 8 voice calls.
controller t1 0/0	Enters controller configuration mode for the VWIC.
clock source	Defines clock source. Available options are line or internal.
cablelength long 0db	Compensates for the reception loss due to the cable length and tries to controls far-end crosstalk.
framing	Specifies a frame type. Available frame types for T1 controllers can be specified as sf for superframe or esf for extended superframe.
linecode	Specifies line encoding for the controller. Line-code values for T1 can be ami or b8zs.
pri-group timeslots	Specifies that the controller should be set up as a PRI interface.

interface serial	Enters serial interface configuration.
isdn switch-type	Defines ISDN switch type.
isdn incoming-voice voice	Enables the port to treat incoming ISDN voice calls as voice calls.
isdn-bchan-number-order	Enables B channel selection for outgoing calls on a PRI interface. Options are ascending (starting from lowest numbered channel) to descending (starting with highest numbered channel).
isdn protocol-emulate user	Configures (Layer 1) port mode emulation as slave. (protocol-emulate network dewfines switch/master side).
no shutdown	Enables T1 port

Figure 13-14 shows E1 PRI interface.

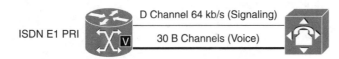

ISDN E1 PRI

D Channel 64 kb/s (Signaling)

30 B Channels (Voice)

Figure 13-14   *E1 PRI Interface*

Example 13-6 outlines a PRI interface configuration for an E1 circuit.

Example 13-6   *PRI Interface Configuration*

```
PRIRouter(config)# card type E1 0 1
!
PRIRouter(config)# network-clock-participate wic 1
!
PRIRouter(config)# controller e1 0/1
PRIRouter(config-controller)# clock source line
PRIRouter(config-controller)# cablelength long 0db
PRIRouter(config-controller)# framing crc4
PRIRouter(config-controller)# linecode hbd3
PRIRouter(config-controller)# pri-group timeslots 1-31
!
PRIRouter(config)# interface Serial 0/1:15
PRIRouter(config-if)# no ip address
PRIRouter(config-if)# isdn switch-type primary-net5
PRIRouter(config-if)# isdn incoming-voice voice
PRIRouter(config-if)# isdn-bchan-number-order descending
PRIRouter(config-if)# no shutdown
```

> **Note**   The commands used for configuring T1 and E1 PRI interfaces is almost similar.
> The major difference is related to framing, linecode, pri-group timeslots, and ISDN
> switch-type.

QSIG is an ISDN-based signaling protocol, based on Q.931 signaling. It is primarily used
for feature transparency between different vendor PBXs. QSIG has two layers of signaling
procedures:

- **Basic call:** Defines the signaling procedures and protocol for the purpose of circuit-switched call control at the Q reference point between private integrated services network exchanges (PINXs) and is explained in Standard ECMA-143.

- **Generic function:** Defines the signaling protocol for the control of supplementary services and additional network features and is explained in Standard ECMA-165.

QSIG features can support the following:

- Basic call features: call completion, diversion, and transfer

- Call identification services

- Message waiting indication (MWI) service

- Path replacement

- Do not disturb and override

Example 13-7 illustrates ISDN-QSIG configuration for a T1 controller.

Example 13-7   *ISDN-QSIG Configuration*

```
QSIGRouter(config)# controller t1 0/1
QSIGRouter(config-controller)# pri-group timeslots 1-23
!
QSIGRouter(config)# interface serial 0/1:23
QSIGRouter(config-if)# isdn switch-type primary-qsig
QSIGRouter(config-if)# isdn protocol-emulate user
```

In Example 13-7, ISDN switch-type primary-qsig defines the signaling as QSIG.

ISDN Dial Plan—Type of Number (TON)

Before proceeding to the next section, it's important to understand the number format
used by ISDN signaling. In the ISDN world, to differentiate between different types of
calls the type of number (TON) [or nature of address indicator (NAI)] parameter is used.
This indicates the scope of the address value such as whether a number being received
or dialed is a "local number format (e.g., 555XXXX), a "national" number format
(e.g. 408555XXXX), or an "international" number format (e.g., 498912345678). This is

relevant for E.164 (PSTN) numbers. Voice gateways must consider the TON when transforming the called and calling numbers for ISDN calls.

> **Note** The calling-party number in ISDN is the automatic number identification (ANI). The called-party number in ISDN is the dialed number identification service (DNIS).

When leveraging an E.164 number plan and digit manipulation, most of the issues with incorrect representation of ANI or DNIS are rectified. For example, some ISDN networks present the inbound ANI as the shortest dialable number combined with the TON which is not a fully qualified PSTN number. This can be a potential problem since it results in an ANI that cannot be called back. Moreover, improper ANI or DNIS representation within and outside of your collaboration network can cause calls to be rejected by the CUCM/carrier.

Examples of TON include the following use cases (using NANP):

- A call is received from the local area with a subscriber TON and a seven-digit number such as 5551234 (ANI). This number only needs to be prefixed with outside access code 9, that is, 95551234; for CUCM to route the call over traditional PSTN or SIP carrier circuit.

- A call is received with a national TON and ten digits. In this case, the DNIS needs to be modified by adding access code 9 and the long-distance number 1, so the call can be completed successfully. For example, 914085551234.

- A call is received from outside of the US with an international TON. For this call, the access code 9 and 011 must be added to the received number (ANI), as a prefix to the country code. For example, 9011498912345678.

Digit manipulation using various mechanisms (voice translation rules and profiles, num-exp, and so on) are discussed later in this chapter.

TON is supported in ISDN circuits, on MGCP gateways, and H.323 gateways. TON is not supported on SIP gateways.

Channel-Associated Signaling

Channel-associated signaling (CAS) is a variant of digital signaling wherein the signaling is carried within the channels themselves instead of reserving a dedicated channel for signaling as in ISDN. CAS is also known as *robbed-bit signaling* because its signaling operates by "robbing" the least significant bit of information from voice channels (every sixth sample of every channel) and using this to send on-hook, off-hook, and busy signal status.

T1 CAS uses in-band robbed-bit signaling. Signaling for a particular traffic circuit is permanently associated with that circuit. Signaling is based on analog signaling: loop-start, ground-start, and E&M variants. E&M supports feature groups such as feature groups D and FGD. Example 13-8 describes the configuration of a T1 CAS circuit.

Example 13-8 *T1 CAS Configuration*

```
CASRouter(config)# controller T1 0/0/0
CASRouter(config-controller)# framing esf
CASRouter(config-controller)# linecode b8zs
CASRouter(config-controller)# ds0-group 0 timeslots 1-24 type e&m-fgd dtmf dnis
```

In Example 13-8, ds0-group configures all channels for E&M, FXS, and SAS analog signaling with DTMF and DNIS support.

E1 R2 is an equivalent of T1 CAS for E1 systems. E1 R2 signaling specifications are defined in ITU-T Recommendations Q.400 to Q.490. E1 R2 supports inbound and outbound digital number identification service (DNIS) and automatic number identification (ANI). The channel in timeslot 0 is used for framing, syncing, and alarms. The channel in timeslot 16 is reserved for signaling. However, there is no link access procedure-D (LAPD). Example 13-9 describes the configuration of an E1 R2 circuit.

Example 13-9 *E1 R2 Configuration*

```
CASRouter(config)# controller E1 0/0/0
CASRouter(config-controller)# framing non-crc
CASRouter(config-controller)# linecode ami
CASRouter(config-controller)# ds0-group 0 timeslots 1-31 type r2-digital
  r2-compelled ani
```

In Example 13-9, ds0-group configures R2 channel-associated signaling on the E1 controller and setup for automatic number identification (ANI) collection.

Note R2 signaling has dialed number identification service (DNIS) support enabled by default.

Non-Facility Associated Signaling

The non-facility associated signaling (NFAS) protocol allows a single D channel to control multiple PRI interfaces. In other words, instead of giving away a D channel on, for example, three PRI T1 trunks, NFAS can be used to tie together all trunks' D channels, thereby using a single D channel on one of the three trunks. A backup D channel can be configured on a T1 trunk other than the primary trunk for resiliency. A sample configuration (for three T1 trunks) is shown in Example 13-10.

Example 13-10   *NFAS Configuration*

```
NFASRouter(config)# isdn switch-type primary-ni
!
NFASRouter(config)# controller T1 0
NFASRouter(config-controller)# framing esf
NFASRouter(config-controller)# clock source line primary
NFASRouter(config-controller)# linecode b8zs
NFASRouter(config-controller)# pri-group timeslots 1-24 nfas_d primary nfas_int 0
  nfas_group 0
!
NFASRouter(config)# controller T1 1
NFASRouter(config-controller)# framing esf
NFASRouter(config-controller)# clock source line secondary 1
NFASRouter(config-controller)# linecode b8zs
NFASRouter(config-controller)# pri-group timeslots 1-24 nfas_d backup nfas_int 1
  nfas_group 0
!
NFASRouter(config)#controller T1 2
NFASRouter(config-controller)# framing esf
NFASRouter(config-controller)# clock source line secondary 2
NFASRouter(config-controller)# linecode b8zs
NFASRouter(config-controller)# pri-group timeslots 1-24 nfas_d none nfas_int 2
  nfas_group
```

Direct Inward Dial

When calling to a voice port, the call is first answered by the gateway itself, and then the matching dial peer expects further digits to be dialed so the call can be routed to the destination extension. This is known as *two-stage dialing behavior*. This is common for any voice port, be it analog or digital. To avoid two-stage dialing and connect directly with the destination number (extension), implement direct inward dial (DID), which allows calls from the PSTN to be routed directly to extensions on the call-control agent. Thus, DID removes the hassle of operator-assisted dialing/ multistage dialing.

The following commands in Table 13-12 can be used to verify the BRI/PRI port and controller configurations, and voice call status.

Table 13-12 *Cisco IOS Gateway Voice Controller and Status Commands*

Command	Description
show voice port [*slot/port* | summary]	Displays configuration information about a specific voice port or a summary of all voice ports
show running-config	Displays the codec complexity setting for digital T1/E1 connections
show controllers bri *slot/port* show controllers T1 *slot/port* show controllers E1 *slot/port*	Displays information about the specified controller
show voice dsp	Displays voice channel configuration information for all DSP channels
show voice call summary	Verifies the call status for all voice ports
show call active voice	Displays the contents of the active call table
show call history voice	Displays the contents of the call history table

Cisco IOS Dial Plan

A dial plan allows people to call each other by dialing a number (or a SIP URI) on the phone. Dial plans include access codes, area codes, and specialized codes. Cisco IOS routers can implement a dial plan to route calls within a site, outside of a site to the PSTN, or to a main site/another remote site. A Cisco IOS dial plan has multiple components, such as:

- **Endpoint Addressing:** POTS dial peers for endpoint ports such as. e-phone DNs, foreign exchange station (FXS) ports

- **Call Path Selection and Call Routing:** Cisco IOS routers (like CUCM) allow call path selection and subsequent routing of calls over the selected (preferred) call path. Call path selection and associated call routing can be done on various attributes such as least-cost routing (LCR) or a circuit/trunk not being available.

- **Dial peer:** Dial peers allow calls to be received from VoIP or POTS at voice gateways and for sending calls from voice gateways to destination devices/trunks. Dial peers can point to or accept calls from an IP endpoint such as H.323, SIP, or MGCP endpoint/call-control or a PBX/PSTN-trunk for example T1, E1, or BRI. Dial peers allow for call routing and path selection

- **Dial plan digit manipulation:** At times it is required to manipulate digits so that the calling/called number can be changed and delivered as required to the destination.

- **Class of restriction (CoR):** Enables limiting incoming/outgoing calls because they are classes of restriction based on dial peers/ephones

The following section gives an overview of IOS dial plan.

Cisco IOS Voice Gateway Dial Plan Overview

This section gives an overview of the Cisco IOS dial plan. The subsequent sections explain the core concepts of IOS dial plan. Figure 13-15 gives an overview of the IOS dial plan and how the Cisco IOS voice gateways interact with elements within and outside of VoIP network.

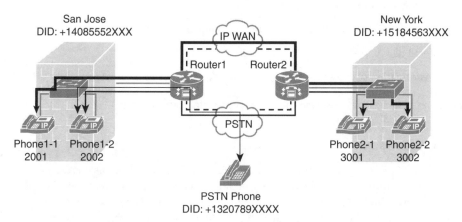

Figure 13-15   *Overview of Cisco IOS-based Dial Plan*

As seen in Figure 13-15 the two corporate locations of an organization in San Jose and New York are connected over an IP WAN and PSTN network. Router 1 and Router 2 offer two distinct call paths between San Jose and New York as well as connectivity to outside world.

Note   It is important to understand that PSTN in context of a modern day collaboration network can be a traditional trunk circuit or an SIP service provider.

When a user in San Jose (extension 2001) wishes to dial a user in New York (extension 3001), to save on toll charges, the call is routed over IP WAN using a multiprotocol label switching (MPLS) network or another way of connecting with ITSP such as digital subscriber line (DSL). However, when the IP WAN network is not available, the call is routed over PSTN. This remains transparent to the end user. On the flip side, if the user at 3001 wants to dial the PSTN phone +1320789XXXX, the call is routed over PSTN. All of this can be done by enforcing corporate-calling privileges via class of restriction to allow or disallow users to dial within and outside of corporate communications network. Moreover, the IOS dial plan allows to present the called number (called party) and the calling number (calling party) where the ITSP or PSTN service provider requires when the call goes over the PSTN circuit/trunk.

Therefore, the IOS dial plan provides the following:

- Connectivity for two or more locations of an organization

- Offers extension dialing so the ephone-DNs and devices connected to FXS ports can be dialed

- Call path selection using varied call-paths

- Digit manipulation for external and internal numbers where required

- Enforce dialing privileges

- Transformation of numbers where required (called and calling party)

The subsequent sections describe the IOS dial plan elements in detail.

Endpoint Addressing

Similar to CUCM, a Cisco IOS router also requires that the internal extensions are assigned a directory number. The directory numbers can be assigned as ephone-DNs in case of Cisco Unified Communications Manager Express (CUCME), which is an IOS-based call-control or dial peers on FXS ports. Endpoint addressing ensures that all endpoints such as IP phones, analog phones, and fax machines; as well as applications such as voice-mail systems, auto-attendants, and conferencing systems are reachable via assignment of directory numbers.

An example of number assignment is shown in Figure 13-16.

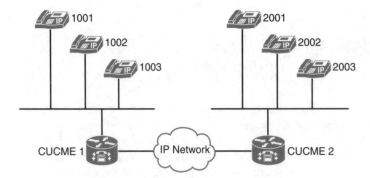

Figure 13-16 *CUCME-based Extension Numbers*

Similar to the CUCM dial plan, internal dialing can be achieved by controlling the number of extensions (4 digits or 5 digits for example), and for incoming calls, the direct inward dialing (DID) can be enabled so that DID numbers are mapped to internal directory numbers.

It is important to understand that while building an endpoint-addressing scheme for a multisite installation, the best practice is to design a flexible and scalable dial plan that has no impact on the end user. As discussed earlier, the endpoint addressing is primarily managed by call agents, such as CUCM, CUCME, or routers in survivable remote site telephony (SRST) mode.

> **Note**   For PSTN-routed calls, digit manipulation should be configured on the gateway to transform the internal numbers to E.164 numbers that can be used in the PSTN.

The next section describes call path selection and call routing which are functions of dial peers.

Call Path Selection and Call Routing

Call path selection and call routing are one of the most important dial plan components that define how and where calls should be routed. A voice gateway might be involved with both call routing and path selection based on the design and implementation. Figure 13-17 summarizes the two concepts.

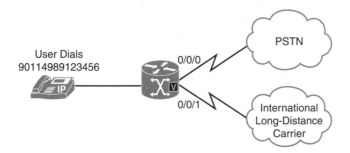

Figure 13-17   *Call Path Selection and Call Routing*

If a user dials an extension number in another location, for example, 408-555-2XXX, the call should be sent over the IP WAN. If the WAN path is unavailable due to network failure, insufficient bandwidth, or no response from remote router, to ensure that the call is completed and the process remains transparent to the end user, the call should be attempted over the PSTN circuit. Moreover, the call path can be defined based on the least-cost routing (LCR) wherein, based on the route that provides minimal cost for call to be completed.

Call routing usually depends on the called number (destination-based call routing is usually performed). This is similar to IP routing, which also relies on destination-based routing. Multiple paths to the same destination might exist, especially in multisite environments (for example, a path using an IP connection or a path using a PSTN connection). Path selection helps you decide which of the available paths should be used.

As seen in Figure 13-17, when a user dials an international number 90114989123456; the router can be setup to select a preferred path such as the international long-distance carrier trunk. Subsequently, the call is routed over the chosen path to the destination. It is important to understand that both call path selection and call routing leverage dial peers are discussed in next section.

Cisco IOS Dial Peers

On Cisco IOS routers, dial peers are used to configure dial plans and to identify call source and destination as well as each call leg in the call connection. Dial peers are a critical component of a Cisco Collaboration network. There are two types of dial peers:

- Plain old telephone system (POTS)

- Voice over IP (VoIP) dial peers

Note   Other dial peer options are Multimedia over IP (MMoIP), Voice over ATM (VoATM), and Voice over Frame Relay (VoFR).

Example 13-11 shows basic configuration for POTS and VoIP dial peers.

Example 13-11   *POTS and VOIP Dial-Peer Configuration*

```
IOSRouter(config)# dial-peer voice 10 pots
IOSRouter(config-dial-peer)# description Calls to internal extension 1111
IOSRouter(config-dial-peer)# destination-pattern 1111
IOSRouter(config-dial-peer)# port 0/1
!
IOSRouter(config)# dial-peer voice 20 voip
IOSRouter(config-dial-peer)# description Calls to external cluster extension 2222
IOSRouter(config-dial-peer)# destination-pattern 2222
IOSRouter(config-dial-peer)# session target ipv4:198.18.133.3
```

As seen in Example 13-11 dial peer is configured using **the dial-peer voice tag [pots | voip]** command. The tag is a number between 1 and 2147483647 that identifies an individual dial peer. POTS dial peers are used to connect a physical voice port to a PBX or to the PSTN provider's switch. VoIP dial peers are used to define packet voice network attributes and map a dial string (number) to a remote router or call-control, for example, CUCM. Table 13-13 describes the various commands used for POTS and VoIP dial peers.

Table 13-13 *Cisco IOS Gateway Voice Dial-Peer Commands*

Command	Description
description	Allows putting a description to the type of dial peer.
destination-pattern	Used to associate a dial string with a particular telephony device. A destination pattern can be either an entire telephone number or a partial number using wildcard digits. For example, a wildcard period character (.) e.g. **destination-pattern 555....**
port	Associates a dial peer to a physical or virtual router port e.g. T1 or E1 port.
session target	Associates a dial peer to a network IP address of another router or device (e.g., CUCM) to which the call should be routed.

Each dial peer completes a call leg. A *call leg* is a logical connection (or segment) between two routers or a router and a call-control such as CUCM. Figure 13-18 illustrates the relationship between call legs and interworking of dial peers in a Cisco Collaboration network.

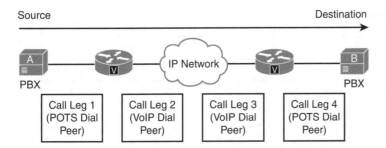

Figure 13-18 *IOS Dial Peer Logic and Call Leg Relationship*

When a voice call enters the network (from an endpoint, such as a phone, trunk, PBX) the router collects digits and the following sequence of events occur.

Step 1.   The originating router collects dialed digits via an incoming dial peer first, and then continues to process until it matches an outbound dial peer.

Step 2.   Upon matching an outgoing dial peer, the router immediately places the call and forwards the associated dial string via a VoIP or POTS dial peer to the next hop. The next hop could be an IP PBX, for example, CUCM, another router, PSTN trunk, or an endpoint.

To further explain the concept of dial peers Figure 13-19 depicts a VoIP network with analog phones connected to Foreign Exchange Station (FXS) ports on Router1 (R1) and Router2 (R2).

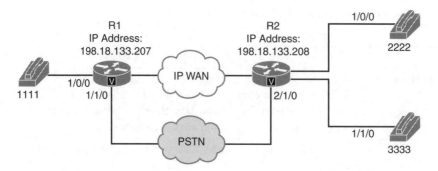

Figure 13-19   *IOS Call Routing*

> **Note**   For illustration purposes (and keeping the scenario simple for explaining call
> flows), the extensions 1111, 2222, and 3333 have been shown to be reachable via both
> IP WAN and PSTN. In the real world, calls via PSTN will need an amended number, for
> example, 914085551111 to be routed over a PSTN network.

Example 13-12 builds on Figure 13-19 to explain the dial peer configuration router R1 for
the call flow between extension 1111, and extensions 2222 and 3333.

Example 13-12   *R1 Dial Peer Configuration*

```
R1(config)# dial-peer voice 1111 pots
R1(config-dial-peer)# description Incoming calls from extension 1111
R1(config-dial-peer)# incoming called-number .
R1(config-dial-peer)# forward-digits all
R1(config-dial-peer)# port 1/0/0
!
R1(config)# dial-peer voice 111 pots
R1(config-dial-peer)# description Calls to extension 1111
R1(config-dial-peer)# destination-pattern 1111
R1(config-dial-peer)# forward-digits all
R1(config-dial-peer)# port 1/0/0
!
R1(config)# dial-peer voice 2222 voip
R1(config-dial-peer)# description Calls to external extension 2222 via VoIP
R1(config-dial-peer)# destination-pattern 2222
R1(config-dial-peer)# session target ipv4:198.18.133.208
R1(config-dial-peer)# preference 1
!
R1(config)# dial-peer voice 3333 voip
R1(config-dial-peer)# description Calls to external extension 3333 via VoIP
R1(config-dial-peer)# destination-pattern 3333
```

```
R1(config-dial-peer)# session target ipv4:198.18.133.208
R1(config-dial-peer)# preference 1
!
R1(config)# dial-peer voice 222 pots
R1(config-dial-peer)# description Calls to external extension 2222 via PSTN
R1(config-dial-peer)# destination-pattern 2222
R1(config-dial-peer)# forward-digits all
R1(config-dial-peer)# port 1/1/0
R1(config-dial-peer)# preference 2
!
R1(config)# dial-peer voice 333 pots
R1(config-dial-peer)# description Calls to external extension 3333 via PSTN
R1(config-dial-peer)# destination-pattern 3333
R1(config-dial-peer)# forward-digits all
R1(config-dial-peer)# port 1/1/0
R1(config-dial-peer)# preference 2
!
R1(config)# dial-peer voice 1 pots
R1(config-dial-peer)# description All incoming calls via PSTN
R1(config-dial-peer)# incoming called-number .
R1(config-dial-peer)# forward-digits all
R1(config-dial-peer)# port 1/1/0
```

Example 13-13 describes the dial peer configuration on R2 router.

Example 13-13   *R2 Dial Peer Configuration*

```
R2(config)# dial-peer voice 2222 pots
R2(config-dial-peer)# description Incoming calls from extension 2222
R2(config-dial-peer)# incoming called-number .
R2(config-dial-peer)# forward-digits all
R2(config-dial-peer)# port 1/0/0
!
R2(config)# dial-peer voice 3333 pots
R2(config-dial-peer)# description Incoming calls from extension 3333
R2(config-dial-peer)# incoming called-number .
R2(config-dial-peer)# forward-digits all
R2(config-dial-peer)# port 1/1/0
!
R2(config)# dial-peer voice 222 pots
R2(config-dial-peer)# description Calls to extension 2222
R2(config-dial-peer)# destination-pattern 2222
R2(config-dial-peer)# forward-digits all
R2(config-dial-peer)# port 1/0/0
!
```

```
R2(config)# dial-peer voice 333 pots
R2(config-dial-peer)# description Calls to extension 3333
R2(config-dial-peer)# destination-pattern 3333
R2(config-dial-peer)# forward-digits all
R2(config-dial-peer)# port 1/1/0
!
R2(config)# dial-peer voice 1111 voip
R2(config-dial-peer)# description Calls to external extension 1111 via VoIP
R2(config-dial-peer)# destination-pattern 1111
R2(config-dial-peer)# session target ipv4:198.18.133.207
R2(config-dial-peer)# preference 1
!
R2(config)# dial-peer voice 111 pots
R2(config-dial-peer)# description Calls to external extension 1111 via PSTN
R2(config-dial-peer)# destination-pattern 1111
R2(config-dial-peer)# forward-digits all
R2(config-dial-peer)# port 2/1/0
R2(config-dial-peer)# preference 2
!
R2(config)# dial-peer voice 1 pots
R2(config-dial-peer)# description All incoming calls via PSTN
R2(config-dial-peer)# incoming called-number .
R2(config-dial-peer)# forward-digits all
R2(config-dial-peer)# port 2/1/0
```

The following steps explain the call flow and dial peer matching for calls from extension 1111 to extension 2222.

Step 1.   Extension 1111 dials extension 2222. Router R1 uses pots dial-peer 1111 to accept the incoming call setup using **incoming called-number**.

Step 2.   R1 matches dial-peer 2222 (higher preference) using **session target ipv4:** and the call is sent over IP WAN to R2.

Step 3.   If IP WAN is unavailable or dial-peer 2222 is disabled; dial-peer 222 (lower preference) is used to route the call to a remote destination PSTN circuit using the **destination-pattern** command.

Step 4.   On router R2 the default incoming (VoIP) dial-peer is used to match the incoming number(s) 2222 from R1. Alternatively, if the call comes over PSTN trunk, its handled by dial-peer 1; leveraging the **incoming called-number**.

Step 5.   R2 matches outgoing pots dial-peer for extension 2222 using **destination-pattern** and routes the call.

Note The same sequence of steps occur for extension 1111, dialing extension 3333 using outbound dial-peer(s) 3333 or 333 on R1 and on R2 incoming default dial-peer or dial-peer 1 and finally dial-peer 3333 to route call from 1111 to 3333.

For incoming calls to R1 for extension 1111 (from R2 extension 2222 or 3333) the following steps explain the call flow.

Step 1. Extension 2222 dials extension 1111. Router R2 uses pots dial-peer 2222 to accept the incoming call setup using **incoming called-number** .

Step 2. R2 matches dial-peer 1111 (higher preference) using **session target ipv4:** and the call is sent over IP WAN to R2.

Step 3. If IP WAN is unavailable or dial-peer 1111 is disabled, dial-peer 111 (lower preference) is used to route the call to a remote destination via PSTN circuit using **destination-pattern** command.

Step 4. R1 receives the call via VoIP or PSTN trunk from R2 for extension 1111. If the call comes over IP WAN it is handled by default VoIP dial-peer. If the call comes over PSTN, its handled by dial-peer 1; leveraging **incoming called-number**.

Step 5. After matching the incoming number to extension 1111 (digit analysis), R1 forwards the call to dial-peer 111 that matches the **destination-pattern** and sends the call to extension 1111.

The next section describes IOS dial peer–matching logic.

Cisco IOS Dial Peer–Matching Logic

Multiple dial peers can be configured with various destination numbers (patterns) and answer-address. As seen in Example 13-12 and 13-13, dial peers with the same destination pattern may be configured for redundancy. Dial-peer selection of the dial peer can be based on the called number, such as DNIS (called number), on the calling number, such as ANI, on both, or based on port. Keeping all this in mind; the rules pertinent to dial-peer matching logic for outgoing and inbound calls are as follows.

Note The following are the matching events in order of preference and are mutually exclusive. If there is a match against the incoming called number, then no further dial-peer matching occurs.

In the case of inbound dial-peer matching, the following rules apply:

1. Called number matching based on the DNIS is performed; based on the most explicit match. This is configured using the **incoming called-number** command.

2. If no dial peer is found, calling number matching based on the ANI is performed; based on the most explicit match. This can be configured using the **answer-address** command.

3. Calling number matching based on the ANI is performed; based on the most explicit match port. This can be configured using the **destination-pattern** command.

4. If multiple dial peers have the same port (POTS dial peer), the dial peer added to the configuration earlier (or in order of addition) is considered. Port-based matching can be configured with the **port** command.

5. If nothing matches, default dial-peer 0 is used.

When matching an outbound dial peer, the router always uses the **destination-pattern** command. In case of outbound dial-peer matching, the following rule applies: the called number is based on DNIS matching the outbound dial-peer destination pattern and most explicit match. Dial-peer routing for POTS is based on the **port** command and for VoIP is based on the **session target** command. In certain cases, two or more dial peers may have the same destination pattern for instance, VoIP dial peers to CUCM subscribers for call processing redundancy. In such a case, the **preference** command can be added to each dial peer to set a priority, with **preference 0** being the default and highest preference. Multiple dial peers can be defined with the same destination pattern with **preference 1, 2, 3**, and so on. Example 13-14 illustrates dial-peer preference configuration.

Example 13-14 *Cisco IOS Router Dial-Peer Preference Configuration*

```
IOSRouter(config)# dial-peer 100 voice voip
IOSRouter(config-dial-peer)# description Calls to Primary CUCM
IOSRouter(config-dial-peer)# preference 1
IOSRouter(config-dial-peer)# destination-pattern 1...
IOSRouter(config-dial-peer)# session-target ipv4:198.18.133.3
IOSRouter(config-dial-peer)# dtmf-relay h245-alphanumeric
IOSRouter(config-dial-peer)# no vad
!
IOSRouter(config)# dial-peer 101 voice voip
IOSRouter(config-dial-peer)# description Calls to Secondary CUCM
IOSRouter(config-dial-peer)# preference 2
IOSRouter(config-dial-peer)# destination-pattern 1...
IOSRouter(config-dial-peer)# session-target ipv4:198.18.133.7
IOSRouter(config-dial-peer)# dtmf-relay h245-alphanumeric
IOSRouter(config-dial-peer)# no vad
```

Note If no incoming dial-peer is matched by the router/gateway, the inbound call leg is automatically routed to a default dial peer (POTS or Voice-Network). This default dial peer is referred to as dial-peer 0 or pid:0.

Table 13-14 explains the various destination-pattern wildcards.

Table 13-14   *Cisco IOS Gateway Destination Pattern Wildcards*

Symbol	Description
.	The period indicates a single-digit placeholder. For example, 5551... (three periods) matches any 7-digit dialed string beginning with 5551
[ ]	Brackets contain a range of digits. A consecutive range is indicated with a hyphen (-). For example, [1-3] indicates that the digits 1, 2, and 3 will be accepted. A nonconsecutive range is indicated with a comma (,). For example, [2,6] indicates that 2 or 6 will be accepted as dialed digits. Hyphens and commas can be used in combination. For example, [5-7,9] indicates that 5, 6, 7, and 9 will be accepted as dialed digits. Multiple brackets can be used within the same destination pattern.
T	Indicates the interdigit timeout value. The router waits a specified time to collect additional dialed digits.

IOS Digit Manipulation

At times, digit manipulation is needed to route calls and translate a number (calling or called party) so that the call is successfully routed to the destination. Cisco IOS gateways have a number of dial plan mechanisms (similar to CUCM dial plan components) to manipulate digits for an outbound or inbound call.

Digit manipulation is possible only on SIP and H.323 voice gateways. For MGCP gateways, the call agent, that is, CUCM must perform digit manipulation as it controls the calls. A voice gateway in SRST mode can also perform digit manipulation and route calls from/to PSTN.

Note   Cisco Unified Communications Manager Express (CUCME) also leverages digit manipulation mechanisms discussed in this section.

The following elements constitute IOS dial plan manipulation.

- Number translation: voice translation rules and profiles
- Number expansion
- Digit stripping
- Prefixing digits
- Forwarding digits

Voice Translation Rules and Profiles

A voice translation rule can manipulate a calling-party number (Automatic Number Identification [ANI]) or a called-party number (dialed number identification service [DNIS]) for incoming, outgoing, and redirected calls. Voice translation profile allows implementing the translation rule to a voice dial peer, voice port, trunk group, SRST implementation, source IP group, and VoIP incoming as inbound or outbound translation rule for a called or calling number. Table 13-15 shows the various regular expressions used for voice translation rules.

Table 13-15 *Voice Translation Rule Regular Expressions*

Character	Description
.	Match any single digit.
0 to 9,*,#	Any specific character.
[0-9]	Any range of characters.
*	Modifier-match none or more occurrences.
+	Modifier-match one or more occurrences.
?	Modifier-match none or one occurrence.
\	In the match pattern, indicates where to slice the number, and in the replacement pattern, indicates where to copy the number to keep.
()	Group regular expressions.
/	Delimiter that marks start and end of both matching and replacement strings.
^	Match an expression at start of a line.
$	Denotes absolute match of digits or characters.

Example 13-15 illustrates voice translation rules.

> **Note**   Example 13-15 shows voice translation rules followed by test commands to demonstrate that the outcome of digit manipulation is as expected.

Example 13-15 *Voice Translation Rule Configuration*

```
Router(config)# voice translation-rule 1
Router(cfg-translation-rule)# rule 1 /\(^[2-9].........\)/ /91\1/
Router(cfg-translation-rule)# rule 2 /^8.../ /9222&/
!
```

```
Router# test voice translation-rule 1 4082228000
Matched with rule 1
Original number: 4082228000      Translated number: 914082228000
Original number type: none       Translated number type: none
Original number plan: none       Translated number plan: none
!
Router# test voice translation-rule 2 8000
Matched with rule 2
Original number: 8000    Translated number: 92228000
Original number type: none       Translated number type: none
!
Router(config)# voice translation-rule 2
Router(cfg-translation-rule)# rule 1 /^9/ //
Router(cfg-translation-rule)# rule 2 /.*/ /2228000/
!
Router# test voice translation-rule 2 94082228000
Matched with rule 1
Original number: 94082228000     Translated number: 4082228000
Original number type: none       Translated number type: none
Original number plan: none       Translated number plan: none
!
Router# test voice translation-rule 2 .
Matched with rule 2
Original number: .       Translated number: 2228000
Original number type: none       Translated number type: none
Original number plan: none       Translated number plan: none
```

As seen in Example 13-15, the voice translation rule 1 concatenates digits as per the expression used. In contrast to translation rule 1, rule 2 removes extraneous digits as per the expression used.

Translation profiles are required to apply the rules at the dial peer or trunk group level for incoming or outgoing calls as required. The following voice translation profiles can be defined:

- **called:** Defines the translation profile rule for the called number

- **calling:** Defines the translation profile rule for the calling number

- **redirect-called:** Defines the translation profile rule for the redirect-called number

Using the previously defined rules as shown in Example 13-15, the profiles can be defined as shown in Example 13-16.

Example 13-16   *Voice Translation Profile Configuration*

```
Router(config)# voice translation-profile PSTN-OUT
Router(cfg-translation-profile)# translate calling 1
!
Router(config)# voice translation-profile PSTN-IN
Router(cfg-translation-profile)# translate called 2
!
Router(config)# dial-peer voice 200 POTS
Router(config-dial-peer)# translation-profile outgoing PSTN-OUT
Router(config-dial-peer)# destination-pattern 9T
Router(config-dial-peer)# forward digits all
Router(config-dial-peer)# port 0/0:23
!
Router(config)# dial-peer voice 201 POTS
Router(config-dial-peer)# translation-profile incoming PSTN-IN
Router(config-dial-peer)# incoming called-number .
Router(config-dial-peer)# direct-inward-dial
Router(config-dial-peer)# forward digits all
Router(config-dial-peer)# port 0/0:23
```

Example 13-16 translation-rule 1 helps to set the outgoing calls (national) with a prefix of 91 and the local calls with a prefix of 9. The translation-rule 2 helps strip 9 from calls coming in with 9 as a prefix; otherwise, for any other match it sets the called number to 2228000. Finally, the translation profiles PSTN-IN and PSTN-OUT apply the rules to dial peers 200 and 201 for outgoing and incoming calls, respectively.

Sometimes sending the numbering plan along with the dialed number (to PSTN) is required. In such a case, the translation rule can be used to append the appropriate numbering plan to different rules so that ANI (calling number) is understood correctly by the PSTN provider. Example 13-17 describes numbering plan manipulation using translation rules and profiles.

Example 13-17   *Voice Translation Rule Configuration with Plan Type*

```
Router(config)# voice translation-rule 11
Router(cfg-translation-rule)# rule 1 /^.*/ /9&/ type subscriber subscriber
Router(cfg-translation-rule)# rule 2 /^.*/ /91&/ type national national
Router(cfg-translation-rule)# rule 3 /^.*/ /9011&/ type international international
!
Router(config)# voice translation-profile PSTN-NumberPlan
Router(cfg-translation-profile)# translate calling 11
!
Router# test voice translation-rule 11 2228000 type subscriber
Matched with rule 1
```

```
Original number: 2228000        Translated number: 92228000
Original number type: subscriber        Translated number type: subscriber
Original number plan: none      Translated number plan: none
!
Router# test voice translation-rule 11 4082228000 type national plan national
Matched with rule 2
Original number: 4082228000     Translated number: 914082228000
Original number type: national  Translated number type: national
Original number plan: national  Translated number plan: national
```

In Example 13-17, translation-rule 11 sets the right numbering plan against local, national, and international calls to the PSTN provider.

Voice translation rules can also be used to block certain patterns as per policy or requirements. The following configuration illustrates voice translation rule setup to reject a particular pattern and provide a cause code of invalid number to the call initiator as shown in Example 13-18.

Example 13-18   *Voice Translation Rule Configuration with Plan Type*

```
Router(config)# voice translation-rule 13
Router(cfg-translation-rule)# rule 1 reject /91408*/
!
Router(config)# voice translation-profile reject-invalid-call
Router(cfg-translation-profile)# translate calling 13
!
Router(config)# dial-peer voice 1001 pots
Router(config-dial-peer)# call-block translation-profile incoming reject-invalid-
    call
Router(config-dial-peer)# call-block disconnect-cause incoming invalid-number
```

Number Expansion

Number expansion changes digits on an outgoing called number only. It is applied to the gateway at a global level and acts on all calls, not just those matching a designated dial peer.

Note   Number expansion manipulation occurs before any outbound dial peer is matched. So, you must configure outbound dial peers to match the expanded numbers, not the original ones. Number expansion can be used to manipulate a number so that the final called number can contain fewer digits than the original, contain more digits than the original, or be a totally different number.

Example 13-19 shows number expansion configuration.

Example 13-19   *Number Expansion Configuration*

```
Router(config)# num-exp 1... 5551...
!
Router# show dialplan number 1111
Macro Exp.: 5551111
!
Router(config)# num-exp 7771... 1...
!
Router# show dialplan number 7771111
Macro Exp.: 1111
```

As seen in Example 13-19 The first **num-exp** expands any four-number extension beginning with 1 to a seven-digit number beginning with 5551. The second **num-exp** changes any seven-digit number beginning with 7771 to a four-digit extension beginning with 1.

Digit Stripping

Digit stripping helps format an outgoing number so that digits that explicitly match their destination pattern are stripped and rest of the number is forwarded to PSTN trunk. For example, if a destination pattern is 5551... as a result of digit stripping, the called number sent to the PSTN would contain only the last three digits and the first four digits, 5551, would be stripped.

> **Note**   Digit stripping is the default behavior of POTS dial peer(s). In contrast VoIP dial peers by default transmit all digits in the called number. Digit stripping can be disabled with the command **no digit-strip** under POTS dial-peer configuration mode.

The following are some use cases of digit stripping.

- Destination pattern 555[1-8]... : 555 would be stripped and rest of digits will be forwarded to PSTN trunk.

- Destination pattern 9.......... : 9 will be stripped and the rest of digits will be forwarded to PSTN trunk.

- Destination pattern 9T: 9 will be stripped and the rest of digits will be forwarded to PSTN trunk.

- Destination pattern 911 (with no digit-strip command under dial-peer): 911 will be sent to PSTN trunk.

Prefix Digits

The **prefix** command does the same job as **num-exp** with a couple of striking differences such as:

- This is a POTS dial-peer based command compared to **num-exp** which is a global command. In other words, prefix adds digits to a called number per dial-peer basis and provides a higher level of control on expanding numbers per-destination basis.

- This command can only append numbers to the called number and cannot discard any digits unlike **num-exp** which can add or discard digits.

A real-world use case for a prefix command is when a call that would normally go across the IP WAN (VoIP) network needs to be rerouted through the PSTN (if the IP network is unavailable). In such case, PSTN switch will not understand the internal dial plan of an enterprise and requires E.164 number format, for example, 914085551111. Hence, the addition of the appropriate area code is necessary and prefix. Example 13-20 illustrates prefix command on a dial peer.

Example 13-20 *Prefixing Digits for an Outgoing Call on POTS Dial Peer*

```
Router(config)# dial-peer voice 900 pots
Router(config-dial-peer)# description Lower preference dial-peer to reach
  extension 1...
Router(config-dial-peer)# preference 2
Router(config-dial-peer)# destination-pattern 1...
Router(config-dial-peer)# prefix 914085551
Router(config-dial-peer)# port 1/0/1:23
```

In Example 13-20, when a user dials the number 1111, the original digit 1 is stripped by the default POTS dial-peer digit stripping behavior, leading to only 3 digits being sent to PSTN. This is where a prefix command comes in and 914085551 is prefixed to the remaining number thereby sending 914085551111 as outgoing number to PSTN switch.

Note The voice gateway prefixes digits after the outgoing dial peer is matched and after any digits are stripped, but before it sends out the call.

Forward Digits

This command has been used in multiple examples earlier in this chapter. The **forward-digits** command lets you specify the exact number of digits to be forwarded to a PSTN trunk. This command takes affect after the outbound dial peer is matched, however, before the digits are sent out to PSTN trunk.

The **forward-digits** command has number of command options such as:

- **Number:** provides the number of digits to be forwarded

- **All:** forwards all digits as is

- **Extra:** forwards any digits longer than the length of **destination-pattern**

Note   When a specific number of digits are configured for forwarding, the count is right justified.

A real-world use case is when dial peers are set up to match the NANP emergency number 911, and that number plus the outside access code, 9911. Example 13-21 shows the use of forward command in both scenarios.

Note   As defined in NANP dial plan 911 is the emergency number, to accommodate user dialing behavior 9911 is also used because a user may dial 9 (by force of habit) before every number.

Example 13-21   *Forward Command for 911 and 9911*

```
Router(config)# dial-peer voice 911 pots
Router(config-dial-peer)# description Emergency calls 911
Router(config-dial-peer)# destination-pattern 911
Router(config-dial-peer)# forward-digits all
Router(config-dial-peer)# port 1/0/1:23
!
Router(config)# dial-peer voice 9911 pots
Router(config-dial-peer)# description Emergency calls with access code 9911
Router(config-dial-peer)# destination-pattern 9911
Router(config-dial-peer)# forward-digits 3
Router(config-dial-peer)# port 1/0/1:23
```

In Example 13-21, dial-peer 911 allows the user to dial 911 and sets the dial-peer to use forward all so that all 3 digits are forwarded to PSTN trunk. On the other hand, dial-peer 9911 allows users to dial 911 with outside access code 9 and yet sends out just 3 digits (right justified), that is, 911 to PSTN trunk.

Class of Restriction

Class of restriction (COR) on IOS voice gateways is analogous to CUCM Partitions and Calling Search Spaces (CSS). COR is implemented at either dial peers or ephone-dns on a voice gateway.

> **Note** Ephones and Ephone-dns are logical entities created to support endpoints such as analog phones or IP phones on a Survivable Remote Site Telephony (SRST) router or Cisco Unified Communications Manager Express (CUCME).

COR provides the ability to deny or allow call attempts based on the incoming and outgoing CORs provisioned on the dial-peers. COR is used to specify which incoming dial-peer can use which outgoing dial-peer to make a call.

The **dial-peer cor custom** command is equivalent to creating a CUCM partition, whereas **dial-peer cor list** is equivalent to creating a CUCM CSS. COR can be implemented on SIP and H.323 gateways and while a gateway is in SRST mode. IOS dial peers can be provisioned with an incoming and an outgoing COR list. The corlist command sets the dial-peer COR parameter for dial-peers and the directory numbers that are created for Cisco IP phones associated with the CUCME. If the COR applied on an incoming dial-peer (for incoming calls) is a super set or equal to the COR applied to the outgoing dial-peer (for outgoing calls), the call goes through.

Example 13-22 illustrates COR configuration on Cisco IOS voice gateway.

Example 13-22 *Cisco IOS Voice Gateway COR Configuration*

```
Router(config)# dial-peer cor custom
Router(config-dp-cor)# name emergency
Router(config-dp-cor)# name local
Router(config-dp-cor)# name long_distance
Router(config-dp-cor)# name international
!
Router(config)# dial-peer cor list emergency
Router(config-dp-corlist)# member emergency
!
Router(config)# dial-peer cor list local
Router(config-dp-corlist)# member emergency
Router(config-dp-corlist)# member local
!
Router(config)# dial-peer cor list long_distance
Router(config-dp-corlist)# member emergency
Router(config-dp-corlist)# member local
Router(config-dp-corlist)# member long_distance
!
Router(config)# dial-peer cor list national
Router(config-dp-corlist)# member emergency
Router(config-dp-corlist)# member local
Router(config-dp-corlist)# member long_distance
Router(config-dp-corlist)# member international
!
```

```
Router(config)# dial-peer voice 911 pots
Router(config-dial-peer)# corlist outgoing emergency
Router(config-dial-peer)# destination-pattern 911
Router(config-dial-peer)# forward digits all
Router(config-dial-peer)# port 1/0/1:23
!
Router(config)# dial-peer voice 9 pots
Router(config-dial-peer)# corlist outgoing local
Router(config-dial-peer)# destination-pattern 9.......
Router(config-dial-peer)# forward digits all
Router(config-dial-peer)# port 1/0/1:23
!
Router(config)# dial-peer voice 91 pots
Router(config-dial-peer)# corlist outgoing long_distance
Router(config-dial-peer)# destination-pattern 91..........
Router(config-dial-peer)# forward digits all
Router(config-dial-peer)# port 1/0/1:23
!
Router(config)# dial-peer voice 9011 pots
Router(config-dial-peer)# corlist outgoing international
Router(config-dial-peer)# destination-pattern 9011T
Router(config-dial-peer)# forward digits all
Router(config-dial-peer)# port 1/0/1:23
!
Router(config)# ephone-dn 1
Router(config-ephone-dn)# number 1001
Router(config-ephone-dn)# cor incoming international
!
Router(config)# ephone-dn 2
Router(config-ephone-dn)# number 1002
Router(config-ephone-dn)# cor incoming long_distance
!
Router(config)# ephone-dn 3
Router(config-ephone-dn)# number 1003
Router(config-ephone-dn)# cor incoming local
!
Router(config)# ephone-dn 4
Router(config-ephone-dn)# number 1004
Router(config-ephone-dn)# cor incoming emergency
!
Router(config)# ephone-dn 5
Router(config-ephone-dn)# number 1005
```

As seen in Example 13-22 the following commands are used to define COR for outbound calls from endpoints (ephones).

■ dial-peer cor custom defines four types of destinations that can be dialed (NANP), such as emergency number 911; local number, for example, 95551111; national number, for example, 914085551111; and international number, such as 9011919999911111.

■ dial peers correspond to the **cor list outgoing** to signify the type of call.

■ Ephone-dns are assigned **cor list incoming** to allow them calling privileges as follows.

  ■ 1001 is allows to call all destinations, such as emergency, local, national, and international numbers.

  ■ 1002 is allowed to call emergency, local, and national numbers.

  ■ 1003 is allowed to call emergency and local numbers.

  ■ 1004 is allowed to call only emergency numbers.

  ■ 1005 has no cor applied, which by default can reach any destination.

Example 13-23 shows output of **show dial-peer cor** command.

Example 13-23   *Cisco IOS Gateway COR Verification*

```
Router# show dial-peer cor

Class of Restriction
  name: emergency
  name: local
  name: long_distance
  name: international

COR list <emergency>
  member: emergency

COR list <local>
  member: emergency
  member: local

COR list <long_distance>
  member: emergency
  member: local
  member: long_distance
```

```
COR list <international>
  member: emergency
  member: local
  member: long_distance
  member: international
```

Cisco Unified Border Element

Cisco Unified Border Element (CUBE) is a Cisco IOS feature that is available in Cisco Integrated Services Routers (ISR), Cisco Aggregation Services Routers (ASR), and Cisco Unified Computing System (UCS) platforms.

Note   CUBE is supported as a virtualized form factor from Cisco IOS XE 3.15S release and CUBE features are integrated into Cisco CSR 1000V Series Cloud Services Routers (Cisco CSR 1000V router). CUBE virtual instance is supported with UCS C-Series servers. Any media resource-based functions such as hardware MTP, DSP-based features, H.323 interworking, and H.323 gatekeeper are not support in virtualized instance.

CUBE enables organizations to use SIP trunking services from a SIP service provider (also known as IT service provider or ITSP) network. CUBE supports IP-to-IP Calls (SIP, H.323) and TDM Voice Calls.

CUBE provides the following functionality and services:

- CUBE acts as a broker between the trusted enterprise network and untrusted public network, thereby offering a security demarcation.

- CUBE offers hiding of internal enterprise IP addresses, presenting a single IP address for signaling and media to the outside world (ITSP). Thus, CUBE acts as a single point for control for signaling and media—in and out of an organization.

- CUBE acts as a mediator for protocol interop for example SIP to H.323, H.323 to H.323, and SIP to SIP. Essentially, CUBE is an IP–IP gateway that can broker connections from one signaling/media protocol to another.

- CUBE offers advanced media interworking features such as background noise cancellation, QOS marking, and sophisticated interface queuing mechanisms. CUBE also offers DTMF interworking, transcoding, and other media functions.

The following sections describe various features of CUBE.

CUBE Protocol Interworking

CUBE can route a call from one VoIP dial peer to another VoIP dial peer; whether the VoIP dial peers be handled by SIP or H.323 protocols. CUBE offers the capability to interconnect VoIP networks using different signaling protocols or VoIP networks using the same signaling protocols; at the same time resolving any interoperability issues. Protocol interworking includes.

- H.323-to-H.323 interworking

- SIP-to-SIP interworking

- H.323-to-SIP interworking

Figure 13-20 illustrates the capability of CUBE to interconnect dissimilar VoIP networks.

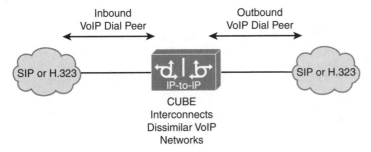

Figure 13-20   *CUBE VoIP Network Interworking*

Table 13-16 illustrates the various interworking mechanisms supported by CUBE.

Table 13-16   *CUBE DO and EO*

Protocol Interworking	Support	Inbound Leg	Outbound Leg
SIP to SIP	Bidirectional	Early offer	Early offer
	Bidirectional	Delayed offer	Delayed offer
H.323 to H.323	Bidirectional	Fast start	Fast start
	Bidirectional	Slow start	Slow start
	Bidirectional	Fast start	Fast start
H.323 to SIP	Bidirectional	Fast start	Early offer
	Unidirectional	Slow start	Delayed offer

CUBE Media Flows

CUBE offers two options for media (RTP) flows. These are:

- Media flow-through

- Media flow-around

Note   CUBE is always involved in the call setup, that is, the signaling part of an audio/video call. However, the RTP (bearer stream) may flow through the CUBE, or it can be routed around the CUBE.

With the media flow-through option, the media packets are passed through the CUBE. RTP streams from audio/video endpoints get terminated at CUBE and re-originate with CUBE's IP address and port number. When using media flow-through, CUBE replaces the source IP address used for media connections with its own IP address. This allows the following two benefits:

- It offers address-hiding. CUBE hides the endpoint's IP address from the remote endpoint(s).

- This solves IP interworking issues in case the same IP address ranges are being used on both ends.

Figure 13-21 shows CUBE Media Flow-Through implementation.

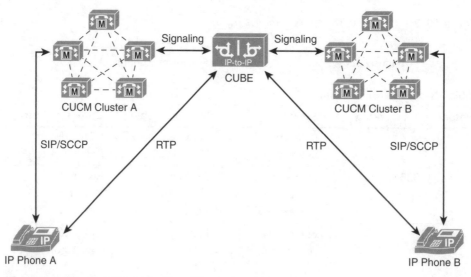

Figure 13-21   *CUBE Media Flow-Through Implementation*

As seen in Figure 13-18, the signaling between the CUCM A and CUCM B clusters is processed by CUBE. CUBE sits between the RTP streams from IP Phone A to IP Phone B and vice versa, thereby replacing the source IP addresses of the endpoints by its own IP address.

Note   Media flow-through has an impact in terms of higher resource (CPU/memory) load on a CUBE router, which in turn decreases the number of supported concurrent flows.

Media flow-around, as the name suggests, terminates the signaling on CUBE. However it allows RTP streams to flow directly between the endpoints. This can be compared to default behavior of CUCM where endpoints have a signaling relationship with call-control whereas they setup RTP between themselves.

Figure 13-22 shows CUBE Media Flow-Around implementation.

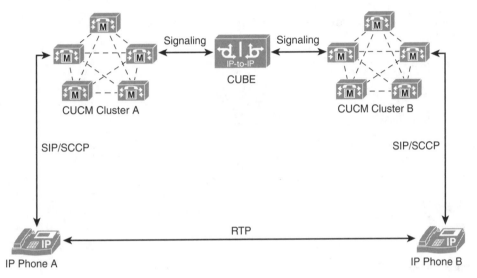

Figure 13-22   *CUBE Media Flow-Around Implementation*

Media flow-around allows the CUBE greater scalability in the number of concurrent sessions that can be processed by the CUBE router.

Media flow-through is most suitable when address hiding and security are the primary concerns because the internal IP addresses are never revealed to the ITSP or the other party. Media flow-around offers little to no protection from the address-hiding perspective, which is suitable for in-house enterprise communications and communications with business partners.

CUBE Early Offer and Delayed Offer

CUBE supports early offer (EO) and delayed offer (DO) calls to/from CUCM/SIP ITSP. More often than not, SIP ITSPs require an EO, and CUCM may require to do both DO and EO to CUBE. However, even if CUCM is sending a DO INVITE, CUBE can reinitiate the call leg out to the SIP SP as an EO INVITE (with SDP). Delayed offer to early offer (DO-EO) interworking can use CUBE flow-through or flow-around. Table 13-17 describes the EO and DO relationship with SIP INVITE (with and without SDP).

Table 13-17 *CUBE DO and EO*

	Early Offer (EO)	**Delayed Offer (DO)**
Offer	SDP in INVITE	No SDP in INVITE
Answer	SDP in 200	SDP in 200

Figure 13-23 gives an overview of a CUCM to CUBE DO and CUBE to SIP ITSP EO call setup.

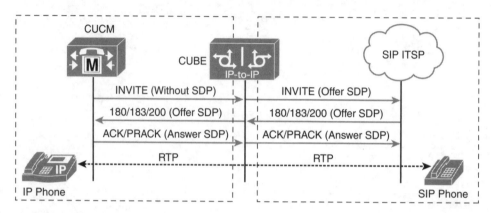

Figure 13-23 *CUBE to SIP ITSP DO-EO*

> **Note**   Not all call-signaling events are shown; the emphasis is on CUBE performing DO-EO for SIP INVITE and consequent events.

Example 13-24 illustrates CUBE setup for EO negotiation:

Example 13-24 *CUBE to ITSP Early Offer Configuration*

```
CUBE(config)# voice service voip
CUBE(config-voi-serv)# sip
CUBE(config-serv-sip)# early-offer forced
```

CUBE DTMF Interworking

At times, DTMF incompatibility may exist between different devices initiating or accepting calls via CUBE. This might be due to the difference in protocols, standards, or the way the collaboration network was setup. In such scenarios, DTMF interworking is required to ensure that caller inputs reach through to the destination application/device.

For example, when an (SCCP/SIP) endpoint registered with CUCM (or CUCME) tries to call a toll-free number in the SIP (PSTN) cloud, the call signaling passes through CUCM to CUBE (via H.323 trunk to CUBE), from CUBE to the SIP ITSP's SBC via SIP trunk, and finally to the destination PBX/phone. On the way, there is a requirement for DTMF interworking between H.323 incoming dial peer on CUBE, and from CUCM, the SIP outgoing dial peer to SIP ITSP. The appropriate DTMF type must be configured at the incoming and outgoing dial peers as shown in Example 13-25.

Example 13-25   *CUBE DTMF Interworking Configuration*

```
CUBE(config)# dial-peer voice 10 voip
CUBE(config-dial-peer)# description Calls To/From CUCM
CUBE(config-dial-peer)# destination-pattern 42618...$
CUBE(config-dial-peer)# session target ipv4:198.18.133.3
CUBE(config-dial-peer)# incoming called-number .
CUBE(config-dial-peer)# dtmf-relay h245-alphanumeric
CUBE(config-dial-peer)# codec g711ulaw
CUBE(config-dial-peer)# no vad
!
CUBE(config)# dial-peer voice 11 voip
CUBE(config-dial-peer)# description Calls To/From  SIP-ITSP
CUBE(config-dial-peer)# destination-pattern 9T
CUBE(config-dial-peer)# session protocol sipv2
CUBE(config-dial-peer)# session target ipv4:100.100.1.100
CUBE(config-dial-peer)# incoming called-number 4085551...$
CUBE(config-dial-peer)# dtmf-relay rtp-nte
CUBE(config-dial-peer)# codec g711ulaw
CUBE(config-dial-peer)# no vad
```

CUBE supports multiple DTMF methods/interworking schemes, as shown in Table 13-18.

Table 13-18   *CUBE DTMF Interworking*

SIP	SIP	H323	H.323	H323	SIP
NOTIFY	NOTIFY	H.245-Alphanumeric	H.245-Alphanumeric	H.245-Alphanumeric	NOTIFY
RFC 2833	NOTIFY	H.245-Signal	H.245-Signal	H.245-Signal	NOTIFY
RFC 2833	RFC 2833	RFC 2833	RFC 2833	RFC 2833	NOTIFY
NOTIFY	KPML	H.245-Alphanumeric	RFC 2833	H.245-Alphanumeric	RFC 2833
RFC 2833	KPML	H.245-Signal	RFC 2833	H.245-Signal	RFC 2833
KPML	KPML	Voice In-Band	RFC 2833	RFC 2833	RFC 2833
Voice In-Band	RFC 2833			H.245-Alphanumeric	KPML
				H.245-Signal	KPML
				Voice In-Band	RFC 2833

CUBE supports DTMF interworking to enable a delay between the dtmf-digit begin and dtmf-digit end events in the RFC 2833 packets or to generate RFC 4733 compliant rtp-nte packets.

The command **dtmf-interworking** command has the following options:

- **rtp-nte:** Used to introduce a delay between the DTMF-digit begin and DTMF-digit end events in the RFC 2833 packet if the remote system cannot handle RFC 2833 packets sent in a single burst. This option is available under (global) voice service VoIP and dial peers.

- **standard:** Generates RFC 4733–compliant packets. This option is available under (global) voice service VoIP and dial peers.

- **system:** Enables global-level DTMF-interworking configuration (derived from voice service VoIP). This is the default configuration under dial peers. This option is available only under dial peers.

Codec Negotiation

CUBE can interconnect VoIP networks, and different VoIP networks may require different codecs (to be negotiated between originating and terminating endpoints). A dial peer can be configured to allow a specific codec (or to use a codec voice class) to specify the choice of codec to be used with other VoIP network. This implies that a dial peer will set up a call leg only if the preferred codec is matched. As a result, CUBE performs codec-filtering. CUBE supports transparent codec negotiations as well, which enables the endpoints to communicate and negotiate codecs, bypassing CUBE as shown in Figure 13-24.

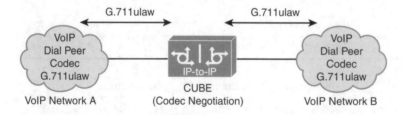

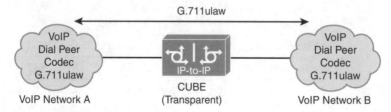

Figure 13-24 *CUBE Codec Negotiation and Bypass (Transparent)*

CUBE supports the following codecs:

- Audio codecs: aacld, clear-channel, g711alaw, g711ulaw, g722-48, g722-56, g722-64, g723ar53, g723ar63, g723r53, g723r63, g726r16, g726r24, g726r32, g728, g729br8, g729r8, gsmamr-nb, ilbc, isac, mp4a-latm, and transparent.
- Video codecs: h261, h263, h263+, h264, and mpeg4.

CUBE Mid-Call Signaling

CUBE supports SIP mid-call RE-INVITE, leveraging the **midcall-signaling** command. In most scenarios, SIP to SIP video and SIP to SIP RE-INVITE–based supplementary services require mid-call signaling to be configured before configuring other supplementary services. CUBE also offers the capability to consume mid-call signaling RE-INVITEs/UPDATEs.

Figure 13-25 depicts the mid-call signaling flows and CUBE intercepting the RE-INVITEs. Mid-call RE-INVITE/UPDATE consumption works only with media flow-through.

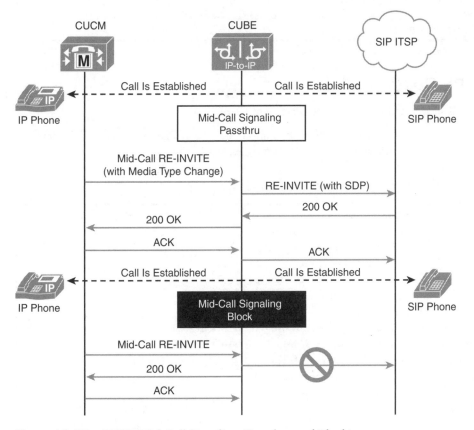

Figure 13-25   *CUBE Mid-Call Signaling (Passthru and Block)*

Mid-call signaling supports the following modes:

- **Block:** Blocks all the incoming RE-INVITEs/UPDATEs; handled locally by CUBE.

- **Passthrough (Media Change):** Optimizes the number of RE-INVITEs/UPDATEs (with SDP) within the call. Mid-call signaling changes are passed through only when there are new media changes, for example, video escalation, fax, and so forth.

- **Preserve-codec:** Helps preserve the established codec and denies any codec (mid-call) changes.

Example 13-26 shows the configuration of mid-call signaling options at (global) **voice service voip** and **dial-peer** level.

Example 13-26   *CUBE Mid-Call Signaling Configuration*

```
CUBE(conf)# voice service voip
CUBE(config-voi-serv)# sip
CUBE(config-serv-sip)# midcall-signaling [block | passthru | preserve-codec]
!
CUBE(conf)# dial-peer voice 180 voip
CUBE(config-dial-peer)# voice-class sip midcall-signaling [block | passthru |
  preserve-codec]
```

CUBE Configuration

This section addresses the configuration of CUBE.

Example 13-27 outlines CUBE configuration to establish a SIP trunk with CUCM in the enterprise network and with SIP ITSP on the external network.

Example 13-27   *CUBE Router Configuration*

```
CUBE(config)# voice service voip
 CUBE(conf-voi-serv)# mode border-element
CUBE(conf-voi-serv)# allow-connections sip to sip
CUBE(conf-voi-serv)# allow-connections h323 to sip
CUBE(conf-voi-serv)# allow-connections sip to h323
CUBE(conf-voi-serv)# allow-connections h323 to h323
CUBE(conf-voi-serv)# sip
CUBE(conf-serv-sip)# bind control source-interface loopback 0
CUBE(conf-serv-sip)# bind media source-interface loopback 0
CUBE(conf-serv-sip)# early-offer forced
CUBE(conf-serv-sip)# pass-thru content sdp
!
```

```
CUBE(config-dial-peer)# session protocol sipv2
CUBE(config-dial-peer)# session target ipv4:198.18.133.3
CUBE(config-dial-peer)# dtmf-relay rtp-nte sip-notify
CUBE(config-dial-peer)# codec g711ulawCUBE(config)# dial-peer voice 50 voip
CUBE(config-dial-peer)# description Calls to/from SIP-ITSP
CUBE(config-dial-peer)# destination-pattern 9T
CUBE(config-dial-peer)# session protocol sipv2
CUBE(config-dial-peer)# incoming called-number 91408555....$
CUBE(config-dial-peer)# session target ipv4:192.168.108.254
CUBE(config-dial-peer)# dtmf-relay rtp-nte sip-notify
CUBE(config-dial-peer)# codec transparent
!
CUBE(config)# dial-peer voice 51 voip
CUBE(config-dial-peer)# description Calls to/from CUCM
CUBE(config-dial-peer)# destination-pattern 408555....
CUBE(config-dial-peer)# incoming called-number .
```

Table 13-19 describes the commands used in Example 13-27.

Table 13-19 *CUBE Configuration Commands*

Command	Description
voice service voip	Defines the voice service parameters (in this case for SIP).
mode border-element	Defines and enables CUBE feature on IOS router.
allow-connections	Allows IP-to-IP connections SIP–SIP, SIP–H.323, H.323–H.323.
bind control source-interface	Binds signaling to the desired interface (in this case loopback 0).
bind media source-interface	Binds media to the desired interface (in this case loopback 0).
early-offer forced	Enables forced early offer for sending SDP in initial INVITE.
pass-thru content sdp	Passes SDP transparently from the inbound leg to the outbound leg with no media negotiation.
session protocol sipv2	Defines the session protocol as SIP to be used on VOIP dial-peer.
dtmf-relay rtp-nte sip-notify	Specifies the use of RFC 2833 in-band DTMF relay as first priority and out-of-band DTMF relay, using the SIP Notify method, second priority.
codec transparent	Specifies CUBE to be transparent for codec negotiation; endpoint codec preference is used for codec negotiation

Follow these steps for configuring CUCM to CUBE integration.

Step 1. A SIP trunk must be defined that points to CUBE (with CUBE's IP address or SRV). This is similar to the SIP trunk configured from CUCM to SIP router earlier in this chapter.

> **Note** The **Redirecting Diversion Header—Inbound** and **Redirecting Diversion Header—Outbound** checkboxes can be checked for inbound or outbound calls respectively. This allows the originating calling party's number instead of relayed diversion information that is passed with SIP invite messages. This is particularly useful for voice messaging and call-queuing systems where original calling party's information helps system invoke the right script or message.

Step 2. To support early offer from CUCM to CUBE, SIP profile for Early Offer needs to be configured. Go to **Device > Device Settings > SIP Profile** to configure a SIP profile. Provide the **Name** of SIP Profile and under **Trunk Specific Configuration**, set **Early Offer support for voice and video calls** to **Mandatory (insert MTP if needed)** as shown in Figure 13-26. Also, under **SIP Information** check the checkbox **Send send-receive SDP in mid-call INVITE**.

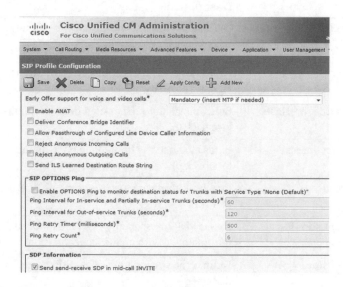

Figure 13-26 *SIP Trunk Profile*

Step 3. Go to **System > SIP Trunk Security Profiles > Non Secure SIP Trunk Profile**, and set the Outgoing Transport Type as TCP or UDP as per the ITSP's settings/requirements as shown in Figure 13-27.

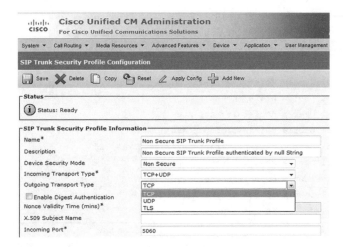

Figure 13-27   *SIP Trunk Security Profile*

At this time CUCM is configured and integrated with CUBE.

CUBE for B2B Video

As discussed earlier, CUBE plays the role of SBC which means its not just audio but also video between two or more enterprises (or as a service offer from the service provider). Figure 13-28 shows a Business-to-Business (B2B) call.

Figure 13-28   *Business-to-Business call*

Example 13-28 shows the CUBE configuration to support B2B TelePresence Calls.

Example 13-28   *CUBE Router Configuration to Support TelePresence B2B Calls*

```
CUBE(config)# voice service voip
CUBE(conf-voi-serv)# rtp-ssrc multiplex
CUBE(conf-voi-serv)# address-hiding
CUBE(conf-voi-serv)# allow-connections sip to sip
CUBE(config-voi-serv)# sip
CUBE(config-serv-sip)# midcall-signaling passthru
CUBE(conf-serv-sip)# session transport tcp
CUBE(conf-serv-sip)# header-passing error-passthru
CUBE(conf-serv-sip)# pass-thru content sdp
```

```
CUBE(conf-serv-sip)# rel1xx disable
CUBE(conf-serv-sip)# bind control source-interface loopback0
CUBE(conf-serv-sip)# bind media source-interface loopback0
!
CUBE(config)# dial-peer voice 1100 voip
CUBE(config-dial-peer)# preference 1
CUBE(config-dial-peer)# dtmf-relay rtp-nte
CUBE(config-dial-peer)# destination-pattern 3…$
CUBE(config-dial-peer)# session target ipv4:198.18.133.207
CUBE(config-dial-peer)# session protocol sipv2
CUBE(config-dial-peer)# codec transparent
CUBE(config-dial-peer)# ip qos dscp cs5 media
CUBE(config-dial-peer)# ip qos dscp cs3 signaling
```

Table 13-20 describes the commands used in Example 13-28.

Table 13-20 *CUBE Configuration Commands*

Command	Description
rtp-ssrc multiplex	Defines pass through for the TelePresence multiplexed RTP stream.
address-hiding	Provides topology (address) hiding.
midcall-signaling passthru	Allows pass-through REINVITEs for session refresh.
header-passing error-passthru	Allows pass through for SIP error codes.
pass-thru content sdp	Allows pass-through SDP content such as KPML (hold/resume)
rel1xx disable	TelePresence doesn't require PRACK
codec transparent	Allows CUBE to be transparent for codec negotiation; endpoint codec preference is used for codec negotiation
ip qos dscp cs5 media	Marks TelePresence media traffic as DSCP CS5
ip qos dscp cs3 signaling	Marks TelePresence signaling traffic as DSCP CS3

Chapter Summary

The following list summarizes the key points that were discussed in this chapter:

- Cisco IOS has a number of features and capabilities that can be leveraged in a Cisco Collaboration network to offer state-of-the-art facilities to users.

- SIP, H.323, and MGCP are the three key voice protocols used in any Cisco Collaboration network.

- MGCP gateway depends on Call-Control (CUCM) for dial-plan and call-routing intelligence.

- SIP gateways work as UA to connect with various entities in the Cisco Collaboration network.

- H.323 gateways can interoperate with H.323 gatekeepers and CUCM.

- Cisco IOS gateway offers many dial plan components which help build an enterprise grade network. Various IOS tools make it possible to manipulate digits being sent within and outside of a VoIP networks.

- CUBE offers enterprise SBC capabilities on ISR, ASR, and UCS (CSR 1000V) platforms.

- CUBE offers features that allow administrators to perform address hiding, demarcation, protocol/DTMF/codec interworking, and much more.

References

For additional information, refer to the following:

Cisco Systems, Inc. Cisco Collaboration Systems 10.x Solution Reference Network Designs (SRND), May 2014. http://www.cisco.com/c/en/us/td/docs/voice_ip_comm/cucm/srnd/collab10/collab10.html

Cisco Unified Border Element http://www.cisco.com/c/en/us/products/unified-communications/unified-border-element/index.html

Review Questions

Use the questions here to review what you learned in this chapter. The correct answers are found in Appendix A, "Answers to the Review Questions."

1. Which H.323 protocol controls call setup between endpoints?

   a. H.225

   b. H.245

   c. RAS

   d. RTCP

2. Which VoIP features are affected most by codec choice? (Choose two.)

   a. Voice quality

   b. Silent packet handling

   c. Voice packet header size

   d. Bandwidth required for voice calls

3. Which protocol is used between CUCM and IOS gateway where CUCM has control over dial plan, call routing, and other characteristics of the gateway?

    a. SCCP

    b. H.323

    c. SIP

    d. MGCP

4. CUBE can perform all of the following functions but one. Choose the function not performed by CUBE.

    a. Register ephones

    b. Offer codec negotiation capabilities

    c. Interwork between networks using different voice protocols

    d. Provide demarcation in VoIP network and address hiding

5. Which audio codecs are supported by CUBE?

    a. iLBC

    b. G.729

    c. G.722

    d. G.711

    e. All of above

6. Which SIP Message indicates a successful connection?

    a. 1XX

    b. 2XX

    c. 3XX

    d. 4XX

    e. 5XX

7. What codec must be configured on CUBE to allow direct media negotiation between originating and terminating entities?

    a. G.711ulaw

    b. iLBC

    c. Transparent

    d. pass-thru

    e. H.263

8. True or false? corlist outgoing should be applied to ephone-dn to allow calls out of a valid dial-peer.

   a. True

   b. False

9. Common Channel Signaling (CCS) uses a dedicated D channel for signaling and B channels for media. What is the CCS configuration for a T1 PRI?

   a. 24B + D

   b. 22B + 2D

   c. 23B + D

   d. 23B + 2D

10. What is not true about NFAS?

   a. NFAS allows binding together two D channels on one of the trunks with other trunks being backup.

   b. NFAS allows binding together one D channel on one of the trunks with other trunks except primary trunk being backup.

   c. NFAS can be configured on both T1 or E1 controllers.

   d. NFAS configuration applies to only channelized PRI trunks.

Answers to the Review Questions

Chapter 1

1. c
2. d
3. c
4. c
5. e
6. a
7. b
8. b and d
9. c
10. c

Chapter 2

1. d
2. d
3. a
4. b
5. b
6. c
7. c

8. b
9. c
10. b

Chapter 3

1. b
2. b
3. a
4. b
5. b
6. a
7. b
8. b
9. a
10. b

Chapter 4

1. c
2. a and b
3. b
4. a and d
5. b
6. a and d
7. a
8. d
9. a
10. c

Chapter 5

1. b
2. a, c, and d
3. a and d
4. c
5. a and d
6. b, d, and f

7. d
8. a
9. c
10. b

Chapter 6

1. c
2. a
3. b
4. a
5. a
6. b
7. a
8. b and e
9. b
10. b

Chapter 7

1. a
2. b
3. b
4. c
5. e
6. c and d
7. b
8. d
9. c
10. b
11. a and c
12. b
13. c
14. b
15. a and c

Chapter 8

1. b and c
2. c
3. b
4. d
5. d
6. a
7. b
8. a
9. d
10. c

Chapter 9

1. a
2. a
3. a and b
4. b
5. d
6. a
7. d
8. a
9. d
10. c

Chapter 10

1. a
2. c
3. c
4. b and d
5. d
6. a, b, and d
7. b and d
8. a
9. b
10. a

Chapter 11

1. a
2. d
3. c
4. a
5. d
6. a
7. b
8. b
9. b
10. d

Chapter 12

1. c
2. b and d
3. c
4. d
5. a and d
6. b
7. c
8. a
9. a
10. b
11. c

Chapter 13

1. a
2. a and d
3. d
4. a
5. e
6. b
7. c
8. b
9. c
10. a

Glossary

1080p30 An abbreviation for video transmission at 1080p resolution at 30 frames per second.

23B+D A designation for an ISDN PRI (T1) implementation including 23 bearer channels and 1 data channel.

2B+D A designation for an ISDN BRI implementation including two bearer channels and one data channel.

30B+D A designation for an ISDN PRI (E1) implementation including 30 bearer channels and 1 data channel.

720p30 An abbreviation for video transmission at 720p resolution at 30 frames per second.

720p60 An abbreviation for video transmission at 720p resolution at 60 frames per second.

802.11a/b/g/n/ac Standards for wireless local-area network (LAN) radio transmission and associated data rates. Typically, devices with wireless network adapters will be listed as 802.11 capable followed by a list of the radios supported. In this case, 802.11a/b/g/n/ac denotes support for 802.11a, 802.11b, 802.11g, 802.11n, and 802.11ac standards.

802.3af PoE A standard for providing a maximum of 15.4 watts of DC power to a PoE-capable device. The 802.3af standard defines only the use of Classes 0, 1, 2, and 3. Class 4 devices require 802.3at.

802.3at PoE A standard for providing a maximum of 25.5 watts of DC power to a PoE-capable device. Class 4 devices must have 802.3at power available to function. This is also known as PoE+.

AAR Automated alternate routing. Used to reroute calls over a traditional PSTN network if bandwidth is not available, as governed by CAC.

Active Directory A Microsoft-based LDAP server. Microsoft AD is a common LDAP server in which CUCM end users are synchronized and authenticated against.

Ad hoc Cisco defines an ad hoc conference as any conference where the participants joining the conference are not scheduled.

ANI Automatic Number Identification.

API Application programming interface. The code-line interface used by programmers and equipment administrators to issue advanced-level commands to the system.

ARJ   Admission reject; part of the H.323 RAS messaging. Sent from the gatekeeper to an endpoint confirming the call attempt failed.

ARQ   Admission request; part of the H.323 RAS messaging. Sent from an endpoint to the gatekeeper to request a call be established.

Auto attendant   A virtual reception available on MCUs. Auto attendants are used as a means for participants to choose what conference they want to join. Auto participants will hear an interactive voice response or IVR, which auto attendants are often referred to as.

Auto-registration   A capability in CUCM that allows for phones to be connected to the network, register, and receive a directory number without any phone-specific administrative configuration.

AVC   Advanced Video Coding. Video compression format that is commonly used for the recording, compression, and distribution of video content.

BAT   Bulk Administration Tool. A method inside a CUCM server for bulk administering settings into the database.

Basic Rate Interface (BRI)   BRI is an ISDN interface to basic rate access. Basic rate access consists of a single 16-kbps D channel plus 2 64-kbps B channels for voice or data.

CA   Certification authority. Entity that issues digital certificates (especially X.509 certificates) and vouches for the binding between the data items in a certificate.

CAC   Call admission control.

Call control   A central or distributed entity that provides signaling, destination route pattern lookup, connection admission control, class of restriction, and other operations associated with call setup, state change, and teardown in telephony or video infrastructure deployments.

CAS   Channel associated signaling.

CCD   Call Control Discovery. Works along with Service Advertisement Framework (SAF) and Global Dial Plan Replication (GDPR) for dynamic dial plan distribution in a collaboration solution.

CFA   Call Forward All. A Cisco IP phone feature to forward all calls to a user-defined number.

CFNB   Call Forward No Bandwidth. A Cisco IP phone feature.

CFQDN   Cluster fully qualified domain name.

CFUR   Call Forward Unregistered. A Cisco IP phone feature.

Cisco ASA   Cisco Adaptive Security Appliance.

CoS   Class of service. An indication of how an upper-layer protocol requires a lower-layer protocol to treat its messages. In SNA subarea routing, CoS definitions are used by subarea nodes to determine the optimal route to establish a given session. A CoS definition comprises a virtual route number and a transmission priority field. Also called ToS.

cRTP   compressed Real-Time Transport Protocol. Specified in RFC 2508, compressed RTP provides a mechanism to reduce the IP/UDP/RTP headers from 40 bytes to 2 to 4 bytes to improve bandwidth efficiency.

CSS   Calling search space. Defines what can be called by an endpoint.

CSV   Comma-separated value. A form of data represented by columns which are separated by commas. Typically, CSV files are used to exchange information between disparate systems. CUCM uses CSV files as an import and export tool.

CTI Computer telephony integration. Allows IP PBX to interact with computers and computer applications.

CUBE Cisco Unified Border Element.

CUCM Cisco Unified Communications Manager is an IP PBX.

CTS Cisco TelePresence Server A scalable videoconferencing bridge that works with Cisco Unified Communications Manager to bring multiparty video to unified communications deployments.

DHCP Dynamic Host Configuration Protocol is a client/server protocol used to provide IP information to a device automatically.

DID Direct inward dialing. Allows a user outside a company to dial an internal extension number without needing to pass through an operator or an attendant. The dialed digits are passed to the PBX, which then completes the call.

DISA Direct inward system access.

DMZ Demilitarized zone.

DN Directory number.

DND Do Not Disturb. A Cisco IP phone feature.

DNS Domain Name System. System used on the Internet for translating names of network nodes into addresses.

DNS SRV Domain Name System Service record. Used to identify system that host specific services.

DSP Digital signal processor. Used to handle analog-to-digital (IP) and vice versa conversion and to handle functions like mixing of voice streams.

DTMF Dual-tone Multi Frequency. Tones generated when a button is pressed on a telephone.

E.164 An ITU-T recommendation, titled "The International Public Telecommunication Numbering Plan," that defines a numbering plan for the worldwide public switched telephone network (PSTN) and some other data networks. E.164 defines a general format for international telephone numbers.

EMCC Cisco Extension Mobility Cross Cluster. This is a feature of Cisco Unified Communications Manager that allows user to log in to an IP phone on a remote cluster.

Expressway-C The internal gateway component of the Cisco Expressway (Collaboration Edge) solution. Cisco Expressway-C and Expressway-E form a secure traversal link to enable video, voice, content, and IM&P services to software clients and endpoints outside the firewall.

Expressway-E The external gateway component of the Cisco Expressway (Collaboration Edge) solution. Cisco Expressway-C and Expressway-E form a secure traversal link to enable video, voice, content, and IM&P services to software clients and endpoints outside the firewall.

FQDN Fully qualified domain name. FQDN is the full name of a system, rather than just its hostname. For example, abc is a hostname, and abc.local.com is an FQDN.

Gatekeeper A call control and CAC mechanism most often associated with H.323 voice and video implementations.

GDPR Global Dial Plan Replication. Allows numbers and patterns to be replicated dynamically using Intercluster Lookup Service (ILS).

H.323 H.323 allows dissimilar communication devices to communicate with each other by using a standardized communication protocol. H.323 defines a common set of codecs, call setup and negotiating procedures, and basic data transport methods.

HTTP Hypertext Transfer Protocol is an application protocol for distributed, collaborative, hypermedia information systems. HTTP is the foundation of data communication for the World Wide Web (WWW). Hypertext is structured text that uses logical links (hyperlinks) between nodes containing text.

HTTPS   Secure Hypertext Transfer Protocol is the use of Secure Sockets Layer (SSL) or Transport Layer Security (TLS) as a sublayer under regular HTTP application layering.

ICT   Intercluster trunk. Allows intercluster dialing between two or more clusters.

ILS   Intercluster Lookup Service. Dynamically networks clusters so that the directory Uniform Resource Identifier (URI) information can be replicated using an ILS network. GDPR uses this service.

IOS   Internetwork Operating System. The operating system used on most Cisco routers and Cisco network switches.

IPsec   IP Security. A framework of open standards that provides data confidentiality, data integrity, and data authentication between participating peers. IPsec provides these security services at the IP layer. IPsec uses IKE to handle the negotiation of protocols and algorithms based on local policy and to generate the encryption and authentication keys to be used by IPsec. IPsec can protect one or more data flows between a pair of hosts, between a pair of security gateways, or between a security gateway and a host.

ISDN   Integrated Services Digital Network is a form of communication over the circuit-switched network, using V.35, PRI, or BRI lines.

ITSP   Internet telephony service provider. Usually a SIP provider.

IVR   Interactive voice response. Term used to describe systems that provide information in the form of recorded messages over telephone lines in response to user input in the form of spoken words or, more commonly, DTMF signaling. Examples include banks that allow you to check your balance from any telephone and automated stock quote systems.

Jabber IM&P   A Cisco Jabber client (desktop or mobile) that is configured to provide only IM and presence services. In IM&P mode, the Jabber desktop client is still capable of providing CTI control of a Cisco collaboration desktop endpoint.

Jabber   A Cisco Jabber client (desktop or mobile) that is configured to provide only voice service.

LBM   Location Bandwidth Manager. Allows enhanced location-based call admission control (E-LCAC) for intercluster calls.

LCR   Least cost routing.

LDAP   Lightweight Directory Access Protocol. A protocol that provides access for management and browser applications that provide read/write interactive access to the X.500 Directory.

LRG   Local route group. A feature of Cisco Unified Communications Manager that allows using a local gateway for PSTN.

MGCP   Media Gateway Control Protocol. A merging of the IPDC and SGCP protocols.

MOH   Music on hold. Plays when a party is kept on hold by the other party. MOH can be unicast or multicast and can be played from a CUCM MOH server or an IOS router's flash.

MPLS   Multiprotocol Label Switching. A switching method that forwards IP traffic using a label. This label instructs the routers and the switches in the network where to forward the packets based on pre-established IP routing information.

MRA   Mobile and Remote Access A core component of collaboration edge architecture (Expressway). MRA allows Cisco Jabber and other endpoints VPN-less registration, call control, provisioning, messaging, and presence services.

MRG   Media resource group. Collection of media resources such as transcoders, conferencing, and MOH resources.

MRGL   Media resource group list. Collection of MRG.

MTP   Media termination point. Helps bridge audio calls with different characteristics.

MVA   Mobile voice access.

MWI   Message waiting indicator. Indicator on a Cisco Unified IP phone to notify the user of a new voice mail.

NANP   North American Numbering Plan.

NAT   Network Address Translation. A mechanism for reducing the need for globally unique IP addresses. NAT allows an organization with addresses that are not globally unique to connect to the Internet by translating these addresses into globally routable address space. Also known as Network Address Translator.

NTP   Network Time Protocol. A protocol that is built on top of TCP that ensures accurate local timekeeping with reference to radio and atomic clocks that are located on the Internet. This protocol is capable of synchronizing distributed clocks within milliseconds over long time periods.

OOB   Out of band. One of the many ways used for management of resources in a network.

OTLD   Organization top-level domain.

PAT   Port Address Translation. Translation method that allows the user to conserve addresses in the global address pool by allowing source ports in TCP connections or UDP conversations to be translated. Different local addresses then map to the

same global address, with port translation providing the necessary uniqueness. When translation is required, the new port number is picked out of the same range as the original following the convention of Berkeley Standard Distribution (BSD).

PKI   Public key infrastructure. System of CAs (and, optionally, RAs and other supporting servers and agents) that performs some set of certificate management, archive management, key management, and token management functions for a community of users in an application of asymmetric cryptography.

POTS   Plain old telephone service.

PSTN   Public switched telephone network. General term referring to the variety of telephone networks and services in places worldwide. Sometimes also called POTS.

QoS   Quality of service. Measure of performance for a transmission system that reflects its transmission quality and service availability.

RAS   Registration, Admission, Status are communication messages sent between devices and an H.323 gatekeeper.

RSIP   Restart In Progress.

RSVP   Resource Reservation Protocol. A network-control protocol that allows endpoints to request specific QoS for their data flows.

RTCP   Real-time Transport Control Protocol.

RTMT   Real-Time Monitoring Tool. A GUI-based troubleshooting tool for Cisco Unified Communications servers.

RTP   Real-time Transport Protocol. Commonly used with IP networks. RTP is designed to provide end-to-end network transport functions for applications transmitting real-time data, such as audio, video, or simulation data, over multicast or unicast network services. RTP provides such services as payload-type identification, sequence numbering, timestamping, and delivery monitoring to real-time applications.

SAF   Service Advertisement Framework. Used to dynamically set up number/ DN distribution in a Cisco Collaboration solution using underlying routing protocols.

SCCP   Skinny Client Control Protocol. A protocol developed by Cisco for its endpoints to communicate with CUCM and other Cisco call controls.

SDP   Session Description Protocol.

SIP   Session Initiation Protocol. Protocol developed by the IETF MMUSIC Working Group as an alternative to H.323. SIP features are compliant with IETF RFC 2543, published in March 1999. SIP equips platforms to signal the setup of voice and multimedia calls over IP networks.

SRST   Survivable remote site telephony.

SRTP   Secure Real-time Transport Protocol.

SSH   Secure Shell Protocol. Protocol that provides a secure remote connection to a router through a TCP application.

SVC   Switched virtual circuit. A virtual circuit that is dynamically established on demand and is torn down when transmission is complete. SVCs are used in situations where data transmission is sporadic. Called a switched virtual connection in ATM terminology.

TDM   Time-division multiplexing. Technique in which information from multiple channels can be allocated bandwidth on a single wire based on preassigned time slots. Bandwidth is allocated to each channel regardless of whether the station has data to transmit.

TEHO   Tail-end hop-off. For LCR of toll calls via IP until the penultimate hop and then hand off to PSTN.

TLS   Transport Layer Security. An IETF protocol.

TMS   TelePresence Management Suite.

TTL   Time to live. A mechanism that limits the lifespan or lifetime of data in a computer or network.

TUI   Telephone user interface.

TURN   Traversal Using Relay NAT.

UCL   User Connect Licensing.

UDS   User Data Services. A REST-based set of operations that provide authenticated access to user resources and entities such as user's devices, subscribed services, speed dials, and much more from the Unified Communications configuration database. UDS is available with CUCM 10.0 and later.

URI   Uniform Resource Identifier. Type of formatted identifier that encapsulates the name of an Internet object and labels it with an identification of the name space, thus producing a member of the universal set of names in registered name spaces and of addresses referring to registered protocols or name spaces [RFC 1630].

UWL   Unified Workspace Licensing.

VCS   [Cisco TelePresence] Video Communications Server.

VPN   Virtual private network. Enables IP traffic to travel securely over a public TCP/IP network by encrypting all traffic from one network to another. A VPN uses tunneling to encrypt all information at the IP level.

VXML   Voice XML.

XMPP   Extensible Messaging and Presence Protocol.

Index

Symbols

A

D

Q

U

V

W-X-Y-Z

Exclusive Offer – 40% OFF

Cisco Press
Video Training
livelessons⊙

ciscopress.com/video
Use coupon code **CPVIDEO40** during checkout.

Video Instruction from Technology Experts

Advance Your Skills

Get started with fundamentals, become an expert, or get certified.

Train Anywhere

Train anywhere, at your own pace, on any device.

Learn

Learn from trusted author trainers published by Cisco Press.

Try Our Popular Video Training for FREE!
ciscopress.com/video

Explore hundreds of **FREE** video lessons from our growing library of Complete Video Courses, LiveLessons, networking talks, and workshops.

CISCO

Connect, Engage, Collaborate

The Award Winning Cisco Support Community

Attend and Participate in Events

Ask the Experts
Live Webcasts

Knowledge Sharing

Documents
Blogs
Videos

Top Contributor Programs

Cisco Designated VIP
Hall of Fame
Spotlight Awards

Multi-Language Support

https://supportforums.cisco.com

REGISTER YOUR PRODUCT at CiscoPress.com/register
Access Additional Benefits and SAVE 35% on Your Next Purchase

- Download available product updates.
- Access bonus material when applicable.
- Receive exclusive offers on new editions and related products.
  (Just check the box to hear from us when setting up your account.)
- Get a coupon for 35% for your next purchase, valid for 30 days.
  Your code will be available in your Cisco Press cart. (You will also find
  it in the Manage Codes section of your account page.)

Registration benefits vary by product. Benefits will be listed on your account page under Registered Products.

CiscoPress.com – Learning Solutions for Self-Paced Study, Enterprise, and the Classroom
Cisco Press is the Cisco Systems authorized book publisher of Cisco networking technology, Cisco certification self-study, and Cisco Networking Academy Program materials.

At **CiscoPress.com** you can
- Shop our books, eBooks, software, and video training.
- Take advantage of our special offers and promotions (ciscopress.com/promotions).
- Sign up for special offers and content newsletters (ciscopress.com/newsletters).
- Read free articles, exam profiles, and blogs by information technology experts.
- Access thousands of free chapters and video lessons.

Connect with Cisco Press – Visit CiscoPress.com/community
Learn about Cisco Press community events and programs.

Cisco Press

ALWAYS LEARNING

PEARSON